VOLUNTEERS

VOLUNTEERS

The Incredible Story of Kitchener's Army in Soldiers' and Civilians' own Photographs

Richard van Emden

Pen & Sword
MILITARY

First published in Great Britain in 2023 by
Pen & Sword Military
an imprint of
Pen & Sword Books Limited
Yorkshire – Philadelphia

Copyright © Richard van Emden 2023

ISBN 978 1 47389 186 9

The right of Richard van Emden to be identified as the Author of this Work has been asserted by him in accordance with the Copyright, Designs and Patents Act 1988.

A CIP catalogue record for this book is available from the British Library.

All rights reserved. No part of this book may be reproduced or transmitted in any form or by any means, electronic or mechanical, including photocopying, recording or by any information storage and retrieval system, without permission from the Publisher in writing.

Typeset by Mac Style
Printed in the UK by CPI Group (UK) Ltd, Croydon, CR0 4YY.

MIX
Paper | Supporting responsible forestry
FSC® C013604

Pen & Sword Books Limited incorporates the imprints of After the Battle, Archaeology, Atlas, Aviation, Discovery, Family History, Fiction, History, Maritime, Military, Military Classics, Politics, Select, Transport, True Crime, Air World, Frontline Publishing, Leo Cooper, Remember When, Seaforth Publishing, The Praetorian Press, Wharncliffe Local History, Wharncliffe Transport, Wharncliffe True Crime and White Owl.

For a complete list of Pen & Sword titles please contact:

PEN & SWORD BOOKS LIMITED
47 Church Street, Barnsley, South Yorkshire, S70 2AS, England
E-mail: enquiries@pen-and-sword.co.uk
Website: www.pen-and-sword.co.uk
or
PEN AND SWORD BOOKS
1950 Lawrence Road, Havertown, PA 19083, USA
E-mail: uspen-and-sword@casematepublishers.com
Website: www.penandswordbooks.com

Title Page: *A lad of the Worcestershire Regiment on board ship and on his way to France in 1916.*

Frontispiece: *Each Recruit means a Quicker Peace: an unknown recruitment officer stands at the door of a recruiting office.*

Dedicated to Marta van Emden and George Robinson

And to the memory of Vic Cole, 1897–1995

1988. Ninety-one-year-old Vic Cole outside his home in Reading.

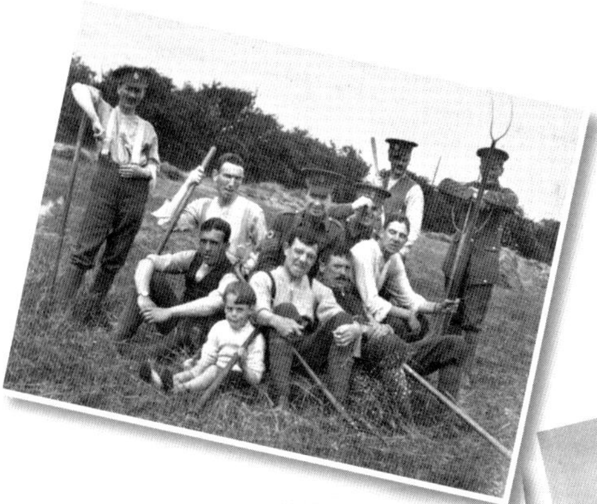
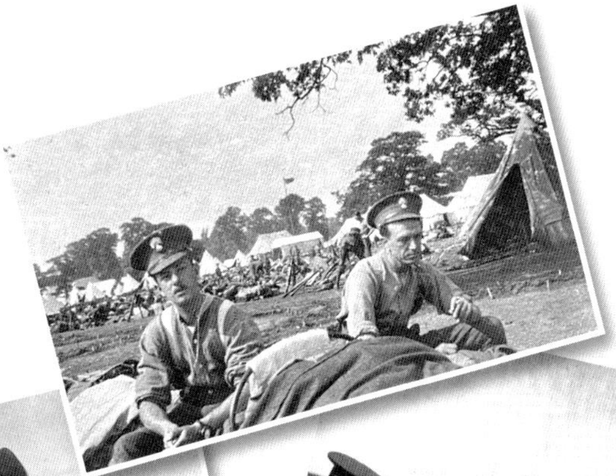
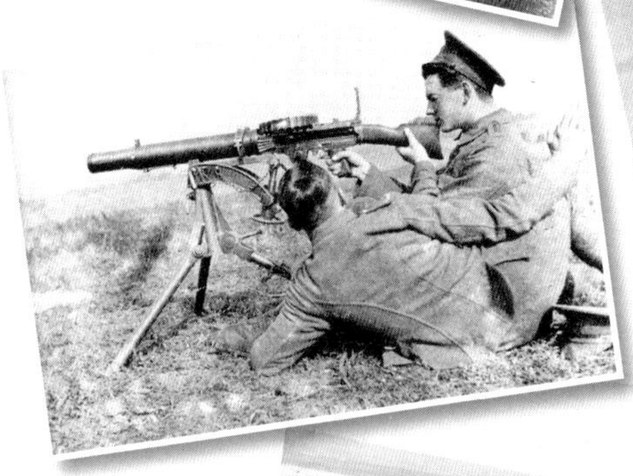
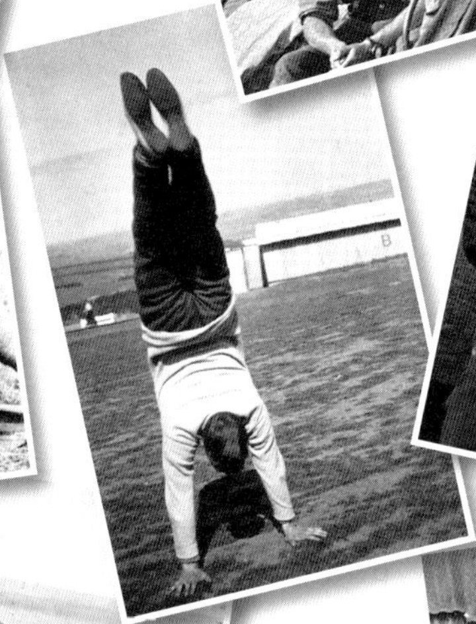
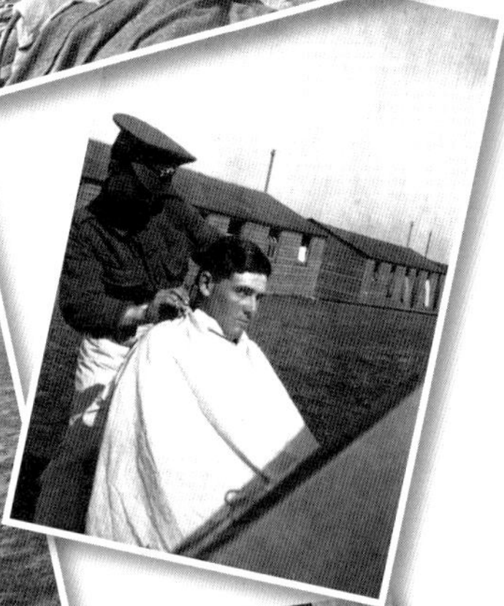
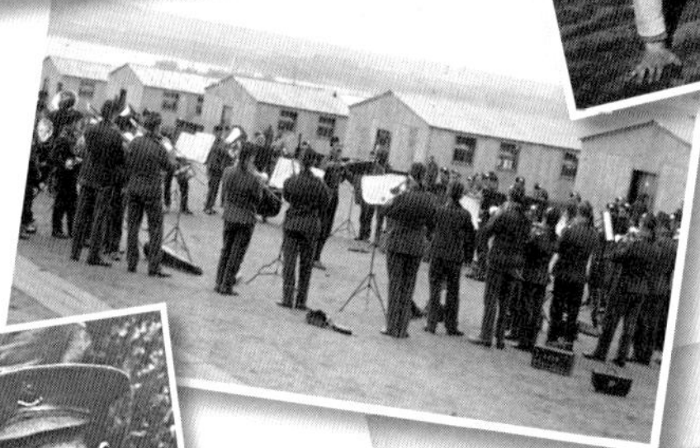
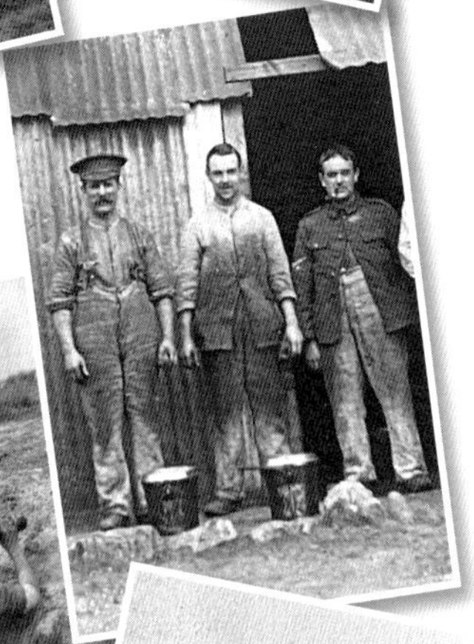
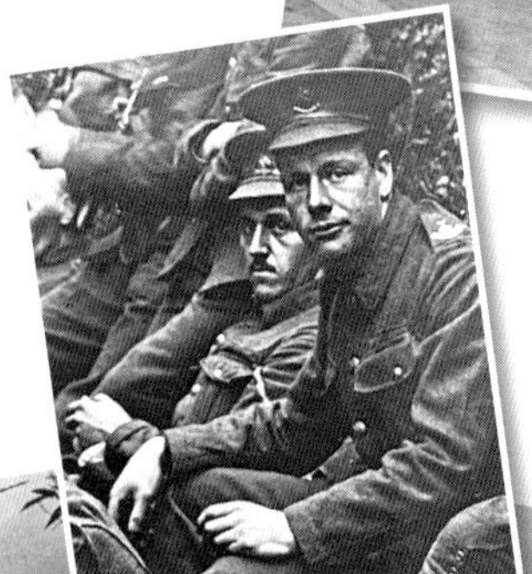
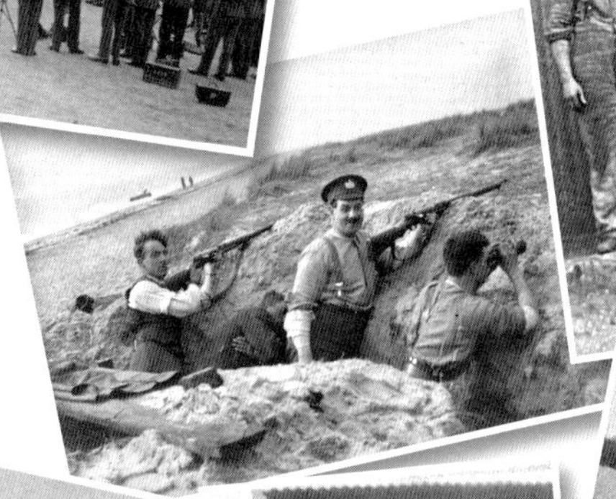
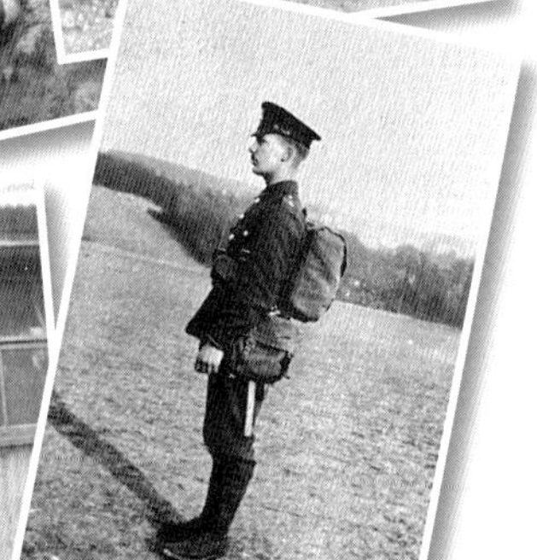
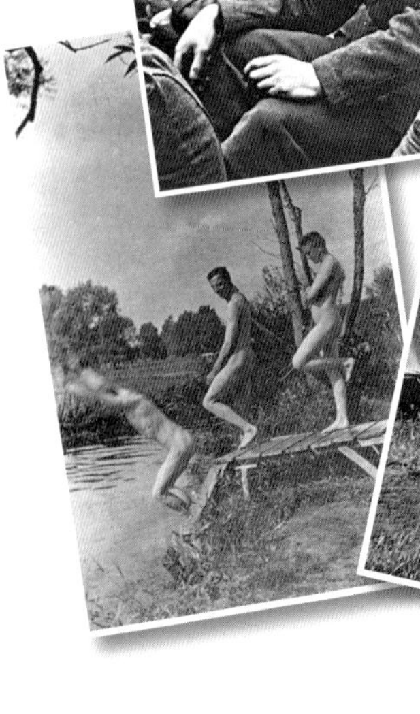
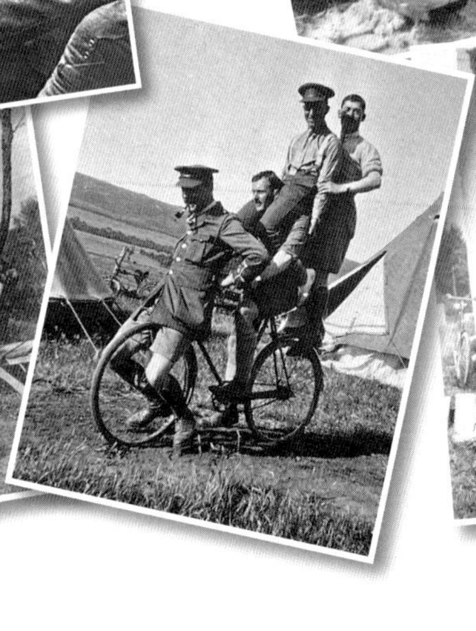
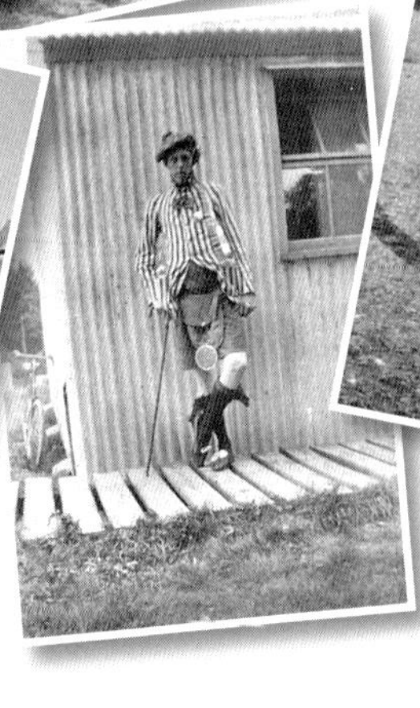

CONTENTS

Introduction		1
Chapter 1	Kitchener's First-born	13
Chapter 2	All up, I Suppose	31
Chapter 3	Crossing the Rubicon	61
Chapter 4	Warts and All	93
Chapter 5	Right Sorts	127
Chapter 6	Taming Lions	163
Chapter 7	Simple Bare Necessities	197
Chapter 8	Living the Dream	233
Chapter 9	Winter Blues	277
Chapter 10	Fiddling About	307
Chapter 11	Grey Waters	331
Acknowledgements		364
Sources and Permissions		365
Index		368

Opposite: A compilation of soldiers' own photographs taken by volunteers in 1914 and 1915 while serving with the Gloucestershire Regiment, the Honourable Artillery Company, the Devonshire Regiment, the Royal Army Medical Corps, and the Warwickshire Regiment.

HUT ORDERLY.

Introduction

'The sudden transformation of several millions of peaceful citizens, most of whom, had they troubled their heads about the matter at all, had regarded the Service as a lazy, almost contemptible method of earning a living, into an enthusiastic and comparatively efficient Army will probably be adjudged by the verdict of history to be the greatest military feat ever accomplished.'

Captain Cecil Street, Royal Garrison Artillery

A retired major of the Royal Corps of Transport once told me how pleasantly surprised he was whenever the British Army successfully deployed on operations. Life's quirks of fate coupled with everyday miscommunications – not to mention 'cock-ups' (I believe he used those words) – caused countless logistical headaches, both at home and abroad. And yet we turned up, he noted with evident pride, pretty much on time, generally prepared, and by and large, correctly equipped: the forces had resourcefully muddled through. His recollections of the 1950s and 1960s, one man's of course, may nevertheless ring bells with serving or former army officers, but they would not reflect the military experience of August 1914.

In one sense and one sense only did Great Britain plunge into the Great War perfectly prepared and ready to go. Tasked by the War Office to devise a plan to mobilise and deploy to the continent a small professional army, Staff officers had come up with a proposal so detailed, so regularly revised and honed that when it was enacted it worked almost entirely as anticipated. In two weeks from the order to mobilise, 80,000 men of the infantry, artillery and cavalry, with all necessary ancillary supplies and equipment – the British Expeditionary

Opposite: Hut Orderly: Private Reginald Birkett, son of a Liverpool architect, took a camera with him after joining the 20th Royal Fusiliers, a Public Schools Battalion. He took the camera to France in November 1915. In 1917, he was commissioned. He survived the war.

Force (BEF) – were transported to France. This was a professional army at its most professional.

And there preparations hit the buffers, for no one foresaw the speed with which Britain's military commitment would develop or the sheer scale of operations that would swamp the forces' capacity to cope. There was no great contingency to expand the army to meet the demands of a vast European war, no plan in place to undertake the full mobilisation of a civil population, if required. Nor was there much preparation to place an economy onto a conflict footing or to adjust national finances to pay for a war of hitherto unprecedented scale and ferocity. 'Business as usual' was the Liberal government's luxury refrain in August and September 1914, on the one hand a sensible policy signalling the continued predominance of free enterprise, neither destabilising the money markets, nor sowing economic uncertainty, but on the other hand a complacent gesture that this was a war that need not be taken *too* seriously. The British navy, always the guarantor of domestic safety and overseas authority, would continue its paternal duty of care. Unlike the rest of continental Europe's competing nations living in close physical proximity, there was no need for a large standing army in Britain: 20-odd miles of water had rendered unnecessary a lot of preparatory hassle.

Into this vacuum strode the one man judged absolutely necessary to take command in a febrile situation: Lord Kitchener, the man of the moment. There was a nationwide sigh of relief when he agreed to become the new Secretary of State for War, taking over from a fraught Prime Minister, Herbert Asquith, who had briefly doubled up on job titles. Newspapers, including *The Times*, had urged the Prime Minster to appoint Kitchener such was his

Lord Kitchener, snapped mingling with families prior to a medal presentation ceremony.

status as a national hero and icon. 'Kitchener meant as much to the British in 1914 as Churchill meant in 1940,' wrote the author and Great War army officer Charles Carrington in the 1960s, pointedly disclosing a reverence still held by an ageing and fast-fading generation.

Kitchener's immediate proposal to create a new volunteer civilian army is his lasting legacy. He foresaw that the war would last years, not months, though he wisely did not posit this view to a general public unprepared, psychologically or otherwise, for such a terrible commitment. By dint of the fact that Kitchener required a civilian army of 100,000 men, very quickly expanded to 500,000, it was clear to those who cared to look that he never believed the war would be over by Christmas, at least not the Christmas of 1914.

This book is not a study of the man himself, but the story of this man's greatest achievement, warts and all, told through the memories of those who enlisted that late summer and autumn of 1914. Their collective accounts are illustrated through the unique photographs these soldiers took on their privately held cameras, as well as by images *of those* who volunteered, taken by civilian photographers. It is not my intention to break down in detail the mechanics by which Kitchener built his army, though important aspects of his strategy are included, but rather to recreate the *atmosphere* of the time, to relive the intense patriotism and camaraderie of 1914, and the myriad frustrations when things went wrong, as they invariably did. Rather than focusing on the types of rifles used, the bayonets, or the logistics of army supply, I lean more towards anecdotes not found elsewhere, the minutiae of a soldier's daily life such as the problems of putting on a kilt in a packed bell tent, or the confusions of a night march over boggy moor.

Above all, this book will tap into the humour of the men who enlisted, men (too often boys) blissfully ignorant of what lay before them on the Western Front and elsewhere. These men represented a comprehensive cross section of British social life and they were launched wholesale into an unprecedented experiment out of urgent necessity. Their letters and memoirs are extensively used in this book.

* * *

On his appointment, Lord Kitchener was elevated to the Cabinet. Owing to his status and military prowess, he dominated those around him, ministers feeling obliged to defer to his expertise. As head of the War Office, he was given an open remit to act, with huge responsibility and power over strategy, manpower and supply. Yet at the same time, he was entrusted with a remit that by its very size created near insurmountable issues, especially for a man who found it hard to delegate.

Fighting on the Western Front was intense. At times, it was also dangerously desperate, particularly in 1914 and in the first half of 1915 as the Germans pressed home their numerical and firepower advantage. Stalemate on the Western Front was hard won. In an effort to find momentum, the Allies opened alternative operations in the Dardanelles, but these quickly bogged down. Logistics were overstretched everywhere, yet at home, Westminster permitted key issues to drift without proper oversight, such as the painfully low and slow supply of ammunition to the front for which the War Office and ultimately Kitchener held responsibility. As early as March 1915, the editor of the influential London *Morning Post*, Howell Gwynne, wrote in a letter to the newspaper's owner:

> The Cabinet have given up to Lord Kitchener all kinds of control which they ought to have kept in their own hands… The truth is that for good or ill Lord Kitchener is trusted absolutely by the people, and we must put up with any mistakes he may make, for no Cabinet, be it Coalition, Liberal, or Conservative, can afford to quarrel with him.

Only in May 1915, amid newspaper controversy over the handling of the war, did the Liberal government fall, and a coalition government form. Kitchener remained in post. Gwynne was wrong; politicians finally roused themselves from their complacency. The need to harness the nation's industrial resources for war was belatedly addressed, and control of munitions was removed from the War Office to a new Ministry of Munitions, although the idea of introducing conscription was delayed amid fears that a freedom-loving country might resist compelling men to fight: the nation was fighting Germany's authoritarian rule, after all.

To what extent Kitchener, with his wide-ranging remit, was truly responsible for problems at the front and at home is an argument that finds supporters and detractors of the great but also fallible man.

There were undoubtedly serious failings and inefficiencies. The free-for-all nature of recruitment to his New Army in 1914 led to a serious dislocation of industry as millworkers, miners, and men from the foundries and steelworks enlisted only to find their collective strength underutilised while the army grappled with issues of accommodation, command, and training. Kitchener could be taciturn and difficult, and sometimes cut a lonely figure. Should he have foreseen the astonishing success of his recruitment drive and the associated problems success would bring? Was there an unquantifiable risk that had he introduced

Drumming up support for the war: a military band plays outside a recruitment office. This image was taken by a French civilian during a visit to London.

controls, checking the pace of recruitment, he might have also lost the zeitgeist? That is for others to decide.

In modern popular culture, Kitchener is remembered not for his military achievements per se, on and off the battlefield, but rather for that one poster, cited by veterans as the reason they felt compelled to enlist, although the poster was less widely distributed than popularly imagined. That poster: the rigid face, the stare, the gun-shot-straight arm and pointed finger with the invocation to enlist, remains totemic of the era. It is still hugely influential and potently used in advertising today, copied, manipulated, bastardised to sell everything and anything.

That poster encouraging civilians to join up, and scores of others published in 1914 and 1915, used varied tactics of persuasion, but all played on the nation's indisputable patriotism. Some posters employed emotional blackmail (Women of Britain say "Go!"), others fostered ideas of lifetime guilt in those who stood back (Daddy, what did YOU do in the Great War?) or there were those that simply made an appeal for all to take part in a collective effort (Each Recruit Means Quicker Peace).

* * *

Prior to 1914, the British Army had not been held in high public esteem and was not, generally, a first port of call for employment, unless a man was down on his luck. As Captain Cecil Street wrote in his memoirs: the public 'regarded the Service as a lazy, almost contemptible method of earning a living'. In August 1914, those negative feelings were partially set aside. Kitchener could not have built his New Army without an extraordinary level of public goodwill and compliance. This is true not just of the men who offered themselves to the country, and the families that bade them farewell, but for the local organising committees that helped raise (and often initially funded) Kitchener battalions as well as the established 'associations' that launched additional battalions of the recently created (1908) Territorial Force. Civic pride and local money often procured for 'their men' the uniforms and equipment the

INTRODUCTION

War Office had neither the means nor wherewithal simultaneously to provide.

The pre-war industrial unrest, the threat of Unionist violence in Ireland and the regular acts of civil disobedience, such as the activities of the Suffragette movement, was indicative to some of a nation struggling for social cohesion. Would the community be willing to pull together in a national emergency? Could people park (temporarily) their rancour towards a resistant political establishment? If any concerns were voiced, then they proved to be unfounded. Forces that bound the nation together proved greater than those that sought, for right or wrong, to question, challenge or even to undermine it. For us today with the benefit of hindsight, it is interesting to see that the success of Kitchener's Army was about not only what it created physically, but also what it said about the country emotionally and psychologically.

A recruitment office festooned with early recruitment posters.

Kitchener, of course, was interested purely in establishing a force that could compete with the massed conscripted armies of Germany and the Kaiser's allies. No one should underestimate this achievement. In excess of 5.7 million men served in the British Army in the Great War, the largest army by far that Britain has ever assembled, trained and deployed, and 66 per cent more than would serve in the British Army in the next, longer-lasting war. Of those who served between 1914 and 1918, over 43 per cent were volunteers, or 2.5 million men, almost all of whom enlisted before the end of 1915.

The raising of Kitchener's New Army, indeed armies, for there were several, sequentially numbered K1, K2, K3 and eventually K4 and K5, and the story of the inspiration for the so-called Pals battalions, is central to the story told here. But the title *Volunteers* is deliberately used to encompass the stories of all those who enlisted without compulsion, thereby including the exponential growth of the Territorial Force, too often sidelined in modern accounts of the time. Although conceived for home defence only, the part-time Territorial Force served overseas in the crucial period between the autumn of 1914 and the summer of 1915, acting as a bridge between the small Regular Army deployed in the first weeks of war and the gradual appearance of the New Army from May onwards: without this bridge Britain would not have survived on the battlefield long enough to witness the arrival of *his* – 'Kitchener's' – men.

Volunteers does not aim to reprise other books that have considered broadly the same story, though I would like to acknowledge the inspiration that I have taken from two volumes in particular: Peter Simkins' wonderful *Kitchener's Army: The Raising of the New Armies 1914–1916* and Charles Messenger's superb *Call To Arms: The British Army 1914–18*.

All of the quotations used here are from diaries, letters, and

Vic Cole, aged 17, shortly after enlistment into the Queen's Own (Royal West Kent Regiment).

memoirs written by men who enlisted voluntarily; none is taken from soldiers who enlisted post conscription (i.e. from 1916 onwards). The quotations are used deliberately close or very close to the time in which they were produced, usually within days or, at most, weeks. Occasionally, when a quote dovetails beautifully with another and is also broadly time and location irrelevant, then I will use them together.

In a slight departure from my other books, I have focused on fewer sources, using the memories of a dozen or so key players who enlisted in 1914, backed up in a supporting role by other veteran memories. The idea is to follow their stories in detail so that the reader not only appreciates the broader historical context in which they served, but is also offered an opportunity to understand them as individuals. Vic Cole, one of the original men of the 7th Queen's Own (Royal West Kent Regiment), and one of the most interesting veterans that I have ever interviewed, is given especial significance in the next chapter, being usefully emblematic of so many of his generation who enlisted that late summer of 1914.

Finally, this book is one of a series I have written over the past decade. *Tommy's War, Gallipoli, The Somme, The Road to Passchendaele* and *1918* have all used the images taken on soldiers' own privately held cameras to tell the story of the war as they saw it and as they wished to remember it. These images are rare, although the photographs taken by soldiers on the home front differ in one respect from those taken abroad: the use of cameras at home was not banned. Cameras were banned on the Western Front from December 1914 onwards, after the army became aware of the intelligence risk of allowing their unfettered use. Some

An officer holding the ubiquitous Vest Pocket Kodak. Thousands of these versatile, easy-to-use cameras were sold to officers and other ranks after the outbreak of war.

Other ranks of the 2nd Birmingham Pals (15th Royal Warwickshire Regiment) contemporaneously named by one of their number. At least three of these men would not survive the war.

of the images that appear in this book were snapped on cameras that were eventually taken illicitly to France, by men who wilfully ignored orders and the risk of court martial for their disobedience.

Soldiers' images are different from those of press photographers. Soldiers' images often give us the names of those captured on film, images placed in post-war albums and annotated by the surviving soldier. Their photographs convey what was important to the men. These might be humorous, sometimes quirky events, moments captured between mates, some of whom would not survive the war. There is a naturally relaxed attitude adopted between men who lived in close proximity for months, an informality that the official photographer could only rarely hope to record.

The pictures published here are overwhelmingly from my own collection. The vast majority of those that have never been published before were taken in Great Britain during training in 1914 and 1915. Most images are attributable to a particular battalion, and the approximate date they were taken usually known. Sometimes the photographer is also identified, and where it seems useful, I have included a man's original hand-written inscriptions.

In addition to soldier's own images, I have chosen to include civilian photographs. Civilian photographers were often present in and around camps, touting for business, selling the opportunity to have a group photograph or one of an individual; images of recruits as they relaxed under canvas, trained in fields or went on route marches. The photographer composed his shots, returning a day or two later with postcards for those who wished to purchase them and send them to loved ones at home. As one might expect, the quality of these images is often high.

* * *

In April 1916, a memoir, *Battery Flashes*, was published to minor acclaim. The book drew together a series of war service letters written by volunteer gunner Cecil Longley, who was serving in the Royal Field Artillery. Midway through the book, and stated as being ten days after leaving England, the author notes the civilian job composition of his battery comrades as they took up position behind the trenches for the first time. Interestingly, in his personal private copy he chose to ink-in the names of his comrades, names presumably missing in all other surviving editions of this book. 'We have a rum lot of occupations in our battery,' Longley wrote.

> A shop manager [Goodwin] was laying A gun, an apprentice engineer [Day] B Gun, an analytical chemist [Barke] C gun, and a mechanic [Fletcher] D gun! The Sergeant-Major (acting) was a solicitor's clerk [Hamer], and the signaller a bank cashier [Longley] and the OC [officer commanding] the son of a late director of Imperial Tobacco Co [James]; I don't know what he is personally. Other gun 'numbers' and signallers were commercial travellers, mechanics, college men, a wine merchant, and a good supply of various clerks.

The names give added poignancy to his published list, and a reminder of the men of all classes and backgrounds who answered their country's call in August 1914. Sadly, as might be expected, not all of these named men survived the war.

Richard van Emden
August 2023

MORNING POST
Milkmaid Milk
Milkmaid Milk
Pears Soap
Pears Soap

1
Kitchener's First-born

'If all kids were brought up not to play at soldiers like good little Fabians, they wouldn't want to play at the same game when they grew up. But then they will never get the particular bite on the apple of life which I have had the last two months, and, by Christ! I wouldn't change places with them even if I am going to be popped to glory in six months.'

Sergeant Frederick Keeling, 6th The Duke of Cornwall's Light Infantry

---

If challenged to provide a description of a typical Kitchener recruit, how would you depict him, his background, his upbringing and his personality? How would you portray the influencing world into which he was born, the sights and sounds, the social milieu, his schooling? As more than a million men voluntarily enlisted in the British Army between August and Christmas 1914, it might seem ridiculous even to try. Those who joined came from all walks of life and from every type of employment and income bracket, from the down-on-their-lucks to the conspicuously well-heeled. Skilled and unskilled tradesmen enlisted, as did the aspiring professional classes, men who were honest and moral as the day was long serving cheek-by-jowl with scallywags and scoundrels. And every age group between 14 and 60 was represented, schoolboys and late middle-aged men alike: all found their way into Kitchener's New Army.

While most civilians would have considered themselves patriotic, predisposed – one might even say socialised – to rally to the nation's defence, many volunteered for reasons other than loyalty to the State. So there is no single photofit, no one-size-fits-most, for a Kitchener recruit. Yet, if pushed, if a broad impression sufficed, then one might choose to look no further than Londoner Victor (Vic) Thomas Cole.

Opposite: *The Strand in London prior to war, with the church of St Mary le Strand in the middle distance.*

Vic was born into a lower middle-class family. His father, Thomas Cole, was aged just 19 at the time, Vic's mother, Charlotte, a year older. In mid-Victorian Britain, Thomas's father John had built a successful ironmonger's business in southeast London, accumulating enough money to purchase a small number of residential properties in West Norwood. But when he died in 1893, the money was divided amongst Thomas's five elder brothers and in such a way that appeared to significantly exclude the youngest boy. Thomas, then aged 16, attended fee-paying Dulwich College, but was withdrawn by the family on his father's death and encouraged to make his own way in life.

Vic was the first of Thomas's seven children; a brood that grew rapidly, indeed too rapidly, for the eldest was packed off to live with his paternal grandmother and aunt in Gipsy Hill. In his unpublished memoirs, Vic attributed the move to his family's tightening fiscal circumstances, but privately he confirmed that the move was occasioned as much by the prospective social embarrassment of his mother's pre-marital pregnancy.

Vic Cole with his parents, circa 1898.

> Mother did once say, 'Oh, you are different, that's why you are living with your grandmother, you are a seven-month child,' in other words I was born seven months after they married. They all loved me, yes of course, but I was illegitimate.

Thomas and Charlotte married in the summer of 1896 and Vic had arrived on 2 January 1897, his Christian name a homage by patriotic parents to the monarch's Diamond Jubilee and a nod to the anticipated national celebrations. In paying this tribute, Vic's parents were by no means alone. In 1897, as was

KITCHENER'S FIRST-BORN

the case a decade earlier, the names Victor and Victoria had been unusually common in the nation's Register of Births.

What is striking about Vic's childhood recollections is the degree to which his life was forged by the reliable presence of paternalistic, conservative, and patriotic social forces; they were imbibed both consciously and subconsciously. His outlook on life, as with so many of his contemporaries, was shaped and moulded by symbols of Britain's imperial power. The presence of the army, with parading troops and marching bands, was a common sight on the streets of southeast London. Vic spent his pocket money on boys' weekly newspapers such as *Chums* and *The Union Jack*, and he remembered how life was underpinned by communal events such as Empire Day and, in celebration of the relief during the Boer War of a besieged British force in a South African town, Mafeking Day. And then there was the Crystal Palace; nothing in London was more grandiose than the magnificent glass and metal structure built in the 1850s at the height of national self-confidence. The landmark stood on Vic's doorstep and in his youth, he attended the spectacular events staged both inside and out.

I remember well the first anniversary of Mafeking Day in May 1901. For many weeks my aunt had been cutting and sewing pieces of bunting that on this great day appeared as a large Union Jack hung from one of the upstairs windows. Most houses in the street had some sort of flag showing – it was a gay scene – my own contribution to it all being a stick with coloured streamers lashed to the top which I waved wildly whenever a uniformed soldier came into sight.

I was born at Thornton Heath in the year of the Old Queen's Diamond Jubilee. The noise of my advent, with its accompanying social upheaval caused by the sudden creation of parents, grandparents, aunts and uncles, had scarcely died away when, a year later, further agitation announced the appearance of my first brother.

He was followed at intervals by a series of lesser disturbances denoting the arrival of my second, third, fourth, fifth, and sixth brothers, each bringing in their wake additional strain upon my father's slender resources. To add further to parental worries I became involved in the untimely collapse of a folding chair, and, at the age of five, I found myself in possession of a fractured ankle.

Victor Thomas Cole

Vic wearing his Sunday best, around 1906.

Whilst convalescing, and I suspect to alleviate a slowly dwindling exchequer, I was packed off to live with my paternal grandmother, Henrietta, who, ably assisted by her only daughter my Aunt Alice, became my guardian.

For some months after going to live at Gran's, I attended a small private school where the tuition fee was sixpence a week, a coin taken on Monday mornings wrapped up tightly in many folds of paper. My efforts at this school were not I'm afraid of much account, thus at the age of six I was sent to the Council School at Gipsy Road where my brother Len was already a scholar.

Although somewhat given to violent combat as a means of settling disputes, they were on the whole a pretty good lot of youngsters. Fights, though frequent, were kept clean and proper by mutual observance of the so-called 'fair play' code which laid down the various conditions under which blows could or could not be exchanged. To strike a boy smaller than oneself was definitely not done! This would bring forth cries of 'coward' and 'bully' or 'hit one yer own size!!'

On the other hand it was considered quite in order to attack any lad bigger than oneself. The unfortunate victim of this assault, being unable to hit back under the code, had either to run away or stand his ground and remain on the purely defensive. This system certainly had the effect of controlling some of the bigger fellows who might otherwise have bullied but it made some of the little fellows very troublesome…

The discipline at Gipsy Road was to be marvelled at. At the first strokes of the assembly bell the kids would drop all games (or fights!) and snap into their class formation like guardsmen. There were several lady teachers who would rap out words of command like sergeant majors. The children would spring smartly to attention at the order,

An Edwardian classroom. Note the patriotic images on the wall, including the portrait of the reigning monarch.

right or left turn as one man, and march into their respective classrooms. At lessons, unless told definitely to relax, they would sit bolt upright, still, and orderly, and listen with apparent breathless interest to each succeeding lesson. The tension would last right through school until final dismissal at four o'clock when the kids would once more become their own little cockney selves again.

Corporal punishment was frequent. There were the liberally applied 'six-handers' as Vic called them, the half-dozen strokes of a cane on the palm that even the 'immediate application of the cold iron of the desk did not stop stinging for hours'. Vic accepted the cane as an occupational hazard, applied typically for truancy or 'hopping the wag', especially in summer months when the temptation to jump over the school wall proved too great for Vic and his mates. Free, they would head into an orchard and down a railway embankment to doze on the grass, munching apples. Truancy would deprive a boy of any chance of winning one of the prized good conduct medals that were worn on special occasions, such as the end of term or Empire Day: 'they were awarded to scholars who had gone through the year without once being absent or late. In time some of the boys had seven or eight, and one paragon I remember had no less than nine.' Vic received none.

When I was eight years old my family moved to West Norwood in order to be near my father's workshop in Chapel Road. This was not far away so I would sometimes spend weekends at home with my parents and young brothers and occasionally they would come to Gypsy Hill to see me. Life with Grandma and my Aunt was vastly different from that at home. At Gypsy Hill we had prayers every day. In the morning we had our breakfast and knelt down to ask for a blessing for the day, then in the evening we would have our supper and we would all kneel again whereupon the old lady would give a thanksgiving before going to bed. Jesus was brought into everything and I got fed up with it.

During the week life was very quiet and after school hours I roamed the garden or read books by lamplight in the dining room. On Sundays there was church twice a day and no noise of any kind to be made by little boys.

At West Norwood things were more free and easy. Father had some boxing gloves with which we would spar or by way of variation we wrestled in imitation of those two heroes of the day, George Hackenschmidt and Madrali the Terrible Turk! [In April 1906, these men fought for the World Wrestling Championship at Olympia.]

On Saturdays, Mother took us to Brixton where she did her shopping. Here with immense delight we wormed our way through dense crowds around the Costermongers' barrows. It was even more interesting after dark; stalls lit by flickering smoky Naphtha flares and costers vying with each other in shouting their wares, beseeching passers-by to buy the very last cabbage or cucumber.

As a contrast to crowded raucous Brixton, hilly old Norwood built upon the slopes and summit of Sydenham Hill and dominated by the Crystal Palace, was one of the quietest and most picturesque suburbs of London.

Gypsy Hill, Gypsy Road, Rommany Road, reflected the area's old-time heritage, in fact when I was a boy there was still an original Gypsy settlement nearby and Gypsies would come round the houses with rabbits to sell, all full of shot. If my grandmother bought one the seller would hook it on to the railings, skin it and take the money and pelt. Selling at the door was normal. The baker's boy made his round with a basket of loaves, and the butcher's trap would appear too. This was driven by the son of our local butcher, George Pulley, and was a two-wheeled box arrangement pulled by a horse with a cold section packed out with ice. George had a scooped out wooden tray with handles at either end on which he would place meat, carrying it on his shoulder down the side passage to the back door. 'What meat do you want today, Mrs Cole?' and she'd pick out pieces of steak, a couple of chops, and then go and pay up at the shop a few hundred yards away on Gypsy Hill. I got to know George well as he was only a year or so younger than me and we often mucked about together.

Anerly Hill with Crystal Palace dominating the horizon.

The many hills of the district made a good training ground for red-coated Volunteers. On Saturday afternoons in summer they came marching up one steep hill or another, shedding perspiration, pipe-clay and profanity along their upward route. Upon reaching the hill top and level ground beyond, the band with a crash would strike up a lively tune and the troops, hill climbing momentarily forgotten, would swing happily along to the general gratification of admiring bystanders.

Sometimes Army Balloon Section Cyclists wheeled along, darting in and out amongst the traffic, casting anxious glances skywards. They were the 'balloon chasers' and following their gaze one would presently see three or four shiny gas-bags sailing gracefully on the wind, apparently oblivious of the plodding cyclists so relentlessly dogging them to their landfall.

There came a growing public interest in aeronautics. Balloons, airships, kites, and that latest contraption the 'aeroplane' were objects of constant discussion and newspaper comment. [Stanley] Spencer's captive balloons were on show at the Crystal Palace and for a shilling or two the daring could risk their necks and ascend to 1,000 feet in the basket of a moored balloon. There they would remain until hauled down, swaying gracefully in the wind, surveying the countryside and, I can well imagine, trying hard not to be sick.

The Crystal Palace was a never-failing attraction. It still retained most of its earlier glamour. The Great Organ was, I believe, the largest in England and in its auditorium, among other musical events, the periodic festival of the *Five Thousand Voices* (mostly school children) was held.

Football finals at the Palace attracted enormous crowds from all over the country and on Bank Holidays it seemed that half the population of London made rendezvous there. Music and dancing was everywhere. People brought their own instruments, accordions or concertinas and where there was music there was dancing, some organised, but mostly impromptu.

After dark, the North Tower Gardens were lit by many thousands of coloured fairy lights and the band, on summer evenings conducted by Mr Godfrey, played soft dreamy music. Electric launches glided along on the artificial lake carrying the more romantically inclined through the dim-lit plaster caverns and quiet lagoons at a shilling a voyage. For

'Electric launches glided along on the artificial lake' at the Crystal Palace.

further amusement there was the Topsy Turvy railway, the Waterchute, the Switchback, the Maze and many other entertainments where for a modest sixpence one could be tossed up, flung down, swung round, pushed, shaken, and jolted.

Thursday was firework night, but they came rather late in the evening and if my Aunt would let me stay up, I watched them rapturously from the bedroom window. Inside the Palace, tucked away in one of the long galleries and always a source of great interest to most boys, was a series of panoramas with life-size models from all parts of the Empire. Street scenes in India, Burma, Hong Kong, and Malaya with the different native types all correctly represented. There were farming and home-steading scenes in Canada, Australia, and New Zealand. In fact I don't think any part of the Empire had been left out. As a boy, I gazed at these marvels for hours on end, transporting myself in imagination to each country in turn as though upon a magic carpet.

Colonel Samuel Cody was a frequent visitor to the Crystal Palace. He was still experimenting with his famous man-lifting kites, which could be seen suspended high in the air, on almost any fine day when there was enough breeze. These kites were usually coupled in 'tandem' of three, supporting beneath them a tiny wicker basket above the rim of which could be seen the head and shoulders of the Aeronaut or 'Tailman' as he was called. These kites had actually been used with good effect during the Boer War by the army for observation work.

It was about this time that the army dirigible *Nulli Secundus* [Second to none] on its way to the Crystal Palace flew right over our house at a few hundred feet.

The army-built Nulli Secundus *drifting over London on its short-lived life before being wrecked in a storm.*

We rushed out into the garden and Grandma waved a tablecloth. To our great joy, as the long cigar-shaped machine sailed slowly overhead, a man leaned out from the gondola and waved back at us. There were four broad white bands round the gasbag. It was most saddening to hear a few days later that a violent storm had totally destroyed this lovely little aircraft as she lay at her moorage in the Palace grounds.

In 1909, my brother Len and I joined the Boy Scouts. We had made a start some months previously by buying *Scouting for Boys* and excitedly reading it from cover to cover. With half a dozen local kids we formed our own Patrol (the Wolf Patrol) and in shorts and wide-brimmed hats, lustily wielding broom-sticks, scouted and skirmished over Streatham and Tooting Commons on all possible Saturday afternoons.

We eventually joined the official Gypsy Hill Troop, which was later taken over by Mr Crisford and called the 1st Crystal Palace Troop.

Scouts parading before local dignitaries. Note the map on the wall showing the extent of the British Empire, coloured in red.

The whole thing then expanded and through the energetic work of Mr Crisford and his assistants we obtained the use of a small building off Westow Hill that finally became the HQ of the 2nd Croydon Troop. We also acquired an ingenious contrivance known as the 'Patrol Wagon'. This appeared to be a species of builder's truck drawn by six scouts (four in the shafts and two at the drag ropes) and whenever we went away we loaded it with our gear. The sides of the wagon were detachable and formed ladders when needed, the rest of it came off in sections, which, when fitted together complete with guys and anchoring pegs, formed a bridge long enough to push across a twelve-foot stream.

We passed the various tests and wore the appropriate badges and stars. To see us marching back to headquarters of a Saturday night, was, I believe, a brave sight! Bugles blowing, drummers beating away for dear life and on their heels the rest of the tired and dusty scouts, patrol colours flying, cart loaded, the whole outfit swinging along, each lad hoping in his heart that admiring mums or siblings would be amongst the citizens lining the kerb.

In the same year Bleriot made his flight across the English Channel. This roused public interest in aviation more than ever, one of those most interested being myself. I conceived the brilliant idea of making a glider of my own and spent several days stretching old curtains upon a framework of wood until I had an apparatus, which with a certain amount of imagination might be supposed to bear some resemblance to an orthodox hang glider. Working on the theory that if the contraption failed to glide it would still act as a parachute, I launched myself off the roof of the potting shed. I crashed! I crashed heavily and awkwardly and when I picked myself up I realised that my left arm was broken. I dragged myself up to the house and my Aunt ran to fetch the doctor, while Grandma attended to the immediate needs of cutting my coat sleeve and cleaning me up.

This broken arm put a stop to schooling for a while but I was able to go to the Scouts' Review at the Crystal Palace. Sir Francis Vane, a leading light in the Scout Movement, shook hands with me and I had to explain to him how I had come to break my arm, which was still in a sling. He laughed and said that one day I might become a famous aviator. I also saw General Baden Powell. He stood on a chair in the centre of a great crowd of boys and gave us a wonderful talk.

Boys' organisations were training and drilling everywhere. 'Lord Robert's Boys' – Boy Scouts – Sea Scouts, and Boys' Brigades. There were exhibitions at Earl's Court and the Crystal Palace where Boys' Cavalry Brigades drilled and paraded, sponsored, I believe, by some of the big daily newspapers.

When King Edward VII died in May 1910, I went up to London with the scouts to see the funeral. We lined a few yards of the route just inside the gates at Hyde Park Corner. As the solemn procession passed, we doffed our hats – there was the gun carriage, the Charger, the Royal Mourners, and Caesar the King's little wire-haired terrier.

With the passing of the King, things seemed to change. There was a different and more serious spirit abroad. Perhaps the change was just in my own mind – I don't know.

The funeral procession of Edward VII in May 1910. After his death, 'things seemed to change', according to Vic.

In December I left the Council School and managed to scrape through the entrance exam for Alleyn's School, Dulwich, which seat of learning I was to attend after the Christmas holidays.

There were six houses at Alleyn's, named after masters and denoted by coloured rings on the school cap. My house was Cribbs and my colour a dashing mauve. Brown was for Brading (a nice old gentleman with mutton chop whiskers), Tulley's was Red (he was my Form Master and had a wooden leg), Yellow was Roper (Doggy Roper, another dear old soul!), Green was for Brown's (a handsome dashing Cavalier of a man – well liked) and White was for Spurgeon who had passed away long before my time at the school.

KITCHENER'S FIRST-BORN

In January 1911, on the opening day of the term, I commenced my studies in Form 3A. There were three other new boys, but they, unlike myself, had all won scholarships to Alleyn's from Council Schools. Tulley the Form Master asked me if I had come from a Council School. I naturally answered 'Yes', he, therefore thinking I was a scholarship boy, always treated me as he did the other three, with that peculiar deference reserved for our supposed 'type'. It is hard to describe this manner, but it seemed that while socially we were supposed to be slightly below the level of the rest of the form, mentally we were considered definitely above it!

Edward VII's favourite terrier following the funeral cortege.

One great difference I now found was the free and easy attitude adopted by my fellow students in class that contrasted greatly with the stiff discipline of the Council School. Here at Alleyn's scholars would interrupt lectures demanding to know the exact 'why' and 'wherefore' of a statement. The masters with supreme patience would laboriously explain every detail. I was somewhat taken aback, I must confess, to discover that a great many of these questions were merely framed to make the master wander from the sometimes dry subject of the lesson to some more interesting topic, or to engage his attention with one particular scholar so that others could relax, close their eyes and dream of more congenial things.

There was no corporal punishment. Punishment was detention, amounting to several hours a week that had to be worked off on Wednesday afternoon (half holiday) or Saturday morning. This was known as Punishment School and three hours at Algebra, German, or some equally tiresome subject on a sunny afternoon with the cries of happy cricketers floating in on the still air was a real punishment.

In 1912, the *Titanic* disaster and the Crippen murder case awakened in Vic an interest for wireless telegraphy. He bought a booklet entitled *Wireless Simply Explained* and he and his father built a set, the wire aerial from which was slung round the chimney and the top branches of a garden apple tree. A licence was bought and to Vic's thrill, they listened in to the Time Signal from the Eiffel Tower. 'I fetched my poor Aunt and Grandmother all the way from the kitchen to attic to listen to this faint high pitched voice from the Eiffel Tower – they listened and went away dutifully marvelling.'

Vic left school shortly afterwards and despite his nascent interest in wireless he was guided towards the haberdashery department of Rushbrooke's, a wholesale drapers in Aldersgate where for eight shillings a week he worked as an assistant. It was a dull job and at lunchtime, he escaped to walk through London's thoroughfares.

Whitecross Street was a popular promenade for clerks and factory hands. It was a kind of Petticoat Lane lined with cheapjack stalls and street entertainers. These ranged from black-faced gentlemen selling toothpaste, to ex-sailors releasing themselves from straightjackets and

London's bustling Whitecross Street, where Vic Cole spent his time during lunch breaks.

knotted ropes for the amusement of the crowds that usually melted away at the first sign of a hat being passed round.

The Professor who sold throat tablets was the star of them all. Crouched dejectedly over the little table bearing his packets of pastilles, with hat-brim pulled down, coat collar turned up and sagging knees, he looked a very sorry object. His patter rolled out in a thick husky voice, punctuated by a ghastly cough, praising the quality of his famous pastilles. Invariably after a few minutes someone in the crowd would shout 'If they are so good why don't you try 'em yourself!' 'Very well, Sir,' the Professor would gasp. 'Just to please you I <u>will</u> try one myself.'

He then placed one in his mouth, threw out his chest and roared in a voice of thunder, 'Gentlemen you now see the tremendous, immediate, instantaneous effect, not only on the throat but on the physical structure of the whole human body!' Folk seeing this stunt for the first time were much amused and usually parted briskly with their sixpence for this astounding elixir.

At this time I began travelling with George Pulley. George did not like his delivery job much and found a position at the General Electric Company in town and we would often take the same electric train from Gypsy Hill to London Bridge. He was a bit of a tear-away. In those days a boy could buy without a licence a long-barrelled Derringer pistol for 7/6. These guns took .22 calibre cartridges, a roundshot with a charge, and when we had a carriage to ourselves he would fire at anything he fancied as we went along, cows, or alternatively into the door of the compartment or partition.

By 1912 there was a great spate of Invasion stories. There was a serial in *Pearson's Weekly* called *Invasion* about the Germans landing in Kent and being foiled by gallant Boy Scouts. Other regular stories were *The Invaders* and *The Riddle of the Sands* and in the Crystal Palace grounds a terrific floodlit open-air play: *The Invasion*. This showed a life-size English village complete with church and pub. Village folk walked slowly from the former and others drank beer outside the latter. Into this peaceful sylvan scene suddenly swooped a German aeroplane (it ran down a wire) and dropped some bombs that exploded with

Opposite: The plinth of Nelson's Column in Trafalgar Square adorned with a war recruitment poster: 'We're both needed to serve the Guns!' Many boys like Vic Cole could not resist their country's call to enlist.

appropriate noise and a great deal of smoke. When the smoke cleared it was seen that German soldiers occupied the village. All ended happily as I remember when the Territorial soldiers arrived and routed the enemy.

In the spring of 1914, Vic left his job at Rushbrooke's. His grandmother and aunt had scraped together enough money to send him on a wireless telegraphy course at the Training School in Clapham Road. Vic proved himself an exceptional student, enjoying not just the practical work on the most modern equipment available, but also the theory. 'In a lecture room a Mr Wicks did his best to draw aside for us [the students] that veil which hid the mysterious workings of atoms, alternating currents and magnetic waves.' In addition, with the experience gained from his scouting days, Vic quickly reached the speed of twenty words a minute in Morse code and before the war broke out, the heady heights of forty words.

Yet, everything was about to change, Vic recalled. 'World events were about to curtail my natural curiosity.'

Overleaf: Off to invade Belgium and France: men of the German 106th (Saxon) Infantry Regiment march through the streets of Leipzig, August 1914.

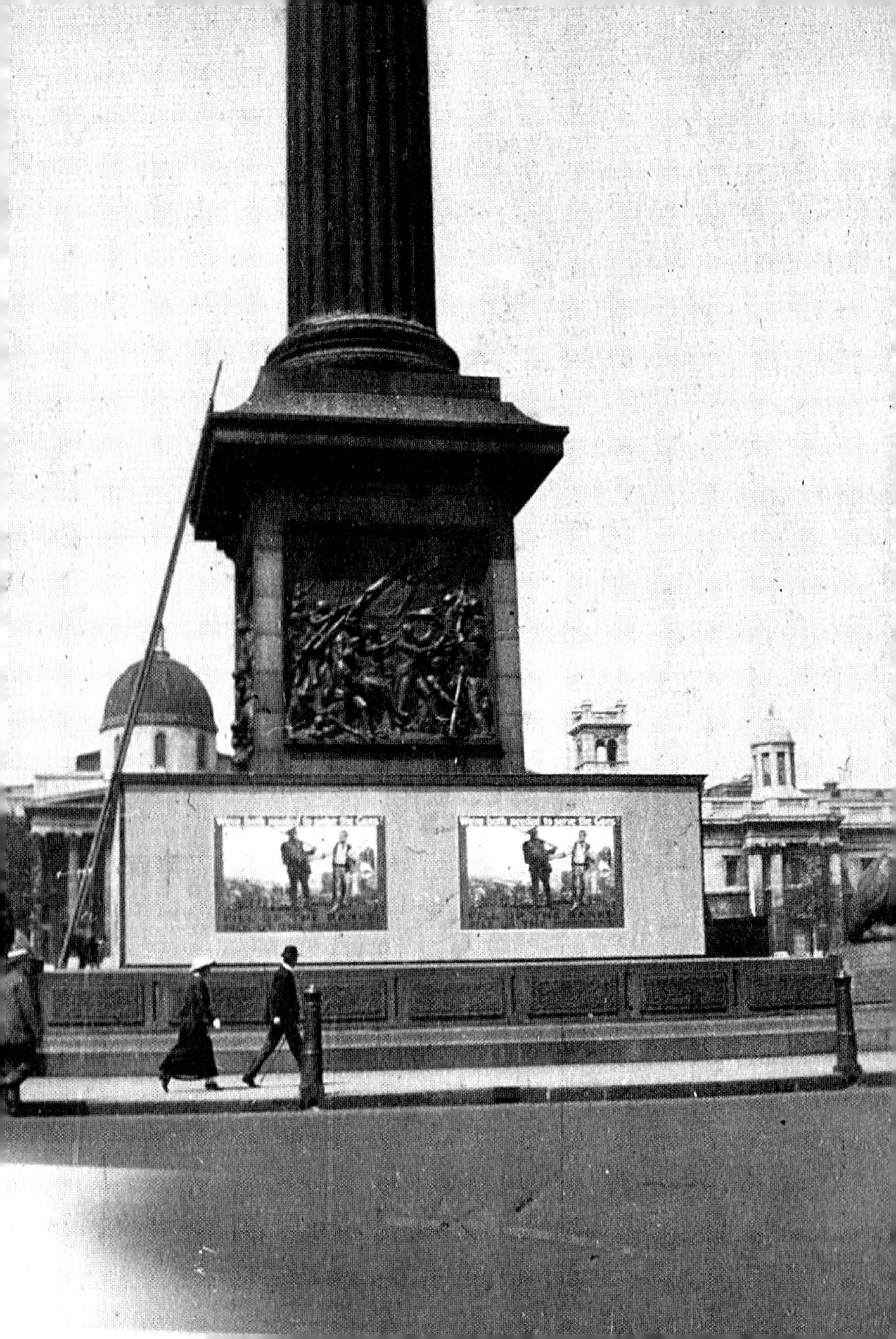

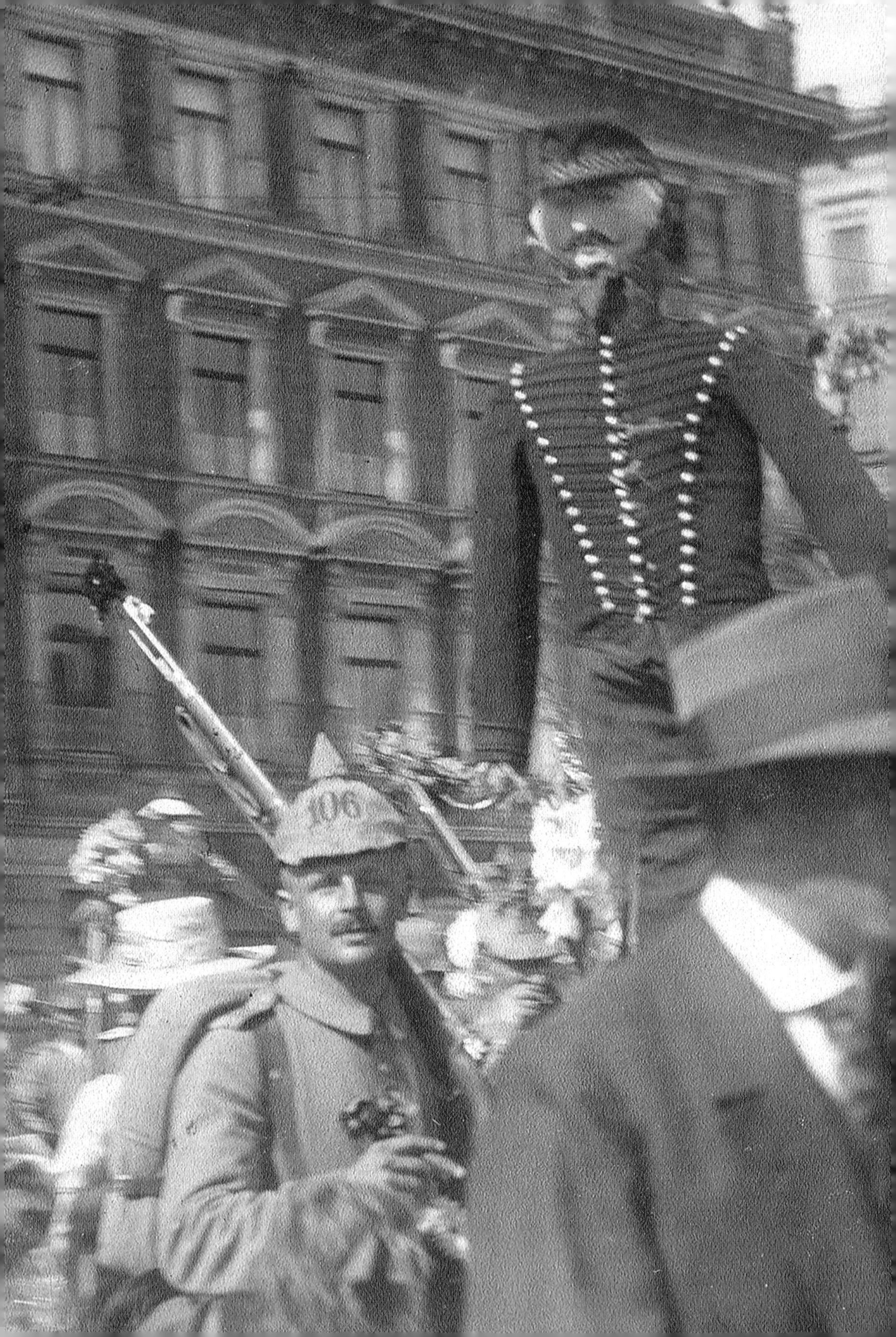
106

2 All up, I Suppose

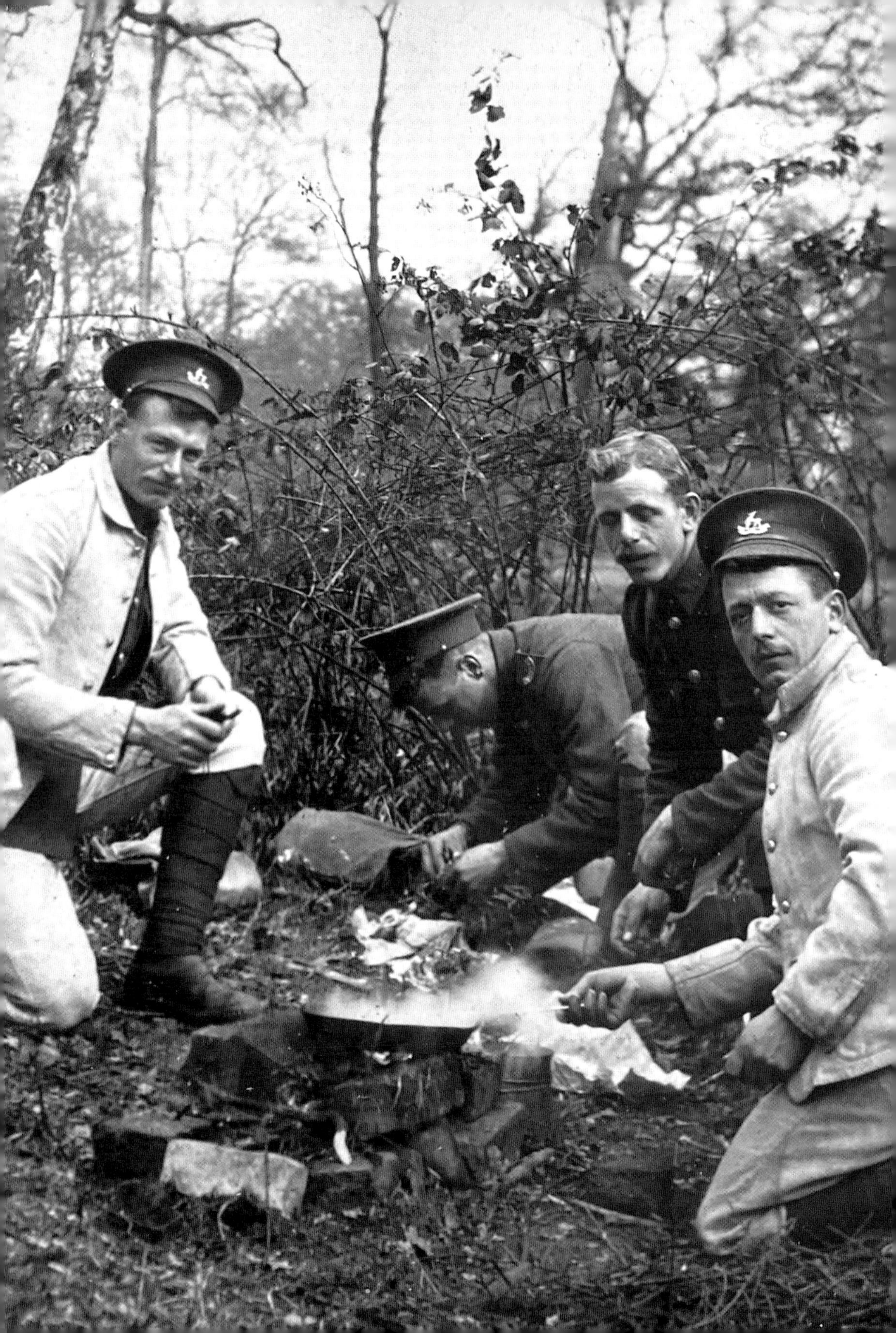

'I maintain that the inevitability of War with Germany was perfectly patent to all men of intelligence years ago. I knew when I was a schoolboy. All my friends knew it. Utterances and actions during the South African War showed very clearly the way the wind was blowing. The History of Germany indicated it positively. Their progressive armaments left no doubt… and in the universal and perfectly frank conversation of any casual Germans one met.'

Charles Jacomb

At the turn of the twentieth century, print media was *the* industry that delivered in-depth political, social, and business news to the public. But while print media did the heavy lifting, the global expansion of telegraphic communication made possible the reach of headline stories not just to a domestic audience but also to those resident or travelling overseas. Within living memory news had been slow fare, taking weeks, even months to skirt the globe: not any more. Throughout the summer of 1914, readers digested stories that charted an inexorable European tumble into conflict. It was now technologically possible for much of the world's population to follow key diplomatic and military manoeuvres in Paris, London, Vienna, Berlin, and Moscow, and in what must have felt like near real time.

On 29 July, businessman Douglas Cuddeford was passing through the West African country of Nigeria just as a European war seemed imminent. His recollections of where and with whom he was travelling are crystal clear, though his memoirs written twenty years later confused the sequencing of two connected historical events, albeit they occurred within days of each other.

Opposite: *Pre-war Regular soldiers belonging to the Royal Warwickshire Regiment, wearing overalls while on camp.*

Douglas Cuddeford

I particularly remember the date because it was my birthday. My German friend and I had been sitting together in the train all the afternoon travelling from Oshogbo to Ibadan, gossiping on every subject except war, and it was only when we were parting that evening that he made the very off-hand remark 'Oh, by the way, have you heard that Germany has declared war on Russia?' [In fact, Austria-Hungary had declared war on Serbia.] He must have got the news earlier in the day from some of his compatriots upline, although we Britishers knew nothing about it at the time.

A few days later and half a world away, Scottish music hall artist Harry Lauder was visiting Australia with his wife and son John. John, an officer in the Territorial Force, had recently joined his parents as they toured the country, and it was in eastern Australia, in the city of Melbourne, that the family learnt of Britain's entry into the now fast-expanding conflict.

Harry Lauder

The next day was the fourth of August, my [forty-fourth] birthday. And it was that day Britain declared war upon Germany. We sat at lunch in the hotel in Melbourne when the news-boys began to cry the extras. And we were still at lunch when the hall porter came in from outside.

'Lieutenant Lauder!' he called, over and over. John beckoned to him, and he handed my laddie a cablegram.

Just two words there were, that had come singing along the wires… 'Mobilise. Return.'

There are two things to take away from Lauder's recollections. The first, how quickly news had travelled, and secondly and more significantly, the astonishing preparedness of the British Army for war; they knew precisely where Second Lieutenant John Lauder was, for when he left Britain he had submitted as required in case of national emergency a detailed itinerary of when and where he would be. It would appear that as quickly as the British Army could call on an officer on holiday in Cornwall or Scotland, it could contact a second lieutenant of the 1/8th Argyll & Sutherland Highlanders, and from the other side of the world.

On the same day, but in Buenos Aires, Argentina, a British priest, the Reverend Claud Burder, was out and about enjoying the city's street life when talk of a cable message from London began to circulate confirming European hostilities. The message was succinct: 'Great Britain has declared war on Germany.' It was of no great surprise to Burder, for although conflict appeared to break suddenly, he, along with many others, had long expected confrontation; it was in the international ether. What may have surprised him was the joyous public support for the fight.

> The pent-up feelings of the crowd at once gave way to delirious manifestations of relief, that will long linger in the memory of all those who were present. Flags of Great Britain, France, Belgium, and Russia appeared on the scene as if by magic, and were carried through the streets of the city by cheering crowds to the accompaniment of the National Anthem of each country in turn.
>
> The following day, life in Buenos Aires continued much as it always had. Apart from the commercial dislocation resulting from any war, there were only a handful of unusual incidents, which was perhaps surprising as about a third of the population was made up of nations that were now at war with one another. I did hear that a blow had been struck for the Fatherland by a German who refused to show his ticket on our local railway line because it was owned and run by the British, but that is the sort of tale that gains in the telling.

— Claud Burder

Five thousand miles away in Nigeria, events were moving quickly.

> All business was thrown out of joint, and we were left in a state of bewilderment by the rapid succession of conflicting rumours that reached us. One day we heard that the German High Seas Fleet had been sunk in the Channel with all hands; again that half-a-million Russians had taken possession of the situation and were going to see the war through for us within a few weeks at the most. In fact, according to those early optimistic rumours we were winning the war hands down.

— Douglas Cuddeford

Twenty-nine-year-old Martin Kirke Smith was in Argentina shortly before war broke out. Like so many others living overseas, he patriotically returned to enlist. He was killed on the Somme in December 1915 while serving with a trench mortar battery.

Hostilities had barely started, but the news alone spurred people into action. The Reverend Burder read that seventy-five volunteers destined for the British forces had set sail within days on the SS *Torakina* from Montevideo to England. 'Newspapers reported that they had paid their own fares,' he noted, with a certain admiration for their zeal.

In Melbourne, Harry Lauder sat gazing at a son transformed by the emotion of the moment. The desire to act in Britain's hour of need would drive John to seek an immediate passage to England.

John's eyes were bright. They were shining. He was looking at us, but he was not seeing us. Those eyes of his were seeing distant things. My heart was sore within me, but I was proud and happy that it was such a son I had to give my country.

'What do you think, Dad?' he asked me, when I had read the order.

I think I was gruff because I dared not let him see how I felt. His mother was very pale.

'This is no time for thinking, son,' I said. 'It is the time for action. You know your duty.'

He rose from the table, quickly.

'I'm off!' he said.

'Where?' I asked him.

'To the ticket office to see about changing my berth. There's still a steamer this week – maybe I can still find room aboard her.'

Harry Lauder

Patriotism gripped members of ex-pat communities and holidaymakers alike, with thousands of would-be volunteers making their way back to their country of origin from across Europe, but also from the Argentine, from South Africa, Australia, and Canada, to name the most reactive. The author and soldier Charles Douie remembered the response in his post-war memoirs: 'The call to arms had sounded afar, and men long absent from their country took the first boat and hurried home,' he wrote, later recalling of his voluntary enlistment:

> On my first night as a soldier, I found myself with a schoolmaster from a remote township on the Amazon, two men just back from the Caspian Sea, and another from somewhere in Canada. Later I met men from much stranger places.

Germans made the same trips, and it was quite possible that ships that bore Britons back to Europe transported equally patriotic Germans. The only issue for all on board was where the ship docked first. Most stopped in British-controlled ports such as Gibraltar and inevitably after an inspection of the ship's manifest, Germans were plucked out for wartime internment. It was always going to be easier for Britain with its vast navy, many colonies and ports to interrupt the passage of Germans crossing the Atlantic than for Germans to effect the arrest of British subjects doing the same.

John Lauder would go back to England to serve on the Somme. He was killed in December 1916. Cuddeford and Burder would enlist too, serving on the Western Front. Both survived the war.

* * *

July 1914: King George V and Queen Mary photographed amongst an adoring throng in George Square, Glasgow. Three weeks later, Britain was at war.

ALL UP, I SUPPOSE

The spark that would ignite the international conflagration – the assassination by a young Bosnian Serb of the heir apparent to the Austro-Hungarian throne – had hardly interested British domestic conversation; in the early days of the crisis, this seemed to be an 'elsewhere' event without wider implications.

> The newspapers were full of the tale of a crime in an odd spot in Europe that none of us had ever heard of before. A foreigner was murdered – what if he was a prince, the Archduke of Austria? We were sorry for the poor lady who sat beside the Archduke and was killed with him. And then we forgot it. There was no more in the newspapers.

Harry Lauder

Not then, not immediately. But as early July and then mid-July came and went, and late July arrived, long-term international political and military alliances came into play, and newspapers returned to report on the darkening diplomatic clouds.

The fallout from the assassination pitted countries against one another and dragged in additional nations too; nations that had agreed to support each other in time of war. Austria-Hungary threatened Serbia, its neighbour, whom it blamed for the assassination; Russia backed the Serbs, its traditional allies. Germany backed Austria-Hungary, and France, an ally of Russia, was bound by treaty to get involved, bringing the prospect of war to Britain's front door.

Controversial and seemingly intractable British domestic issues, such as the question of Irish Home Rule, that had bedevilled parliamentary politics for months, slid down the political agenda now war loomed. A general European-wide conflict that once seemed plausible but inconceivable morphed into 'plausible but improbable' then morphed again to 'highly likely'. As diplomats from across Europe strove to find an eleventh-hour solution, the British waited with rising anxiety as to the outcome of international posturing, direct threats and finally, ultimatums.

* * *

Towards the end of July, Britain's part-time Territorial Force had gone on its annual summer camp. Across the country, civilian soldiers were enjoying the

A Territorial Force officer in and out of uniform, photographed during the annual summer camp.

break from everyday work to practise their martial skills in nigh perfect weather. In Scotland, the 1/6th Argyll & Sutherland Highlanders were training happy warriors between Campbeltown and Machrihanish. War was still far from everyone's mind, according to the commanding officer, Lieutenant Colonel Craig. At the day's end, the men were heading off towards their camp and the scores of perfectly aligned bell tents. '[It would be] the same canvas city gleaming white in the last rays of the setting sun, the same military routine, the same cheery mess tents, and the same holiday spirit and jolly comradeship of many old friends,' Craig would recall fondly.

One afternoon I remember an officer reading aloud a small paragraph from the daily newspaper which hinted at the possibility of a European War. The reader remarked that in this event we would all be at Auchterarder, which was our War Station, within ten days. This remark was greeted with a round of incredulous laughter and ridicule, but he only miscalculated the date by about a week.

I can vividly recall our last field day, and our return across the sand dunes towards the camp with feelings of thankfulness in our hearts that another training season was well over, and we could safely count on a long rest from military duties until next spring. Some of those due to leave camp early packed up; rose next morning and dressed in mufti, preparatory to catching the mid-day boat to Cambeltown, only to be told on arriving at the mess for breakfast that all leave was stopped, and that the battalion was under orders to return to headquarters, with all the war stores, as quickly as arrangements could be made for transportation.

Which of us will ever forget the tense anxiety and excitement of the following weekend, the hurried visit to places of work, so that we might be left free for whatever the ensuing week would have in store… In addition to arranging our own private affairs, we, who were Territorials, had much to attend to at Battalion and Company Headquarters, and every person there was on the 'qui vive', awaiting the final signal which would transfer us from civil life to His Majesty's Service.

Lieutenant Colonel J. Craig, 1/6th Princess Louise's (Argyll & Sutherland Highlanders)

Saturday, 1 August was the first day of the British summer bank holiday weekend. The beautiful weather continued unabated with near cloudless skies. Those who could took the opportunity to swarm across public parks or headed by train to the beach to enjoy the sun. War was imminent but while civilians may have appeared parochial, they were not unaware of the dire international situation. Instead, 'they clung to what they knew', wrote observer William Scott in a reflective post-war book of remembrance.

William Scott

Above: *The calm before the storm: a friends' picnic, circa 1914.*

Determined holidaymakers had gone to the coast and the inland resorts for the weekend with somewhat of a feeling that, whatever happened, the customary outing must not be missed.

All had a certain foreboding and those who stayed at home, perhaps felt the position the more keenly. On the Sunday [2 August] in the churches and chapels there were prayers for peace; and invariably the first thing with which one person greeted another had some reference to the awful possibilities. Special Sunday editions of the local newspapers increased the tension and were bought up feverishly… Everywhere there was the sense of impending disaster.

That Sunday, on the Isle of Wight, Frederick Keeling, socialist and assistant editor of the *New Statesman*, penned a letter to a friend.

ALL UP, I SUPPOSE

I have come down here for a couple of nights to get a little opportunity for peaceful reflections. War news has been trickling through ever since I left London at five o'clock yesterday morning. When I reached Basingstoke they gave notice that Portsmouth harbour was being closed up. I was going by Southampton in order to get the pleasant trip down Southampton Water. Today I met a postman on special duty taking round mobilisation notices to Naval Reservists. This morning I heard that Germany had given twenty-four hours' notice to Russia and France to cease mobilising, and tonight there is a rumour that she refuses to recognise Belgian neutrality, and has already entered Belgian territory. If so it is all up, I suppose.

Frederick Keeling

The next day, he wrote again.

What I have seen today has given me a painful impression of English insularity. I spent a couple of hours in the crowds at Cowes. I had not seen an English Bank Holiday scene for many years and I was glad to be mixed up with it. The patient, courageous, placid stolidity of the crowd was amazing. But the insularity, the inability to get a glimmering of this appalling situation!

Frederick Keeling

The British public flocked to the coast the first bank holiday weekend of August 1914, despite the imminence of war.

Ivor Hanson, a 15-year-old clerk at the Port Talbot Steelworks, had headed with friends to the beach. It was a halcyon day if ever there was one, yet one tinged with sobering signs of impending war.

Ivor Hanson

Today we had a picnic on the expansive, golden sands of Morfa Mawr… It was a scorching day and we bathed in a placid, turquoise sea whose single, foamy breaker tumbled on to the sands and in flecked wavelets flung forward in rapid little advances. We played games, ate enormously but behind all the hilarity loomed the ominous shadow of war. Across the Bristol Channel, Somerset and Devonshire were dimly visible and some steamships stood out faintly against the coast. They were too far away for us to determine their class, but Davies [a friend] thought they were warships, and my heart swelled with pride at the thought of Britain's glorious naval traditions. [He] said that the government would soon be asking for volunteers for the army and navy, and that if necessary he was quite prepared to enlist.

Not everyone had got away to the coast as many bank holiday railway excursions were abruptly cancelled, with trains held in readiness for troop mobilisation.

There was a palpable sense of both excitement and anxiety across the country, though pockets of resistance voiced their objections. That last weekend of peace, 16-year-old Harold Bing attended a demonstration at which the former leader of the Labour Party, a well-known pacifist, spoke out against war.

Harold Bing

When I heard that a big anti-war demonstration was to be held in Trafalgar Square on Sunday 2nd August, and that Kier Hardie was to be one of the speakers, I walked up from my home to Trafalgar Square – about 11 miles – took part in that demonstration, listened to Kier Hardie and of course walked home again afterwards, which perhaps showed a certain amount of boyish enthusiasm for the anti-war cause. It was quite a thrilling meeting with about ten thousand people there and certainly very definitely anti-war.

ALL UP, I SUPPOSE

On the continent, it was all too late. Now at war, Germany would immediately deploy its blueprint for military operations. Known as the Schlieffen Plan, this detailed document had been frequently revised in anticipation of a conflict jointly with Russia and France. The plan demanded a quick and decisive war against France before the full might of the German Army be turned on Russia. In order to execute this plan Germany would use Belgium as a convenient back door to northern France with the ultimate aim of pouring in sufficient troops to sweep all before them and seize Paris. The invasion began on the morning of 4 August. Britain had stayed its hand until the Kaiser's troops violated Belgian sovereignty, a country whose territorial sanctity Britain co-guaranteed through international law. An ultimatum was given to Germany to withdraw its troops immediately. They did not.

'It was 11 o'clock at night – 12 by German time – when the ultimatum expired,' wrote the then First Lord of the Admiralty, Winston Churchill, in his memoirs.

> The windows of the Admiralty were thrown wide open in the war night air. Under the roof from which Nelson had received his orders were gathered a small group of admirals and captains and a cluster of clerks, pencil in hand, waiting. Along the Mall from the direction of the Palace the sound of an immense concourse singing 'God Save the King' floated in. On this deep wave there broke the chimes of Big Ben; and, as the first stroke of the hour boomed out, a rustle of movement swept across the room. The war telegram which meant 'Commence hostilities against Germany', was flashed to the ships and establishments under the White Ensign all over the world.
>
> I walked across Horse Guards Parade to the Cabinet room and reported to the Prime Minister and the ministers who were assembled there that the deed was done.

— Winston Churchill

Despite the sizeable protest in Trafalgar, war-fever was the pre-eminent emotion on conflict's eve. In London and on The Mall heading up to Buckingham Palace, civilians flocked to their monarch. One anonymous witness wrote:

One could not stay in the house… There was a feeling of an inner smouldering that at moments burst out into intense excitement. Crowds of people were in the streets. The red geraniums outside Buckingham Palace looked redder than they had ever looked before. The Palace, seen against the sky, appeared as if cut out of steel. It seemed as if inanimate things might suddenly become alive and do something.

Outside Buckingham Palace, 17-year-old Vic Cole was amongst the crowds milling about in anticipation of an announcement. At times, he must have been just yards away from another lad, Jim Davies, a struggling actor by trade and a would-be recruit if called upon by his country.

Vic Cole

In the afternoon I went up to town and wandered about in front of Buckingham Palace and down the Mall. There was a great crowd of people outside the Palace, roaming around down the Mall and other crowds were congregating in Whitehall and towards Westminster. We got down into Trafalgar Square and then into Whitehall and Palmer Street. It was a very friendly atmosphere, everyone talking to each other and then all of a sudden someone said in a confirmatory, slightly resigned voice, 'It is war, it's war.' It was midnight and word was going around that the ultimatum had expired so we were now at war with Germany. I don't remember getting home but I was terribly excited, the thing that people had been talking about for years had at last come about and at any moment (I thought) the invasion of England would begin! I conjured up brave visions of myself lying behind a hedge, rifle in hand, firing round after round at hordes of Germans advancing through the fields of Kent on their way to besiege London.

Jim Davies

We expected war to be declared, so I rushed down by 11 o'clock to Big Ben. The crowds were there and as Big Ben struck 11 everybody cheered! We sang *Rule Britannia* and *Britons never shall be slave*s ['La Marseillaise' was sung too] and then someone said, 'Let's march back to Buckingham Palace.' We all marched back, right down Whitehall, down the Mall. It was very late then, getting on for midnight, and we were shouting for the King and singing songs. I'd met a couple of medical students and we climbed up by the big gates. The King came out and the Queen and we all cheered and sang some more. We said we'd join the army the next day: full of enthusiasm – not drink – just enthusiasm. Next day I thought, 'Christ, I'm going to join the army, I've got to give two weeks' notice in.'

Journalist Frederick Keeling remained in refined and cultured Cowes as war news filtered through.

Thank Heaven there is no Mafficking [wild celebrations], except a few crowds largely composed of boys. What we have got to do in the interest of Europe is to fight Germany without passion, with respect and with all our might, but without bitterness. Did you see that horrible Daily Mail poster on Monday, 'Greedy Germany'? I respect the magnificent confidence of Germany daring the whole ring of nations all round her. I feel rather ashamed at not being in a position to be called up. I don't value my life much just now, and I would be game for anything desperate that was of use.

Frederick Keeling

To fight Germany 'without passion' would have been a recipe for defeat, and 'without bitterness', a laudable hope, but a sign too of Keeling's failure to grasp the essence of war: destruction and death often on an industrial scale, and bitterness. Bitterness came with the territory.

Turning on Germany was analogous to a calamitous disagreement with a close relative or dear friend. The links between the two nations were not just familial – the veins of the British Royal family flowed with German blood – but also deeply social and commercial. Each year in spring and summer, wealthy British holidaymakers made a beeline for German spas while German tourists flocked to cosmopolitan London to be attended to by German waiters serving in some of the best London hotels: The Ritz, no less, was managed by Theodore Kroell, of German heritage. In private, German governesses were in high

King George V and his cousin, Kaiser Wilhelm of Germany, ride side by side in London. The king made a state visit to Germany as late as 1913.

Emily Galbraith

demand in the best British homes. Culture rubbed shoulders with *Kultur* in art galleries, theatres, opera houses, and concert halls. German brass bands played in British bandstands, and British choirs sang in German cathedrals.

Despite this significant cultural exchange there had been an all-pervading impression that conflict was coming. Even children had picked up on the public's pent-up enthusiasm for a military reckoning with Germany. Emily Galbraith was the daughter of a Methodist minister living on the outskirts of London.

In 1901, I was at a good fee-paying school in London. In class we had dual desks and I sat next to a German girl and she used to tell me that her king was coming over here to fight my king and her king was going to win. We sat in these desks and I used to have a ruler and poke her and say my king would win and she used to poke me until we both got sore. Then after school, on the way home, I took the train from Fenchurch Street Station. Now, on this train you went into a cabin before stepping into the main carriage. Boys used to congregate in these cabins and as the train went along we would pass over fog signals. As the train passed each signal it made a very loud noise, a hefty bang, and the boys used to shout into the carriage, 'The Germans are here! The Germans are here!' It was just a bit of fun. But you see, we knew that war was coming, we knew long before it happened.

When I was a youngster, I was helping a greengrocer to get food put on a stall when who should come down the Oxford Road on horseback but King George. And who should be with him but the Kaiser, stuck up there wearing a great big cape and a helmet and wonderful medals on his chest. Well, our own king George, he looked absolutely way out of his depth. When I got home I told my father and he said, 'Oh, there's going to be a war and not so very long either. That bloke's not over here for nothing.' This was in about 1913.

Percy Johnson

Nevertheless, everything had carried on as normal right up to the moment of war. Annually, hundreds of young British businessmen went to Germany in an open exchange of industrial ideas, while many more attended German universities, just as Germans attended British ones. Germans settled in Britain in ever-growing numbers (they were the third largest immigrant population in Britain by the late nineteenth century) building successful businesses from pork butchers to barbers, from owning lace-making factories in Nottingham to building world-beating petrochemical conglomerates. It was inevitable that many people in Britain and Germany would feel keenly the rupture.

Nineteenth-century British capital had helped build the German economy in tramways, cotton mills, gas and waterworks, and in return, Britain purchased cattle, corn, and wool: the two economies were deeply and successfully intertwined. By 1911, Britain and Germany controlled nearly 40 per cent of world trade, Britain two-thirds of that, and the two countries owned 53 per cent of the world's merchant ships. Yet, festering jealousies between them had grown over the years and the balance of power was changing. Nations on the turn, nations on a slow, relative industrial decline would eye suspiciously the rise and rise of aggressive competitors, and Germany was a self-assured if not bellicose new nation state with a rapidly growing military capacity. To British eyes, Germany was the boorish, over-confident and acquisitive upstart that would not temper its ambitions and overfamiliarity had seeded contempt where it mattered most in the incapable and unpredictable hands of Kaiser Wilhelm, a monarch bent on German expansion.

In her diary, 44-year-old socialite Georgina Lee encapsulated the British antipathy towards the man:

> The Emperor, or Kaiser Wilhelm II, has thrown off at last the mask of peacemaker he has worn for ten years and shown himself in his real light… [He] has long thirsted for an opportunity to hurl his gigantic army and his fleet, at the whole of Europe.

The arms race that had broken out between the two countries in the 1890s intensified in the first years of the new century, with Germany's navy perceived as a serious threat to British global maritime interests. Ironically, had a military conflagration not broken out it was entirely possible that Germany with its much larger population would have won the industrial and commercial war in the short to medium term without ever resorting to force. As it was, the conflict of August 1914 was the culmination of a growing public conviction, at least in Britain, that to lance the boil, war was a necessity. As Georgina Lee added: 'there is not one of us in the country who is not thankful at heart that the great fight is to take place at last. The strain has been too great for many years.'

Why otherwise would so many people greet the prospect of war with such unalloyed joy? War had come as a 'relief', Burder had written in faraway Buenos Aires, a word that revealed so much.

*   *   *

Most British civilians believed the country acted as an honest international broker, a guarantor of global free trade and prosperity, and a reassuring presence in an unpredictable world. 'We had been taught to worship God one day a week but to worship Country and Empire seven days a week,' wrote one young man, Hugh Nisbet, a product of Marlborough School and destined for

Posing for a portrait with the Union Jack draped behind: patriotism was ubiquitous in 1914, but there were myriad reasons for enlisting once war was declared.

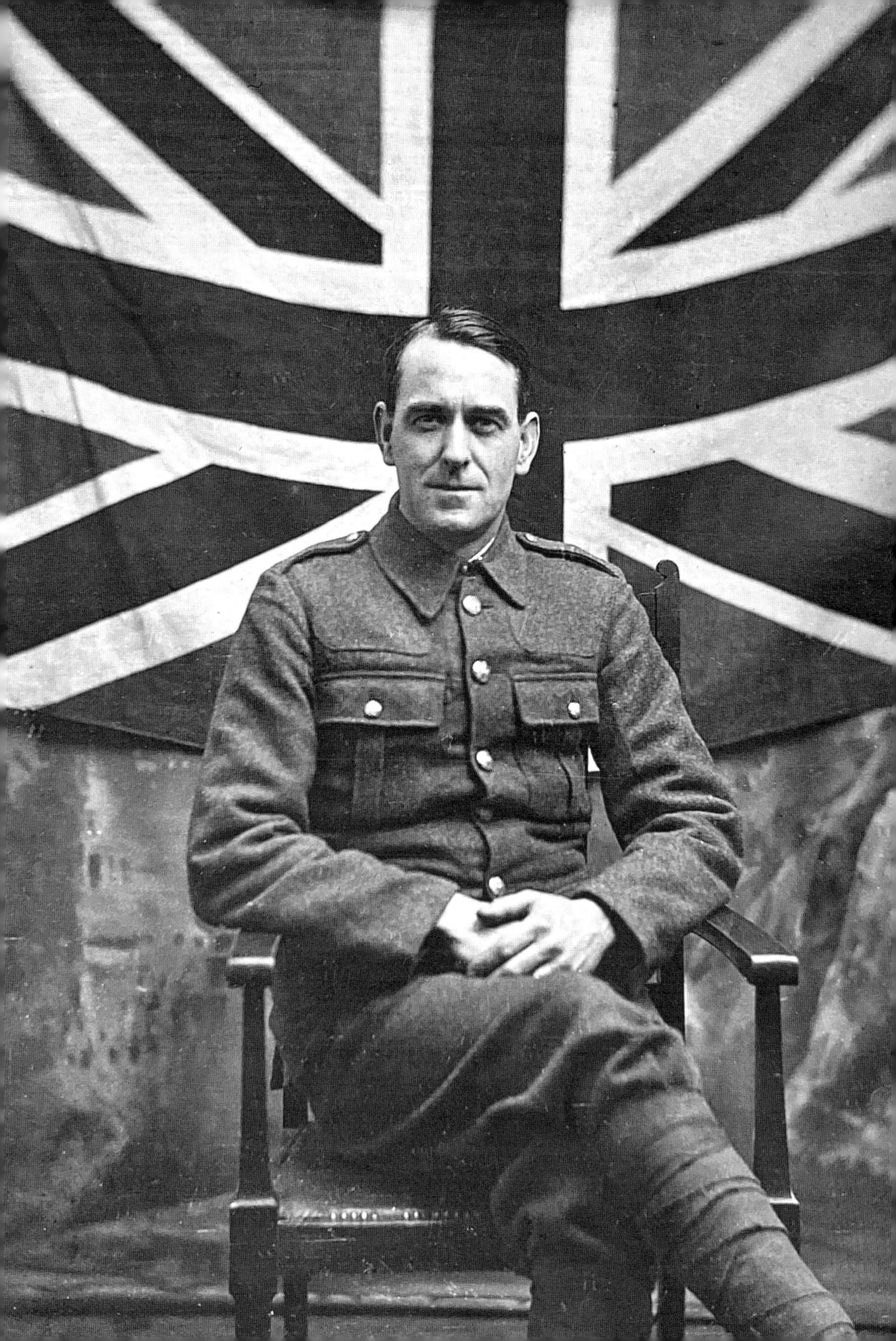

a commission in the Queen's Own (Royal West Kent Regiment). 'The British Empire was the greatest empire the world had ever known, and its greatness was due to the superior qualities of the British. Foreigners weren't cast in the same mould.'

While some people lamented war with Germany, few disagreed that Britain was right to take up the sword of justice. 'It wasn't a matter of "our country, right or wrong",' argued Nisbet, 'our country was 100 per cent right and Germany 100 per cent wrong. We were fighting to uphold the principles of justice and freedom, and international morality.'

'To have asked questions about [British] society would have been to show oneself a fool,' believed Alan Thomas, another young man soon to join the forces.

Alan Thomas

One might as well have asked questions about the Bank of England or the ground beneath one's feet. Doubt and uncertainty about the future there was none. We [amongst the middle classes] knew, each of us, how our paths were set, what careers we were to follow, or at all events what careers were open to us. We knew though we never thought about it – that we belonged to a respected class whose members it was customary for waiters, railway porters and such like to address as 'sir', and we knew that whatever happened we must always be true to the code. The nature of this code had been defined for us [by the Headmaster of Malvern School] in three words, 'Christian English Gentleman' or by [the House Master], with greater economy, in two, 'Old Malvernian'. These things we knew. Once they had been grasped, all extra knowledge could be looked upon as trimmings.

Nisbet and Thomas were products of their time. They were public schoolboys and ideal for the part of British subaltern. Nisbet would be commissioned before the year was out. Even Frederick Keeling, a man who felt a genuine kinship with Germany, was in no doubt where his ultimate loyalties lay.

Frederick Keeling

You know my feelings; my sympathies are all on the other side, except so far as my own country is concerned. I have a sort of secondary patriotism for Germany, and it seems to me madness that we should be fighting on the side of the Russian barbarians and the French, who have caused most of the wars of the last three centuries…

Has ever a nation gone into war more cold-bloodedly and reluctantly than we are going?… Men whom I knew as raving anti-Germans five years ago have now lost every trace of such sentiments, and even *The Times* can't pump much enthusiasm for France. Well, perhaps there will be some mess to be cleared up after it all where I shall be able to help.

I have long looked forward to a predominantly Teutonic Central European State stretching from Antwerp to Trieste. I wrote a long letter to *The Nation* on the subject two or three years ago, but I am enough of a Liberal and Constitutionalist to object to the foundations of such a state being laid upon a blood-and-iron policy. It is not good for Europe or for Germany, which I feel to be my own country after England… Germany naturally determines to strike as hard as she can and as soon as she can and that involves invading Belgium. But the practical inevitability of this first step… doesn't make it any more acceptable.

Keeling was not the only one who felt conflicted fighting the Germans. Eliot Crawshay-Williams, a 44-year-old former army officer and Liberal MP, did not wish to fight but: 'As long as smiters smite it is futile and wrong to turn the other cheek to them.'

It has often interested me to reflect in what spirit I shall wage war when it comes to the point. I have absolutely no antipathy against the Germans. I do not think it is possible to hate a people any more than it is possible to indict them. Individual Germans I may dislike, but so I do individual Englishmen. Certain traditionally German characteristics I also dislike, but not more than I do certain traditionally English characteristics. I do not like to see a fat lower-middle-class German eating soup, but I also do not like to see a fat lower-middle-class Englishman eating peas.

Eliot Crawshay-Williams

This was a war that would have to be fought to a successful conclusion. The attitude was almost dispassionate. But those who welcomed war, even reluctantly, outgunned those committed to peace by an order of magnitude, as schoolboy and would-be soldier Basil Peacock acknowledged.

Basil Peacock

Although there was a section of the population, some of the intelligentsia, who detested the idea of war for any reason, I can remember at the school only one boy, who came from a family of Fabians, who said that war was foolish and wicked, and that we would never take part in it. Oddly enough, we excused his attitude on the grounds that he was physically unfit, thinking his remarks were sour grapes.

* * *

Most recruitment offices did not buckle under a surge of besieging patriots that first day of war. Crowds of men milled around the entrances to barracks, but it was often to discuss the latest news and to cheer Regular soldiers who sauntered by, rather than to offer themselves there and then.

As the Regular Army readied itself for war, small numbers of men offered themselves for enlistment, but those were typically the unemployed and the

High levels of poverty gripped Great Britain, encouraging enlistment amongst the young, feckless, hungry and unemployed.

unattached, the feckless and the hot-headed: men and boys with few arresting responsibilities. Otherwise, Britain's men stood back to see how things developed. What would family members say if a husband or son enlisted without anyone's prior knowledge or consent? Working men were also conscious of how a spur-of-the-moment visit to the recruitment office might play out with employers to whom they had afforded neither due consideration nor notice.

War anxiety affected business. Since the first ultimatum made by Austria to Serbia on 23 July, the markets had become jittery as investors rushed for liquidity, dumping assets. In Britain, the international turmoil forced the London Stock Exchange to close its doors for the first time in its 117-year history; as it turned out, it would not reopen for five months. The public bank holiday weekend was extended by three days while the Treasury sought to ward off a financial crisis. The banks closed, not just on the holiday Monday but also for four days: a moratorium was proclaimed, protecting the banks from a run on their deposits. Contracts were suspended, debtors protected.

One Barclay's Bank manager, Andrew Buxton, noted the instability.

> We live in exciting times in the financial world… How dearly I should like to enlist at this moment, but it is impossible to leave the bank at so critical a time… The summary actions taken by the War Office, etc. are all good. I have just heard of a man driving with carriage and pair to a Surrey county station and having his horses commandeered and so left stranded! In this office we have several amusing incidents in the form of offers from aged (quite safe!) spinsters offering to help if it will enable the clerks to enlist. The question of enlisting is very difficult, both as to myself and the clerks, I am bound to drag on, anyhow for a few days, and see how the bank will be able to manage with a smaller staff.

— Andrew Buxton

> No one could guess how the war would affect their lives and no one knew what should properly be done. Some people prudently bought up everything in the shops in case there should be a food shortage, others in shocked tones denounced them as public enemies for doing so. Rather vague committees sprang up to organise relief work – but for whom? – and offers of all sorts were made to patriotic funds.

— Charles Carrington

There was still a nascent public sense of unreality and unease: social stability was needed and a sense of order and control established.

Geoffrey Fildes

England, as a people, had hardly begun its education in war. A few startling pages had been read, but beyond a certain feeling of great unpleasantness, the public had no real conception of the book before them. The country was at war, fighting for a somewhat vague object – was it Belgium? The forces arrayed against us were recognised to be immense, yet there was no understanding of the need for conscription. That, we were informed, was precisely what we were fighting against. The German Army was, according to popular fancy, above all continental armies, the outcome of this pernicious measure. Conscription and Militarism were unquestionably a pair of Potsdamese twins, both highly objectionable.

In Lord Kitchener, the government had appointed the one man who could exude the requisite resoluteness and calm; one of a small cohort of senior military officers with publically acclaimed battlefield victories and fame on newspaper front pages. His particular successes culminated with victory at the Battle of Omdurman in 1898, an event witnessed and reported on in the *London Gazette* by a young journalist called Winston Churchill. Kitchener had served in the Second Boer War (1899–1902) and in 1909 was rewarded with the highest military rank of field marshal. His height, 6 feet 2 inches, and his steely appearance helped maintain his public persona of a steady and effective soldier. He was an officer untainted by military failure and owing to his years overseas, was never involved in political intrigue.

The British Prime Minister was lucky to have him at hand. Kitchener just happened to be in England on leave from his post as consul general in Egypt. On 3 August he was found impatiently walking the deck of a steamer in Dover port when a message arrived ordering him to remain in Britain. On returning home, he found a note from Asquith: 'I am very sorry to interrupt your journey today… But with matters in their present critical position I was anxious that you should not get beyond the reach of personal consultation and assistance.' Kitchener met with Asquith on the evening of 4 August.

Though he may have appeared the best candidate for the job, the candidate was initially reluctant to take the position.

'[He] was not at all anxious to come in, but when it was presented to him as a duty he agreed,' wrote the Prime Minister. In brief negotiations, Kitchener made it clear that he should either be allowed to go back to Egypt or be given full powers as Secretary of State for War. With press clamour for his appointment, Asquith acceded to his subordinate's demands. The next day he entered the Cabinet as a non-party, politically neutral soldier.

Kitchener had long predicted a protracted conflict with Germany. Even during the Boer War, he espoused this view, and nothing in the intervening years had changed his mind. In 1908, he opined to a German officer that the war would last three years at least. Interestingly, he foresaw no clear victory for

On 4 August, Lord Kitchener arrived back in London reluctantly to take up the post of Secretary of State for War.

either side but an inevitable seeping of world influence and power to the USA and Japan. If he still held such views in 1914, then he was careful what he said. At his first Cabinet meeting, Kitchener told the assembled ministers that to defeat Germany a new army would have to be established immediately.

One million men were needed with an initial call for 100,000 volunteers aged between 19 and 30. Service length was set for 'a period of three years or until the war concluded'. These men would be enlisted through an expansion of the Regular Army and by the ordinary process of recruitment, overseen by the Adjutant General's Department within the War Office. Divisions would precisely replicate those of the British Expeditionary Force embarking for France, with new divisions containing three infantry brigades each of four battalions, and with all the necessary artillery, engineers, and field ambulances needed for independent action. All new battalions, or 'Service' battalions as they were called, would be placed within the British Army's existing structure of line regiments.

In London, the Cabinet needed to be apprised of the military situation and to hear home truths. Britain would have to commit fully to the struggle, Kitchener warned ministers. New divisions made up of enlisted civilians would continuously reinforce the existing fighting men: the British Army would reach its combat zenith in 1917. In the end, millions of men would be deployed overseas. The Cabinet is reported to have listened to Kitchener in near silence and then gave him their collective approval.

The Secretary of State for War wasted no time. On 6 August, he ascended the steps of the War Office and began work in earnest and with energy seldom witnessed before at the government department. On 7 August, the newspapers published his 'call to arms':

> An addition of 100,000 men to His Majesty's Regular Army is immediately necessary in the present grave National Emergency. Lord Kitchener is confident that this appeal will be at once responded to by all those who have the safety of the Empire at heart… God Save the King.

The same day the press announced the formation of the New Army, the House of Commons voted to authorise the expansion of the Regular Army by 500,000 men.

Enlistment into the New Army would follow the voluntary method of recruitment only. Kitchener accepted the Cabinet view that any recourse to compulsory service might prove politically and socially divisive when the need for national unity was paramount. In the meantime, the Secretary of State for War fully expected the navy to protect Britain's shores. His decision to establish his New Army through the huge expansion of the Regular Army betrayed how little trust he had in the efficiency of the relatively new Territorial Force, or the 'Town Clerks' Army' as he is said to have disparagingly called them. In the event of a German invasion, the Territorial Force would be vital to national survival, but it would not be improved militarily if it were suddenly inundated with vast numbers of recruits, he believed. In this opinion, he would ultimately be proved wrong.

Overleaf: Men queue up for a medical assessment at a recruiting station in Birmingham.

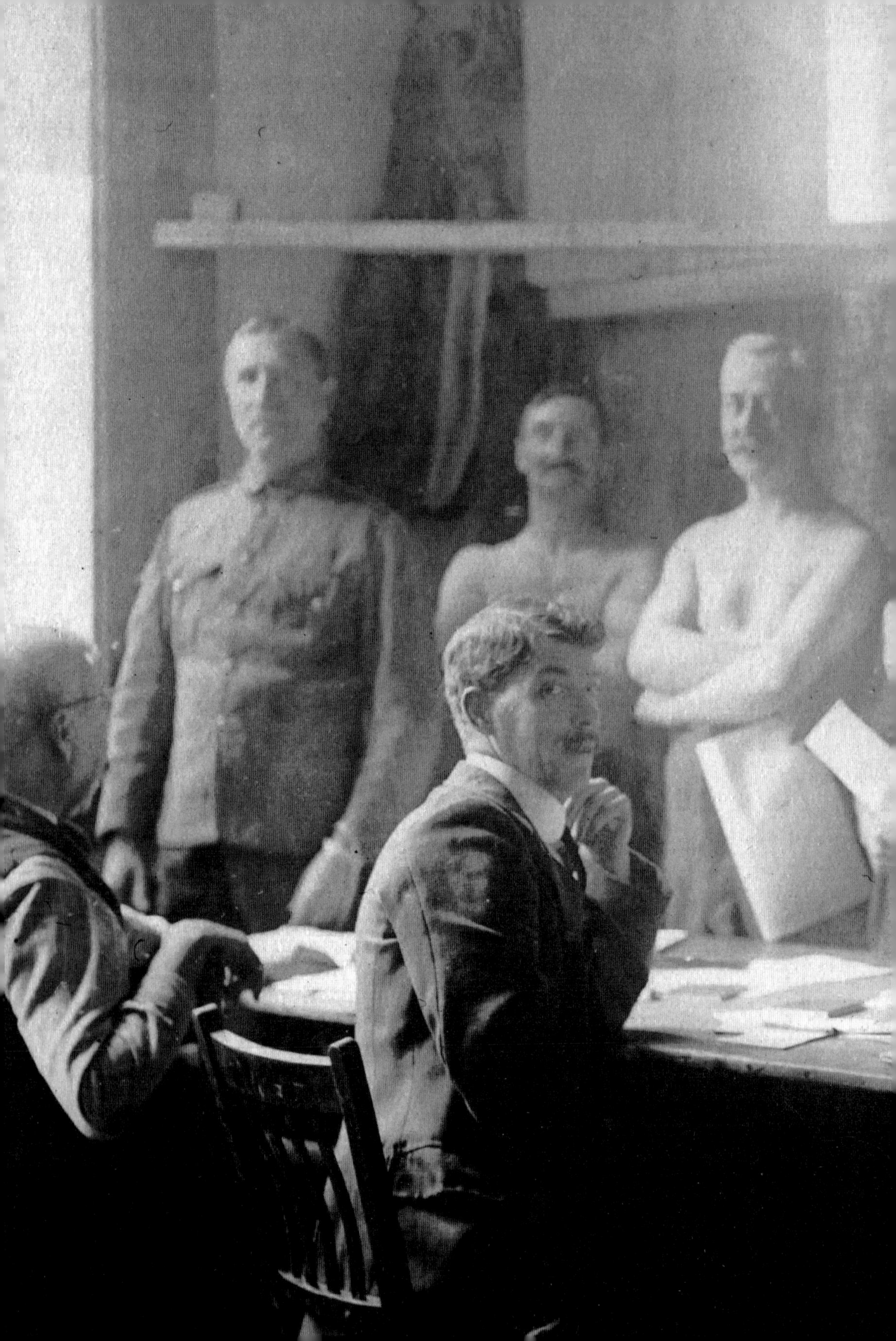

3 Crossing the Rubicon

> **PRESENTED TO**
> **Alderman EDWARD ANSELL, J.P.**
> October 17th, 1914.
>
> **BY THE**
>
> Officers and Staff of N°3 Recruiting Station at the Technical Schools, and Curzon Hall, Birmingham, in grateful recognition of the valuable services he rendered to recruiting by his generosity in providing refreshments, both for Staff and Recruits, during the great stress imposed upon them in the early stages of the War.
>
> Signed on behalf of donors,
> Charles J. Hart, Colonel
> J. Hall-Edwards, Major R.A.M.C.

'It seems pretty clear that the Germans have no friends anywhere in the world, except perhaps in Turkey, and possibly Bulgaria. Of course, one will wait to learn the German version of the whole story after the war, before finally accepting the British version.'

Frederick Keeling, 7 August 1914

John Laister, a 17-year-old lad originally from Attercliffe in Yorkshire, was amongst the very first to volunteer that August. His father, a merchant navy ship steward, had died overseas in 1906, leaving a wife and three sons. She had quickly remarried a man ten years her junior, moving to be near her paternal family in Langley, Worcestershire. John had left school and found work. His was an unrewarding job, and with no one depending on his lowly wage, he enlisted, perhaps feeling no need to defer first to a stepfather.

I was employed at Oldbury [railway] Carriage Works as a fitter and turner from six in the morning until six at night, with a long walk to and from work. I was on my way home and I'm looking at the evening paper and there was a picture of men queuing up to join the army in James Watt Street in Birmingham. 'I'd like to join the Army better than slogging down at the Works for a few shillings a week,' I thought, so without telling Mother I got my bike in the morning and went to enlist. I never bothered telling my employer what I was up to; I didn't feel I owed them anything.

The number of men who enlisted nationwide in the first week of war was far in excess of the hundred men a day the army recruited in peacetime, but the numbers were as nothing compared with what was to come. John Laister joined up on 11 August, one of 7,020 men nationwide to do so.

John Laister

Opposite: *The pictures in this chapter were used in a commemorative album given to Colonel and Alderman Edward Ansell, owner of Ansell's Brewery. He provided the recruiting staff with 'refreshments' during the first months of war.*

Recruits preparing to volunteer for service are reminded of their duty towards the sovereign by a large painting of George V.

John Laister

In James Watt Street, recruitment was being conducted on the first floor of a building, and volunteers were being let in on a 'one in, one out' basis, suggesting an orderly and unhurried process.

The sergeant major opened the door. 'Come in.' As soon as I got in he says, 'Take your clothes off.' It wasn't too warm and there were two doctors in white coats and an officer sitting behind this table and they examined me and measured me. I was five foot one inch tall. I didn't think I was so small. The officer looked up. 'How old are you?' 'Nineteen sir.' 'Are you sure you're nineteen?' 'Yes, sir.' 'Well, I'll tell you what. You come back here in about two years' time and then perhaps you will have filled out.'

So I'm making for the door with tears in my eyes, and a corporal who was there said, 'Half a minute' and he went to the sergeant major and he whispered something, and he went in front of the officer, saluted and said, 'Do you think he'll fill out, sir?' 'Well, I don't know,' replied the doctor. 'Oh, all right, put him in the Army and let them sort him out.'

In Dundee, recruitment appeared buoyant. The war was a day or two old when journalist William Andrews arrived to offer himself. Though he was not confident of his martial qualities, physically he was likely to have been a cut above much of what was being offered the country at this time.

The scene was the swarming street outside the recruiting-office. I struggled in a mob of old militiamen and unemployed to reach the recruiting sergeant. I was twenty-eight, unmarried, teetotal, vegetarian, a quiet, spectacled Yorkshireman. My shorthand was good, but I had never dug even a garden-bed.

A gaunt man in a muffler towered over me. He looked down, and said, not without sympathy: 'Out o' work, chum?'

William Andrews

Andrews was not without work; on the contrary, he was happily employed as the News Editor of the *Dundee Advertiser*, but being single, he did possess one of the characteristics of early recruits.

'Then you make way for us lads wi'out jobs,' the recruiting sergeant had suggested and Andrews was hustled to the back of the crowd. The next day he tried again, and then the day after. In a local drill hall, he was finally accepted.

[I] joined with an extremely mixed mob, passed the doctor, took my military path, and remained for some days under the impression that I was a Regular, or at least a Kitchener man, a sort of temporary regular. I had been asked to help recruiting by writing for the Press, and I signed my articles, 'By One of Kitchener's Hundred Thousand'. Then it turned out that I was only a Territorial.

You will think this was stupid on my part. You will think it a proof that I was extraordinarily ignorant of military terms. I was, but really the mistake arose from the unprecedented confusion of recruiting-offices and barracks in those days. Men were pouring in, overwhelming the ordinary staff. Men were ready to sign anything and say anything. They gave false names, false addresses, false ages. They suppressed their previous military service, or exaggerated it, just as seemed to promise them best. Recruits had to sign as fast as they could. They did not trouble to read their papers. Most of them were more eager in those early days about getting food than about their commitments to King and Country. Whether our motives were to defend Britain, see the War, or get free food, we bundled ourselves into the Army.

William Andrews

In the west of Scotland, close to Glasgow, the companies of the 1/6th Argyll & Sutherland Highlanders would concentrate on Paisley, as provided for by Mobilisation Regulations. The men would be sent to prearranged billets including school buildings while the work of fitting out the battalion was undertaken. The battalion was slightly below the usual war establishment of 1,000 men, numbering 30 officers and 800 other ranks, though not for long. With war and with Kitchener's call to arms, the commanding officer, Colonel Craig, found himself under siege from willing recruits, leaving him a free hand to choose whom he liked, men with previous military service being given preference.

Lieutenant Colonel J. Craig, 1/6th Princess Louise's (Argyll & Sutherland Highlanders)

We had no lack of applications for enlistment, it is true, but very often these were from men who were not suitable for our ranks. We had to refuse the services of many engineering and shipyard apprentices; and, as the maximum age limit was then very low, and the standard of medical fitness very high, these circumstances reduced our field of selection very considerably.

Nevertheless, and leaving out men for sickness and others found more generally unfit for military service, the battalion quickly reached the numbers required and left for Auchterarder to join up with additional Territorial units of the regiment.

James Hall did not need to join up; he was not hungry for one, nor was he unemployed. He was an American citizen and could have avoided war altogether for he had a ticket for a ship about to leave for the United States. War curiosity rather than war fever had turned his head and after days of resisting the public appeal, he gave in.

James Hall

It was on the 18th of August 1914 that the mob spirit gained its mastery over me. After three weeks of solitary tramping in the mountains of North Wales, I walked suddenly into news of the Great War, and went at once to London, with a longing for home which seemed strong enough to carry me through the week of idleness until my boat should sail. But, in a spirit of adventure, I suppose, I tempted myself with the possibility of assuming the increasingly popular *alias*, Atkins. On two

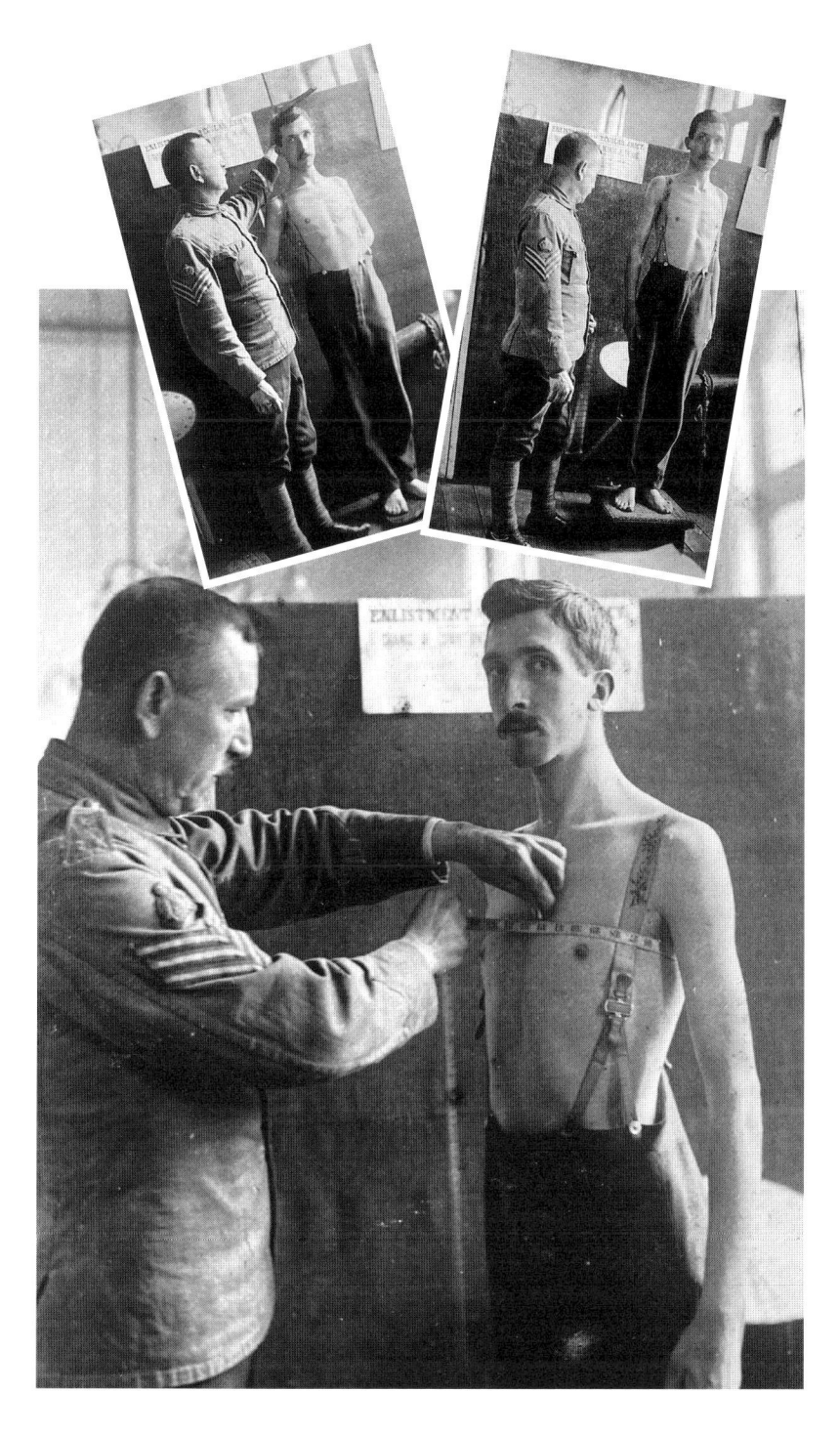

Undergoing medical tests. The minimum chest measurement for acceptance was set at 33 inches. This man appears to barely make the grade.

successive mornings, I joined the long line of prospective recruits before the offices at Great Scotland Yard, withdrawing each time after moving a convenient distance toward the desk of the recruiting sergeant. Disregarding the proven fatality of third times, I joined it on another morning, dangerously near to the head of the procession.

'Now, then, you! Step along!'

There is something compelling about a military command, given by a military officer accustomed to being obeyed. While the doctors were thumping me, measuring me, and making an inventory of 'physical peculiarities, if any', I tried to analyse my unhesitating, almost instinctive reaction to that stern, confident 'Step along!' Was it an act of weakness, a want of character, evidenced by my inability to say no?

I was frank with the recruiting officers. I admitted, rather boasted, of my American citizenship, but expressed my entire willingness to serve in the British army in case this should not expatriate me. I had, in fact, delayed, hoping that an American legion would be formed in London as had been done in Paris. The announcement was received with some surprise. A brief conference was held, during which there was much vigorous shaking of heads. While I awaited the decision, I thought of the steamship ticket in my pocket. I remembered that my boat was to sail on Friday. I thought of my plans for the future and anticipated the joy of an early homecoming. Set against this was the prospect of an indefinite period of soldiering among strangers. 'Three years or the duration of the war' were the terms of the enlistment contract. I had visions of bloody engagements, of feverish nights in hospital, of endless years in a home for disabled soldiers. The conference was over, and the recruiting officer returned to his desk, smiling broadly.

'We'll take you, my lad, if you want to join. You'll just say you are an Englishman, won't you, as a matter of formality?' Here was an avenue of escape, beckoning me like an alluring country road winding over the hills of home. I refused it with the same instinctive swiftness of decision that had brought me to the medical inspection room. And a few moments later, I took 'the King's shilling'.

RECRUITS RECEIVING MEDICAL CERTIFICATES.

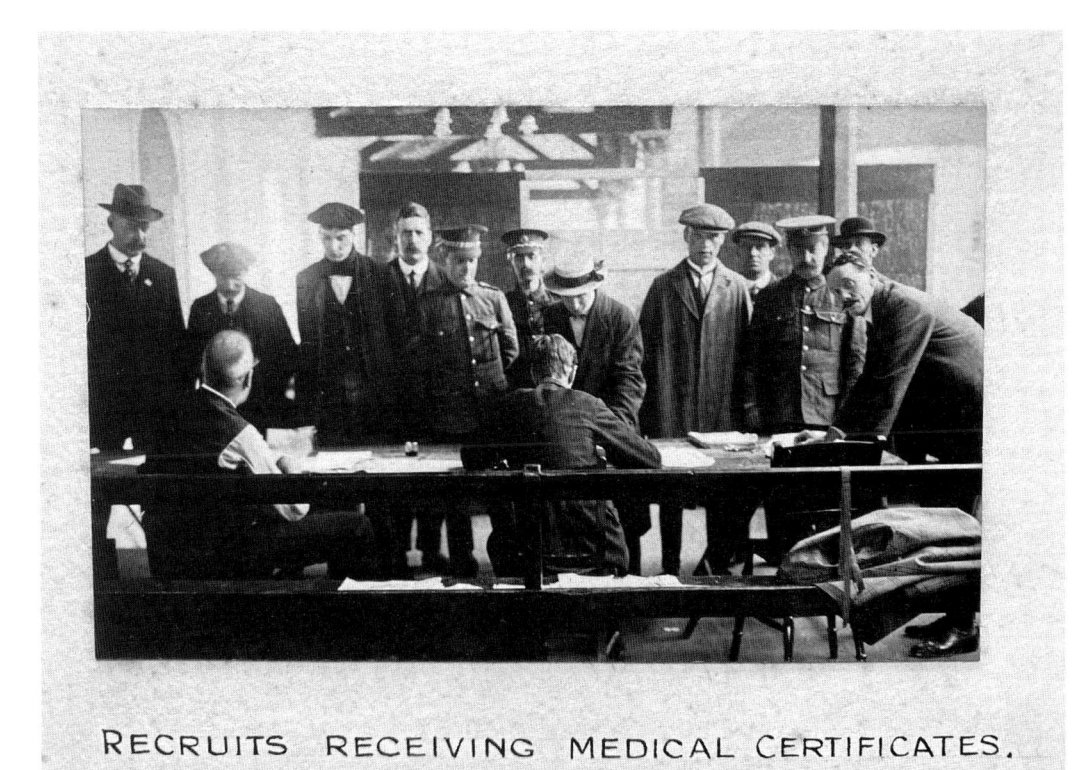

Not everyone was so obliging, happy to bend rules to find a keen young man a position in the army. Stuart Dolden, a recently appointed assistant solicitor in the Great Eastern Railway, sought out a regiment that had traditionally prided itself on being highly selective.

I announced at breakfast that I was going to join the Army. I sensed from my parents' silence that they were not too keen on the idea. However, they did not say anything to deter me. I was of slight and not robust build, and one of my brothers' friends expressed the opinion that 'I would not stay the course', so with that depressing thought I set off to 59 Buckingham Gate, in south-west London, with the object of joining the London Scottish Regiment.

    I took my place in the queue with a number of others wishing to volunteer, and eventually found myself in front of the Medical Officer.

A. Stuart Dolden

When I was turned down on the grounds that my chest measurement was two inches under requirement, I felt absolutely shattered, and decided there and then that something had to be done about it. Accordingly, I went to a Physical Culture Centre in Dover Street, London, which was run by a Dane called Muller.

The course was prohibitively expensive, and Dolden knew he would have to turn for the money to his already reluctant father. With much negotiation on price, a fee was agreed, and a three-month course was conveniently truncated to ten days. Dolden's father agreed to pay.

A. Stuart Dolden

I had an individual instructor and no apparatus was used, for the treatment consisted merely of deep breathing, in conjunction with the appropriate manual exercises. The tenth day arrived, and to my great relief my chest had attained the required two inches in expansion.

Another hopeful, Aubrey Smith, had returned to work in mid-August after enjoying two weeks' annual holiday only to discover that a number of his firm's colleagues had enlisted: two had been accepted into the Artists Rifles and three others into the London Rifle Brigade (LRB). Smith and a work associate were anxious that such a drastic reduction in staff numbers might mean the office would deem them indispensable: 'the firm lost no time in assuring us that we were not.'

Aubrey Smith

We therefore went round to the Headquarters of the L.R.B. and craved permission to enlist, in a manner that would have won the hearts of recruiting sergeants in later days. The L.R.B., however, did not seem any more anxious for our services than the office was: they were over-strength and had closed their roll. Nevertheless, as a special favour, they allowed us to put our names down on the waiting list for the 2nd Battalion, having ascertained that we had been to public school and that we would sign on for foreign service.

The London Rifle Brigade, like the Artists Rifles, was a prestigious organisation, both battalions formed in the mid-nineteenth century as volunteer units. The LRB's members were all 'men of good position' in the City, the Artists Rifles, as the name suggested, set up by painters, poets, sculptors and musicians. Both units were discerning as to whom they chose, opting to maintain the social composition of their respective battalions at the outset of war. The London Scottish was intent on doing the same, charging 'customers' for the honour of a space in the ranks.

Back I went to 59 Buckingham Gate the next day and, not disclosing I had been before, I again confronted the Medical Officer. This time I sailed through with flying colours, and after swearing the Oath of Allegiance, I found myself a soldier on one shilling a day pay. I also had to pay one pound for the privilege of joining the London Scottish Regiment. At the time I thought this was rather odd, but looking back over the years I realise that in view of the bond of comradeship created during the War, and which has continued ever since, that it was indeed a privilege to have belonged to such a Regiment.

A. Stuart Dolden

The Artists Rifles had agreed to take journalist and devout Socialist Frederick Keeling. He enlisted amongst men the vast majority of whom would be offered commissions when the army looked round for additional officers. The poet Rupert Brooke (a friend of Keeling's) was already serving in the battalion, though he departed soon after.

Keeling's political views were no block to him serving in the ranks of the Artists Rifles, though he quickly hankered after a change, seeking to join a Kitchener battalion. Owing to Lord Kitchener's jaundiced view of part-time soldiers, no restrictions had been placed on men jumping ship to the New Army. Once there Keeling could serve alongside the rank and file, the everyday manual worker turned soldier with whom he felt a certain kinship. His letters, published posthumously, are very much of their time: archaic and rather pompous in style, but sentiments that would be quite reasonable to those he addressed back in 1914.

Frederick Keeling

I was rung up today by an Oxford man in the Board of Trade who heard I was thinking of going into the ranks of the Kitchener Army, and wants to come with me if he can get permission. He is a very good fellow and would make a good comrade-in-arms. We both had the idea of going and enlisting in a country district – West of England, Sussex, or Westmorland.

The men who are being enlisted in London are in many cases rather awful types, much farther off the decent workmen than we are from the latter. I saw a good deal of the type at the starting of the Exchange in Leeds. Countrymen or miners of any set of men from a district, with something of a traditional standard of comfort would make much better fellow-soldiers, and I don't see the point of running up against the worst types of proletarians…

I should be happier with a decent sort of workmen than with the middle-class young men in the Artists. And I think the Kitchener Army will get tougher work and training; we shall be the professionals

Frederick made his decision and with two friends went to enlist.

Frederick Keeling

As one of a party originally numbering three, I made a preliminary visit to the Scotland Yard Recruiting Station before actually being sworn in. Each of us was about six feet high, and we were at first pressed by the recruiting officer to enlist in the Guards. 'That's the place for fine young fellows like you,' he said. We were flattered, but deterred by imaginary visions of ceremonial drill. As we were all moved by a terror of horses, the cavalry was out of the question. I had a weakness for the artillery, but a musician in the party objected to being deafened. We therefore decided by a method of exclusion on the infantry. 'Well, then,' said the recruiting officer, 'why not try a county light infantry regiment? You'll like it better than a regiment recruited from London or a big town.'

We hit more or less by accident on the [Duke of Cornwall's] Light Infantry, and four days later returned to Scotland Yard at 8.45 am for the purpose of being sworn in. In connection with the preliminaries to this process, some of us protested against the official system of religious classification. 'What religion?' said the inquiry clerk. 'No religion,' I replied firmly. 'Come, come, you must have some religion,' he urged. 'Well, atheist, if you like,' I said. 'That isn't a religion,' he said. I didn't want to clog the machine, so I said, 'Well, you can call me a bit of a Unitarian, if you like.' (After all, any one can be 'a bit of a Unitarian'.) 'Well, I'll write in "Unitarian" specially to oblige you,' he said, 'but that isn't really in the list either.' As we don't attend Church Parade till we get our uniforms, I have not yet discovered what provision the Army makes for Unitarians. To avoid trouble, I have decided in the last resort to go with the Presbyterians. After being sworn in and receiving our first day's pay, we were sent off to the regimental depot.

Most men were not so combative; they knew what they were whether they truly believed in a god or not. Those not overly concerned with a particular faith could try to second-guess what advantages might accrue with a 'right' answer, as Stuart Dolden recalled.

Eastwood, when asked for his religion replied, 'What are you short of?' He finally settled for Roman Catholic in the belief that as we were a Scottish regiment he would not have to attend church parades. But alas! The following Sunday he was mustered and marched off with the other Roman Catholics to a service about five miles away. On Monday he changed his religion; I have never seen such a dramatic conversion and all without the aid of prayer!

A. Stuart Dolden

One of hundreds of general medical practitioners brought in to examine the recruits that summer was 53-year-old Dr Herbert de Carle Woodcock. In 1914, he worked in a Leeds recruitment office, helping to alleviate the pressure on the army's medical officers.

Any medical man who could spare the time to examine recruits was welcomed. These boys lined up naked against the walls of the Tram

Dr Herbert de Carle Woodcock

A civilian doctor drafted in to help pass recruits listens to the heart of a middle-aged volunteer.

Offices. How I remember them! How anxious they were to join up! A whole bunch of them swerved over to the group of medical men because we were rejecting few and passing recruits in quickly. One drunken volunteer was turned out by an austere doctor who said the army must not be degraded by 'drink'. However, the recruit came up again. I saw him enter the room, and in a few minutes he was in the army. One old man who had been at Tel el Kebir [1882] came before me. When he was rejected as far too old he said, 'You'll want me before you've finished.'

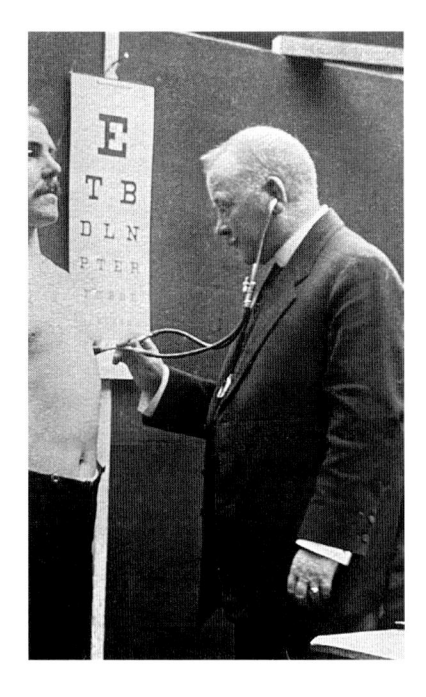

The examination was a strange one. Men who could jump and hop and shout 'Who goes there?' were thought by some examiners to be strong in wind and limb, strong enough to fight, whilst men with the classical faults of the recruiting tests, variocele, flat foot, varicose veins, and the like, were rejected in large numbers. All these faults were subsequently ignored, and recruits who could shoot and march, whose internal organs were capable of bearing strain, were accepted.

In Hampshire, Lieutenant Arthur Martin, a professional soldier of the Royal Army Medical Corps, was awaiting orders to embark for France. In the meantime, he and one other doctor were drafted in to help examine the recruits and separate the wheat from the chaff.

Lieutenant Arthur Martin, Royal Army Medical Corps

Each doctor takes five at a time. At the word of command they strip and the doctor begins. He casts a professional eye rapidly over the nude recruit. A general look like this to a trained eye conveys a lot. The chest is examined, tongue, mouth, and teeth looked at. The usual sites for rupture are examined. About three questions are asked: 'Any previous illness?' 'Age?' 'Previous occupation?' A mark is placed against the name, the nude Briton is told to clothe himself, and the examination is over. It is done at express speed, and although the examination is not very thorough it is sufficient to enable an experienced man to detect most physical defects. If a man passed, he was put down for foreign service. Some had slight defects and were put down for home defence. Some had glaring defects and were turned down altogether.

Even the chaff might be usefully employed, Martin was advised. 'The first call to arms generally brings in a very motley crowd,' he noted, confirming that the 'best' volunteers generally held back until domestic affairs, such as knowledge of the army's quoted separation allowances for wives and children, were settled, which guaranteed an income at home while a man was away.

We had all sorts of derelicts turn up. One weary-looking veteran, unwashed and with straw sticking in his hair, indicative of a bed in a haystack the previous night, was blind in one eye and very lame. A draper's assistant from a London shop had a twisted spine, an old soldier had syphilitic ulcers on the legs, some had bad hearts from excessive smoking, some bad kidneys from excessive drinking, some young men were really sexagenarians from hard living, and so on. They were old men before their time. The occupations of our recruits were as diverse as their shapes and constitutions – a runaway sailor, a Cockney coster, a draper's assistant, a sea cook, a medical student, a broken-down parson, an obvious gaolbird, and a Sunday-school teacher.

Before the doctor the son of a prizefighter makes a better showing than the son of a consumptive bishop. We had orders not to be too strict with our physical examination. We were not to turn a man down if he could be usefully employed in any State service during the war. For instance, many of the 'weeds' amongst the young men, the cigarette victims, the pasty-faced, flat-chested youths, those who had lived down dark alleys and in unhygienic surroundings all their lives, were all capable of being made into better men. Regular meals, plain food, good quarters, baths, cleanliness, and hard work, marching, drilling, and gymnastics, made these slouching, dull-eyed youths into active,

Lieutenant Arthur Martin, Royal Army Medical Corps

smart men. They then held their heads up, breathed the free air, lost their sullenness, and became cheerful.

Some of the recruits were not fit to be made into soldiers, and work could always be found for them. There are so many openings for the willing man at this time, be it cook's assistant, mess servant, officer's servant, orderly, or bootmaker's help.

Back in Leeds, Woodcock noticed that while many men came to the recruitment office they did not all fall in line or step inside. Some were clearly conflicted, unsure if enlisting there and then was the right thing to do. In the street outside the office stood 48-year-old policeman Robert Bretherick and, according to Woodcock, he proved 'a valuable recruiting agent', turning unsure bystanders into recruits.

Dr Herbert de Carle Woodcock

Bretherick was too old to enlist but he sent his son and son-in-law. He told the crowd of waiting lads thus. And his eloquence was simple and direct. 'You've come here to enlist, and that's all you've come for, so march in!' And big lumps melted off the crowd and pushed through the door. Some were a little sheepish, some had flushed and some had pale faces; some were big, many were small. Many were rejected on account of tuberculosis.

The general health of these early recruits, like 5-foot 1-inch, 7½-stone John Laister, was at best indifferent and very often extremely poor. Woodcock refers to one 'thin lad suffering from phthisis'. Woodcock mentioned to the boy his diminutive statue and his lack of fitness, to which the lad replied: 'I know I am, but I thought I should get in, I could do something.' Phthisis was pulmonary tuberculosis, or consumption as it was better known, typified by a chronic cough and weight loss, amongst other things. The men or boys who suffered were usually rejected within a week or two as medically unfit, even if they had initially passed a medical and had been recruited. Of those discharged, many attempted to enlist again if their condition stabilised or even improved, 'the men slipping out and slipping into the Army', noted Woodcock. 'Later, the nation and the Army came to regret this, but who could blame the fiery enthusiasts who took the patriotic course.'

John Laister was one of many discharged within days being deemed medically unfit. He was also one of many who sought to re-enlist a week later. Despite his obvious frailties, John was accepted and sent to the depot of his chosen regiment. By November, he was serving in France.

In London, American James Hall was not filled with patriotism; there was no reason to be, but he was excited and curious. He had taken the plunge and enlisted though he was now kicking his heels while he awaited further orders.

During the completion of other, less important formalities, I was taken in charge by a sergeant who might have stepped out of any of the 'Barrack-Room Ballads'. He was true to type to the last twist in the s of Atkins. He told me of service in India, Egypt, South Africa. He showed me both scars and medals with that air of 'Now-I-would-n't-do-this-for-any-one-but-you', which is so flattering to the novice. He gave me advice as to my best method of procedure when I should go to Hounslow Barracks to join my unit.

"An 'ere! Wotever you do an' wotever you s'y, don't forget to myke the lads think you're an out-an'-outer, if you understand my meaning, – a Britisher, you know. They'll tyke to you. Strike me blind! Be free an' easy with 'em, – no swank, mind you! – an' they'll be downright pals with you. You're different, you know. But don't put on no airs. Wot I mean is, don't let 'em think that you think you're different. See wot I mean?'

I said that I did. 'An' another thing; talk like 'em.' I confessed that this might prove to be rather a large contract. "Ard? S'y! 'Ere! If I 'ad you fer a d'y, I'd 'ave you talkin' like a born Lunnoner! All you got to do is forget all them aitches. An' you don't want to s'y "can't", like that. S'y "cawrn't". I said it. 'Now s'y, "Gor blimy, 'Arry, 'ow's the missus?"' I did. 'That's right! Oh, you'll soon get the swing of it.' There was much more instruction of the same nature.

By the time I was ready to leave the recruiting offices, I felt that I had made great progress in the vernacular. I said good-bye to the sergeant warmly. As I was about to leave he made the most peculiar and amusing gesture of a man drinking.

James Hall

'A pint o' mild an' bitter,' he said confidentially. 'The boys always gives me the price of a pint.'

'Right you are, sergeant!' I used the expression like a born Englishman. And with the liberality of a true soldier, I gave him my shilling, my first day's wage as a British fighting man.

The remainder of the week I spent mingling with the crowds of enlisted men at the Horse Guards Parade, watching the bulletin boards for the appearance of my name which would mean that I was to report at the regimental depot at Hounslow. My first impression of the men with whom I was to live for three years, or the duration of the war, was anything but favourable. The newspapers had been asserting that the new army was being recruited from the flower of England's young manhood. The throng at the Horse Guards Parade resembled an army of the unemployed, and I thought it likely that most of them were misfits, out-of-works, the kind of men who join the army because they can do nothing else. There were, in fact, a good many of these. I soon learned, however, that the general out-at-elbows appearance was due to another cause. A genial Cockney gave me the hint.

"Ave you joined up, matey?' he asked.

I told him that I had.

'Well, 'ere's a friendly tip for you. Don't wear them good clo'es w'en you goes to the depot. You won't see 'em again likely, an' if you gets through the war you might be a-wantin' of 'em. Wear the worst rags you got.'

I profited by the advice, and when I fell in, with the other recruits for the Royal Fusiliers, I felt much more at my ease.

It was two weeks since the outbreak of hostilities and British infantry had not fired a shot in anger: there remained a sense of war unreality back home. With no news of casualties to stir emotions, no battlefield setbacks, no reports of enemy foul play to galvanise young men to action, there appeared to be no pressing need to enlist. The public assumed the war would not last and recruits were unlikely to see action before Germany sued for peace.

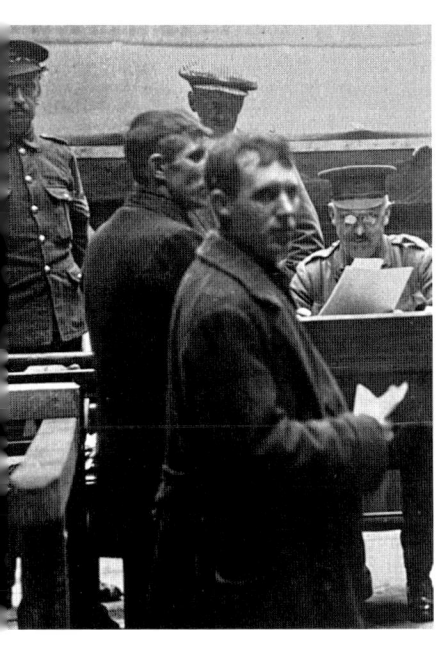

It was only as newspapers reported the fighting around Mons and the retreat of the British Expeditionary Force towards Paris that the atmosphere changed. It was clear that while the Germans were undoubtedly suffering heavy casualties at the hands of British infantry, the BEF was under severe stress, outnumbered and outgunned. Only as a more accurate picture emerged from the fighting in France and Belgium did recruitment numbers rise exponentially. Early September saw the greatest daily influx of volunteers, numbers outstripping the army's capacity to cope; more recruits enlisted on 3 September than the army received annually in peacetime.

The paymaster's office: handing out the traditional shilling given on enlistment, constituting a man's first day's pay.

One of the 32,000 recruits that day was Londoner, 19-year-old Jack Davis, an employee of a popular West End club.

I was in the Boys' Brigade and was a member of the athletics club too, so I both accepted discipline and had an organised life. The call of the army quite naturally attracted me. I enlisted in New Scotland Yard with thirty of my colleagues, waiters, wine waiters, valets, en masse, because our manager at the Liberal Club was a patriotic Frenchman and so we had no difficulty in joining up and letting the women take over our jobs. Then we had a night out, the group of us, for once you accepted the traditional King's shilling, you're in. So, it being our last night of freedom, we made the best of it with the boys.

Jack Davis

Vic Cole's work at the Wireless School of Telegraphy was suffering.

We had gone back to school, but we were mucking about, nobody knew what they were doing, but I wanted to be in the army with a gun in my hand like the boys I had so often read about in books and magazines.

Spurred on to fight, he made his way to the Crystal Palace where a twice-daily recruitment rally was held. 'It was a good spot because the trams came up and disgorged people there while others were making their way to the Palace proper: there were always crowds.' On his way, he bumped into his friend George Pulley, and Vic suggested they went together.

Vic Cole

Saturday night September 5th, George Pulley and I attended our first and last recruiting meeting at the top of Anerley Hill, by the south tower of the Palace. A leather lunged gentleman was going on about this Kaiser and keeping the Germans off the green fields of old England and telling us how beautiful it was to be in the army. He was standing on the seat of an open car, and was urging the crowd to throw up their jobs, join Kitchener's Army and fight for King and Country. The way he spoke it was just a matter of coming up, drawing a rifle and ammunition and proceeding straight away to France to fight the Germans. George and I considered the matter, well, he more or less egged me on to do it, and so we made our decision and approached the Sergeant who already had his eagle eye upon us. He was most pleased to see us, possibly because out of all that crowd, I discovered, we were the only ones to join up that night.

Lolling back on the nice cushioned seats of a fast car we were rushed off along Crystal Palace Parade, down West Hill to a nearby hostel in Penge called *The Crooked Billet*. We were shown to an upstairs room with several long tables upon which various people were signing forms: this was the Recruiting Office. We stood before the

A medical officer of the Royal Army Medical Corps and a local dignitary in an official car used to ferry would-be volunteers to recruiting offices.

Recruiting Officer who demanded particulars. 'Age?' 'Nineteen years and nine months' (I was actually two years less than that). 'Occupation?' 'Student.' 'What regiment do you wish to join?' George behind me whispered 'West Kents' so I said, 'Make it West Kents.' The R.O. with a smile (looking back on it I feel inclined to say with a sinister smile) said 'Sign this form.' I did so. He handed me a railway warrant and a slip directing me to report at Bromley Drill Hall at 9 am on the 7th inst. George had similar instructions, so off we went to spend our last few hours as civilians.

My poor Aunt and Gran could scarcely believe their ears, when, hardly waiting to close the door, I called out, 'I've joined the army!'

'Oh dear, oh dear' said Gran 'my poor boy' neither of them were at all demonstrative but when I sat down Gran put her arm about me for a moment. My Aunt shed a tear and then said, 'Well, I suppose you'd like a cup of tea now.'

Neither Vic nor George were given a medical, simply signing enlistment papers before going on their way. Medical officers were not always on hand to pass recruits and it was evident that in some cases pub rooms doubling up as pop-up recruiting offices were keen to get a man's legal commitment so he could no longer back out. Dealing with the issues of fitness and mental capacity could come a day or two later.

The oath taken by every recruit on attestation was succinct. A man would read out or repeat the words of a sergeant, swearing to pay true allegiance to His Majesty, King George the Fifth, his Heirs and Successors:

> I will, as in duty bound, honestly and faithfully defend His Majesty, His Heirs and Successors, in Person, Crown and Dignity, against all enemies, according to the conditions of my service.

The officer's voice ceased, and with it our repetition, leaving our group awaiting the next formality. For an instant his glance swept our ranks, then: 'Kiss the Book.'

One by one we did so, as it came to each in turn. Thus we became recruits in the Territorials. So quickly had one event followed

Private Geoffrey Fildes, 2/28th The London Regiment (Artists Rifles)

Holding the Bible while recruits repeat the oath of allegiance.

another through the last half-hour that I could hardly realise the momentous change that had come into my life. The medical examination, the filling in and signing of attestation papers, and, lastly, this ceremony of being sworn in, all impressed a civilian mind by their unfamiliarity and gravity.

'Party – 'Shun!'

A sergeant, instructed by another officer who had preserved hitherto an air of detachment, called our squad of raw recruits to attention; thereby banishing individual thoughts.

'Parade 9 o'clock, Russell Square, tomorrow morning; wear anything you like. On the command "Dismiss", turn smartly to your right and dismiss.'

'How does one do that?' I wondered.

'Party – Dis-miss!'

We turned as ordered, horribly uncertain whether to salute or not. For a moment we stood there wavering, then, our civilian habits overcoming our doubts, we fell out.

Fildes was all too aware of having just crossed one of life's significant Rubicons.

Private Geoffrey Fildes, 2/28th The London Regiment (Artists Rifles)

Proceeding homewards, one could not help feeling that henceforth everything was changed. So great did the change in my own lot seem, that I fancied something of it must be visible to every passer-by. For oneself, during the last month, the world had turned upside down, and the incident just finished seemed to complete the final overthrow. As I made my way toward the 'Tube', it seemed incredible that the surrounding world could continue in just the same leisurely fashion as before. Surely so great a crisis should leave some token of its presence, some fresh landmarks on the scene?

But along the streets, little or nothing in the outward appearance of things served to indicate the great catastrophe which had visited us. True, the crowds had a sprinkling of khaki, but nothing more that suggested the new epoch. Buses, taxicabs, and pedestrians wore just the same aspect of unconcerned preoccupation as ever.

However, Trafalgar Square revealed signs of the war's presence in our midst, for, above a crowd of bowler hats and caps, the red coat of a Chelsea pensioner was visible. He, at least, had grown restless at the tramp of marching feet. The Past, no less than the Present, had called to him 'Fall in!', and so he had taken the field once more. The sight of him beneath the shadow of the Nelson Column still haunts my memory: gloriously decrepit, he was still strong enough to preach the new crusade.

In the cathedral city of Ely, 21-year-old Sydney Fuller cycled over to the old militia barracks and offered himself up for the Royal Garrison Artillery. He was medically examined and passed fit and his papers marked 'Good'. By early afternoon he had been sworn in, the ceremony conducted in an office of the local brewery. By mid-afternoon, he along with other volunteers was being directed to the depot of the Suffolk Regiment in Bury St Edmunds. Although a local boy, he did not find it odd that he was being sent to the home of the Suffolk Regiment but he was surprised when perfunctorily informed on arrival that his first choice of the Royal Garrison Artillery was 'full up', as was that of the Royal Field Artillery. 'I did not greatly care at the time, so made no demur.' Fuller accepted his fate. The Suffolk Regiment it would be.

All volunteers had the right to choose the regiment or corps they wished to join, but periodically the authorities opened and closed access to certain branches deemed temporarily full. Whether or not all branches of the artillery had reached capacity, it does appear that the army was not willing to pass up a recruit who, on being told his first choice was unavailable, could feasibly walk away. Like Sydney Fuller, local boy 17-year-old Reginald Spraggins was keen to join the artillery, although legally too young to enlist.

Reginald Spraggins

At a recruiting office in Ipswich an officer asked me how old I was. I told him the truth. He said, 'That's no good, you must be nineteen to join the Army. I'll tell you what' – and this is what he said – 'Go out of that door and come back in this one. Once you come back in this one if you're nineteen you can go and join the Army.' So I did that. 'How old are you?' 'I'm nineteen,' I said. 'Just what we want!' he replied.

He then asked me, 'So first of all, what do you want to join?' 'The Royal Field Artillery,' I replied. 'I want to drive horses because I'm used to doing that.' So he said, 'That's all right. Well, first of all you have to go to Bury St Edmunds and then when you get there you tell them you want to go to the Royal Field Artillery and that's where they will put you, but first of all you have to go to be trained.' And that's the last I ever heard of the Royal Field Artillery. I was in the Suffolk Regiment and I had to stay in the Suffolk Regiment.

As newspaper reports of setbacks grew ever more dark and worrisome, men who initially stood back began to struggle with their emotions. Thirty-four-year-old Andrew Buxton, the Barclay's Bank manager, was unfit, a heavy smoker, and to his mind not an obvious recruit for the army.

Andrew Buxton

Sunday, August 30
I smoked my first cigarette since Friday after supper here and sweet indeed it is. It has been hard work not to have a smoke before, but I must now get fit for military duties, which I am confident are incumbent upon me, unless a very different turn takes place from the German awful move onward.

August 31
I know you don't want me to enlist, but I can't help thinking it my duty from every point of view to do so soon – say next week or the following. I am not a born soldier, but I am a bachelor and I have an idea of rifle shooting, and with every available man being required I cannot stand out. There is a Corps called 'The Artists', which rather attracts me, as I should not, I think, try for a Commission. It would,

no doubt, mean three or four months' training, and then choice of volunteering abroad or not.

One of Lord Kitchener's issues with the Territorial Force was the existing conditions of service under which men served; they could not be forced to go overseas. Instead, they would have to agree to new terms, signing a form agreeing to deployment abroad. Many Territorial units would only accept new recruits if they were willing to sign up to the new conditions: Andrew Buxton was still under the impression that he could train and then decide.

September 4

Andrew Buxton

I have not yet enlisted. I went up last night to Lord's Cricket Ground where a good many of the Artists are quartered on the practice ground and sleep in booths, etc. all round where tea parties usually reign supreme… Of course my intention is to join the ranks and not try for a Commission. This will be all right, provided I get in with nice men. I am now using endeavour to get men I know to arrange to come into the same Company with me. The disadvantage of waiting to enlist is that the probability of getting to France is more doubtful. This, as you can imagine, I should wish to do.

Buxton's age and fitness was a stumbling block to recruiting officers who could afford to be stringent with whom they signed up. Andrew was rejected by one doctor 'who absolutely refused' to accept him, but managed to find another more lenient

The last moments of a man's civilian life.

one who passed him. In the end Andrew did not join the Artists Rifles but a newly established Kitchener battalion raised on 11 September at Epsom: one of four University and Public Schools Battalions (UPS) of the Royal Fusiliers, as equally selective a unit as the Artists Rifles or the London Rifle Brigade.

Andrew Buxton

I feel my course has been right, and if not taken, to be endlessly regretted, though how to shoot or bayonet a German will, I think, continue an endless problem till the time comes, and then it has got to be done, even though conscious that he may have a mother who loved, in some degree, as mother does! Am I sentimental too much? I fear I am.

Far too young to imagine the implication of such terrible actions, Vic Cole and George Pulley had enlisted, being directed to turn up at Bromley Drill hall two days later.

Vic Cole

Early on Monday morning then, George and I, our pockets stuffed with sandwiches, went forth to war.

Arriving at the Hall without incident, we found some fifty other fellows wandering about in various stages of undress undergoing medical inspection. Our turn came. We dutifully walked on our toes, exhaled and coughed when ordered, read jumbled letters on a card and passed as fit. George and I then stripped and waited for the doctor. As we stood there, George looked me up and down, and then at my chest. 'I haven't got much up here, you're all right,' he whispered, 'you've got some muscle,' clearly he was a bit anxious. He was sixteen and he was a little bit skinny.

Once stripped, each man stepped behind a screen to test for rupture, the doctor putting two fingers either side of the testicles and ordering us to cough twice. Apparently if you have a rupture the bone in your crutch moved and they didn't want ruptured men going to the front. Ordeal over, we dressed and six at a time entered a small room to kiss the Bible and repeat after the Sergeant the words of an oath.

Thomas Lyon, the son of a builder, enlisted in early September in his home city of Glasgow. He joined the Highland Light Infantry and within weeks began writing personal sketches for his local newspaper, the *Kilmarnock Standard*, developing into a series of articles that became the basis for a memoir published in 1916. He and his comrades were amongst the battalion's first recruits, 'the rawest of the raw', he called them. In those early days, and in order to encourage additional volunteers, Lyon and his new comrades spent time marching around the city, 'basking in the grateful sunshine of popular esteem'.

Promptly at ten o'clock every morning we assembled in the great drill hall at the headquarters of the battalion, close to Glasgow Green. The spectacle that we presented as we formed ourselves into long lines, more or less straight reminded one of a scrum in a game of Rugby football more than anything else – so great was the shoving and jostling in order to get beside one's friends. Having been numbered

Private Thomas Lyon, 2/9th The Highland Light Infantry (Glasgow Highlanders)

Men from all walks of life quietly queue with their medical forms in hand.

off, we were counselled to form fours, which we succeeded in doing with something approaching spontaneity and precision, after several abortive attempts and as many sharp reprimands from the Sergeant-Instructor.

Then our triumphal march began. We were taken by devious ways to various quarters of the city, tapping a different district every day, and learning much of the local topography of which we had hitherto been ignorant. As day succeeded day our procession became longer: from five hundred we swelled to a thousand strong. The plan of attracting attention to the battalion by marching us through the city succeeded; other young men joined our ranks.

Oh, yes, we knew that we presented a very impressive sight as we swept through the city streets, each man trying to adopt the air of a martial hero and wondering in his own heart if the onlookers noticed the remarkable resemblance between him and Lord Kitchener or Napoleon. It was fine to march along Argyle Street or Sauchiehall Street and to see at each corner a long line of cars and other vehicles being held up until we should pass; it was fine to see and hear the crowds of people ranged on either side of the street that cheered us as we went by. Every door and every window was crowded with men and women waving handkerchiefs and shouting words of encouragement and benediction, and we acknowledged their greetings by asking them if we were downhearted, and, before receiving their reply, we ourselves assured them most emphatically that we weren't. Then those of us who could threw our chests further out, and those of us who couldn't did the next best, and threw out our stomachs, and we one and all tried to look like 'boys of the bulldog breed'…

Assuredly there was romance in the situation. Only one short week before, we were all unknown and unhonoured: city clerks, salesmen, lawyers, stockbrokers, accountants, pressmen, students – a hotch-potch of young men of different characteristics and calibre, but all equally obscure; and now we were being acclaimed – *en masse* if not individually – in the streets of Glasgow as martial heroes; or, at least, so the cheers of the assembled citizens seemed to betoken. Therefore we developed strong convictions regarding our present ability to pulverise the Germans; in the daytime, in the sight of the multitude, we flattered ourselves in respect of our military bearing and fitness.

The first-line Territorial battalions, those that existed on the outbreak of war, were directed to their war stations. Fear of a German invasion was real, and the Territorial Force was required within striking distance of the east coast, principally Suffolk and Kent, where invasion was most likely. In addition, a number of Territorial battalions would be sent overseas, not to the Western Front, but to countries such as Egypt, Malta, Gibraltar, and India, releasing Regular units on Garrison duty to return to Britain.

Second-line Territorial units and those newly established remained close to home, where they could be sustained by the associations legally charged with their care and maintenance, the 2/9th Highland Light Infantry remaining close to Dunfermline.

New Service battalions of Kitchener's New Army would experience life a little differently from those of the Territorial Force.

Within a day or two of enlistment, recruits to the infantry and artillery were directed to their respective regimental depots. If train travel was necessary, and in most cases it was, a railway warrant was issued before the men set off to undertake the rudiments of basic training.

Depots were for the purpose of receiving the recruit from the moment of his enlistment, training him in the elementary drill in which it is necessary for men of all arms to become proficient, to allow of their being 'handled' either singly or in mass, and providing him with a uniform and other articles of clothing… The man himself underwent a course of drills, physical training and lectures until he had reached a standard of efficiency that would warrant his being sent to his unit; when he attained this proficiency he waited until the Depot was ordered to send a draft to the unit, and then formed a member of it. With this moment his actual training as a recruit ceased.

These preliminary stages in the conversion of a civilian into a soldier were the main duty of the Depots, but apart from that, they had

Captain Cecil Street, Royal Garrison Artillery

another different function to perform. Upon a soldier terminating his service with the colours, he gave up his uniform and equipment, and these were carefully stored at the Depot during the period in which his service in the Reserve lasted. The Mobilisation Store at a big Depot was a very interesting sight, with a certain space allotted to each Reservist attached to the Depot, and in it his uniform, kit, and equipment, most carefully labelled and numbered, ready for instant issue. It was the pride of the Quarter-master's heart…

This then was the condition of the Depots on the outbreak of war, and this the purposely deliberate procedure that governed the training of recruits. Time was of no importance compared with the attainment of efficiency, *festina lente* [make haste slowly] was their motto. And now let us see how this well-oiled, slow-moving machinery answered the test of mobilisation, and how it was accelerated to meet the thousands per cent overload imposed upon it.

* * *

On Monday, 7 September, Vic Cole and George Pulley turned up as directed to Bromley Drill Hall, where both passed their medical examinations and with other recruits destined for the Royal West Kent Regiment they caught a train for Maidstone.

Vic Cole

We waited around in that drill-hall for some time until all had undergone the formalities of enlistment then found ourselves sharply ordered outside into the sunlit street and lined up in two ranks by a very smart khaki-clad Corporal of the West Kents, whose exceedingly pleasant and friendly manner gave us the optimistic but mistaken impression that life in the army was not so bad after all.

We numbered down, formed fours quite creditably and marched off en route from Bromley Station where, having dispersed about the platform to await the train for Maidstone (the West Kent Depot) we listened to a moving speech by His Worship the Mayor, who, addressing us as Men of Bromley, wished us all the best of luck and a safe return.

At the conclusion of this address, there was a great deal of singing and cheering, accompanied on my part by a slight altercation with a battered gentleman smelling strongly of hops, who, insisting that I bore a resemblance to a Sergeant-Major of his acquaintance, was, for that reason, going to punch me on the nose. The train came in at this moment however, and in the ensuing rush for seats, the beery one was swept away out of sight.

Vic and George were on their way.

Overleaf: *Crowds of onlookers watch and cheer volunteers making their way to enlist, ultimately into the 36th Ulster Division.*

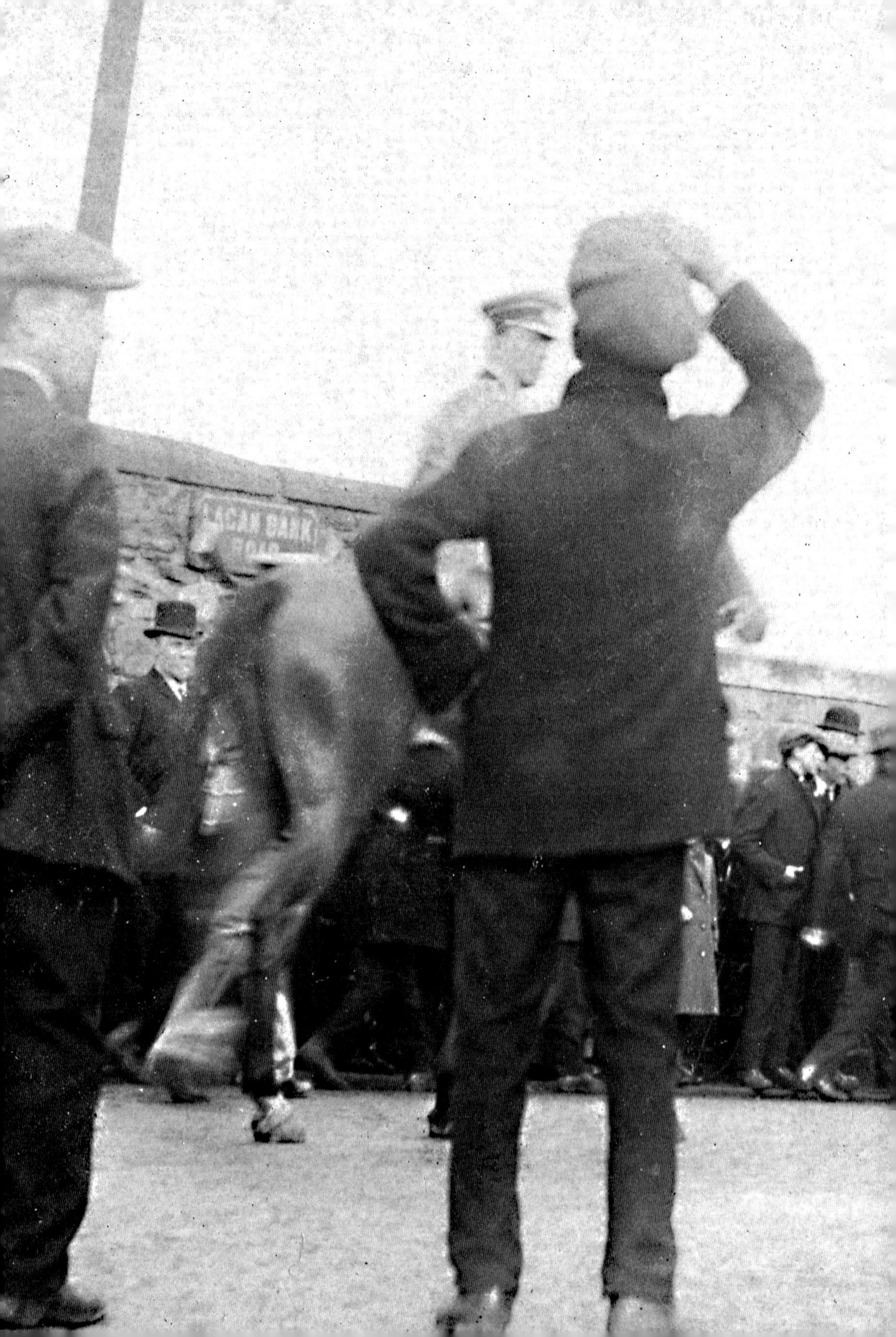

4 Warts and All

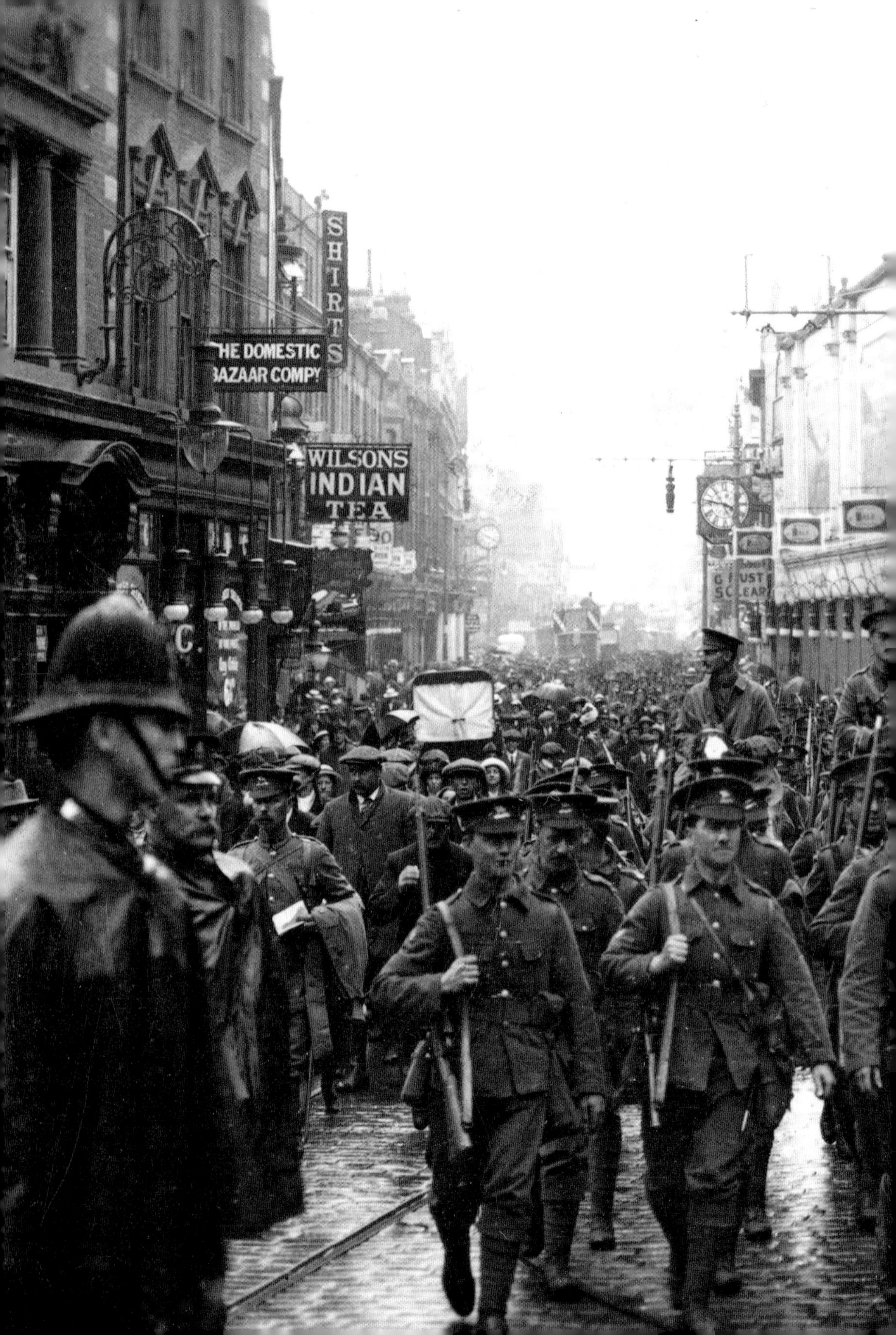
SHIRTS
THE DOMESTIC
BAZAAR COMPY
WILSONS
INDIAN
TEA

> 'There are many funny stories about these men when they first joined the army. It was a common thing for a man to call an officer "Your honour", and one who wished to be particularly respectful is said on a certain occasion to have addressed the Colonel as "Your Reverence".'
>
> Lieutenant Colonel Rowland Feilding, 6th The Connaught Rangers

---

'Peace became in an instant the most strenuous preparation for war,' wrote Captain Cecil Street, recalling the frenzy of activity triggered by the War Office order to mobilise.

Across the country, the army's depots dealt with an immediate surge of Reservists heading back to barracks, the 'first flood', as Street called it. These were men sometimes long into retirement, frequently veterans of the Boer War who had completed their service in the Regular Army before returning to civilian life.

Accommodation had to be found for them, barrack-rooms improvised out of dining rooms and sheds, tents pitched upon the hitherto inviolate cricket ground, even for a while upon the barracks square itself. Night and day the deluge continued, the weary staff toiled incessantly at the monotonous task of marshalling a disorderly rabble into squads and companies, inventing ways and means of cooking their food and serving it in as civilised a method as possible. It almost seemed as though human endurance had reached its limit.

Captain Cecil Street, Royal Garrison Artillery

Reservists drew their uniforms and equipment from the quartermaster's stores and revived their technical knowledge with prompting and encouragement. Although these men were equipped with 'every art of the old soldier for

Opposite: Territorial soldiers in Croydon march to their headquarters after general mobilisation.

escaping arduous duties', as Street was well aware, they had at least been taught 'with sufficient of the old tradition to allow their being led by a determined hand'. These men slotted back into place amongst old friends. And then, within days they were gone, leaving, briefly, a virtual ghost town staffed by a small cadre of experienced officers and NCOs.

Days after mobilisation, men of the Honourable Artillery Company camp on their parade ground at their headquarters in City Road, London. Within weeks, these men would be in France.

No sooner had the pressure upon the staff been relieved by the drafting of the more efficient of the mobilised Reservists to service units than the scheme for the New Armies came into operation…

The second flood were pure civilians, drawn to the colours by their sturdy patriotism… They were keen, enthusiastic, pathetically anxious to learn, but utterly unmanageable from their very ignorance of discipline and its formulae. In them was no leavening of experience that should help the whole on their first most difficult steps in the path of military knowledge, they flowed in too fast to allow of minute subdivision into squads to be carefully nursed by an experienced NCO, even had such been available.

Captain Cecil Street, Royal Garrison Artillery

In Kent, a train full of these enthusiasts was on its way to the depot of the Royal West Kent Regiment and included childhood friends Vic Cole and 16-year-old George Pulley.

It was three weeks since the depot had received the first Kitchener recruits, all destined for the regiment's 6th Battalion. Anticipating the rush, the staff had quickly processed them, sending batches of 80–100 men to board trains for Colchester and a fast-growing tented encampment. Before they left, each man had drawn a uniform from stores.

Only at Colchester was the battalion effectively established, leaving urgently required room at the depot for Vic and his mates to join the regiment's 7th Battalion, born officially on 5 September. It must have seemed to the overworked depot staff that the numbers arriving would never end, an effective conveyor belt of recruits, for within days an 8th Battalion took root. At its most chaotic moment, Maidstone Depot would handle 1,400 men, which was far in excess of peacetime capacity.

What with manipulating our sandwiches, scrambling at the stops for cups of tea and yarning away with our new-found friends, the journey soon passed and we were detraining at Maidstone. Up the sloping street and across the bridge (still singing but not so loudly) until at last with a left wheel we swung through the gates of Maidstone Barracks. Here, after falling out for a brief rest we were called to the Pay Office

Private Vic Cole, 7th The Queen's Own (Royal West Kent Regiment)

window to receive our first Army pay. This was the sum of 2/9 (the King's shilling plus one day's pay plus one day's ration money). For this we were called alphabetically and after drawing the pay we were paraded for the first time and formed into sections and the next day put through our first drill on the barrack square. Sadly, in dividing us up I became separated from George and it was only very occasionally that I ran across him after this.

Sydney Fuller, thwarted in his wish to join the Royal Field Artillery, began life in the infantry at the Suffolk Regiment Depot in Bury St Edmunds.

Private Sydney Fuller, 8th The Suffolk Regiment

On arrival, we were marshalled in some sort of order by a few NCOs and marched to the barracks where we were met by a sergeant armed with a small book, in which all our names were duly entered. This business over, the sergeant said, 'Right! There's your hotel,' and indicated a large marquee, erected in the barrack grounds. We then obtained one blanket per man, and, as it was getting dark and we were tired, we made ourselves comfortable on the ground in the marquee. This was packed like a sardine tin, and many and strong were the criticisms of the way the country treated 'men what volunteered to fight for their King and Country'. Many and strong were the smells that thickened the air, feet (sweaty) being an easy first. Several men had evidently celebrated the occasion in a drink (or several) before arriving, and some of these insisted on singing in very untuneful voices, one (a Cockney) keeping it up until about midnight.

In Bodmin, the home of the Duke of Cornwall's Light Infantry, the regimental staff was also dealing with an avalanche of volunteers. Men were already sleeping in the depot's married quarters, in the gymnasium and detention rooms when journalist Frederick Keeling and hundreds of additional recruits arrived from London. The train journey had taken seven hours, and so packed were the carriages that there had been insufficient space for many to sit.

Before starting we each received sixpence ration money, but sixpence does not go far in a railway refreshment-room. Fortunately, when we arrived a committee of ladies of the town provided us with an excellent supper at the station. After three cheers for our hosts, we marched up to the barracks, received a blanket, and then marched back to the local assembly rooms. There the Major in charge of the depot addressed us. He explained that the accommodation in the barracks was intended for less than two hundred men, but that over two thousand were on his hands. He appealed to us, for the sake of the honour of the regiment, not to wreck the hall, a feat which he evidently expected us to perform.

Of course, the place was in a state of pandemonium even before the Major had finished, and when the lights were put out, the high-spirited youth of Poplar and Stepney only substituted cat-calls for conversation across the hall. I did not expect a wink of sleep. But the noise did gradually subside, in spite of repeated cheers at the offer of a sergeant to fight any one who wanted to speak. Actually I slept well and woke to the sound of an impromptu game of football in the road outside. We fared better than the thousand or so recruits in the barracks, many of whom slept on the grass under trees.

For breakfast we obtained loaves of bread, torn up at ease on the grass, and rumours of butter and tea. The dinner [lunch] was an excellent stew of beef and potatoes. Few of us could obtain knives or forks, but a hungry man can dispense with these. Tea a good many of us missed owing to the prolongation of the medical inspection, but for threepence one could buy an excellent meal of cocoa, corned beef, and bread in the canteen.

Private Frederick Keeling, 6th The Duke of Cornwall's Light Infantry

George Butterworth, composer and erstwhile music master at Radley public school, joined the same battalion. Butterworth was a good friend of Keeling's. In a letter, he recalled the raucous, happy band of men who drank and sang their way to Cornwall aboard the Paddington to Bodmin train.

Private George Butterworth, 6th The Duke of Cornwall's Light Infantry

Recruits of the 11th Welsh Regiment in September 1914. Although they appear fit and well, the reverse of this photograph indicates that they were 'nearly starving'.

Our reception [at the barracks] was not encouraging; at the gate we were each presented with one blanket, and told that the sleeping accommodation was already over-full, and that we must do as best we could in the open. Some 20 of us accordingly stationed ourselves under a small group of trees. Food was the next question; although we had been given no opportunity for a meal since Paddington, nothing was provided for us. Luckily, the canteen was still open, and by dint of much pushing we managed to secure a tin of corned beef and bottle of beer. Considering the situation in which we found ourselves – the night was a distinctly cold one for September – it was not surprising that certain of the rougher specimens partook rather freely.

Although he managed to remain amongst his friends, George was introduced to new comrades from all walks of life. It was a shock.

> It so happened that we shared our 'pitch' with a rabble from Handsworth, Birmingham – a district which is, I believe, notorious. These worthies kept us supplied with a constant stream of lewdness, mostly of a very monotonous kind; there was one real humourist who made some excellent jokes, but they are scarcely repeatable. At about 2 am we were joined by several unfortunates who had found their tents already occupied (by lice) and preferred the open air and the wet grass. Altogether it was a remarkable experience, the most surprising thing about it being the complete absence of any attempt at discipline.

Private George Butterworth, 6th The Duke of Cornwall's Light Infantry

Bodmin took in hundreds of men in public rooms, school halls, and church buildings, but in the end some men had to be moved to other regimental depots, not locally (they were generally overwhelmed too), but to Ireland and the depots of both the Dublin and the Inniskilling Fusiliers. Meanwhile, six Metropolitan police officers were dispatched to help act as temporary instructors and six clerks from the Army Service Corps drafted in to help with the completion of attestation papers.

In Maidstone, Vic Cole was finding his feet. At least he and his mates would be properly accommodated on their first night.

> In our new-formed sections we marched across the barrack square to a vast room in the main building where we were shown our beds and left to our own devices. I was tired, and, having found out how to arrange the two parts of my iron bedstead and adjust the three 'biscuits' (small mattresses) I crept between the blankets and – failed to sleep for many hours! To begin with, clad only in my shirt, the coarse texture of the blankets was most uncomfortable against my bare legs. Also, my bed being installed at the end of the room, I found myself only a few feet from that unsavoury barrack-room utensil the 'night-tub' [urinal], which placed just inside the door seemed to be in use throughout the night.

Private Vic Cole, 7th The Queen's Own (Royal West Kent Regiment)

Next morning, just prior to Reveille we were awakened by shouts of 'Gunfire, Gunfire' which I discovered to be the signal for early morning tea, otherwise known as 'Gunfire Tea'. This we swallowed steaming hot whilst lying in our beds and later a small collection was made as recompense to the cooks for their extra work. Routine jobs followed – tub-emptying, bed-making and floor-sweeping, the first tasks of every day.

Another underage soldier, George Coppard, a lad from Croydon, arrived at the depot of The Queen's (Royal West Surrey Regiment), Stoughton Barracks in Guildford. Describing himself as 'an ordinary boy of elementary education and slender prospects', George had been thrilled by the military bands on his town's street corners, thrilled enough to enlist.

> I had no fixed ideas of what branch of the army I wanted to join and considered I would be lucky if I was accepted at all. Although weighing over ten stone I was very much a boy in heart and mind.

Aged 16, George had trodden the already well-worn path by lying about his age, the recruiting sergeant winking as he handed over the King's shilling. That same day, 27 August, George with a 'crummy and unwashed crowd' took the train to the regimental depot and bedded down for the night.

Private George Coppard, 6th The Queen's Own (Royal West Surrey Regiment)

Reveille was at 5.30 am next morning and, after a night on the floor with half a blanket, I didn't feel too good. Word flashed round that 'gunfire' (tea) was available in the cookhouse. A scramble followed, but there were few mugs to drink from. I drank mine from a soup plate, not an easy task at the first attempt. After a day or two of this kind of thing, I realised that I had left the simple decencies of the table at home. One had to hog it or else run the risk of not getting anything at all. I learnt that lesson quicker than anything else.

Like George, Ernest Parker had everything to learn about the army. On his train ride to the cavalry barracks in Bristol, a middle-aged man cautioned him: 'The Army makes or mars,' he had said, leaving Ernest to wonder what his fate would be. The next morning the new recruits looked for signs of breakfast. There would be no timidity or respectful queuing for food amongst these men..

Sharp eyes kept scanning the door of the cookhouse and when a line of buckets glinted in that direction everyone was afoot and each orderly was surrounded by a struggling mob of untidy, unshaven men. I didn't have a chance in that scramble and, more or less a spectator, I watched the lucky owners of mess tins making for safety out of the crowd. More often than not they lost the contents of their tins on the way! When the bread ration followed, that too went to the strong, some of whom found it possible to get two or more shares, which they wolfed ravenously.

Private Ernest Parker, 15th (The King's) Hussars

An impromptu toilet in the morning, as no soap or towels were obtainable, and hardly anyone had brought these with them. Happy was the man who had the wherewithal to wash, for he had many friends… Food and drink, or rather, rations were distributed by parading the crowd and marching one rank on either side of a line of tables, on which were basins of tea, loaves of bread, and tins of herring – one of each for every two men. An NCO stood on a table at the end of

Private Sydney Fuller, 8th The Suffolk Regiment

The arrival of food always delivered an anxious crowd, with the youngest too often being shoved out of the way by more experienced and aggressive recruits.

each line, keeping two eyes on the rations and nipping in the bud any attempts at 'coming the double'. The sergeant in charge of the table I got my rations from had a fine flow of language, of which he gave the full benefit whenever there was any sign of rushing. He threatened to brain some of us with his stick, and to turn the table over.

By evening, more bell tents were made available and Sydney was able to get a decent night's sleep. The weather was fine and warm and many men remained outside, sleeping on the grass, two waking to find a hedgehog for a bedfellow.

Private George Butterworth, 6th The Duke of Cornwall's Light Infantry

Morning found most of the crowd considerably sobered – not to say depressed. Breakfast was long delayed, and when it came consisted of loaves of bread thrown about indiscriminately, and large dishes of tea (mixed with milk and sugar) one dish to eight men. We eked out this allowance with the remains of last night's supper.

The proceedings of the day were irritating and futile in the extreme – endless 'parades', and very little business done. Amongst other things we were all medically inspected again, this time to see if we were fit for foreign service. But, curiously enough, this inspection was much less thorough than the one in London.

Meals were a great difficulty and the conditions generally pretty bad, and I believe not a few actually deserted on their second day of service.

The men were unimpressed and there was an evident need for someone in authority to check the rising disaffection.

Private George Butterworth, 6th The Duke of Cornwall's Light Infantry

If the Government says they require half a million men they must be prepared to receive them in large numbers. If they have no room they ought to start a waiting list. I understand that Bodmin was not by any means the worst of the depots; at Reading, for instance, men had to sleep in the open without even a blanket. The conditions were all the worse because recruits had been specially told to bring next to no luggage, as they would receive their full kit directly on reaching the depot, whereas, in fact many received nothing for days, and even weeks, and thus had absolutely no change of clothes.

After breakfast came the order to parade at the Quartermaster's stores for an issue of clothing. The Q.M stores were much depleted. We drew just the articles that could be found to fit us with most commodities available only in outsizes. Personally I did pretty well with a set of underwear, khaki tunic and trousers and a pair of heavy boots. Some fellows acquired hats only, some only trousers, others just tunics. I donned my uniform but could not bring myself to wear the boots which I later swopped for a much lighter pair, in the meantime my civilian boots did me quite well.

Private Vic Cole, 7th The Queen's Own (Royal West Kent Regiment)

'Some misfits,' states the caption to this photograph, showing men laughing at their tight or outsized khaki uniforms.

Most of the men, obeying instructions had made parcels of their civilian clothes and had sent them home, others had done business with the secondhand clothes dealers in the town: in any case, except for hats and caps which some men had retained they were all now dressed in oddments obtained from the stores. Some had civilian trousers and coloured socks with khaki tunics, while others sported khaki trousers, civilian coats, and boots. One man in a tight fitting tunic and bowler hat struck up a popular music hall song and the rest, with much laughter at the aptness of the words, joined in the chorus 'I can't do my bally bottom button up!'

The human flow into depots was constant, though as time went on there were attempts to stem numbers by raising and lowering the useful bar of minimum height and chest measurements. At the artillery depot where Cecil Street worked, he noted with interest the mixed calibre of the recruits and the times when the next influx of men might be predicted to appear. It was not an exact science and Street was not explicit as to why he believed daily numbers fluctuated, but patterns were recorded and predicting numbers helped smooth depot logistics.

Captain Cecil Street, Royal Garrison Artillery

It was some time my duty to register the recruits as they came in, and this I did daily at 8 am, classing the recruits who had arrived during the preceding twenty-four hours as having joined the previous day. In an experience extending over more than a dozen weeks, I found invariably that Sunday's total was the minimum of the week, Monday's considerably higher, Tuesday's considerably higher again, indeed the maximum for the week, Wednesday's slightly less than Tuesday's, Thursday's very much less again, Friday's showed slight recovery, and Saturday's a rapid decline. We were always enabled to predict, within a fairly small margin, the number of men for whom we should have to provide, unless our calculations were upset by one of the periodic rushes, of which, of course, we had no previous warning. Our system was to keep the gymnasium, cleared of its apparatus, as an emergency-room, and on the first symptoms of a rush to lay straw mattresses upon the floor. Then as the men arrived, they were give a bowl of hot cocoa, and a mattress allotted to them, until in the morning [when] they could be sorted out.

With experience came a modicum of order, but in early September experience was lacking. Despite accommodation in Bodmin's assembly halls and churches, the men were hardly more content than those left lying under trees. On 4 September, George was one of 500 men returned to Aldershot. Given the journey's length, it may have felt as though trains were being used as temporary accommodation. 'We were not sorry to leave Bodmin,' George wrote, noting that his group of friends had expanded to include three other musicians (Francis Ellis, Morris, Toye), a civil servant (Woodhead), an engineer (Roland Ellis), and university teacher (Brown), and one journalist: the journalist was Frederick Keeling.

To the lay mind it is not clear why we were sent three hundred miles from London and then, equally unequipped and untrained, another two or three hundred miles to Aldershot. But 'you must all go through the depot' there is no getting behind that.

Arrived at Aldershot in a special train, we found ourselves almost the last detachment in a camp of 2,300 men, nearly all recruits from London and Birmingham. The first night in the camp is as indelibly stamped on my memory as the first night in Bodmin. Our party of ten friends had secured a tent to ourselves and were mostly asleep, when suddenly a head appeared in the aperture. 'Who are you?' we asked. 'Well, they calls me Joe,' replied a voice, 'but I am the Police. Are you all right?' 'Yes, we're all right.' 'Have you got any whisky?'

Unfortunately we hadn't. 'What do the Police do at night?' I asked, being eager to lose no opportunity of extending my military knowledge. 'Well,' said Joe, 'we mostly 'unts the bushes for women, and foilers the sound of our own footsteps round the camp.' And then followed an illuminating disquisition on the ins and outs of military discipline, which kept us in roars of laughter for an hour, until Joe became rather too muddled and was finally induced to depart.

Private Frederick Keeling, 6th The Duke of Cornwall's Light Infantry

Overleaf: *'Recruits from Gray's & District for Lord Kitchener's Army,' says the accompanying caption. The photograph is dated 1 September 1914, and shows new volunteers being marched off to their regimental depot.*

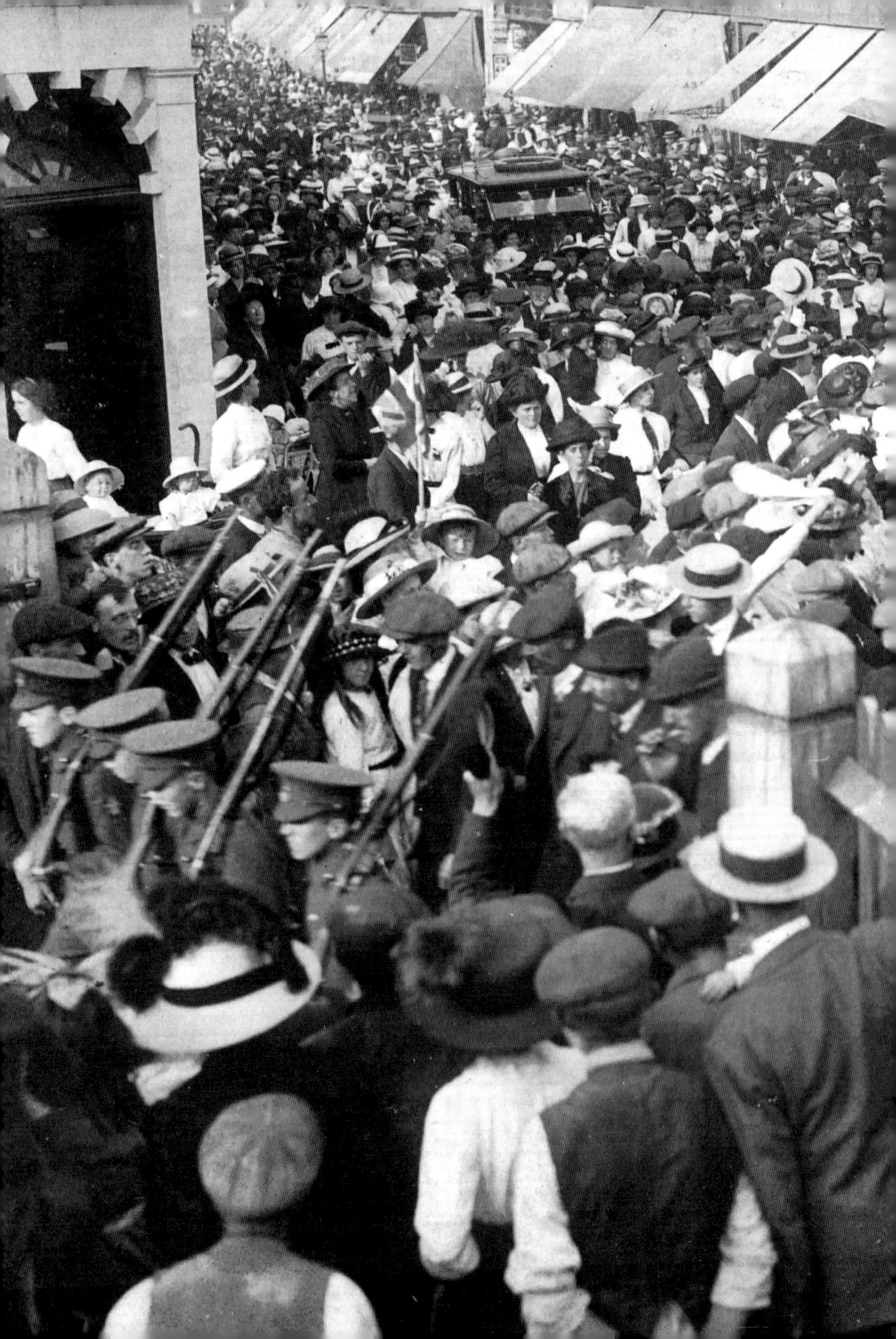

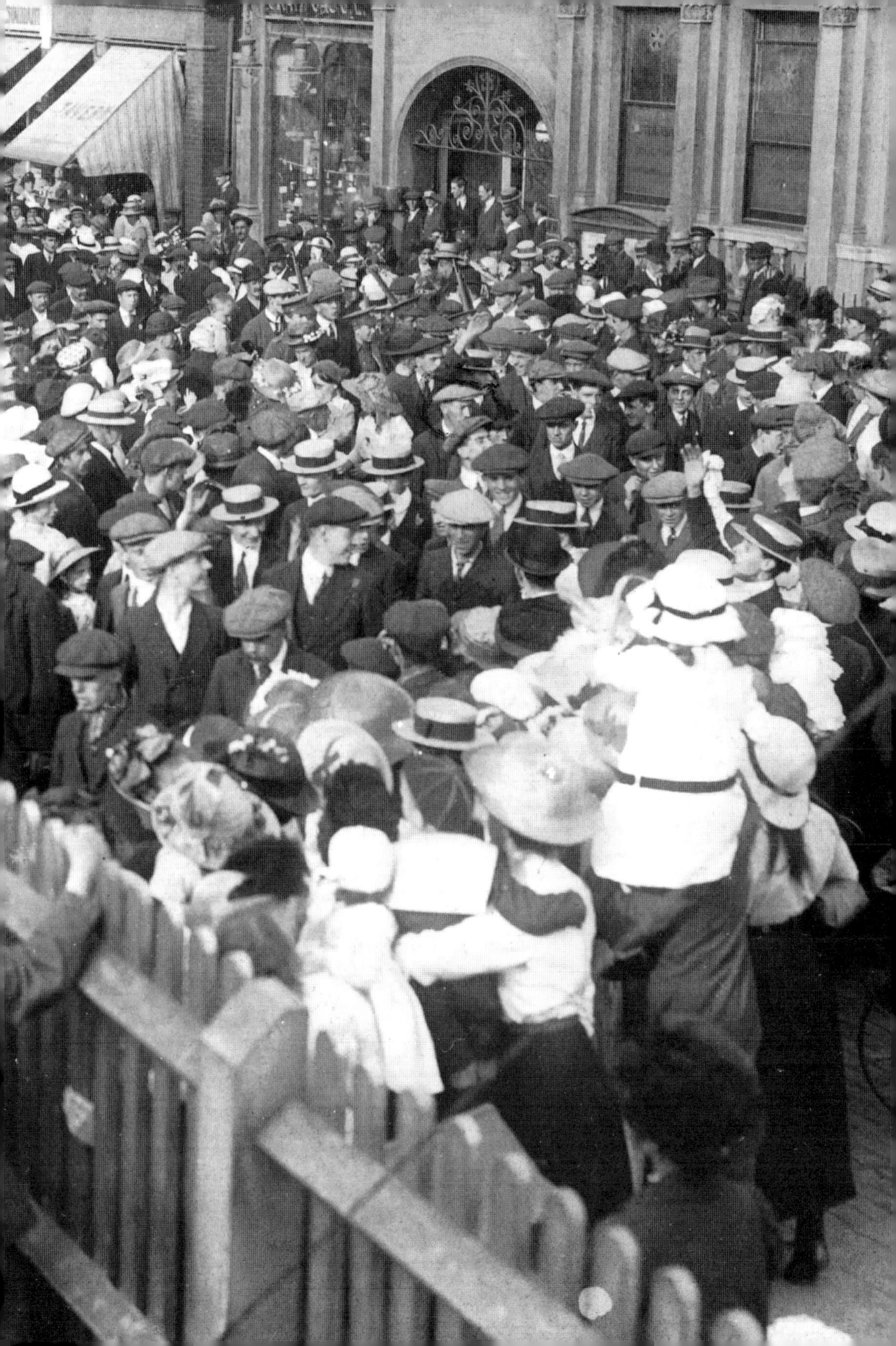

In London, James Hall's journey to Hounslow Barracks had been but a short ride. Hall and the other volunteers were fortunate to find that the depot held appreciably large stores of khaki service dress uniforms, though the boots issued were handed out without much care or attention. 'We squeak-squawked across the barrack square in boots which felt large enough for an entire family of feet,' he wrote. He described his mates as simply a 'mob… herded together like so many sheep'.

Private James Hall, 9th The Royal Fusiliers (City of London Regiment)

We must have been unpromising material from the military point of view. That was evidently the opinion of my own platoon sergeant. I remember, word for word, his address of welcome, one of soldier-like brevity and pointedness, delivered while we stood awkwardly at attention on the barrack square.

'Lissen 'ere, you men! I've never saw such a raw, roun'-shouldered batch o' rookies in fifteen years' service. Yer pasty-faced an' yer thin-chested. Gawd 'elp 'Is Majesty if it ever lays with you to save 'im! 'Owever, we're 'ere to do wot we can with wot we got. Now, then, upon the command, "Form Fours", I wanna see the even numbers tyke a pace to the rear with the left foot, an' one to the right with the right foot. Like so: "One-one-two!" Platoon! Form Fours! Oh! Orful! Orful! As y' were! As y' were!'

Private George Parker, 3rd The Sherwood Foresters (Nottinghamshire and Derbyshire Regiment)

'Orful! Orful!' Recruits parade, ready for an NCO's traditional verbal assault.

Once in the barracks, we were under Army rule, and we soon found that out! Lined up on the barracks square, we gave our names to a Sergeant who then handed us over to another Sergeant, a red-headed one, who was to be the bane of our lives for a time. He walked up and down the line of objects he had taken over with a look of hopeless disgust on his face…

'Redhead' started speaking softly, then gradually rose in volume to a bull-like roar. He had never had the misfortune to see such a bunch in his life. We were a misbegotten, useless lot; we had no mothers or fathers – we were not born but spawned against a wall. He had been given the hopeless job of making soldiers out of a lot of no-good layabouts and, by God, he would do it if it killed us! He strode up and down the line, snatching off the various headgear and throwing them on the ground, but when he came to a bowler hat, his eyes seemed to pop out of his head. He snatched it off and stamped on it. 'A soldier,' he snarled, 'in a bowler hat!' In the guardroom nearby was an open fire. We were ordered to march there and watch, while the poor bowler-hat owner cast it into the flames. His first sacrifice for his country!

In the Guards, new recruits were put through their paces at Caterham Barracks. Norman Cliff may have been inspired to become a Kitchener volunteer, but he had been directed towards one of the toughest regiments of the British Army.

From arrival at Caterham, Cliff and his fellow recruits had been chivvied and chased, shouted at, and verbally mauled, and then, as Cliff described portentously, 'Sgt. Baker happened'.

We noticed that most of the barking NCOs were tall, lean men, as stiff as pokers from the waist up, bellowing as though their throats would burst. Baker was a more elastic figure, blond with a ruddy complexion, a close-clipped moustache and an aggressive expression. First contact with him came as an electric shock.

'Squad, 'tion! As were! 'Tion! As were. Good God! See what the Lord has sent me. What have I done to deserve this? You're a nice looking mass of bloody wrecks, aren't you? And they expect me to make soldiers of you. Alas, my poor regiment, that it should come to this. Thank God we've got a Navy. Looks as though you've all jumped over the wall from the bloody looney bin next door and you'll all be jumping back before I've done with you. You may be God Almighty in Civvy Street but you're fuck all here. I'll make you sweat blood. We tame lions here.'

Guardsman Norman Cliff, 1st Grenadier Guards

Poking a recruit in the ribs with his swagger stick; 'Do you know Mrs Baker?'

'No.'

'No, what?'

'No, Sergeant.'

'Then you'll bloody soon know her son.'

Catching sight of a man with a mop of hair: 'Hi, what were you on civvy life? A poet? Get this wool off by tomorrow morning, d'ye hear?'

Returning all the way from Nigeria to enlist, businessman Douglas Cuddeford was at Caterham Barracks too. He could not help but be impressed at the sight of the NCOs.

Guardsman Douglas Cuddeford, Scots Guards

I'm quite sure they were the pick of the best type of the old-time foot-guardsman. Many of them had re-enlisted for active service, but had been retained at the Depot because they were of more use there than at the front. Most of them, I must say, were the usual foul-mouthed pre-war soldier, but they were the very men for the job, which was to convert recruits in the quickest time possible into well-trained drafts for their regiments.

Private James Hall, 9th The Royal Fusiliers (City of London Regiment)

If there was doubt in the minds of any of us as to our rawness, it was quickly dispelled by our platoon sergeants, regulars of long standing who had been left in England to assist in whipping the new armies into shape. Naturally, they were disgruntled at this, and we offered them such splendid opportunities for working off overcharges of spleen.

We had come to Hounslow, believing that within a few weeks' time we should be fighting in France, side by side with the men of the first British expeditionary force. Lord Kitchener had said that six months of training, at the least, was essential. This statement we regarded as intentionally misleading. Lord Kitchener was too shrewd a soldier to announce his plans; but England needed men badly, immediately. After a week of training, we should be proficient in the use of our rifles.

In addition to this, all that was needed was the ability to form fours and march in column of route, to the station where we should entrain for Folkestone or Southampton, and France.

The naivety was almost touching.

The barrack square was enough to break an old soldier's heart. In one corner would be a squad of some fifty men, the last joined, arrayed in all the splendour of their own particular fancies. It was nearly always possible to tell their previous occupations from the clothes they wore. The stable-boy, in his Newmarket coat, breeches, and gaiters, the labourer in corduroys, the gardener in well-worn trousers and brand-new coat, the chauffeur in his black semi-livery, the mechanic in blue 'boiler creepers', the loafer in a seedy-grey suiting, even the clerk in a smart well-cut coat and trousers, all were represented. And the hats! I had no idea that so many different forms of headgear were possible, from shiny 'topper' to the coal-heaver's shovel-hat. One sportsman joined in stockings, yellow breeches, black mourning-coat, and an opera hat!

How awful were the first cautious movements of the last-joined squad! Their instructor, an old retired sergeant, lately a market-gardener, arrayed in a neat brown suit and a bowler, would patiently string them out into two comparatively parallel lines (I dare not call them ranks) and initiate them into the dark mysteries of turning and saluting and standing at ease. After a few painful hours, the squad had learnt to do much the same thing at any given word of command. Every few minutes they would be allowed to stand easy, and then their thoughts would wander to the old days, so far away, when a man who wished to change the direction in which he was facing might do so in any way that seemed good to him, without incurring reproof from a little man with a voice like a bull.

Then suddenly would come a sharp bark: "Shun!" and each man's scattered wits would cause him to perform a different evolution. Some, the more hard-hearted, would assume a position of excruciating

Captain Cecil Street, Royal Garrison Artillery

rigidity, their faces bearing a look as of a tortured martyr, others would turn, right, left, or about, others again would salute with their right or left hands, remaining in the ridiculous attitude affected by the stage soldier, or would take a step backwards, forwards, or to one side. The resulting effect upon the beauty of the squad may better be imagined than described…

The gunner is never an adept at infantry drill, at the best of times, and as the drill itself had been altered many times since the original retirement of the NCOs from the service, I fancy that some of the evolutions would have seared the brain of an infantry Adjutant as with a red-hot iron. However, if a gunner can be got to form fours correctly, it is about all that is ever expected of him, so perhaps it did not matter much.

At Street's depot, the recruits were held for around a month before being sent to batteries, a period of time far longer than recruits were held at infantry depots. It meant that the men established routines including the regular addressing of both gripes and infractions.

Captain Cecil Street, Royal Garrison Artillery

The scenes in the Depot office, and the humours of the administrative side, almost baffle description. To the staff, many of whom were working sixteen hours a day, they came as a blessing, even though the incidents that composed them usually involved a certain amount of extra work. Perhaps the hours in the evening from six to seven, when the Adjutant with a view to helping recruits as much as possible held a sort of levée, at which any man who wanted advice or nursed a grievance was entitled to be heard, was the most amusing. One man would come in, the picture of indignation, declaring that some one had stolen his socks, and on being informed that unless he could give some clue the task of tracing them amongst a couple of thousand men might prove somewhat beyond human ability, would depart uncomforted.

His place would be taken by another, who would unfold a fearfully complex genealogical table, apparently utterly irrelevant, until the sting that lay in the tail protruded ominously; why had Gunner Williams

J.'s mother's cousin's wife not received her separation allowances last week? This was easier than it seems to deal with, hand him over to the Pay-Sergeant and let them wrangle until one or other lost patience. Next please.

There were plenty of reasons for recruits to vent their spleen, though theft was usually near the top of their grievance list. In Scotland, the recruits of the Black Watch had made a mess of everything, to William Andrews' obvious disgust. He groaned:

> The dirt! Your mental picture of barracks is of spotless, rectangular dormitories, but that drill-hall, with all the dust, stirred up by the tramping, and with roisterers being sick at night where they lay, and many of them prematurely lousy, struck dismay into my heart.

Andrews had chosen to dress down, wearing old clothes for sensible reasons, though he did have a fine pair of boots.

We had to continue wearing civilian clothes, and as it was a waste to wear good ones amid all that dirt, I put on an old golf jacket and tennis shirt, grey flannel trousers, and a pair of expensive new fishing boots which I thought would be useful for heavy route marches. The boots vanished after a couple of days. I asked a sergeant what I should do. 'Watch yourself, laddie,' he said, 'they'll steal the milk out of your tea in this mob.' And that was that.

Private William Andrews, 2/4th The Black Watch (Royal Highlanders)

'An old golf jacket and tennis shirt… and a pair of expensive new fishing boots' distinguished Andrews from the vast majority of his comrades.

The morning wash: facilities in the first weeks were not always so salubrious for recruits.

Private William Andrews, 2/4th The Black Watch (Royal Highlanders)

In soiled garb I began to feel unhappy. I had never realised what a difference presentable clothes make to a man. I used to pay £4 for a suit in those days, a modest enough price, but one that bought more than the suit itself. It gave me self-confidence and a certain amount of public respect. In my civilian days, as an Englishman in Dundee, I had been impressed by the general courtesy to a stranger. If I wanted information, everybody seemed anxious to oblige. I felt happy among Dundee people, but what a difference there was when I went out in shabby and dirty war clothes! The cold shoulder replaced a smiling welcome.

You young gentlemen who read this, and pride yourself that the world looks kindly upon you because of your conspicuous merit, don't be too sure. It may be that the world welcomes you, not because of your character, not because of your brains, but because your clothes make you look so well and prosperous. You would find it hard to look impressive in a shabby suit.

If I found many of my comrades strange, I am sure they found me stranger still. There was I with no friend at hand, a man of queer habits, a vegetarian (though I now tried hard to take Army stew, for Britain's sake), teetotal, and a queer twist of speech, for I am not Scots but pure Yorkshire.

It was a cultural shock literally rubbing shoulders with men from an entirely different class and upbringing, an experience frequently referred to by recruits in letters and memoirs. Teenager Basil Peacock, a middle-class lad from Newcastle upon Tyne, was taken aback by what he heard, though familiarity never bred contempt.

Private Basil Peacock, The Royal Fusiliers

I found myself in a room with much rougher types… The soldier who slept next to me had lately been released from jail and still had jail-cropped hair. He was a rough little cockney, about my height, addressed as Twig, quite illiterate but very talkative. It was distressing to hear him try and express himself with his very small vocabulary, which was made up mostly of four-letter words. To colour his conversation, he would insert them even between the syllables of words. His favourite expression was 'fuckee says I'. He would gabble off a sentence such as, 'I says to fuckee corporal when he tells me to scrub fuckee floor – what's the i-fuckee-dea? I was on fuckee fatigue yesterday – fuckee says I to him.'

Twig and I got on splendidly after a couple of days: I liked him and he had a generous nature and was never surly. We helped each other to clean and assemble our kit, and though he was naturally suspected of being a barrack-room thief, he stole nothing from me and guarded my belongings when I was absent. He was so unlearned that he looked upon me as a man of great education, and I was touched when he asked me childish questions about something he could not understand or to read about something he could not. When I answered he would exclaim, 'Blimey, Bas, fuckee says I if you ain't a fuckee scholar.'

By the second week of September, Frederick Keeling had returned from Bodmin to a tented village on Watts Common, near Aldershot. Getting to know some of his comrades proved illuminating.

I am not really any more intimate with any of the seven Oxford men than with the friends I have made among non-coms [non-commissioned], old soldiers, navvies, painters, shop assistants, and all sorts of fellows here. My opinion of the human race, at any rate of the common Englishman, goes steadily up from being herded with him. But of course it will be best to wait till one has had many rainy days before forming a final opinion.

Private Frederick Keeling, 6th The Duke of Cornwall's Light Infantry

A hat said much about the recruit and his erstwhile position of authority in civilian society. The right hat was often enough to win a man promotion to lance corporal when the platoon officer needed an immediate command structure.

Curiosity cut both ways. Being teetotal and a vegetarian made Williams Andrews 'different'. Yet, was there another, ulterior reason why this obviously educated, bespectacled Yorkshireman had chosen to serve in a Scottish Regiment?

Private William Andrews, 2/4th The Black Watch (Royal Highlanders)

An order came that Captain Rose wanted to see me. I was to know him well afterwards, and to love him for his courage and unselfishness, but [he] was of anxious temperament, diffident and roundabout in his speech, and worn by the burden imposed on him in those recruiting days.

He began to question me in such a transparently guileful way that I felt an overwhelming desire to be mysterious. Our interview went something like this:

Officer: 'You must forgive me if – er – I appear to be a little preemptory in my questions, a little, what shall I say? Excessive. I think you know what I mean?'

W.L.A. 'Yes, sir. You mean you would like to ask me questions, and yet you don't like to ask them.'

Officer: 'This is a question of military duty. I shall not allow my personal wishes to interfere with my duty. I must ask you your motive in joining the battalion. Certain reports have reached me – I will not say that I place full credence in them, but these reports have reached me, I must ask you what was your motive in joining this battalion.'

W.L.A.: 'Must I answer this, sir? Do I understand that anything I now say may be taken down in writing and given in evidence against me in support of any future charge?'

Officer: 'Well, er –. I am not asking you for confidential information.'

W.L.A: 'Then surely I am entitled to know what the charge is.'

Officer: 'There is no charge. There is merely a – how shall I put it? – excited suggestion among the men that you are not what you appear to be.'

The suggestion was that Andrews might be a spy. In response, he passed on the names of former employers in order that his background might be checked, whilst noting how he enjoyed being a player in what felt like an 'old-fashioned melodrama'. Andrews believed the officer had been set up as 'fair-game for the [battalion's] practical jokers'. When an English artist, Joseph Gray, arrived there would be another interview. Gray's crime: the possession of a strong English accent and the rumour that he had been seen reading a German newspaper.

Andrews' isolation amongst comrades was short-lived. To his joy, additional recruits from his newspaper, the *Dundee Advertiser*, joined the battalion. 'It seemed to me that this intolerably filthy and brainless life would now be mitigated by true comradeship... My colleagues were the most welcome rescue-party that ever surprised a prisoner. We must keep together at all costs.'

Some of the cleanest men, at least as far as clothes went, were the men of the Artists Rifles. Frederick Keeling had wished to forgo the unit's manifest homogeneity in order to serve amongst traditional working men, whereas Geoffrey Fildes was entirely at home amongst those with whom he worked and socialised. There appeared no question of suspicion or mistrust amongst this like-minded group.

A large proportion of my comrades were aspirants for a commission, engaged 'for the duration', volunteers for foreign service. I do not recollect many of us who had not been through a well-known school or university. Our uniforms were mostly procured from private tailors, but our equipment followed sooner than we had dared hope for. The 2nd Battalion, to which we belonged, presented at the beginning of October quite a military appearance. Its physique was noticeable, for my company itself, out of eight that comprised the battalion, could boast of nine [Oxford and Cambridge] 'Blues'.

Private Geoffrey Fildes, 2/28th The London Regiment (Artists Rifles)

For the time being, the men of the Artists Rifles remained in their own homes, proceeding every day except Sundays to meet at various points announced in 'orders', including Russell Square for squad drill and Hampstead Heath for route marches.

Russell Square, Hyde Park, Regent's Park, even Holland Park, were soon trampled bare by the mobs of London recruits… These hordes of lusty men, whistling on the march the newly discovered air of the 'Marseillaise', or the popular 'Tipperary', swinging along with measured step would have been laughable had they not been sublime. Average Londoners are not prone to demonstration, but the passage of a battalion of 'Kitchener's' men, as they were popularly called, was in

Private Geoffrey Fildes, 2/28th The London Regiment (Artists Rifles)

those days greeted with uncovered heads. Recognition of their spirit was general everywhere, and familiarity with it had not yet dulled the first instincts of spectators. I never saw more than three officers in one of these battalions until October. Their discipline, taught by those few they could boast of, was maintained by the men themselves. A number had grown up under the codes of our public schools, and the vast majority asked no more than to be made trained soldiers as soon as possible.

James Hall's New Army battalion had little in the way of discipline, at least not the discipline that could be shown to onlookers. Hall and his comrades had marched around London as they waited to reach establishment, but they did not fool anyone as to their martial aptitude, least of all Hall's platoon sergeant, who openly fretted about the quality of men before him.

Private James Hall, 9th The Royal Fusiliers (City of London Regiment)

As soon as the battalion was up to strength, we were given a day of preliminary drill before proceeding to our future training area in Essex. It was a disillusioning experience. Equally disappointing was the undignified display of our little skill at Charing Cross Station, where we performed before a large and amused London audience. For my own part, I could scarcely wait until we were safely hidden within the train.

It was a logistical necessity that the army moved these men to the vast camps springing up across the country in order for real training to begin. James Hall and his comrades were heading from Charing Cross into the wilds of Essex.

Private James Hall, 9th The Royal Fusiliers (City of London Regiment)

During the journey to Colchester, a re-enlisted Boer War veteran from the inaccessible heights of South African experience enfiladed us with a fire of sarcastic comment. 'I'm a-go'n' to transfer out o' this 'ere mob, that's wot I'm a go'n' to do! Soldiers! S'y! I'll bet a quid they ain't a one of you ever saw a rifle before! Soldiers? Strike me pink! Wot's Lord Kitchener a-doin' of, that's wot I want to know!'

The rest of us smoked in wrathful silence, until one of the boys demonstrated to the Boer War veteran that he knew, at least, how to use his fists. There was some bloodshed, followed by reluctant apologies on the part of the Boer warrior. It was one of innumerable differences of opinion which I witnessed during the months that followed. And most of them were settled in the same decisive way.

In Kent, Vic Cole and the men congregating to become the 7th Royal West Kent Regiment left the depot in Maidstone and marched to Gravesend and a ferry that would take them across the mouth of the river Thames.

The weather was fine and sunny; as we crossed the river I sat myself on a handy bollard and looked round at my comrades-in-arms all dressed in their oddments (I almost said remnants) from the QM stores. We were such a mixed crowd, university men, butchers and bakers, and men from all over the country, including a lad from Northumberland and another from Cheshire. A group had come down from Scotland, one, a lad about my age, told me he had wanted to travel. He'd joined up with two mates near Glasgow, Bonnybridge asking for the West Kents because they wanted a free ride to London.

Leaving the ferry, some well-informed person discovered that our destination was Purfleet Camp, and after a short train journey we found ourselves tramping down a cinder track in clouds of black and clinging dust towards a distant canvas city and a double row of bell tents. These tents were to be our new homes, and so, one section to each canvas residence we entered into occupation.

Private Vic Cole, 7th The Queen's Own (Royal West Kent Regiment)

Sixteen-year-old George Coppard had joined the Royal West Surrey Regiment, being sent initially to Stoughton Barracks. For a week, the new recruits had done elementary drill and fatigues before they too arrived at Purfleet.

Our first job was pitching a lot of bell-tents under the supervision of a batch of NCOs, some of whom were regular army and others re-enlisted men. They proceeded to treat us in the traditional manner as if we were a music-hall joke. The tent-pitching job gave them the opportunity to administer a sort of baptism of fire, and by the time the tents were up I was almost wishing I had never enlisted.

Private George Coppard, 6th The Queen's Own (Royal West Surrey Regiment)

Private Vic Cole, 7th The Queen's Own (Royal West Kent Regiment)

We found that each tent was to have a wooden floor. The wood, already cut into four sections, had been brought in by train and stacked up ready for us to go and help ourselves. These were put together with the centre cut out to take the tent pole and onto which were hung meat hooks to lift our gear off the floor. The group in my tent was pretty good. I remember those first few nights we were all talking posh together, being very polite.

Each bell tent was designed to comfortably take twelve men and their possessions, though more could squeeze in if required.

Private George Coppard, 6th The Queen's Own (Royal West Surrey Regiment)

As tents were in short supply, the maximum number of recruits was allotted to each one. Not having been in a tent before, I had no idea that it had twenty-two separate pieces of canvas sewn together to form the roof. The flap was the point of entry and, with men stampeding to get in, somebody had to get the flap division as his portion of territory. I got it. This meant that I couldn't lie down at night until everyone was in the tent.

Above: Heaton Park Camp: men of the Manchester Pals raising bell tents above the segmented wooden base.

At Watts Common, the 6th and 7th battalions of the Duke of Cornwall's Light Infantry were sorting themselves out into some semblance of a structure, namely sections, platoons, and companies.

Each Company has a Captain (why we are also favoured with a Major I don't know), four lieutenants (young officers), one to each platoon, and similarly four sergeants (NCOs), who are, so to speak, parallel with the lieutenants, though under them: the function of the lieutenants seems to be to keep in touch with the captain, while the sergeants are more directly concerned with the men. That, at least, is how it strikes me at present, though I believe in the field the lieutenant directs the platoon, and the sergeant only steps in if the officer should be incapacitated.

After an incredible amount of sorting out which took, literally, days, we were at last put into platoon number 16 [D Company].

Hounslow Heath, 22 August 1914: 'Just a few tent mates. What do you think of them?' A recruit sends a picture of his new friends on the day the Regular Army fired its first shot in anger on continental Europe.

We were just a mob walking around until we were properly organised for the first time, a sergeant major dividing us up as we stood there. 'Right, the first twenty, you will be no1 Platoon, A company, the next twenty, you'll be no2 Platoon, and so forth.' I was put in 'B' Company. There were just a couple of platoons to each company because more chaps would be coming in all the while to make up the numbers. Then Major Whittaker came out, our Company officer, aged about 75 it seemed, with a chest full of medal ribbons going back to the Afghan wars I would think. The order was given to stand to attention and Whittaker turned to one of the NCOs: 'Right, corporal, you take that platoon there.' So this corporal came and stood in front of us: 'Now, come on you lot,' he was a proper cockney bloke. We rather looked at each other. 'Right, what I tells you, you gotta do,' and he gave us our first training.

Private Vic Cole, 7th The Queen's Own (Royal West Kent Regiment)

Removed from everyday civilian life, albeit surrounded by civilians, the recruits craved any communication from home. Letters arrived soon enough, though their distribution could be slapdash.

Recruits gather round to open their mail.

Private Sydney Fuller, 8th The Suffolk Regiment

September 9th. Received my first letter from home. Mail was distributed by the postman personally. He simply came down the lines with his bag, deposited it on the ground between the rows of tents, took the letters out a handful at a time, and called the names. Needless to say, there was a great crowd round him at these times, and sometimes a good deal of confusion. No regimental numbers having been allotted to any of the new soldiers, a man often got a letter addressed to someone else of the same name. (The postman was often too harried to call out Christian names or initials.) As a result, it was the regular practice of anyone who had not received an expected letter to make a round of all whom he knew to have the same or a similar surname to himself, after the postman had gone, to see if it had gone astray.

Into this nascent search for order officers were constantly arriving to take charge of platoons and companies, the vast majority were newly commissioned men as ignorant about training as those they were about to command.

Private George Butterworth, 6th The Duke of Cornwall's Light Infantry

Hammond is the only young officer in camp who has had any experience worth speaking of, and there again we are lucky. He also seems to be a good fellow, but of course we are not personally acquainted with him, for it is contrary to military etiquette for an officer to have any except purely official relations with privates.

When we first came here there was a great shortage both of officers and NCOs – the vacancies have been gradually filled… Major Barnet invited applications for commissions from the members of our party, and Toye put in for one and was promptly accepted. He is now in command of a platoon of B Company. The rest of us, after much consultation, decided that the most important thing for us was to keep our party intact; having arranged to serve together it would obviously be unfair on those who might be left if some of us became officers – (Toye, having joined at the eleventh hour, was held to be free).

In the meantime there has been a great influx of young lieutenants, most of whom have obviously had little, if any, training; there is one who is drilling in the ranks with us, and who had to be shown how to 'form fours'.

How all this will turn out, heaven only knows; personally I should feel uncomfortable at taking on a responsible job without any proper opportunity of training for it. Toye will be all right, for he is amazingly quick and facile, and full of self-confidence; but I am doubtful about some of the others.

For the laudable reason of wishing to stay together, Butterworth and friends missed an opportunity. In the earliest days of a battalion's life, taking a commission within the unit was relatively painless, as Private Toye had discovered, but the openings grew fewer as the War Office sent additional officers to fill them. To demand that all six or none of Butterworth's group be taken on was unrealistic. It was a decision that would later cause unnecessary ill will and antagonism for all concerned.

Most new battalions recruited well beyond the established figure of 1,000 men. According to Butterworth, both the 6th and the 7th battalions of his regiment were 1,200 strong, a similar figure common to other regiments. Throughout the autumn of 1914 there was much chopping and changing as individuals were weeded out as unfit, or surplus groups of men were sent to help make up the numbers in an under-strength battalion, sometimes in an entirely different division.

The army was directing men to where need was greatest, taking recruits and experienced men to form the nucleus of the next crop of new battalions. In the late autumn of 1914, two officers and fifteen NCOs (including a company quartermaster sergeant) were taken from the 6th Battalion Royal West Kent Regiment and sent as far away as Dublin to help with the formation of the 10th Battalion of the Royal Dublin Fusiliers. Not all appreciated the move as they were separated from friends, but the army was dealing with huge and competing demands, making it nigh impossible for those moved to usurp orders.

The overall success of training and the speed with which it could be accomplished would ultimately depend on the quality of those relied upon to take charge. Some were undoubtedly highly experienced, adaptable men, and a few would prove to be a downright hindrance.

Overleaf: Epsom, September 1914: 'This is where we turn in, of course we tidied up for the occasion,' wrote one of these men to his parents. Even for these well-to-do young men, possibly of the 18th Battalion, The Royal Fusiliers (1st Public Schools) Battalion, facilities were sparse.

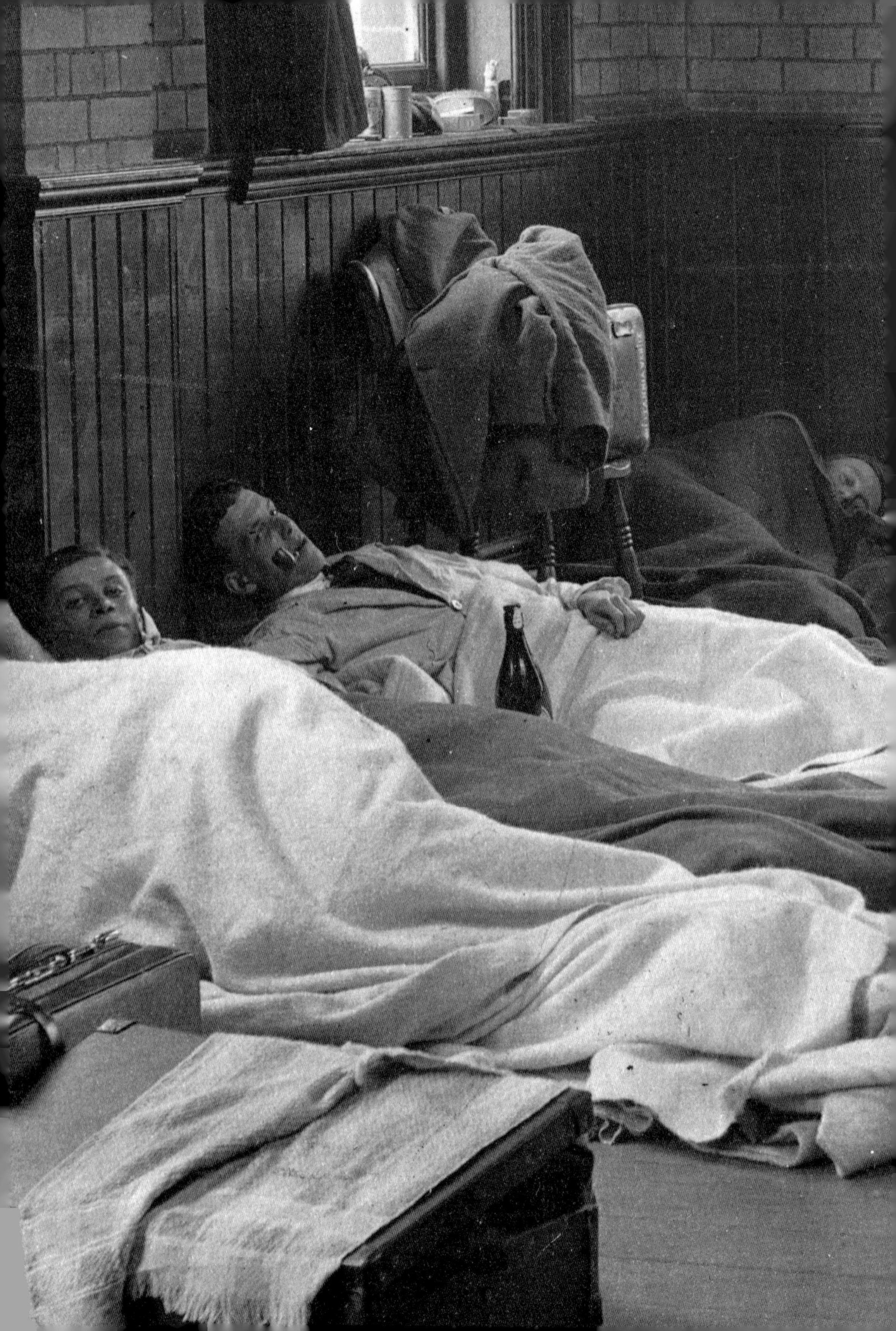

5 Right Sorts

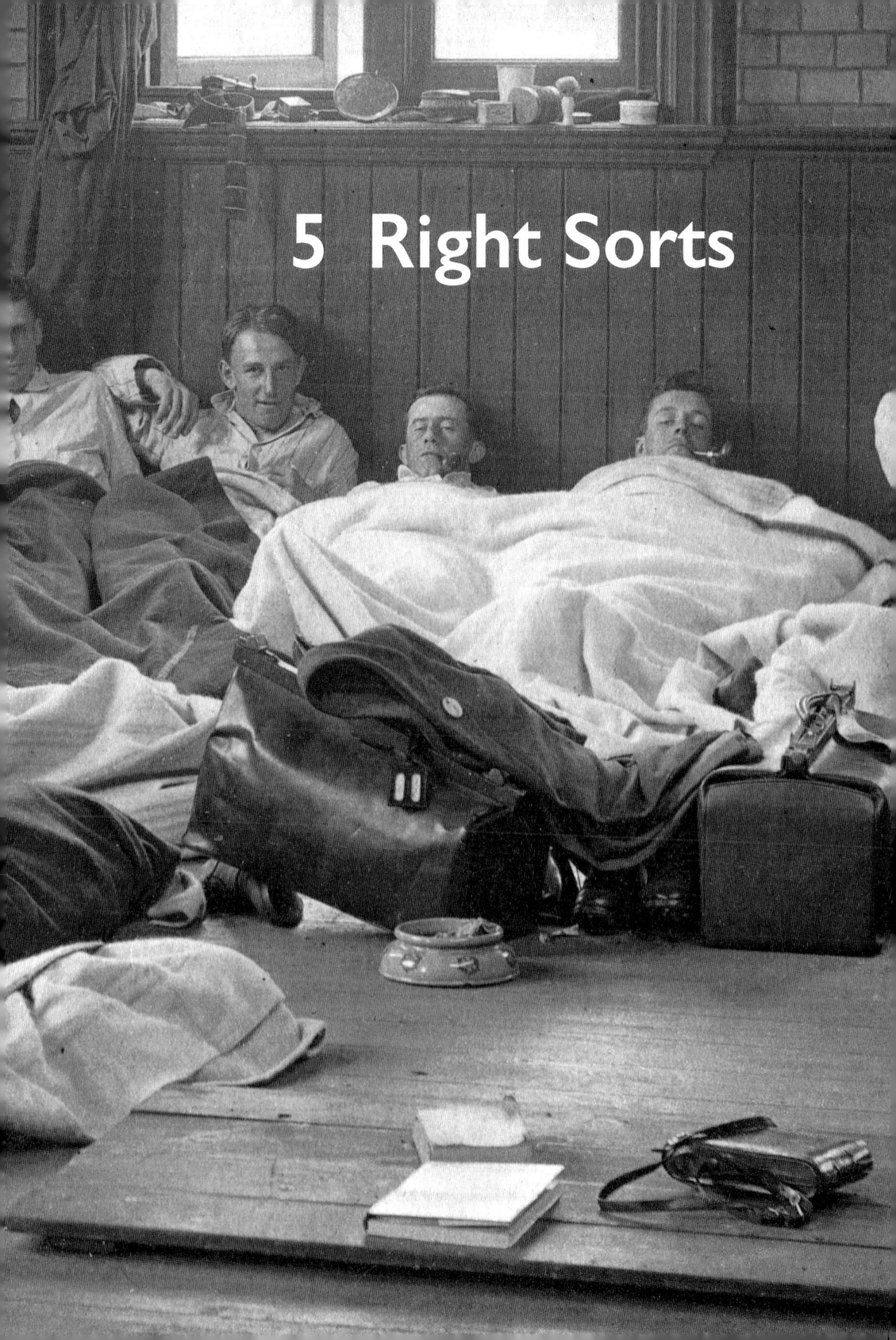

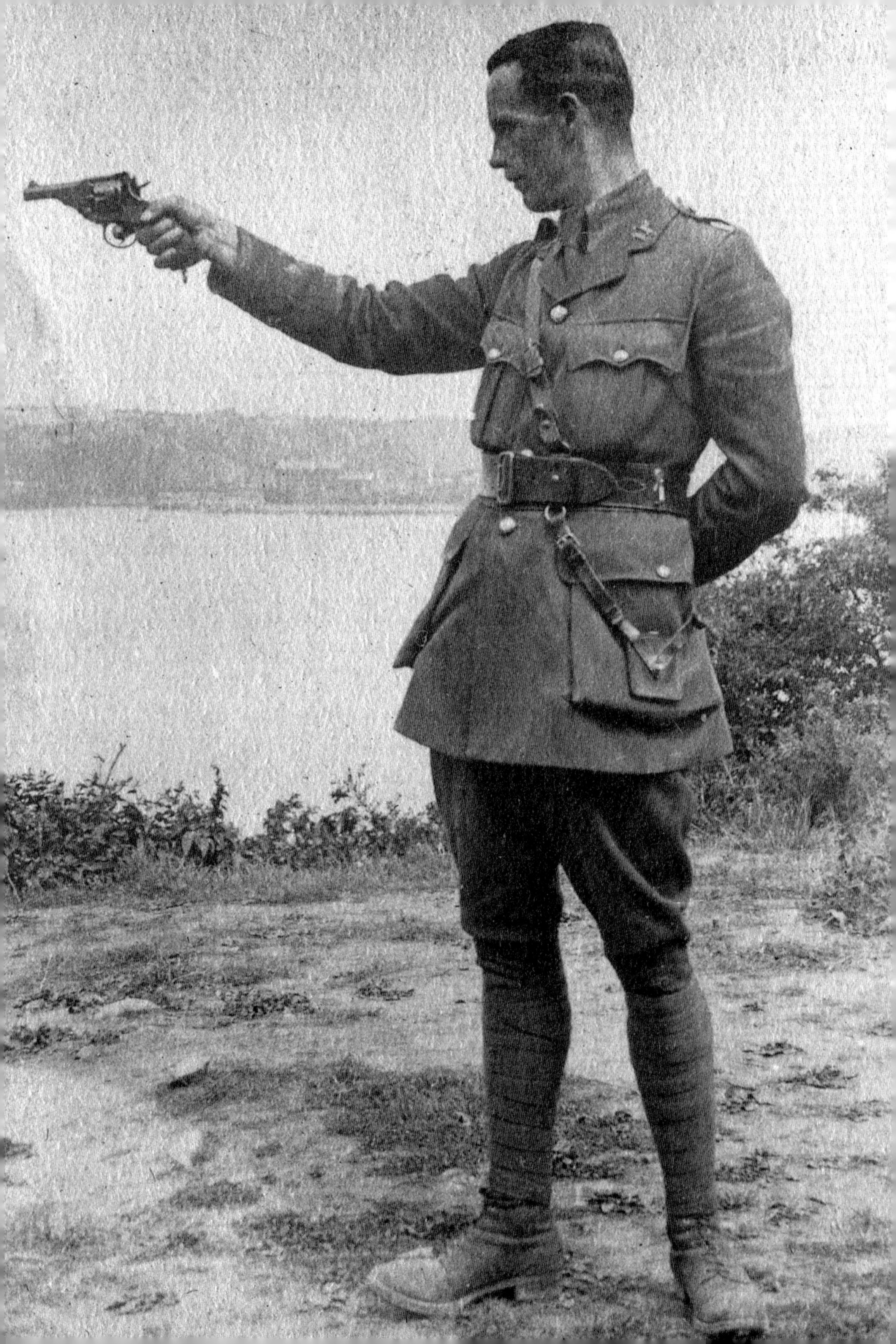

'I have been taken after all for Kitchener's Army. I go off to training camp at Churn for a month or six weeks; after that I have to attach myself to some regiment… Personally, I expect to be sacked in a week.'

Arthur Heath

A key pressure facing Lord Kitchener was finding the requisite leadership for his New Army divisions, a primary focus in his eyes, and for the scores of additional Territorial infantry battalions, something of rather secondary importance. At the very least he would need to double the number of serving officers from 23,000 in the Regular Army and Territorial Force (with a further 5,700 on the Reserve), in order to provide the required command structure within each new unit, and notwithstanding the ongoing attrition amongst the officer corps in France and Belgium. These casualties, unpredictable in number as they had to be, would have to be replaced immediately if Britain were to maintain a disciplined and cohesive presence on the battlefield.

In their enthusiasm to fight, many young men suitable for the officer corps took the plunge and enlisted into the ranks or were threatening to do so. In early August 1914, Lancelot Spicer was due to be in Scotland but instead went straight to Cambridge and his University Officer Training Corps where he and a friend put their names down for a commission. Naively, they expected a positive reply by return of post, but after a week there was nothing. 'We began to get anxious lest the war be over before we had joined up!'

Four weeks after the declaration of war, Spicer heard that a Public Schools Battalion of the Middlesex Regiment was taking shape and he wondered whether he should enlist as a private. The unit was drawn from Spicer's social contemporaries and for that reason, it had great appeal. For a moment, he hesitated. The son of the Liberal Member for Hackney, Spicer decided it might be prudent to see his father and made his way to the House of Commons, waiting in the lobby. It was while he was sitting there that an old family friend, Thomas Mckinnon Wood, the Secretary of State for Scotland, walked by.

Opposite: *An unknown officer of the King's Liverpool Regiment holding a recently outdated Mk 5 Webley revolver.*

Lancelot Spicer

'Lance, what are you doing here? – Why aren't you with your family in Scotland?' I replied that there was a war going on in Europe, and that I was trying to get a commission to serve in the Army, but that it was taking so long I was considering *enlisting*. The moment I said I was going to enlist, he took me by the arm and led me into a corner. 'You are *not* to enlist,' he said, 'only this morning I was at a Cabinet meeting and Kitchener told us how concerned he was at the way you young men are enlisting. This war is going on for two or three years at least and you will be badly wanted as officers. So DO NOT enlist, promise me you won't do so.' I replied that if so, he must speed up the granting of my application for a commission… He asked me for my particulars and said he would do what he could.

To those working with him, Kitchener's weighty concerns were all too evident. Before the British Expeditionary Force left for France, he had ordered that each infantry battalion must leave behind three officers and several NCOs in order to form the nucleus of each New Army battalion. These officers and NCOs, usually disgruntled at being held back, would be supplemented by Regular officers on leave from the Empire's outposts, in particular India, but farther afield too. One officer, a Lieutenant Butler of the 1st Battalion of the King's Own Yorkshire Light Infantry, had just arrived from Singapore when he was ordered to remain in Britain, just one of around 500 officers usefully retained at home.

On 10 August, Kitchener appealed in the press for 2,000 men to take temporary commissions until the war's conclusion. These men had to be unmarried and aged between 17 and 30 and 'Cadets or ex-Cadets of the University Training Corps of a University'. In addition, 'Other young men of a good general education should apply in person to the Officer Commanding the nearest depot.' In other words, even men with no prior military experience could apply if from the right background.

Julian Tyndale-Biscoe had just finished OTC camp when he saw the appeal. He had army connections and wired a relative commanding the King Edward's Horse to see if there was an opening. 'He replied, "Regiment full strength – join something."' That 'something' took Tyndale-Biscoe to barracks at both Bedford and Hertford, but to no avail. He then contacted his Uncle Albert commanding a reserve brigade of the Royal Field Artillery, but his advice was to undertake a shortened course of training with Albert's son, Norman. This course would last no less than six months. 'I thought that much too long because the war would probably be over by then.'

Expressing reservations to his uncle, Tyndale-Biscoe was given a 'kindly' letter of introduction to give to a Major Dooner at The War Office.

I went there straight away and was finally ushered in.

He asked me what school I was at, and when I told him Trent College, he said: 'Oh! I inspected your Corps last June.'

'Good Lord, Sir! So you did,' I replied, and felt a fool for not having recognised him at once, especially as I was one of those who had been called out to command the Company on field manoeuvres.

From a remark made, he evidently thought pretty highly of our Corps.

He then asked me my rank and other questions. When he learnt that I had Certificate A [basic training's military proficiency award] and was in the shooting eight, etc., he gave a grunt and told me he would arrange for my name to be gazetted during the next week or so.

Julian Tyndale-Biscoe

Members of the Downside School Officer Training Corps and School Band, many of whom would be destined for war service as junior subalterns.

Julian Tyndale-Biscoe was duly gazetted on 12 September. Lancelot Spicer's string pulling also worked, Spicer joining a New Army battalion, the 9th King's Own Yorkshire Light Infantry.

Making use of contacts was often the only shortcut to quick success. Richard Hawkins from Chelmsford in Essex, the son of a chief accountant, had attended King Edward VI Grammar School serving as a sergeant in the Cadet Corps. Desperate to serve, he walked out on his engineering apprenticeship, much to the ire of his boss:

> He called me a number of rather unpleasant things, saying that I was an ungrateful so and so. I didn't have much of a vocabulary but I told him what I thought of him and left. It was my duty to leave, nothing out of the ordinary, it was obvious. I was a prize-winning shot at school too, so I thought I'd have no trouble getting in.

In September, the recruitment offices were being overwhelmed but eventually he took the King's shilling at Hounslow Barracks, enlisting as a private in the Royal Fusiliers.

Richard Hawkins

By chance I met one of the Governors of my old school. He was an old soldier and he asked me what I was doing. 'Well I said, I've spent all my time, sir, trying to get into the army. At last I've managed it and now I've got a few days' leave.' 'Look,' he said, 'I've got a son-in-law who's been sent back from India to Colchester to a huge canvas camp there to command a battalion. He's got a second in command, he's got an adjutant, he's got a quartermaster, but he hasn't got a battalion. Go off down there and tell him I sent you. Get over to see him, quick.'

So I borrowed my cousin's motorbike and went down there and was interviewed by Lieutenant Colonel Carr, who gave me a chit to take to somebody in the War Office. That Sunday afternoon some young man, a clerk probably, took me through the medical inspection, asked all my details, my military experience, and my schooling. I was given £30 and told to buy my uniform and a Webley Revolver for £3. I was nineteen years old.

Richard Hawkins' close friends. L to R: friends Bernard Ashmole, Richard Vaughan-Thompson and Walter Hoare, 11th Royal Fusiliers. Thompson and Hoare would die on the Somme and Ashmole would be badly wounded in 1917.

Hawkins returned to Hounslow before being ordered to report to the Battalion and Lieutenant Colonel Carr. Travelling to Essex with two other men, he arrived to a reception he was not quite expecting.

We were given a pretty cold reception. When we arrived an officer shouted, 'Some more of these damned young officers have arrived.'
  '"Tell them to go away," came the reply!'

Richard Hawkins

Richard Hawkins was only briefly disconcerted. He reported and was given command of 16 Platoon, D Company, 11th Royal Fusiliers.

Attendance at the right school was necessary but not necessarily sufficient for a commission to be recommended. One senior officer, Brigadier General Trevor Ternan, took it upon himself to determine that no subaltern in his brigade of the Northumberland Fusiliers would be considered unless they had previous military or OTC experience, though as it turned out, he might be willing to turn a blind eye to age.

A young man presented himself at Brigade Headquarters in Alnwick, and said that he had come up from London with a view to obtaining a commission in the Tyneside Scottish. His testimonials were excellent, and from his build, general appearance, and manner one judges his age

Brigadier General Trevor Ternan, Commanding Officer, 123rd (Tyneside Scottish) Brigade

to be about nineteen or twenty. He had previous experience in a Public School OTC and would have been accepted had I not noticed to my surprise that the official application form signed by his father showed his age to be a little over sixteen, which the boy at once admitted to be correct.

In view of the War Office orders that no one under the age of nineteen was to be appointed, I had regretfully to inform the youth that under the circumstances he could not be accepted. A few days later he again arrived from London with a new form made out, on which the date of his birth as given by his father showed his age to be now nineteen. I thereafter accepted him, and appointed him to one of the Battalions. He soon proved a most useful young officer, and later gained the Military Cross for his work in the field. I feel the moral of this story is obscure.

Many superficially suitable men went unrewarded. After seeing the advertisement in *The Times*, Charles Carrington and a friend were convinced they were precisely what the army was looking for.

Charles Carrington

We jumped on our bicycles and rode over to Aldershot to enquire, and, knowing no better, we asked advice of a redcap (military policeman) at the corner of Queen's Road. He looked at the newspaper and gave the professional opinion that this would be a matter for the Adjutant-General's branch. Believe it or not, we battered our way into the office of the Adjutant General on the sixth day of mobilisation.

The room was full of bustling staff officers in khaki, wrestling with mountains of lists and schedules and files. Though we were not inside for five minutes, some young staff officers took an interest in us. Two or three left their work for a moment to look with a kindly eye at these lanky schoolboys with their absurd enquiry. Warning us off Aldershot, they advised us to try the depot of the Rifle Brigade at Winchester.

Next day we took a train to Winchester with a letter of introduction and actually persuaded an elderly colonel 'dug out' from retirement to put our names on a list… I returned to Fleet to wait with what little patience I could muster, and was soon consumed with chagrin on realising that the authorities were not tumbling over one another to find a military appointment for Charles Carrington, aged seventeen and quite unqualified.

At least Carrington had made a list; Robert Sherriff did not even make that. This former captain of school games, fit and strong and with a sound education, discovered he was not on the army's approved schools list when he visited the headquarters of his county regiment.

'School?' enquired the adjutant. I told him and his face fell. He took up a printed list and searched through it. 'I'm sorry,' he said, 'but I'm afraid it isn't a public school.' I was mystified. I told him that my school [Kingston Grammar School] though small, was a very old and good one – founded, I said by Queen Elizabeth in 1567. The adjutant was not impressed. He had lost all interest in me. 'I'm sorry,' he repeated. 'But our instructions are that all applicants for commissions must be selected from the recognised public schools, and yours is not among them.'

    And that was that. I was told to go to another room where a sergeant major was enlisting recruits for the ranks.

Robert Sherriff

Sherriff was naturally dejected with his bald dismissal, but on reflection, he understood the reasons.

Naturally the authorities wanted the new officers to be men with the same background as those of the Regular Army, with a dedication to their duty that was ingrained in a Sandhurst cadet long before he was considered fit to join a regiment… Officers had to be made quickly, with the least possible trouble. The Army command had to find some sort of yardstick, and naturally they turned to the public schools.

    Most of the generals had been public schoolboys before they went to military academies. They knew from first hand experience that a public school gave something to its boys that had the ingredients of

Robert Sherriff

leadership… At school they gained self-confidence, the beginnings of responsibility through being prefects over younger boys. Pride in their schools would easily translate into pride for the regiment…

It was a rough method of selection, a demarcation line hewn out with a blunt axe; but it was the only way in the face of a desperate emergency.

In 1914, the army was not going to bend the rules much on who was or was not an officer *and* a gentleman. Centuries of tradition could not be ignored or altered overnight. For most men this separation between those who commanded and those who were commanded was entirely right and proper. It took an American to articulate the pros and cons of this historic arrangement. 'The officer class and the ranker class are east and west, and never the twain shall meet, except in their respective places upon the parade ground,' he observed.

Private James Hall, 9th The Royal Fusiliers (City of London Regiment)

I had to accept, for convenience' sake, the fact of my social inferiority. Centuries of army tradition demanded it; and I discovered that it is absolutely futile for one inconsequential American to rebel against the unshakeable fortress of English tradition. Nearly all of my comrades were used to clear-cut class distinctions in civilian life. It made little difference to them that some of our officers were recruits as raw as were we ourselves. They had money enough and education enough and influence enough to secure the king's commission; and that fact was proof enough for Tommy that they were gentlemen, and, therefore, too good for the likes of him to be associating with.

'Look 'ere! Ain't a gentleman a gentleman? I'm arskin' you, ain't 'e?' I saw the futility of discussing this question with Tommy. And later, I realised how important for British army discipline such distinctions are.

So great is the force of prevailing opinion that I sometimes found myself accepting Tommy's point of view. I wondered if I was, for some eugenic reason, the inferior of these men whom I had to 'Sir' and salute whenever I dared speak. Such lapses were only occasional. But I understood, for the first time, how important a part circumstance and environment play in shaping one's mental attitude. How I longed, at times, to chat with colonels and to joke with captains on terms of equality! Whenever I confided these aspirations to Tommy he gazed at me in awe. 'Don't be a bloomin' ijut! They could jolly well 'ang you fer that!'

Norman Dillon from Newcastle upon Tyne had attended one of the 'right' schools and came with a semblance of military knowledge too. On the encouragement of his parents he had served in his school's OTC, though the training was 'sporadic' and annual manoeuvres he described as being meaningless. No one knew what to do, including the organising schoolmasters: it hardly set Dillon up for command.

I did not require any encouragement to put down my name when an urgent call was made for officers or those with OTC Training at Public Schools. After an interview in mid-August with an elderly officer of the Northumberland Fusiliers' Depot at Fenham Barracks, Newcastle, who asked me where I had been educated, my standard of sportsmanship and my OTC training, I was told to go home until I heard further. A fortnight later I received my commission as Second Lieutenant from the War Office. I was then 18 and one month.

Norman Dillon

The British Army admonished its officers to 'play the game', an allusion to the grand idea of war being merely an extension of sport. Playing the game included looking and acting in a way expected of aspirant officers, and while the facts of background and schooling were critical to an appointment, a man's deportment carried some weight too.

Frederick Roe was enjoying Bristol University's OTC summer camp when he, along with other cadets, was taken to Windmill Hill Camp on Salisbury Plain by their commanding officer, Major William Christie, a Regular soldier of the Royal Warwickshire Regiment. On arrival, Christie presented application forms filled out for temporary commissions, save for the cadet's signature. 'We all signed,' wrote Roe, 'and they were dispatched to the War Office.' Owing to the nationwide glut of applications, nothing further was heard so with permission, Roe and a friend, Claude Hughes-Games, headed off to the nearest Territorial Force headquarters in Bristol to see the adjutant. They were placed in an outer office and left to sweat with apprehension.

Frederick Roe

The Adjutant, a regular officer longing to get back to his battalion, looked at me without any sign of greeting and just said, 'You,' and to Hughes-Games, 'Not you,' then to me, 'Follow me!'

Suddenly he flung open a door and said, in a parade voice, 'Take over!' I found myself at one end of a large drill hall where a warrant officer was drilling about 100 recruits. Fortunately, I remembered to stand strictly at attention, to keep my thumbs down the seams of my trousers, and took over. I thought it a cruelly hard trick but after a few minutes during which nothing got really snarled up, the Adjutant told the warrant officer to 'carry on, sergeant major,' and we went away to his office. Before he sat down he said, 'I'll have you.' I remembered to say, 'Thank you, sir,' saluted, and departed.

With determined disregard for the usual channels and with renewed enthusiasm I sent a telegram to the War Office: 'have been accepted for commission in 6th (Territorial Battalion) The Gloucestershire Regiment.' I later read in *The Times* of 1 October 1914 a copy of *The London Gazette* appointing me to a commission as a second lieutenant in that unit.

Roe could not have *known* why his friend was not interviewed, but he speculated that as Hughes-Games had forgotten to put his hat on when addressed by the adjutant, while Roe had never taken his off (for fear of forgetting to put it on), that that small error may have made all the difference.

Madly keen though many men were to enlist, other candidates for commission were entirely phlegmatic about their prospects. Arthur Heath kept in touch with his family writing good-humoured letters that made it clear that he neither 'needed' to be accepted, nor would he be disappointed if he were not.

Camaraderie amongst the young officers of the 8th King's Own Scottish Borderers. Lieutenant Charles Murray, book in hand, was killed on the Somme in September 1916.

Arthur Heath

Mr A.G. Heath has been before the Board recommending for commissions. They gave few signs whether he was likely to get his job or not, but from private inquiries he is not hopeful. The only thing that pleases him is that he was passed as fit by a medical officer who really examined his candidates – at least five minutes each – and did not merely ask whether they were well… Now, if his country refuses his services, it will be with her eyes open and a plain warning in her ears.

Kitchener's appeal drew in far more applicants than the published figure of 2,000. It was a good start, but it would take months to turn them into officers capable of commanding in the field. Meanwhile, hundreds of officers were needed in France. Less than a month after the Battle of Mons an additional 600 were sent overseas from the dwindling band of competent Regular officers at home: within six months, 6,000 officers would be killed, wounded or taken prisoner; the vast majority had to be replaced. This logistical tension was a never-ending source of anxiety for Kitchener. He could hope to withdraw more officers from overseas territories and turn around lightly wounded officers sent home to recover, but invariably this was sticking-plaster management.

Despite the evident problems, Kitchener would not restrict the establishment of further New Army divisions, forcing him to 'find' senior officers to take command. A small number could be withdrawn from France, but in the main he would have to encourage out of retirement men, many aged in their late fifties and early sixties, with military knowledge learnt in the Sudan, Egypt, South Africa, and India.

Second Lieutenant Richard Hawkins, 11th The Royal Fusiliers

I was on parade with my company one morning, and Major Walters came in, nothing to do but he'd come back to serve his country. I said, 'Um, excuse me, Sir, what medals are represented by those little ribbons you are wearing?' 'Well,' he said, 'one is the King's South African Medal and the other's the Queen's. I'm not quite sure which is which. All I can tell you is that my life was never in danger for one moment. I'm not sure I ever heard a shot fired.'

These officers with their antiquated military experience could still offer effective leadership. Many proved successful appointments, though by no means all. A few 'dugouts' (as old time-served officers were known) proved irascible and difficult. A few of the most awkward would be quickly re-retired.

Colonel [William] Mclean was a rather aged and violently tempered old gentleman. We only saw him on battalion parades and manoeuvres – thank goodness… He was always mounted on his horse and from that vantage point would scream at us in a very shrill and terrifying manner, calling us all the foul names he could muster up. If he could find no valid excuse for this he would soon make one up. Woe-betide anyone who had the misfortune to go before him on a charge – his sentence was always severe. Probably his irascibility was due to the fact that his advanced age prohibited him from going to France, in spite of his numerous pleas. After the War the old rascal took up Holy Orders and

Second Lieutenant Richard Hawkins (circled) with the officers and men of his company.

Private John Tucker 3/13th The London Regiment

Sir Robert Gordon-Gilmour, aged nearly 60, had served in the Anglo-Zulu War of 1879, the Sudanese campaign 1884–85 and the Second Boer War, 1900–1902. In December 1914, he was given command of the 118th Infantry Brigade.

one day the newspaper placards bore the legend in huge type 'Clergyman Assaults his Housekeeper'. I do not remember the outcome of the case.

To find additional officers capable of commanding at battalion and company level, Kitchener ordered the Post Office to procure names from letters addressed to colonels, majors, and even captains. These men would be politely invited to offer their services if they had not already done so. The army was not used to employing such unorthodox methods. Nevertheless, they were necessary and they worked.

BRIGADIER SIR GORDON GILMOUR DSO

As recruitment of other ranks overwhelmed expectations, four Kitchener Armies were soon established with K1 (launched 21 August) followed soon afterwards by K2 (11 September) and K3 a few days later. K4 was established towards the end of October. Inescapably, first come came to be first served. The new battalions grouped under K1 received the bulk of the 'left-behind' Regular officers and NCOs as well as the pick of those recently reawakened from retirement, with K2 receiving far fewer officers though appreciably more than K3. K3 began life starved of serving officers, making do at first with truly 'vintage' commanding and company officers and a sprinkling of those newly commissioned. As the number of battalions in K3 grew, so the overall dilution of experienced officers in all three armies continued apace with a drip-down approach established: as soon as they might be spared, serving, experienced officers in K1 were given to K2 and then to K3 to provide the requisite backbone.

Owing to the parochial way in which Pals battalions were raised, latitude was given in the appointment of officers. Until the War Office officially recognised these battalions in late 1914 or 1915, each was permitted to establish its own command structure, relying on local knowledge and connections for selections. Not even the appointment of commanding officers would be London directed, but rather through the local recommendation of a city mayor or raising committee. Names were submitted to the War Office for almost certain 'rubber stamp' approval.

The 11th Border Regiment, known as the Lonsdale Battalion, was formed at the instigation of Lord Lonsdale, a peer and hugely wealthy Cumberland landowner. 'Are you a man or a mouse?' was his inspiration for a recruiting poster printed in his racing colours of red, yellow and white, an appeal responded to by the region's miners, steelworkers, farm workers and office clerks. On his own initiative, Lonsdale appointed a retired lieutenant colonel, Percy Machell, to command and was instrumental in the appointment of additional officers, none of whom had ever served in the Regular Army. Lonsdale paid for uniforms, rifles and kit, funds eventually reimbursed by the War Office. Battalion headquarters was Carlisle Racecourse, upon which the men camped. It was fortunate for all that Machell was a workaholic.

> Every detail had to be taught by him, for the officers, with very few exceptions, knew no more than the men and had to be taught themselves before they could teach. The simplest orderly-room work, such as making out 'crimes' 'guard reports', and 'details' etc., were done by him… And he always checked each of the returns personally. All attestations were made out and recruits personally approved by him, while the separation allowances claimed his particular attention. He organised the feeding of the men… he arranged for the hutting, the clothing, the water supply, the lighting, and conservancy of the camp, and he it was who averted a strike that threatened over the wages question among the men engaged to build the huts. These things alone would have occupied the activities of six ordinary men, but in addition to all this the CO was constantly on parade, training and smartening up both officers and men, drawing up the programmes of work and seeing that they were carried out.
>
> Captain Philip Diggle, 11th The Border Regiment (Lonsdale)

Machell was 52 years old, a stripling compared to other once-retired officers, whose physical fitness and cognitive strength wildly varied. Most 'dugouts' would never see active service, though Machell would. He went to France with the battalion and was killed in action on the first day of the Battle of the Somme.

In addition to the local appointment of men accepted to be the right calibre and educational background to join a Pals battalion, over 20,000 members or former members of the OTC were granted commissions in the first seven months of the war. These came from the senior (university) and junior (public and grammar school) divisions of the OTC, as well as recruits from the Inns of Court. Even so, overall numbers were still below what was required.

As Kitchener knew, the problem was plugging the leak of candidates from private schools, many of whom believed (often erroneously) that getting to France quickly was contingent upon enlisting in the ranks. Top public schools such as Marlborough and Charterhouse were proud of their boys who were accepted for a commission, although almost a fifth of pupils still enlisted in the ranks. From smaller, less well-known private and grammar schools, the figures were broadly reversed, with the majority enlisting as privates.

In their desire to serve overseas, boys kept a close eye on ever-changing dynamics, noticing who got overseas and when. Charles Carrington had applied for a commission but initial failure meant he enlisted as a private. Then he identified a new opportunity. 'On the whole, the best way to jump the queue for France was to get yourself selected for an officer's commission, since young officers had the heaviest casualties and the highest replacement rate.' He then prevailed upon an uncle 'to pull strings'.

Carrington was correct. Becoming a junior officer increased the chances of being killed or wounded if his service was in the infantry combined with the Western Front. Young officers were brave to the point of recklessness, as John Lucy, a hardened Regular soldier, witnessed in 1914: they were, he wrote, 'extraordinarily gallant, and their displays of valour often uncalled for, though thought necessary by them'. For more than a year, officers would wear uniforms that clearly identified their rank and were duly picked off by the enemy in disproportionate numbers. Until many adapted their uniforms, procuring other ranks' tunics and losing conspicuous insignia of status, they would continue to fall in unsustainable numbers.

Just as the War Office had approached the Post Office to forward letters to retired officers, so it made direct approaches to public schools asking for recommendations for commission, targeting boys who had served in the OTC and who held Certificates A and B (Certificate B denoting a higher degree

Men of the Artists Rifles briefly resting by the roadside in September 1914. Almost all of these men would be offered commissions.

of training). Recommendations received, commissions were offered to lads, many of whom were already serving in the ranks. Popular middle-class and upper-middle-class battalions, such as the Artists Rifles, endlessly retarded their development owing to the constant drain on their rank and file.

Private Geoffrey Fildes, 2/28th The London Regiment (Artists Rifles)

The company on an early morning parade began to present a new interest. Gaps appeared, and the absence of familiar faces began to be noted from day to day. These indicated the arrival of commissions for the more fortunate of us. One, we would learn, had gone to join a brother in his Regular battalion; another had had access to the colonel of a Territorial unit in process of formation. Every day changes were to be found among our ranks.

Lieutenant Colonel J. Craig, 2/6th Princess Louise's (Argyll & Sutherland Highlanders)

The 1/6th Argylls at Bedford apparently considered that our main duty was to furnish them with good recruits, commissioned and otherwise; and, if I may be permitted to say so, their requests were by no means easy to meet… I do not err in estimating that we transferred at least four hundred men to the 1/6th Argylls prior to this battalion's departure for France.

Such loss frustrated any commanding officer eager to establish a battalion of which he could be proud; one that he might hope to lead overseas. Pals battalions selective in their recruitment, such as the 10th Royal Fusiliers, unofficially known as the 'Stockbrokers' Battalion', were in equal danger of seeing commands dwindle as those of the Territorial Force that had chosen to be similarly discerning.

The 16th Battalion of the Middlesex Regiment sought only former public schoolboys and their only authorised recruitment office at which recruits could apply given as 24 St James Street, an impressive building on the edge of Mayfair and close to Buckingham Palace. When the battalion's platoons and companies formed, the men waited in civilian clothes, but rather than the tatty clothes seen elsewhere, the men wore breeches, tweed jackets, and even spurs. Bowler hats, tweed caps, and Homburgs were everywhere: these were all solidly middle-class men. Many of these recruits would soon seek a commission though the commanding officer had proved reluctant to forward applications. Private Charles Lawson, who desired a transfer to the Essex Regiment, remembered his commanding officer increasingly agitated by any diminution of his command and all that had meant for his wish to lead the battalion overseas.

To me, he was a man facing disappointment in all his dearest hopes, at a time when many thought that a modern war could not possibly last more than a few weeks, or months at the most. He was not alone. Many of us sought commissions urgently for the same reason… As his dream of an outstanding command faded away and the iron entered his soul, Colonel Hall became less well liked.

Private Charles Lawson, 16th The Duke of Cambridge's Own (Middlesex Regiment)

It must have been with some trepidation, that Lawson approached his commanding officer with a view to a move.

The CO, Colonel Hall, must have received orders from the War Office, who knew the real casualty figures amongst junior officers, so (at this stage) he did not impede those who sought commissions, but they were not popular with battalion headquarters who believed that those who applied were undermining the chances of the battalion going to the front as a crack unit. To apply for a commission from the ranks of the PSB [Public Schools Brigade] you filled in a form giving details of your education, training, etc., and it had to be supported by the signature of someone like a mayor or JP. The Commanding Officer could refuse to forward it on. His only comment to me was that the Essex Regiment was taking a lot of casualties so I would get what I wanted. At that stage demand exceeded supply. No CO was pleased to see his command disappear, or becoming an OTC. My application only went forward when I brought in a recruit to take my place. This I did by going to the nearest recruiting office and giving the Recruiting Sergeant ten shillings for his next recruit. By the time I received my commission many of my fellow originals had gone the same way.

Private Charles Lawson, 16th The Duke of Cambridge's Own (Middlesex Regiment)

The commanding officer could not stop the exodus from the battalion. By the end of the year no fewer than 360 NCOs and men had left to take up commissions elsewhere. The unit's stated restriction to public school applicants only was necessarily dropped.

The four battalions of the University and Public Schools Brigades were suffering too, and they did not like it. One, the 20th Battalion, prided itself on having guardsman NCOs and a Guard's adjutant for whom 'Spit and Polish were the first two gods of war', according to one of the recruits. 'The UPS' smartness on the square was something to take a proper pride in,' he wrote, lamenting the loss of men to other battalions.

Private Reginald Birkett and friends in the 20th Royal Fusiliers. On the right is Private Edmund Wrigley from North Wales. Wrigley died of spotted fever on 26 April 1915.

Private Ashley Gibson, 20th The Royal Fusiliers (City of London Regiment) (3rd Public Schools)

Months before embarkation, our brigade began to lose its advertised character. From the ranks our brightest and best were gazetted out in scores to officer newer units of K's mushroom army. The War Office began to behave as if we were an OTC, which hadn't been what we wanted.

Ashley Gibson would be commissioned too, though he remained within the battalion. By January 1915, commanding officers within the brigade were clamping down on the exodus. 'In the Public Schools Corps they are now putting the drop on taking commissions which is obviously necessary or otherwise with continuous recruits coming in no training can be completed as a Corps,' wrote one former private who had himself only just taken up a commission in the Rifle Brigade.

Commanding officers' resistance was hardly surprising or uncommon; after all, there was nothing in it for them to let promising men go to another regiment. George Butterworth was invited to take a commission with five of his friends by the commanding officer from an entirely different brigade and in an entirely different division, an offer the men accepted. In today's vernacular, it appeared to be a blatant case of 'tapping-up'.

> During the first week of October, [Brigadier General] General Ovens, head of the 68th Brigade [23rd Division], offered commissions to self and five friends. This offer was generally accepted, subject to the sanction of the DCLI officials. The latter, however did not show us much goodwill as I expected. Our company commander [Major Barnet] lodged an objection – trivial as well as inaccurate – on the ground that we had already been offered commissions in the DCLI and refused them. To this we replied that we had not previously been given the opportunity en bloc, and had not cared to risk breaking up the party by accepting offers singly.
>
> The situation was a curious one. General Ovens, having once made up his mind, stood by us splendidly. I kept up communications with him by means of Ellis's motorcar, which carried messages to and from Bullswater [Camp] (General Oven's headquarters) almost daily, and for a whole week a ridiculous three-cornered correspondence went on. General Ovens would send me what practically amounted to a command to join; this I passed on to the Commanding Officer, who invariably ignored it. Why he was so anxious to keep us I cannot conceive, but I fancy it was just a bluff, his only object being to save the face of our company commander by making things as difficult for us as possible.
>
> However, one day a more than usually firm message came from the General, we were all called off parade and ordered to report ourselves as soon as possible at our new headquarters.

Private George Butterworth, 6th The Duke of Cornwall's Light Infantry

Butterworth wrote that he was 'not sorry' to leave the battalion and in the end the battalion might not have been sorry to see Butterworth and his friends leave. They were hardly representative of the unit's general rank and file, and this may have begun to cause needless friction. In mid-September, when Roland Ellis went down with influenza, he was sent to his tent. His brother, Francis, lodged a 'respectful but firm protest' and got permission to remove him to a private room in Aldershot. 'This, of course was a special favour; an ordinary private would have been kept in the camp until dangerously ill,' wrote Butterworth.

Ellis was away two days.

Private George Butterworth, 6th The Duke of Cornwall's Light Infantry

In the afternoon Roland Ellis returned to the tent, having recovered very quickly from his bout of influenza, but almost at the same time Morris was knocked over with it, and was removed to a hotel in Aldershot.

The right to shift into private quarters during illness has apparently been established for our party, which is a relief, but it does no credit to the authorities.

It seems reasonable to suppose that Ellis's car had been used in both cases, to transport the patients away from the camp for recuperation elsewhere.

A group of the most junior ranked soldiers expecting and receiving preferential treatment may have been grudgingly permitted while the battalion was young and while order was being established. Some leniency may have been given too when there was a thought these men would take the commissions offered to them. Major Barnet had indeed approached Butterworth and his band of brothers about a commission, but the group had only offered themselves if all were taken. 'Naturally enough, that was considered as equivalent to a refusal,' wrote Butterworth, a refusal that would hardly have endeared the men to Major Barnet.

Weeks later, when the question of commissions came up again, the group debated amongst themselves. These would be 'elsewhere' appointments, there being no longer vacancies within the battalion.

Private George Butterworth, 6th The Duke of Cornwall's Light Infantry

We have all been wavering in our minds about it for some time, and seeing crowds of beardless youths shipped down here as officers has made us rather less satisfied with our position as privates: the climax

Captain Richard Vaughan-Thompson, 11th Royal Fusiliers, in his private car, photographed by Second Lieutenant Richard Hawkins.

came when the most incompetent of the lot who actually had his first lesson in soldiering only a few days ago in the ranks of our platoon was officially appointed as our platoon officer.

Interestingly, Butterworth claimed that several of the group had received approaches from 'different quarters'. Brigadier General Ovens was perhaps only the most high-ranking officer to make an offer.

Private soldiers did not correspond with brigadier generals unless comfortable communicating with people at a senior level, and Butterworth and his group were well connected, confident, and upper middle class. One former officer wrote, albeit in a novel based on his experiences, that it had become 'the thing to get "asked for" by some particular colonel who was training a new battalion'. In other words, an indirect 'fishing-style' approach would be made to signal that a man was keen to move.

'By any chance [do] you know a Colonel of a regiment who would like my services? It would be a great kindness to give me a letter of introduction,' wrote one well-connected private serving with the Public Schools Brigade in a letter to a friend in the Coldstream Guards. It is easy to see how moves were engineered.

How contact was first made with Brigadier General Ovens is unclear, though he is likely to have received a recommendation that Butterworth would make good officer material. The first letter Butterworth received from Ovens had also asked him to name others of the party for an approach.

Private George Butterworth, 6th The Duke of Cornwall's Light Infantry

After some discussion, it was decided that I should follow this up, and propose the names of Morris, Brown, Woodhead, and the two Ellises; as we considered it improbable that all would be accepted, I grouped the names in pairs – Morris with myself, Brown and Woodhead together, with the two Ellises together – so that no one should be left in the lurch. The only remaining member of our party (Keeling) is now a corporal, and prefers in any case to remain with the DCLI.

General Ovens had told me to write to the Brigade Major at Pirbright, but, after consulting the officers here, we decided that a personal interview would be simpler. Accordingly F[rancis] Ellis and myself were given leave to go over to Pirbright in Ellis' motor car, which he has been keeping with permission at Farnborough.

We had a memorable afternoon. At Pirbright village we stopped for a beer, chiefly for the sake of seeing once again the inside of a country inn, and arrived at the camp of the 68th Brigade at about 4.30… The Brigade Major is the officer temporarily in charge of the whole camp, and we went off to his tent rather uncertain how to approach so exalted a person. We had no need to be so nervous; the sentry, whom we had first to satisfy, turned out to be a seedy Tynesider with a two-day's beard; an intensely comic picture. The Brigade Major himself – though more respectable – was scarcely more formidable; what is familiarly called a 'dug-out'. Like everyone else in the camp he was dressed in mufti, and appeared to be very vague on the subject of commissions. One theory of his was that all the second lieutenancies were filled up, but that we could probably become first lieutenants or even captains if we chose!

The commanding officer of the 6th DCLI had openly resisted losing the group, but his obstinacy may simply be indicative of his annoyance at having his men 'picked off' rather than of any great desire to keep them, especially if he had a full complement of officers. In the end, his hand was forced. All six men were accepted into the 68th Brigade, and divided between three battalions.

Some men of identifiable officer quality *chose* to remain in the ranks despite attempts to persuade them otherwise. Frederick Roe noted that 'Many men just wished to serve their country without any wish to exercise command, enduring the experience of living in tents or barrack rooms with other soldiers of markedly different ways of life'. In his Territorial battalion, the adopted heir of the author Thomas Hardy refused all attempts to send him to officer training, despite the fact that he struggled on long route marches in full kit.

> After every long march the varicose veins of both his legs stood out like pipe stems and he invariably soaked them in a bucket of warm water for each leg to reduce the swelling. He never went or would go sick.

Private Bell, a member of the Three Nuns Tobacco family, also resisted pressure to take a commission, preferring to serve in the ranks.

Amongst his peers in one of the Public Schools Battalions of the Royal Fusiliers, bank manager Andrew Buxton would not have stood out other than for his middle age, and it was perhaps this that led to his being approached, not to become an officer but an NCO. In time, Buxton would be willing to take a commission, but right then and there, he felt painfully aware of his limitations as a soldier: the idea of command at any level unnerved him.

> This morning I had, for some unknown reason, an honour paid to me in being ordered with one other man to fall out with the Non-Commissioned Officers and told they would like me to become one. I am glad to say I was able to get out of it, though at the time I did not think I could work getting off. Non Commissioned Officers have already had a lot of training and the responsibility of being in charge of fourteen men has duties which I do not consider without previous training that I was able to completely fulfil.

Private Andrew Buxton, 21st The Royal Fusiliers (City of London Regiment) (4th Public Schools)

Experienced NCOs were a godsend to the New Army. These four served with the 8th (Service) Battalion, Devonshire Regiment. The man second from the left is wearing the ribbon of the Queen's South Africa Medal.

Finding capable NCOs presented yet another problem for the army to solve. As with retired officers, there was a slush fund of ex-Regular NCOs, no longer on the Reserve but who were willing to re-enlist and be utilised straight away. The upper age limit for re-enlisted soldiers was quickly raised from 45 to 50 and anyone who chose to return could expect to be given at least the rank held when he had left the forces. In the hunt for additional NCOs, requests were made for drafts to be sent home from battalions in India, while both the police and prison warder services, organisations that traditionally attracted former servicemen, were contacted to release men to the depots to help in the basics of drill. The experience of these men was vital when so many newly commissioned officers were going to be ignorant of anything and everything. That NCOs training, like that of retired officers, might be ten or twenty years out of date, was an issue that became apparent on the parade ground.

There were not enough experienced NCOs to go around. New ones would have to be found from amongst those who appeared suited to responsibility. Once again, the process of selection seemed arbitrary, even unfair to some overlooked men, but the army had to begin somewhere.

RIGHT SORTS

There was a general parade after breakfast, at which it became evident that the main part of the camp was composed of raw recruits like ourselves. The remainder consisted of a sprinkling of 'Regular' soldiers, the majority of whom were either 'old sweats', or young soldiers who were, presumably, too young for service overseas with their battalions, unless urgently needed. These were to have the pleasant (?) duty of initiating us in the preliminary duties of soldering. At the general parade certain of the officers were sent along the lines to select the most intelligent-looking of the new recruits for the purpose of 'promotion' as, in our very raw state, we had to begin drill in very small squads, and there were not nearly enough old soldiers.

So, along the lines came these officers, and when they came to any particularly bright-looking object, they asked what his previous occupation had been. If he said the occupation was one which was reputed to require a small amount of brains, the person was invited to 'take a stripe', and in the event of his doing so he was presented with a piece of pink tape which was tied around the upper part of the right sleeve, thus making him a lance corporal forthwith. Any experience in the Boy Scouts or the Boys' Brigade was a great qualification for this kind of promotion. The man next to me on my right happened to be the Cockney who had been so full of beer and songs on the first night at Bury St Edmunds, and he gave his profession as 'glorseblower', and became a lance corporal in a jiffy. Then came my turn. The officer looked me over, and then asked what I had been. 'Good,' I thought, 'I *look* alright anyway.' I replied, 'A farm labourer.' The officer said, 'Oh,' very expressively, and went on to the next man, leaving me more or less squashed, nipped in the bud, as it were.

Private Sydney Fuller, 8th The Suffolk Regiment

In the 10th Essex Regiment, promotion was about looking the 'right sort', as the commanding officer made clear, although previous military experience had helped too.

Unknown officer, 10th The Essex Regiment

A few regular NCOs had been sent to them and such of them who were Lance Corporals were raised to the proud and dizzy rank of CSM upon the spot. Men who knew the difference between 'Form Fours' and a 'Four by Two' were seized upon feverishly, and their arms blossomed immediately into the glory of three stripes. But even this scanty military knowledge was possessed by few, and a straw hat or a bowler determined the choice of the lance corporal, while a really clean white collar in addition to a decent hat was the sure passport to the rank of corporal.

Friends often chose to remain together, resisting any offer to promote one man over another.

In the 12th West Yorkshire Regiment, a novel way of differentiating between men and their class and therefore suitability was discovered entirely by accident.

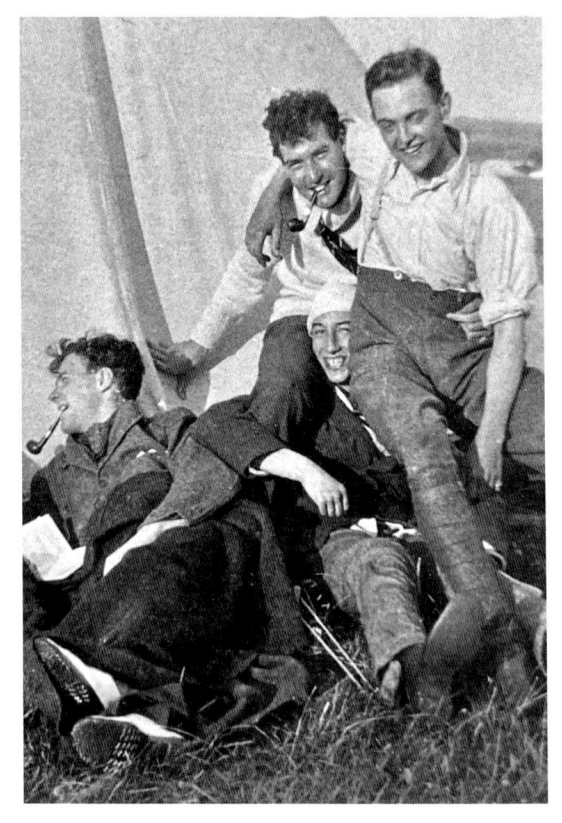

There was no use picking out a few bright-looking chaps and telling them that they were corporals, for there was no way of indicating their rank. We did not even have brassards with stripes on them that they could wear over their coat sleeves. So I counted the men who had moustaches and found that I had just enough, so I made them all lance corporals there and then… Actually I did not realise it at first, but I had hit upon a wizard idea. Nearly all the men were coal miners and coal miners do not have moustaches because of the coal dust. At any rate not those who go underground. So the chaps at the pitheads and in the mine offices sported moustaches – I suppose to show off that they were superior beings; so I had automatically selected the brainworkers to be my lance corporals.

Lieutenant Harold Hemming, 12th The Prince of Wales's Own (West Yorkshire Regiment)

Simple yet subjective methods of promotion did not always work out as expected. In the traditional pecking order of civil employment, a man's position in the business hierarchy was broadly reflective of his age. Amongst the volunteers, this social norm was regularly usurped with younger men being given a lance corporal's stripe ahead of older peers. It was what Private Thomas Lyon called the New Army's 'topsy-turveydom'.

Lyon noted the 'nasty jar' that could happen when civil society's set hierarchy was flipped. He recalled one stockbroker turned private, a man possessed of 'a rotund figure, a motor car, and a tolerably high opinion of himself'. He was 'flabbergasted and worried' as he sought 'to adjust his mental vision to the suddenly altered aspect of his little world'. Lyon recorded in the stockbroker's own words the anguish.

'Only a little while ago the sergeant was strutting up and down in gorgeous raiment before the entrance to a "movies" palace, holding open the swing doors and saying to me as I entered, "Good evening, sir! Yes, sir! Lots of good seats in the balcony, sir! Paybox on the right, sir!" – and today the beggar actually addressed me as, "You – the fat one in the bashed hat!" and ordered me to pick up all the papers and cigarette ends lying on the floor of the hall, and to jump to it lively. And I had to jump to it lively too. It's a most extraordinary state of affairs.'

Private Thomas Lyon, 2/9th The Highland Light Infantry (Glasgow Highlanders)

The same inversion of status could affect officers as well as NCOs. It was probably wise never to exploit what might amount to a temporary ascendancy in the army over one's boss in civil life.

Private Thomas Lyon, 2/9th The Highland Light Infantry (Glasgow Highlanders)

Yet another private I know is in times of peace the head of a department in an important manufacturing business, and his former office boy is now a second lieutenant and his superior officer. It's funny to witness the apologetic and deferential manner in which the young subaltern issues his commands to his former governor. 'I guess he knows', said the latter once, 'that if he tries to swank it before me I'll take the dust out of him when we get back to the office. He knows better than to shoot out his neck at me.'

And at the end of the day's drill one may see privates – the one-an'-tuppence-a-day men – drive off in elegant motor cars, while their officers walk to take the democratic tram car!

If only I could set it to music!

Such disparity of wealth that ran diametrically opposed to the rank held was unusual but by no means unique, as Francis Ellis's private car proved. In the ranks of one of the three Birmingham Pals battalions (the 14th, 15th and 16th Royal Warwickshire Regiment) was a lad whose appearance did not belie his background, according to fellow Private Harold Drinkwater. 'I found out the fellow next to me had never done a day's work in his life. He had had something in the nature of a valet to do it for him. He was barely seventeen.'

Those men who actively sought out promotion or who accepted an offer of a stripe or perhaps two were not guaranteed to enjoy success. Being seen to 'get ahead' was not an attribute always welcomed by contemporaries.

Private Donald Hankey, 7th The Rifle Brigade

The young lance corporal who is put in charge of a section has absolutely no prestige… Of the work he knows little more than the men. He lives and sleeps and messes with them. They know all his faults and weaknesses a great deal better than he does himself. They are inclined to be jealous of him, and have no respect for him except what he can inspire by his inherent force of character. They can cover his deficiencies or emphasise them as they like. If he tries to establish his authority by reporting them, he can by no means count on the sure support of his superiors. Unless they have a very high opinion of him, they will be quite likely to conclude that he is more bother than he is worth, and reduce him to the ranks.

Of course the types vary enormously. At first it is generally the men who want promotion that obtain the stripe, and they mostly belong to one of two classes. They are either ambitious youngsters or blustering bullies. The youngster who wants promotion has probably been a clerk and lived in the suburbs. He is better educated and has a smarter appearance than the general run of men. He covets the stripe because he wants to get out of the many menial and dirty jobs incidental to barrack life; because he thinks himself 'a cut above' his fellows and wants the fact to be recognised; because, in short, he thinks that as a lance-corporal he will find life easier and more flattering to his self-esteem. He soon finds his mistake. He annoys the sergeant major by his incompetence and the men by his superior airs. Soon he gets into a panic and begins to nag at his men. That is just what they hate. The whole situation reminds one of nothing so much as of a terrier barking at a herd of cows. As soon as the cows turn on him, the terrier begins to waver, and, after trying to maintain his dignity by continuing to bark, ends by fleeing for dear life with his tail between his legs…

The career of the bully is different. He is generally a vulgar, pushing fellow, who likes boasting and threatening, likes to feel that men are afraid of him, likes to be flattered by toadies, and likes getting men punished. The men hate him; but he sometimes manages to bluff the officers and sergeants into thinking that he is a 'smart NCO'. Usually he comes to a bad end, either through drink or gambling. Then he is reduced to the ranks, his lot is not an enviable one.

A deplorable number of those who are first promoted finish by forfeiting their stripe. Then comes the turn of the man who does not covet rank for its own sake, but accepts it because he thinks that it is 'up to him' to do so. Generally he is a man of few words and much character. He gives an order. The man who receives it begins to argue: it is not his turn, he has only just finished another job, and so on. The

A bond of friendship: mates together serving in the 2/6th Gloucestershire Regiment.

NCO looks at him and repeats: 'Git on and do it.' The man 'curls up' and does as he is told. An NCO of this sort is popular. He saves any amount of wear and tear, and this is appreciated by the men. He gets things done, and that is appreciated by the sergeants and officers.

Finally, there is the gentleman, who is the most interesting of all from our point of view. He is generally a thoroughly bad disciplinarian in the official sense, and at the same time he is often a magnificent leader of men. He is fair and disinterested. He has a certain prestige through being rather incomprehensible to the average private. He does not care a scrap for his rank. He is impervious to the fear of losing it. He takes it from a sense of duty, and his one idea is to get things done with as little friction as possible.

RIGHT SORTS

It was not necessarily obvious what sort of NCO a man might become. First impressions were not always lasting ones, either for good or for bad.

In the Royal Warwickshire Regiment, Private Harold Drinkwater had watched with interest as platoon commander Lieutenant Rubery invited any man on parade who would like a stripe to step forward.

We thought this is going to be a short war, quick training, over to France and back again, finished… With the foregoing in our minds and the fact that for the most part we were fellows with something in common, we decided in the main that as we had joined as privates we would remain privates.

It was some moments before there stepped forward a pale, anaemic, undersized fellow who might have been eighteen for Army purposes, but actually looked barely sixteen. We looked aghast at this boy when we thought he might be made an NCO. We were staggered a few days later when we found he had been made a lance corporal and, still worse, in charge of the section we were in, but we agreed that we had had an equal chance and it was therefore up to us now to play the game.

In a month we liked him, in six months we said he was as good as any other NCO in the battalion, in twelve months' time we were glad to help him carry out any difficult command he had to obey, in eighteen months we would have cleaned his boots. He had a great hold on us, this young fellow.

Private Harold Drinkwater, 15th The Royal Warwickshire Regiment (2nd Birmingham)

The young lad was willing to set an example to other men and setting high personal standards, not shirking difficult tasks would naturally appeal to those who followed him. The anaemic looking lad who took a stripe turned out to be a superb NCO and leader of men at home and, critically, in France.

Overleaf: A break after a hard morning's work: men of the 20th Royal Fusiliers resting on Salisbury Plain.

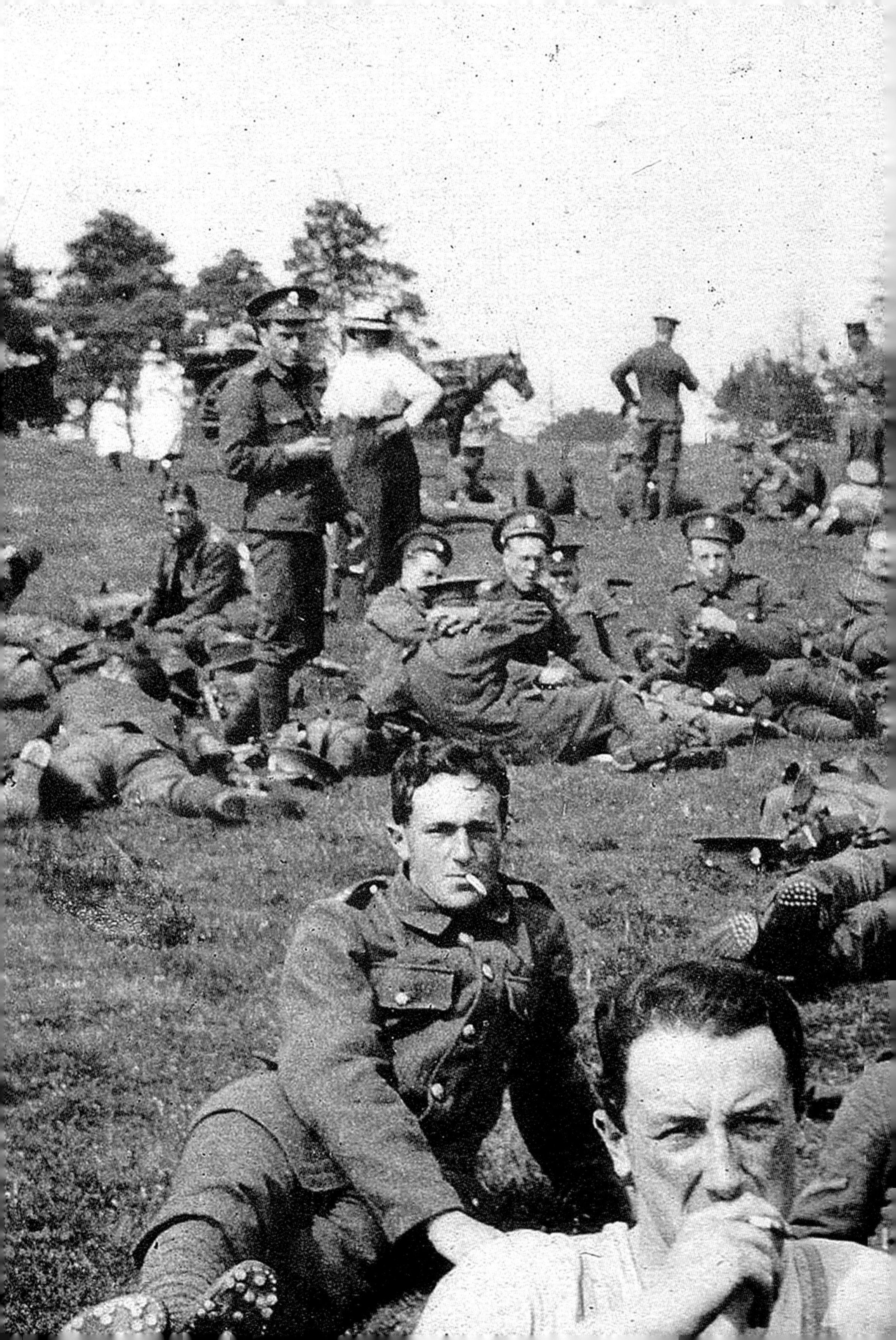

6 Taming Lions

WE'VE HAD A HARD CAMP HERE MOTHER!

'The recruit stands loosely. He is never still. His expression is always changing. His eyes are restless. Now he is interested, and his pose is alert, his eyes fixed on the instructor. Now his attention is distracted elsewhere, his attitude becomes less tense, his eyes wander. Now he is frankly bored, his head and shoulders droop forward, he stands on one leg, his eyes are fixed on the ground. His movements reflect every passing mood. His will is untrained, his character unformed, his muscles undeveloped.'

Private Donald Hankey, 7th The Rifle Brigade

You'd probably like to hear about the men. Well, they're not the 'flower of English manhood' or, if they are, I pity the weeds. But the regular officers think them better than ordinary recruits, and they really are showing considerable keenness. A full eight hours a day on parade is double the ordinary recruits' course, and they are living of course in much less comfortable ways than if they were in barracks. But there is only a small percentage of the men who are not throwing themselves really hard into the work.

Second Lieutenant Arthur Heath, 6th The Queen's Own (Royal West Kent Regiment)

To his evident surprise, Arthur Heath's application for a commission had been accepted and he was gazetted and ordered to join his battalion at Purfleet Camp. The recruits were in their first weeks of training and broadly reflected the sort of men who had enlisted early on, including many likely to be living on society's margins. The battalion sported a few experienced officers although one of these, a dugout major eight years in retirement, died suddenly in camp.

Second Lieutenant Arthur Heath, 6th The Queen's Own (Royal West Kent Regiment)

The men here are more the ordinary recruiting class, and it's a newer and more interesting experience to have to deal with them. They are not – with a few exceptions – unemployables, but they are not 'gentlemen'. They remind me more of some of the Oxford village labourers than of any other class, though they have a touch of London smartness to help them. One or two are comparatively swells, but I shouldn't think that many of them have earned more than 30 shillings a week…

As soon as they found I knew how to form fours they put me in control of the platoon, fortunately under one of their regular officers who was recalled from the transport ship at Southampton to command this company, and I have been spending a good deal of the week in learning the general control of my platoon: inspecting their feet and their boots and their rifles and their dinners and their invisible tooth-brushes, urging doctors to discharge a man with only one kidney, signing their passes for Saturday night, looking after blankets and boot-polish, recovering marriage certificates for a man who could not get his separation allowance, and all sorts of little details like that.

Right across the country, officers and men were learning the ropes. John Hay Beith described the obvious challenges when dealing with recruits, imposing rules that grated with men so recently civilians.

Second Lieutenant John Hay Beith, 10th Princess Louise's (Argyll & Sutherland Highlanders)

You may not spit; neither may you smoke a cigarette in the ranks, nor keep the residue thereof behind you ear. You may not take beer to bed with you. You may not postpone your shave till Saturday; you must shave every day. You must keep your buttons, accoutrements, and rifles speckless, and have your hair cut in a style which is not becoming to your particular style of beauty. Even your feet are not your own. Every Sunday morning a young officer, whose leave has been specially stopped for the purpose, comes round the barrack-rooms after church and inspects your extremities, revelling in blackened nails and gloating over hammer-toes…

In the Army we appear to be nobody. We are expected to stand stiffly at attention when addressed by an officer; even to call him

An officer uses a safety razor before the day's work begins.

'sir' – an honour to which our previous [civilian] employer had been a stranger. At home, if we happened to meet the head of the firm in the street, and none of our colleagues was looking, we touched a cap furtively. Now, we have no option in the matter. We are expected to degrade ourselves by meaningless and humiliating gestures. The NCOs are almost as bad. If you answer a sergeant as you would a foreman, you are impertinent; if you argue with him, as all good Scotsmen must, you are insubordinate; if you endeavour to drive a collective bargain with him, you are mutinous; and you are reminded that upon active service mutiny is punishable by death. It is all very unusual and upsetting.

The barracks were full of authorities far more peremptory and potent than foreman or father. There was the corporal of his [the recruit's] room, who unsympathetically kicked him [the recruit] out of bed in the morning – bed being a mattress on the floor – and made him wash and do his share of the cleaning up of the room. There was the sergeant who made him march up and down the square all the morning, doing what he was told, and in intervals lectured him on his duties, his morals, and his personal cleanliness. There was the sergeant-major, a terribly

Private Donald Hankey, 7th The Rifle Brigade

awe-inspiring person, to whom even the sergeant was deferential, and to whom the corporal was positively sycophantic. There were subalterns, whose business in life seemed to be to preserve an attitude of silent omniscience and to criticise his personal appearance. Instead of freedom he found discipline. His uprisings and his outgoings, and all the smallest details of his being, even to the length of his hair and the cleanliness of his toes, were ordered by Powers against who there was no appeal. They held all the trump cards. He could not even 'chuck the job' in the old lordly way, without becoming a criminal… Submission was obviously the only course; and by degrees he learnt to do more than submit. He learnt the pride of submission. He came to believe in the discipline.

Second Lieutenant Arthur Heath, 6th The Queen's Own (Royal West Kent Regiment)

In my own platoon, three thoroughly bad men and three rather bad instantly disclosed themselves even to the eagle eye of a junior subaltern. But even of these one is not really slack so much as imbecile. Not so imbecile as another man who was in the company for a little time, but then discharged as 'unlikely to become an efficient soldier'. He had only got in by accident. He was a mad organ-grinder, and, according to his own account, had been kidnapped and enlisted by press-gang methods. Anyway he has now been weeded out, and if I might only weed out about five more I think something might be done.

These were new and exciting times and recruits were at their most enthusiastic and pliable. Frederick Keeling, a man who by background and education could have remained in the Artists Rifles and been commissioned, opted instead to remain in the ranks. He was happy to leave command and control to what he saw as a promising assortment of officers and NCOs.

Private Frederick Keeling, 6th The Duke of Cornwall's Light Infantry

In the course of a fortnight we have certainly made some progress in the way of transformation from a rabble into a military unit. Reveille is at 6 am, parade at 7, breakfast at 8, morning parade from 9 to 1, and afternoon parade from 2 to 5. The training in Kitchener's Army must strike every one as being above all practical and to the point, at any rate in a battalion which is so fortunate in its nucleus of trained officers and sergeants as our own. Little time is wasted in ceremonial drill. The number of formal rifle exercises to be learned is reduced to an absolute minimum. Extended order drill, taking cover, and skirmishing are practised almost from the first day of training. And we are already becoming proficient in certain new movements which have been devised in order to meet special features of the tactics adopted by the Germans during the present war, and on which the commanding officer gave an excellent lecture to all officers and NCOs.

The apparent pace with which Keeling's battalion developed was unusual. Much depended as to who was available to train the men and what facilities were on hand. While Keeling recorded that little time was wasted on ceremonial drill, others felt that was all they seemed to do.

The monotonous work of getting fit under the watchful eye of an NCO and a few passing civilians.

In Glasgow, the Highland Light Infantry's march around the city's streets had proved rewarding with more and more men falling in step to enlist so that the battalion quickly reached establishment. Now 'our little hour of glory is over,' wrote Lyon, 'a period of humiliation and self-abasement has come.'

Private Thomas Lyon, 2/9th The Highland Light Infantry (Glasgow Highlanders)

On the east side of Glasgow Green there is a vast, stony wilderness, plentifully wooded with goalposts, and it is here that we are being daily taught the toilsome rudiments of the business of soldiering. Any morning or afternoon you may see, scattered over this unlovely expanse of ground, ten squads of a hundred men each, all hot and perspiring in their efforts to become worthy soldiers of the King.

The cheering crowds have gone, and their place has been taken by gamins [locals] from the adjacent Saltmarket, who, as we march to and from the drilling ground, shout comments more candid than encouraging – 'Aw, luk at that big yin there; the German'll take 'um for a telegraph powl.' – 'Hi, sir, ye'd better tak' yer mither's paurlor carpet wi' ye for a kilt!' – 'Haw, here's speccy Dan! Kill yin or twa Germans fur me, purfessor!' – 'Dis yer mither ken ye're oot, you wi' the bald heid?'

These recruits were proud to strut along the busy roads of Glasgow, sucking in the popular adulation, but after two weeks of the new regime, reality had bitten hard. 'We have no illusions left as to our supreme martial qualities; we look green and we taste raw even to ourselves.'

Private Thomas Lyon, 2/9th The Highland Light Infantry (Glasgow Highlanders)

Company drill is not an exhilarating pastime – for the recruit, at least, however it may be for the instructor. In various formations each company of the battalion moves to and fro, now at the quick and now at the double, across the same little patch of ground for hours upon end – until in time I think each recruit knows every peculiarity and irregularity of the earth's surface and every stone that cumbers the ground…

Extended order drill is a breathless variation of company drill, and our first attempts at it must have seemed to the onlookers remarkably like complete routs; for when the order to 'extend' had been given

TAMING LIONS

and acted upon one would see little bunches of men scattered all over the field; of any definite company formation there was none. Once I had the misfortune to be at the end of the front rank, and upon the command being given I 'extended' so zealously that I found myself completely isolated from my fellows, being separated from the nearest by a distance of fifty yards or so. And as I doubled back to my place I heard the Sergeant shout that if I deserted again he'd have me court-martialled. As a result of this form of drill all the men on our company are now suffering from cricks in their necks through slewing their heads round to see what signalled instructions the Sergeant will give next.

The training of a week of peace had now to be concentrated into a day or two, and monotonous enough the work was to the instructors through whose hands batch after batch of recruits passed in steady succession. The recruit himself knew only that for one puzzled month

'The Battalion parade ground. Some of the boys at drill,' is the contemporary description on the photograph's reverse. Men of the Northumberland Fusiliers close to Alnwick Castle.

Captain Cecil Street, Royal Garrison Artillery

he drilled continuously from sunrise to sunset, with hurried intervals for meals, in wet weather or fine. He scarcely had time to think; before he was aware of it he found himself converted from an aimless lounger through life into a disciplined atom of a great, powerful army. How it had happened he hardly knew, these things cannot be taught, drill can merely convey to the mind the coherence between certain words of command and their appropriate muscular movements. The question of his development, if it troubled him at all, must have been surrounded with mystery.

Frustrated in his attempt to gain promotion to lance corporal, Private Sidney Fuller was training under the guidance of those who had.

Private Sydney Fuller, 8th The Suffolk Regiment

The day was spent in learning how to 'form fours' and 'about turn', under one of the new NCOs, who had had (so he said) considerable experience in the Boys' Brigade, and who no doubt knew all about it… Our new NCOs were inclined to adopt rather a superior air, having been selected from the common herd. In our undisciplined state, that was ever and anon resulting in 'plain English', and sometimes even an offer of battle, from one of the said 'herd' who had been especially snubbed. However, in spite of these little differences, we began to do our little drills in something like the proper order. At first, many were the collisions, falling over one's own or someone else's feet, and misunderstandings.

Aubrey Smith had also been thwarted, not in promotion but in his desire to join the First Battalion of the London Rifle Brigade: with hindsight, he was indeed fortunate to get into the Second as this proved the better move. All the focus was on the First Battalion, allowing the Second to enjoy a 'gentle[r] introduction to the rigours of army discipline and discomforts', as Smith described them. But it was hard to expect much of the men when those in charge were struggling themselves.

Our officers came along in driblets, and, though most of them had territorial or similar experiences, they managed to get us into hopeless tangles in our drill and constantly consulted the NCOs as to the best means of extracting us. Our NCOs consisted partly of those recruits who had a smattering of drill and partly of people who possessed an aptitude for bawling loudly.

Rifleman Aubrey Smith, 2/5th (City of London) Battalion (London Rifle Brigade)

NCOs had had years perfecting their quips and sleights: oft repeated, they remained freshly funny or intimidating (or both) to those that had not heard them. Every squad was 'the worst' the NCO had had the misfortune to train, every individual 'the worst' to set foot on his parade ground. Secretly, the NCOs would have been disappointed if the men had not found their insults amusing, but heaven help anyone who smirked or laughed. 'What are you laughin' at, you in the rear rank? An' what are you ginnin' at, pantomine-face. Ye've got nuthin' to laugh at.' Thomas Lyon remembered the sergeant's words close to verbatim.

When we had marched round the park several times in different formations we'd get the command to halt. 'Dress by the right!' Immediately we hopped, skipped, and jumped in an endeavour to 'touch in' to our neighbour and to form a straight line. 'Huh!' snorted the Instructor. 'Call that a straight line!... You! fat one in the centre! Back a bit. You're putting the whole line out. You better dress by yer belly instead o' yer face.'

Soon he'd give the order, 'Hats, coats, an' weskits off an' lay 'em on the ground,' and we'd know that we were in for a stiff hour of drill, and some would begin to wish that they'd put on a clean shirt that morning, or that they'd got that missing button sewn on to their trousers, or perhaps they wondered if their old braces would outlast the hour.

'Look sharp there,' said the sergeant. 'I asked ye to take of yer coats an' vsts; I didn't tell ye to make yourselves look pretty. Never mind smoothin' back your hair, you in the rear rank! I'll put it out of curl for ye before the hour's over, I'll bet.'

Private Thomas Lyon, 2/9th The Highland Light Infantry (Glasgow Highlanders)

A platoon sergeant leads recruits over a hedge.

When not forming fours, recruits would be taken on a run: fitness would come. In the meantime, the NCOs were offered easy targets on which to vent their comedic spleen.

Private Thomas Lyon, 2/9th The Highland Light Infantry (Glasgow Highlanders)

Away he took us at the double. And after ten or twelve minutes' running, and when we were all breathless and perspiring, he put us through a series of exercises that lacked nothing in strenuousness, his commands the while being interlarded with priceless gems of criticism and comment. At one exercise our hands were placed on the ground and the entire weight of our out-stretched bodies rested on our arms and our toes. 'Now, keep yer bodies perfectly straight,' said the Sergeant. 'I don't want to see a row of Ben Nevises up in the air, and – there's a feller with 'is knees on the ground!'

Into this dynamic world walked young, newly commissioned subalterns. Having firstly acquired a uniform paid for by government grant, 19-year-old Second Lieutenant Norman Dillon arrived at Berkhamsted in Hertfordshire to join the 14th Battalion, Northumberland Fusiliers.

TAMING LIONS

I forgot how I found my Company Officer as everyone was in billets, and nobody knew where anything was. I was told to turn up on a local football field at 8 am the next morning. There I found the adjutant, who told me I was in charge of C Company, some 250 men drawn up in two lines. They were nearly all miners from the Morpeth area – they had been told to go in their old worn-out clothes because uniforms would be issued to them. Needless to say, this was one of the War Office's confidence tricks, and no uniforms were issued for months.

When I arrived what was obviously an old soldier from the South African War judging by the medal ribbons on his civilian jacket gravely saluted me and asked for instructions. 'Where is the Company Commander?' I asked. He told me there wasn't a Company Commander and that until my arrival he was commanding. Having no instructions, and not knowing what to do, I temporised and suggested that until orders were received the men should sit down. So I learned early that useful command 'Carry on, Sgt. Major'. (He was a Corporal as it happened.) Seeing other companies dispersing, I told him to end the parade, not knowing how to do it myself. This put me in a fix, and I was determined to be able to do the elementary movements of

Second Lieutenant Norman Dillon, 14th The Northumberland Fusiliers

An elderly officer examines a Vest Pocket Kodak while being photographed. He is wearing a pre-1912 service dress jacket with a high collar. Most units allowed officers to wear these jackets as working dress until they wore out. The other officers are wearing the recently re-modelled jacket, worn with a collar and tie.

drill myself. I should explain that in 1914 foot-drill and steadiness on parade were the only things that really mattered.

My first action after breakfast was to go to the railway station bookstall and buy a War Office manual called 'Infantry Training'. There, set out quite clearly (for once), was the whole procedure of falling-in a company and how to manoeuvre it on the parade ground. Next morning, I was on the ball and divided the company into its four platoons and started to show them how to form fours (this at least I knew). In this, I had some training at Haileybury OTC. I spent a lot of time with this manual, drilling imaginary troops represented by matchsticks until I was fairly proficient, and so each day I managed a new manoeuvre, and I doubt if those concerned knew that I was only one [step] ahead of them.

This drill, which was really a sort of ritual dance, was considered of great importance. One had to be capable of forming a line into four platoons, one behind the other, and again in a column of four platoons each split into four sections. The problem was to get them all back into line with every man in his original position. It wasn't difficult if one learnt it step by step and I always took note of the man who was No.1 in the line, so as to make sure the situation was restored with my marker where he should be.

At Deepcut Barracks, Hampshire, Julian Tyndale-Biscoe arrived wearing his OTC uniform as the one he purchased on receiving his commission was not ready. 'I was in great glee about being posted to the RHA [Royal Horse Artillery], having great visions of galloping about with a fully trained battery.'

On reporting to the officers' mess, Tyndale-Biscoe was escorted by the adjutant to the battery.

Second Lieutenant Julian Tyndale-Biscoe, Royal Horse Artillery, 14th Division

Where were the guns and horses? All I could see was a large crowd of men in their civilian clothes marching unendingly to the voice of various sergeants on a large gravel square, much to the detriment of their boots. The Major said, 'Here is the Battery – I would like you to train these men.' When I told him that I had had no artillery training,

TAMING LIONS

he said, 'Oh, that does not matter, you just watch the others do it, and then do it yourself.'...

After spending three or four miserable days there watching the men being marched everlastingly round the square, feeling as sorry for them as I was for myself, I again broached the subject with the Major about getting some training. He thought it unnecessary, but finally agreed to ask the Colonel. I hear that my major retired from the Army *before* the Boer War!

An elderly captain in the 8th The King's Own Scottish Borderers. His son was serving in the same battalion.

To his intense relief, Tyndale-Biscoe was ordered to leave for Woolwich and an eight-week training course.

In Aldershot, the 7th Rifle Brigade had received a new officer, Second Lieutenant Ronald Hardy. Hardy had served in the Territorial Force and on the outbreak of war sought a commission in the New Army. He was much older than many of the junior officers around him. Aged 32 in August 1914, he arrived just as the men began their recruit drills. One of them, Private Donald Hankey, a retired army officer who had chosen to re-enlist in the ranks, watched in fascination as Hardy learnt his craft, alert to every detail.

He used to watch us being drilled by the sergeant; but his manner of watching was peculiarly his own. He never looked bored. He was learning just as much as we were, in fact more. He was learning his job, and from the first he saw that his job was more than to give the correct orders. His job was to lead us. So he watched, and noted many things, and never found the time hang heavy on his hands. He watched our evolutions, so as to learn the correct orders; he watched for the right manner of command, the manner which secured the most prompt response to an order; and he watched every one of us for our individual characteristics. We were his men. Already he took an almost paternal interest in us. He noted the men who tried hard, but were naturally slow and awkward. He distinguished them from those who were inattentive and bored. He marked down the keen and efficient amongst us. Most

Private Donald Hankey, 7th The Rifle Brigade (The Prince Consort's Own)

of all he studied those who were subject to moods, who were sulky one day and willing the next…

For a few days he just watched. Then he started work. He picked out some of the most awkward ones, and, accompanied by a corporal, marched them away by themselves. He explained that he did not know much himself yet, but he thought that they might get on better if they drilled by themselves a bit, and that if he helped them, and they helped him, they would soon learn. His confidence was infectious. He looked at them, and they looked at him, and the men pulled themselves together and determined to do their best. Their best surprised themselves. His patience was inexhaustible. His simplicity could not fail to be understood. His keenness and optimism carried all with them…

Then he started to drill the platoon with the sergeant standing by to point out his mistakes. Of course he made mistakes, and when that happened he never minded admitting it. He would explain what mistakes he had made, and try again. The result was that we began to take almost as much interest and pride in his progress as he did in ours.

Only a few officers could hope to be this inspirational.

In the army, newly commissioned officers had always had their metal tested, their character examined by being thrown in at the deep end to see how they coped with stress. They were tested by senior officers and sometimes very senior officers, who saw no reason to make life palatable for underlings, firing verbal volleys at them for the minor indiscretions and using the tool of humiliation, sometimes carried out in front of the men.

Second Lieutenant Norman Dillon, 14th The Northumberland Fusiliers

I met my first Brigadier-General and he was true to the music hall caricature of his kind. I was drilling my platoon before breakfast, as was the rule, when Brigadier-General Armstrong rode up on his horse and abused me because my men were clad in rags and tatters. He said there were plenty of uniforms available in the stores and I had only to ask for them. This was untrue…

The Divisional Commander, Major General Hutton was not much better. He was sitting on his horse by the roadside whilst we marched

An unknown major addresses a junior officer and his platoon.

past. He hauled me out and bawled, 'What did your men have for breakfast?' Of course I didn't know, and was too inexperienced to invent a menu, but it was a mean thing to do to a young officer. He knew perfectly well that it was the duty of the Orderly Officer of the day to visit meals, take complaints and see there was enough. Soldiers do not like all their officers round their ears at meal times. However, it gave him a chance to work off his early morning liver. Oddly enough it had the reverse effect on the men, who muttered thinly disguised sympathy for me and dislike for the General. That sort of behaviour was particularly bad for a citizen army that needed understanding and help, not browbeating and bullying.

At interview for a position in the Gloucestershire Regiment, Frederick Roe had been treated with thinly veiled disdain. He only just passed muster, chosen for a commission while his friend was entirely overlooked for the most inconsequential of reasons, Roe had conjectured.

As a new officer, Roe was considered the lowest of the low. His company commander, a man in his mid-thirties, referred to Roe on and off parade as nothing other than 'Wart', a name Roe discovered was a 'dubious privilege' ladled out to all junior officers.

Second Lieutenant Frederick Roe, 1/6th The Gloucestershire Regiment

I accepted it as a heavy corrective of my own idea of the status of a newly joined ensign. For example, he regularly threw a batch of his own private letters upon the hall table and sharply ordered the 'wart' to go out and post them.

I think that the reason for his conduct was that we were at odds from the beginning of our few months together. In our OTC at Bristol University we had been instructed in the brand new 1914 Infantry Training… But when I joined the battalion I found that the Territorial Force was still using the 1911 edition. The result was that with abysmal lack of judgement but with genuine keenness I drew my company commander's attention to this one evening off duty in the billet, with special reference to rifle inspection on parade. 'For inspection port arms!' was the order that brought the rifle forward to what was called the high port, a position which had been changed in the 1914 edition so as to make it much easier for the inspecting officer to look down the barrel of the rifle.

Correcting his commanding officer on technical details had not been appreciated, even in private.

When it came to the parade ground, dugout officers could appear almost as clueless as new officers, conversant only with outdated modes of drill. At Purfleet Camp, Vic Cole witnessed at first hand the problems bedevilling young and old officers alike.

Private Vic Cole, 7th The Queen's Own (Royal West Kent Regiment)

With everyone being proficient in section drill, the battalion was paraded as one body for the first time. This took place in the meadow in front of the officers' mess where sections combined to form platoons and platoons to form companies. The Commanding Officer (seventy-three year old Major Whittaker, a Boer War veteran whom we never saw again) called us to attention and gave the order 'Attention, Shoulder Arms,' whereupon another officer, one of the younger ones, said quietly, 'Sir, Sir, it's slope arms' and addressing us as the Seventh Battalion Major Whittaker gave us a short pep talk on regimental history and tradition. The 'Arms' which we sloped so smartly were merely wooden ones issued to learn drill; it was a long time before we got real rifles.

We had several officers like Whittaker, none of whom came out with us when we went to France. The Colonel, named Prior, was another very old timer, a bandy looking man, he must have been aged 70, I should think, but we were also so young and judging age in those days was difficult: we felt people were old at 40. [Lieutenant Colonel Arthur Prior was 58.]

This would not be the last time that Vic witnessed unwitting ignorance amongst older soldiers when an instruction went round to find suitable men for the battalion's Signal Section. With his work in wireless telegraphy, Vic was perfect for the job.

The signals officer approached a sergeant and told him he wanted some men to be signallers, so the sergeant came and said to us one by one, 'Well, what are you? Boy Scout? Good. Ok, you. What are you?' and he came to me and I said, 'Wireless operator'. 'Oh, we don't want you,' dismissing me out of hand. He didn't know anything about it,

Lance Corporal Vic Cole, 7th The Queen's Own (Royal West Kent Regiment)

Seventeen-year-old Lance Corporal Vic Cole with his signal section. Vic was acutely aware of his relative youth. Only one man in the section, David Stalker, was killed during the war. In order to enjoy a free train ride, David had come down from Bunnybridge in Scotland to enlist with six friends. Top L to R: David Stalker, 'Deafy' Smith, Jack Day, Vic Cole, Freddie Bayliss, Tom Ryder. Bottom L to R: Bill Faulkner, Percy Wright, Fred Maylam, Slim Wadhams.

didn't know there was such a thing as wireless. I thought, 'that's funny,' until the officer said, 'Right, is there anyone else?' And I said, 'Yes, sir, I know morse and semaphore,' and he said, 'Why didn't you say? Ok, well, come on then!'

To my consternation I was made Lance Corporal of the Signal Section. A special hut was assigned to us and we ceased parading with ordinary mortals and became part of Battalion Headquarters. There were about twenty of us, including an officer, whom we seldom saw as he probably had another job, and a loveable old-time sergeant, Patsy Sheen who wore the Indian Frontier Medal and had a seemingly unquenchable thirst.

I appeared to be the only one with any authority and was well aware that my poor dog's leg [lance corporal's] stripe was not very popular as most of the men were older than me, some ten years older, and objected to being ordered about by a kid of seventeen.

Although Second Lieutenant Dillon felt sufficiently confident to drill men on the parade ground, there was no disguising his broader dearth of knowledge.

Second Lieutenant Norman Dillon, 14th The Northumberland Fusiliers

I was completely ignorant of military procedure other than to salute senior officers. On the way to parades I would meet a distinguished looking officer with many medal ribbons and mutton chop whiskers. I used to salute him and he would return this with dignity. One day I had a friend with me and we met this tremendous personage. I duly saluted him. 'What did you do that for?' said my friend. 'Don't you know who that old b…. is?' He said, 'It's the Quartermaster.' However I continued my practice and it paid dividends, because I could often get things refused to others.

Second Lieutenant Julian Tyndale-Biscoe, Royal Horse Artillery, 14th Division

A rather nice description of the gunner officers that is going the rounds is that the subaltern knows nothing and does everything, the captain knows everything and does nothing, the major knows everything and does everything, and the colonel knows nothing and does nothing! There is an element of truth to it.

TAMING LIONS

'I've been wondering why Great Britain hasn't declared war on Sweden,' mused Private Thomas Lyon. Swedish Drill was introduced into the British Army as a means of improving the physical fitness of recruits by means of exhaustingly repetitive exercises.

Second Lieutenant Arthur Heath, 6th The Queen's Own (Royal West Kent Regiment)

If you are a second lieutenant your lot depends a good deal on the temper of your commanding officer – luckily mine is suave. But the other side is what you have to insist on in other people… I shall soon be saying to men, as my captain said the other day to one unfortunate creature who had fallen out during a route march. 'There's no such thing as falling out on march. In my regiment no man ever falls out unless he falls down unconscious.' I find it difficult to talk like that at present, but no doubt it will come with practice. The route marching, by the way, was pretty good. We did twelve or thirteen miles between 9.30 and 2.0, and could certainly have marched seventeen miles in the day without too great an effort. As far as I gather, no ordinary recruits would do anything like as well.

The recruits were expected to give everything to shed their civilian lethargy. Swedish Drill, a form of physical education designed for fitness but also to instil obedience on command, was a gruelling exercise used on all.

Private Thomas Lyon, 2/9th The Highland Light Infantry (Glasgow Highlanders)

I've been wondering why Great Britain hasn't declared war on Sweden. I've seen a hundred men so exhausted after an hour of this form of physical culture that they hadn't breath enough left among the whole company to blow up a confectioner's paper bag.

You know the kind of thing it is: you shoot out your arms from the shoulder with as much force as the heroine of a melodrama does when she points the finger of scorn at the villain – only you keep on shooting them out and drawing them back until you've no pith left: you bend your body from side to side till your ribs creak like rusty hinges: you lie on your back on the ground and raise and lower your legs until all your money – that is, provided you have any of your weekly eight-an'-tuppence left – rolls out of your pocket on to the grass and the next man pinches it: then you get up and 'mark time' at a furious pace, raising your knees as high as possible in an apparently senseless endeavour to hit your chin. At the end of an hour or so of this you have about as much physical stamina as a wet rag…

From foggy morn to ink-black eve we wear down our shoe leather and our energies on Glasgow Green… I'm willing to bet a silk hat to an Iron Cross that not many men in our battalion ever worked to such excess that they fainted from sheer exhaustion – that is, until they joined the Army. But fainting has become quite a hobby with us… 'That's them bleeding cigarettes again,' says the Sergeant by way of sympathy when the martyr is carried out of the ranks; and, 'The Lord help you when you run up agin somethin' really severe in the way of work or 'ardship,' he says tenderly, while he wipes globules of perspiration from his own forehead.

The Sergeant is not a lily-lipped or honey-mouthed individual, but he *does* know his business… 'If the General or Sir John French himself were on parade on this squad just now,' he told us the other day, 'he'd have to ask my permission before he could fall out, for I'm in command here, an' don't you forget it. Squad – ''Shun!' And obediently we ''shunned', duly impressed by his omnipotence.

He kept us ''shunning' and 'stand-at-easing' for ten full minutes, and until every man's back ached. ''Shun!' he roared… 'Oh! Keep yer heads up an' yer chins tucked in. Ye would think that some o' you fellers had the weight o' the National Debt on your shoulders.

'You at the end of the front rank – straighten yourself, man! Don't stand there like a half-shut knife. Throw your chest well out, you've got a hump like a camel… An keep yer eyes off the ground – there ain't no threepenny pieces lyin' about here… Here, you with the brown jacket in Section Four, who the hell told you you could blow your nose?'

A man was slaughtered for blowing his nose while standing at attention. It happened that the CO himself was taking the parade and he made an example of this unfortunate man by ordering him to report to Duke's Road at 6 am every morning for a month. We thought this very harsh. But the 'let it drip' order was just another peculiar rule of this new school and was accepted as such. A dripping nose might be ungentlemanly, but it was obviously better than having to be on parade every morning at six, so we dripped.

Private John Nettleton, 2/28th London Regiment (Artists Rifles)

Guardsman Douglas Cuddeford, Scots Guards

I had qualms as to how I would stand the rigorous training and general hardships of military life after my eight years in West Africa. At first I found it very hard indeed; harder than I ever supposed any work could be, and the discipline was, to say the least, irksome at the beginning. After a week or two, however, I was surprised to find that I could go through the heaviest day without being unduly distressed. At the same time I think I must have shed pounds and pounds of flesh in the form of sweat on that accursed parade ground. It was not always we older men (I was twenty-eight then) who could bear fatigue least. Some of the young chaps, artisans and manual workers who in civil life were accustomed to hard work in the open air weren't worth a rap in the gymnasium.

Private James Hall, 9th The Royal Fusiliers (City of London Regiment)

It was interesting to note the physical improvement in the men wrought by a life of healthy, well-ordered routine… Many of them had been used to indoor life, practically all of them to city life, and needed months of the hardest kind of training before they could be made physically fit, before they could be seasoned and toughened to withstand the hardships of active service.

Men who toiled down mines, laboured in cotton mills, or sweated in iron foundries knew what body-aching fatigue was like at the end of a working day. By contrast, gruelling physical activity daunted sedentary office workers who quickly discovered muscle groups they never knew they had. And yet, a tough physical regime on the parade ground did not disconcert all such men, in particular those used to coping with mental as opposed to physical stress.

A battalion of 'Scotties' on the march near Codford Camp, Salisbury Plain, in the summer of 1915. Note the extraordinary mass of telephone wires above their heads.

After the wearing discipline and incessant activity of a newspaper office, our training early in the war was like a great lark. It was just like being back at school. Responsibilities had been lifted from our shoulders… Learning how to quick march was kindergarten stuff after my nightly anxiety of getting a paper to press to catch trains. No longer were there moments of sick dismay with which I realised that the rival sheet had beaten us hollow. We had heard of the severity of military discipline, but it was nothing to that of a business office…

We marched out on those smiling August and September days on to country roads, halting where it pleased us best. When we bun-wallahs announced that it was time to clear the dust from our throats, a willing sergeant stopped the march and postponed training for half an hour. If we had not been eager to learn, soldiering would have been like a practical joke. But we picked up the rudiments of the job with some enthusiasm.

Private William Andrews, 2/4th The Black Watch (Royal Highlanders)

Rather than finding army life a chastening experience, many men found it broadened their horizons, giving them time and space to reconsider their lives.

It has really been nothing but beer and skittles so far; even the dullest operations have been tinged with novelty… One feels one could value real intimacy in such circumstances. Under this glorious sky and in this scenery, and with all the varied interests of the new life, I thought I should never want it.

One might be tolerably happy at this game all one's life, but one can't cast out the personal and complicated from one's life altogether. The view over Laffan's Plain, on which we drill, and the sunset and delightful early misty mornings bring one back to the old grubbing in one's own wretched soul. However, it's a long, long way to Tipperary, and one's soul belongs to the Army as well as one's body.

Private Frederick Keeling, 6th The Duke of Cornwall's Light Infantry

Private William Andrews, 2/4th The Black Watch (Royal Highlanders)

The change from the old routine broadened us physically. It also broadened us or rather, loosened us mentally. Most of our little crowd were determined not to go back to the old life in Dundee. We felt we had been released from it forever. Some of us had.

It was inevitable that civilians would take civilian attitudes into the army, attitudes that would only be tolerated when everyone was still finding their feet. The NCOs were dealing with men who at any other time would never have chosen the army as a profession. They were willing soldiers certainly, but it would take time to turn around men who could be obstreperous one moment and charmingly naive the next.

Private Tom Easton, 21st The Northumberland Fusiliers (2nd Tyneside Scottish)

Very few of us knew the meaning of military discipline. A sentry in B Company was pacing up and down in front of Rowton House when a new officer arrived. Approaching the guard, who never saluted, he asked, 'Don't you know who I am?' The sentry said, 'I don't know who ye are.' 'Well,' he said, 'I am Captain so and so,' and the sentry put out his hand and said, 'Well, I am pleased to meet you. I am private so and so, and you'll have a great time among this mob!'

William Andrews fondly recalled one friend, a journalist named Nicholson (Nick), described as having 'a gentle soul', and 'a sweet artless way' about him.

Private William Andrews, 2/4th The Black Watch (Royal Highlanders)

One day the Regimental Sergeant-Major stopped him with a bark as he was entering the officers' mess. 'Who gave you permission to go in there?' he roared, for to him the officers' mess was as sacred as the high alter in a cathedral. Nick was unconscious of impiety. 'That's quite all right, Major,' he said. 'I've been put on guard tonight, and I'm going to ask the Colonel to let me use his telephone to put off an appointment.'

What can you do with such innocence? The RSM, though a grizzled old regular of the fire-and-brimstone tradition, must have liked that slim lad who was eager to speak to his girl. He told him to go and ring up from a public call-office, and gave him a pass to leave the drill-hall.

Opposite below: An old-style, experienced company sergeant major photographed in 1915: a senior NCO and one critically important to the success of Kitchener's New Army.

Habits of a lifetime were hard to dispense with, even in the Guards.

The first NCO to have charge of our squad was a Corporal Booth, a typical pre-war guardsman of the old school; foul-mouthed and coarse, fairly honest, but a good-hearted and decent fellow for all that. I remember I made rather a *faux pas* the first time we were paraded… I was passing out of the [barrack] block when Booth shouted at us to 'Get fell in'. He asked me where I was off to, and I replied that I was just going across to the dry canteen for some cigarettes. He gaped at me open-mouthed without a word, whilst I proceeded to the canteen, bought my cigarettes, returned, and got 'fell in'.

Guardsman Douglas Cuddeford, Scots Guards

A Territorial or New Army RSM might give a man leeway for such innocent impudence but surely not in the Scots Guards? Cuddeford does not record Booth's retribution. However, he did note: 'A bad NCO had it in his power to make life a perfect hell for any recruit to whom he took a personal dislike or had a grudge against.' Apparently, Booth was not one of those.

The discipline of the New Armies is different from that of the old Regular Army because the conditions are different. One of the natural bases of discipline, the subordination of rank to rank more or less according to seniority of service, is necessarily absent in battalions composed almost entirely of men who enlisted en masse as raw recruits.

Private Frederick Keeling, 6th The Duke of Cornwall's Light Infantry

A morning inspection of kit.

Private William Andrews, 2/4th The Black Watch (Royal Highlanders)

In many ways we still had civilian habits of mind. Some important officer was inspecting us one day and had a look down Joe Lee's rifle. 'Filthy,' he said in a voice of thunder. 'Oh, no,' said Joe, easily. 'I think you'll find it's only a little superficial dust.'

Private Thomas Lyon, 2/9th The Highland Light Infantry (Glasgow Highlanders)

At rifle inspection the officer glances through the barrel of your rifle, and – 'Filthy,' he says again, 'absolutely filthy! If you don't keep that rifle properly cleaned I'll give you a week's c.b.' [Confined to Barracks]. You look through the barrel and its shininess simply dazzles your eye. It is only when you have strained your optic nerve after ten minutes of close gazing that you see one tiny spec of dust in the barrel, and it seems quite pathetically lonely amid all the gleam and glitter surrounding it.

Private Frederick Keeling, 6th The Duke of Cornwall's Light Infantry

There is a perpetual chatter in platoons which are supposed to be standing or marching at attention, and a pestilent minority of slackers only intermittently trouble to keep in step on the march. Several men have taken French leave for two or three days, and only been punished by loss of pay. Probably a majority of the battalion would welcome a tightening up of discipline in most directions.

In Territorial and Pals battalions where men knew each other, sometimes from earliest childhood, informality was as natural as it was common and 'chat' between privates and officers hard to eradicate.

I overheard a young private the other day tell his company commander 'not to be a silly ass', and when I subsequently remonstrated with him on his lack of respect he laughed and said, 'Oh, he's engaged to my sister, so it's all right. I can say anything I like to him when we're not on parade. He wouldn't dare to give me any jaw, or I'd give it him mighty hot once the war's over. And I can give the beggar nine strokes at golf and beat him, anyway.'

Private Thomas Lyon, 2/9th The Highland Light Infantry (Glasgow Highlanders)

Amongst the youngest recruits, those who held romantic ideals as to how soldiering should be, lax discipline was exasperating. Horace Calvert from Bradford enlisted into his local Territorial battalion, lying about his age. Most of the NCOs were re-enlisted men, brought back to pass on their knowledge: 'They were very easy going with you, knew you was fresh and everything was new and they tried to take you by stages; there wasn't any bullying.' To most recruits this may have sounded rather pleasant, but not to 15-year-old Horace; he was fed up with the tolerance.

Two young lads serving in the 2/6th Gloucestershire Regiment. Young lads liked to feel as well as look like soldiers and often disliked sloppy discipline and easy-going chat amongst men of different ranks.

In our own way, we thought we were a good battalion but the discipline wasn't there from my point of view. The men were all wool merchants and worked in the warehouses, and the boss was on first-name terms with the staff and of course you got that in the regiment, calling one another Bill or Jack, even if he was a corporal or sergeant. I would have

Private Horace Calvert, 2/6th The Princess of Wales's Own (West Yorkshire Regiment)

preferred orders to have been given in a proper way and then carried out, instead of 'all right, Jack, I'll do it'. To me that wasn't military discipline or the sort of discipline that shows up in a tight corner.

Horace deserted and found his way into the Grenadier Guards. There he would find the discipline he craved – in abundance. Another deserter who looked to find a better 'fit' was Frank Lindley. He had joined the Royal Field Artillery aged 14 but soon decided that it was not for him. 'Of course we saw a gun or two, but we didn't have much training on them. I used to think, "this is not being a soldier".'

With several friends Frank disappeared one night. One, nicknamed Hoppy, subsequently enlisted with Frank into the 14th York & Lancaster Regiment, better known to posterity as the 2nd Barnsley Pals. By deserting, the boys had committed a serious military crime.

Private Frank Lindley, 14th The York & Lancaster Regiment (2nd Barnsley)

We were marched into 'clink'. We knew what it was for; they'd caught up with us. We never wrote home, [so] how they found out goodness knows. We were having dinner in the Public Hall when this orderly sergeant came up and said, 'Come on here you two, in "clink"'. The unfortunate thing was that the lad whose number came between mine and Hoppy's on the [muster] roll was called Lindley as well. They tapped him and Hoppy on the shoulder and took them in. Well, when I'd done my dinner I went to the guardroom and said, 'Here's their dinner, I've brought it. It's me you want.' The sergeant of the guard said, 'I thought it was, I recognised the way you drilled when you were forming fours.' He was a very old soldier was Sergeant Bullock, he recognised the way we were moving. He used to say, 'What the hell are you two doing? That's artillery formation.'

Frank and Hoppy remained in the infantry but the punishment was draconian: three months' pay stopped and twenty-eight days in confinement.

During the day, we had a short lecture from one of the 'old soldiers', a sergeant, the subject being 'Discipline'. The lecturer did not dwell so much as he might have done on the <u>necessity</u> of discipline, but was very emphatic as to the results of disobedience, the penalties of which he recited with relish, especially the extreme one of shooting at dawn.

Private Sydney Fuller, 8th The Suffolk Regiment

The British Army would heavily rely on a cohort of competent, resourceful NCOs who would find their own idiosyncratic ways to instil the required discipline in the ranks. The best NCOs acted as glue, holding things together when everything else appeared to be in such a state of flux.

Their [the NCOs'] methods with the raw material were a wonder to behold, an eternal tribute to 'militarism' that teaches a man tact and patience and self-restraint. Those willing to learn they encouraged at the expense of their own time, those unwilling they showed by an exhibition of firmness that it was unwise to disobey them. The more apt among their pupils they used as examples to the more backward, upon whom they lavished a patience that an archangel might envy. So, by rapid stages, in huge unmanageable hordes, the recruits first straggled helplessly like a leaderless host of the blind, then they walked irresolutely, then marched with quite a large percentage in step with one another, and finally manoeuvred, proudly, steadily, a compact body of men.

Captain Cecil Street, Royal Garrison Artillery

A lovely portrait of two experienced sergeants. The man on the left has crossed swords above his stripes, denoting that he is a Physical Training Instructor.

In the Queen's Own (Royal West Kent Regiment), scores of former NCOs, many long retired from service, re-enlisted to train recruits. Over ninety former NCOs and privates were sent to join the 6th Battalion, thirty-four of whom had at one time held the rank of either corporal or sergeant.

Second Lieutenant Arthur Heath, 6th The Queen's Own (Royal West Kent Regiment)

In my platoon one section stands out above the rest simply because it has been run by a lance-corporal, who is an elementary schoolmaster by profession. His military experience is antiquated; but he certainly has arranged to train his men in every way. The contrast between him and the miserable old idiot who has medals and years of service behind him is the most striking proof I've yet seen of the advantages of education.

Passing on their practical expertise to the new generation of NCOs chosen from amongst the ranks was vital. Frederick Keeling might have eschewed any idea of being an officer, but he would be happy to become one of these men. Within weeks, his talents had been spotted and he was promoted to a corporal; days later and he would be made a sergeant.

Corporal Frederick Keeling, 6th The Duke of Cornwall's Light Infantry

The regimental sergeant-major, whom we all regard as the perfect type of soldier and who is in addition almost the most perfect physical specimen of a man I have ever seen, instructs a special class of about thirty lance-corporals and possible lance-corporals every afternoon and evening on such subjects as musketry, judging distance, patrols, and bivouacking. Judging distance, by the way, is the point upon which most emphasis is placed in our training, and we have all laid to heart the regimental sergeant-major's dictum that after this war it will be considered more important than accuracy in firing.

Sober, competent NCOs were the backbone of the British Army, men that everyone else could rely on. Competent ones but with private issues were a problem, and not all old soldiers who returned to the army did so without 'personal baggage'. In the 1/6th The Gloucestershire Regiment, Frederick Roe found that his platoon sergeant was a decidedly mixed blessing.

[He] was a middle-aged ex regular soldier, incomparable as a senior NCO, a fine scout especially in night operations and a strict disciplinarian. He had been made a sergeant nine times, he said, regularly court-martialled and reduced to the ranks after a colossal drunken spree which knocked him out for four or five days; I suppose he would today be labelled a chronic alcoholic. Inevitably, he repeated this performance. He was duly reduced to the ranks and we found him a job that he liked in the battalion cookhouse.

He begged that he should never be promoted.

Second Lieutenant Frederick Roe, 1/6th The Gloucestershire Regiment

Overleaf: *Heaton Park Camp, 1914: the tents of the 1st and 2nd City battalions of the Manchester Regiment.*

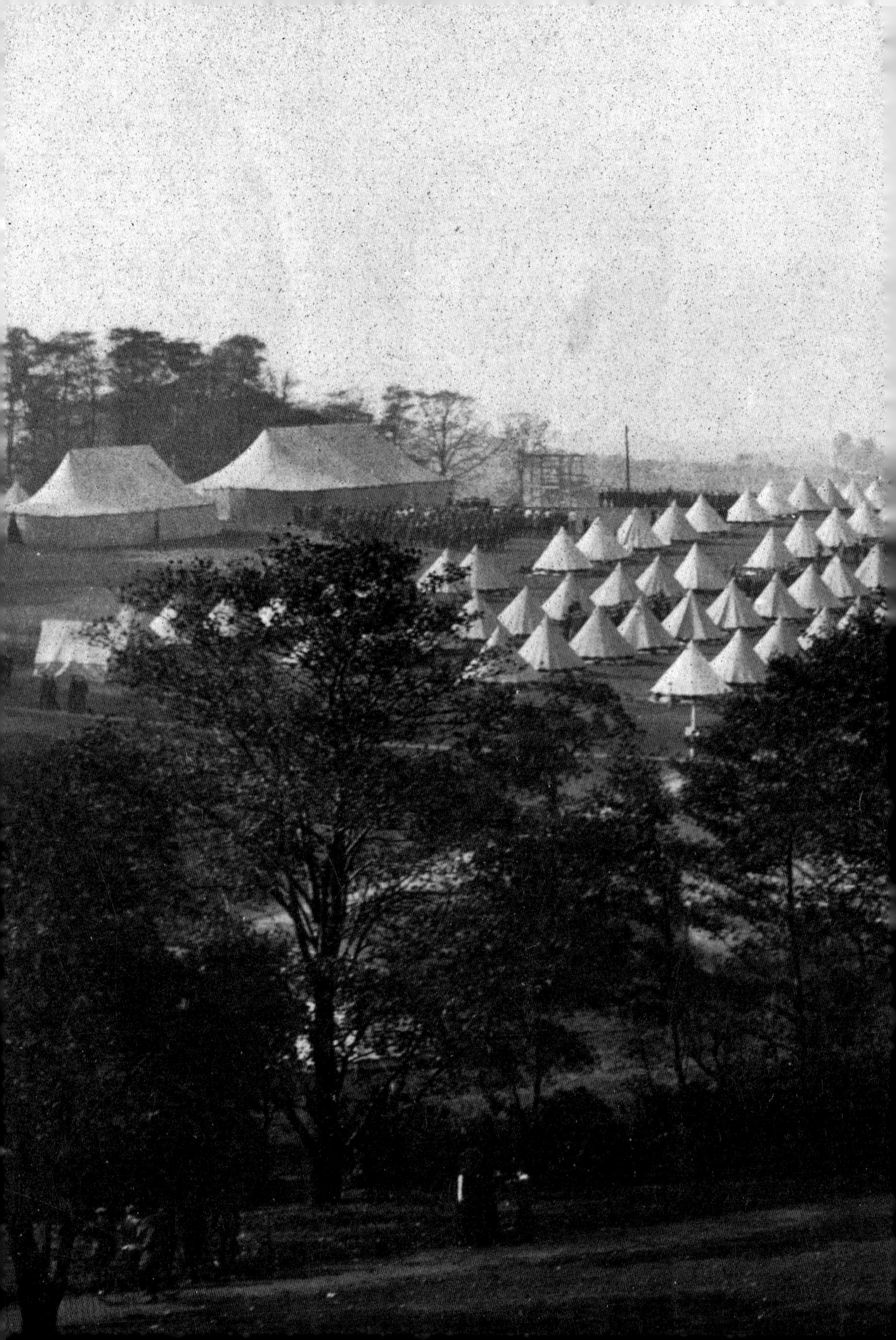

7 Simple Bare Necessities

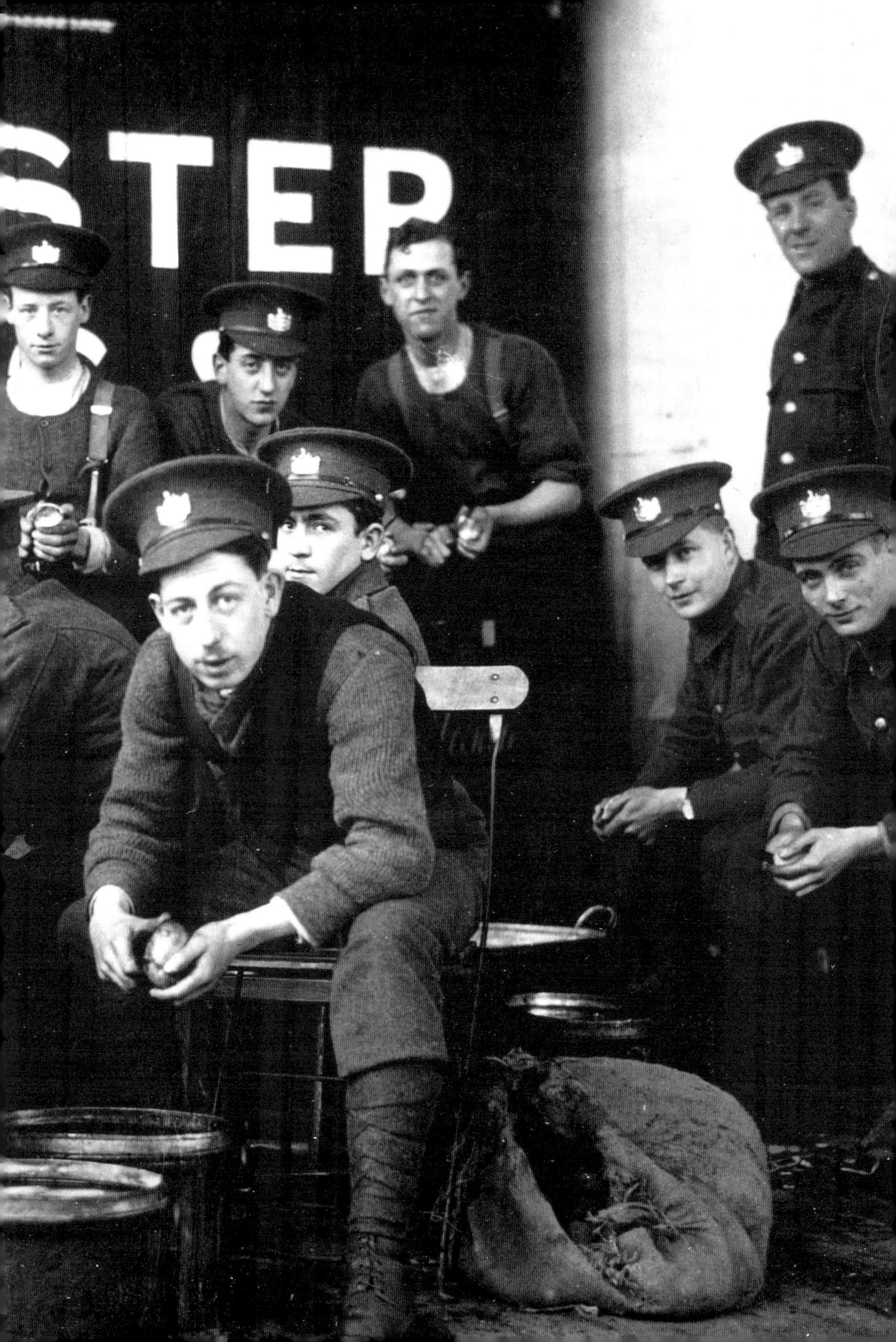
STEP

'The [men] other than the newly-arrived recruits, have almost been in a state of mutiny, as we have a beast of a Colonel, and they have been at meal-times shouting in chorus, to tune of 'Holy, holy, holy', the song I detail over:

> Starving, starving, starving, always bloody well starving,
> From reveille to lights out we're always bloody starving.
> Starving, starving, starving, always bloody well starving,
> We shall be glad when our time's up, we'll starve no bloody more.'

Gunner Cecil Longley, 1st South Midland Brigade,
Royal Field Artillery

Opposite: *The daily chore of spud-peeling undertaken by men of 'B' Company, 12th Gloucestershire Regiment, 'Bristol's Own'. Sitting far right is Private William Smallcombe, who later smuggled a camera to France. He suffered shell shock while serving on the Somme in 1916. He survived the war and lived until 1992, when he died aged 99.*

A Rugby scrum isn't nearly so exciting as the mere effort to buckle on one's kilt in a tent in which are eleven other men engaged in the same operation. And simply to comb one's hair calls for as much courage as it required to face a band of 'penny dreadful' Indians – for one is liable to be scalped at any moment. Such a jostling and scrambling and pushing and shoving and bumping can hardly be conceived, much less described. The air resounds with – 'Beg pardon!' – 'Sorry, old chap!' – 'You clumsy idiot, what the blinkety-blank are you playing at?' In the midst of all the confused bustle three heroes stand grouped around the tent pole, stoically shaving. Bravery can go no further.

Private Thomas Lyon, 2/9th The Highland Light Infantry (Glasgow Highlanders)

Such scenarios were being played out across the country, men struggling to find enough room for themselves in bell tents. Vic Cole's memory that all his comrades had been terribly polite was merely indicative of men getting used

Below: All smiles for now, but autumn was around the corner and life in bell tents was about to become much harder.

to the company of strangers and such courtesy was never going to last. How tolerable life would remain depended much on the make-up and density of the crowd in occupation.

Getting the best pitch was key and the ideal spot was to be as far from the tent flap as possible, avoiding nighttime draughts and, as importantly, the stumbling, indelicate feet of a comrade requiring the toilet. Wily older men forced youth to the strategically worst place, although there was an upside to being near the tent flap and that was the opportunity to poke one's head outside to breathe early autumn's uncontaminated fresh air.

Private Thomas Lyon, 2/9th The Highland Light Infantry (Glasgow Highlanders)

We sleep twelve in a tent – twelve great hefty fellows in a circular tent twelve feet in diameter. Between 9.20 and 9.30 each evening these twelve big fellows file one after another through the open flap of the tent, and at 9.35 they are all huddled together within the canvas walls, each hurrying frantically to get his blankets down on the floor and his clothes off – for experience has taught that the man who lies down first has the best chance of being able to stretch his legs, and of ensuring that his entire body shall rest on the floorboards, and not one-half of it on the floor and the other half on his neighbour.

And in this fearful scramble to get undressed and to prepare one's couch everybody gets in everybody else's way and everybody mistakes everybody else's blankets and kit for his own, and everybody tries to explain the exact amount of space to which everybody else is entitled and to demonstrate just how everybody else is usurping more than his fair share while he (everybody) hasn't as much room as a flea could gambol in comfortably; and everybody calls everybody else soldierly epithets; and there are continual bumpings of heads and tramplings on toes; and every little while the candle is overturned and a stream of molten tallow gutters down some inoffensive man's tunic or rifle, and the tent is plunged in darkness, and the confusion is worse confounded.

The number of occupants of our tent was now 15, so we did not feel any draughts at night – there was no room in the tent for <u>them</u>. During the night the part of the tent floor round the centre tent pole was occupied by a pile of feet, which pile was in a state of perpetual motion. The unfortunate owner of the lowermost pair of feet would stick it as long as possible, and would then withdraw his more or less flattened feet, and place them on top of the pile. Soon the next man would do likewise, and so on, to the accompaniment of many comments of a forcible nature throughout the hours of 'rest'.

Private Sydney Fuller, 8th The Suffolk Regiment

You draw your blankets more closely around you, and you give them a strong pull and tuck them in, when an angry voice sounds just beside you, 'Here, who the burning brimstone has pinched my blankets? Oh, here they are! – that's better.' And you feel the whole mass of blankets slide off you, and then you have a squabble with your bedmate, and each eventually falls asleep while waiting for the other fellow to fall asleep so that he may 'win' a blanket from the unconscious one.

Private Thomas Lyon, 2/9th The Highland Light Infantry (Glasgow Highlanders)

My previous experience of sleeping under canvas had been to have one of these tents to myself, with plenty of ventilation. It was a very different thing to share a tent with eleven others who were afraid of draughts and who did not appreciate the need for a daily, or even weekly tub. That night haunts me yet; the hot smell and human noises

Private Thomas Nash, 1/6th The Gloucestershire Regiment

banished rest. Few of us were able to sleep while those who did made night hideous by snoring.

Private Thomas Lyon, 2/9th The Highland Light Infantry (Glasgow Highlanders)

Between two and four am you awake out of the horrid dream in which you imagined you had been locked up in a refrigerator. You are cold all over, and though you try to cuddle up closer to your next bed-fellow that part of your anatomy farthest away from him feels as though a chunk of ice were upon it. The floor seems even harder than floors usually are, and you feel confident that your body must bear an exact pattern of the grain of wood and of all the little irregularities of surface. Your back aches dreadfully, and then you discover that you have been lying on the hilt of your bayonet. The man on your right snores stertorously, and suddenly with a savage grunt he heaves himself into the air and comes down on your tenderest rib with an appalling thud.

Private George Coppard, 6th The Queen's Own (Royal West Surrey Regiment)

Outside the tent flap within a yard of my head stood a urinal tub. Throughout the night boozy types would stagger and lunge towards the flap in order to urinate. I got showered every time and, worst of all, it became a joke. At last revulsion overcame me, and one night I suddenly went berserk and lashed out violently at someone. There followed a riotous eruption and the tent collapsed.

Private Sydney Fuller, 8th The Suffolk Regiment

There was a 'dust-up' in the tent next to ours. We heard an argument start about 9.30 pm, and it rapidly got warmer, ending in a scrap. 'Lights out' having gone some time before this, everyone was in bed, and the combatants trampled all over the other occupants of the tent to judge by the yells. After about three minutes, the police (Kitchener's) arrived, and removed one of the combatants to the police tent. The remaining warrior was threatened with various unpleasant things by those who had been trodden on in tender spots and things quieted down.

Whether men got enough sleep in such circumstances depended much on the individual. Many men simply lay there waiting for the order to rise, grumpy before the day had even stated.

Reveillé sounds at 5.30. Ere the last note of the bugle has died away the droning of a pipe is heard and the nerry skirl of 'Hey, Johnny Cope, are ye waukin' yet?' destroys all possibility of an extra five minutes snooze. The Orderly Officer and the Orderly Sergeant for the day walk around the lines, smiting the canvas walls with their canes and shouting in rasping tones, 'Come on, show a leg there! Open all these flaps!'

Private Thomas Lyon, 2/9th The Highland Light Infantry (Glasgow Highlanders)

Bugler William Normington, 13th York and Lancaster Regiment, a printer by trade. He died of wounds, 6 November 1916.

Morning parade generally included half an hour's physical exercise followed by a wash and shave. Only then was breakfast taken, one of three meals provided: breakfast, lunch (or dinner as it was called) and tea. In all armies, morale was maintained (or degraded) by the quantity and quality of the food, by its fair and timely distribution, and the cleanliness with which cooks handled the utensils and ingredients. Failure on one, two, or all of these points was a shortcut to discontent in the ranks.

Breakfast might be bread and tinned meat, fried bacon, or porridge. Dinner was likely to consist of stewed beef, potatoes and vegetables, whereas tea would be bread, butter, jam and tinned fruit. Sugar-laced Gunfire tea was always served though not necessarily in the volume to meet demand. Whether served up beneath canvas marquees, huts or in individual tents, the meals' ingredients were meant to be broadly the same. Quality and speed of delivery differed from camp to camp.

There is a shout of 'Here's Paw!' from the Orderly, who staggers into the room with a pail in either hand. And someone asks, 'Paw Who?' and receives the answer in joyful accents from a dozen voices, 'Why, Paw-Ridge!' Then there is a scramble for bowls, and the men line up in a queue and are rapidly served by the orderly with porridge and milk. And very good porridge it is usually.

Private Thomas Lyon, 2/9th The Highland Light Infantry (Glasgow Highlanders)

A dixie of hot tea is then brought in, and bread and butter and a ration of ham are served out. Two ounces of ham per man per day – *perhaps*. That's the army order: but apparently army ounces are variable quantities, though they certainly never vary in the circumstance of being under standard weight.

Bugle calls notified men when food was ready. Indeed, calls were used for almost everything: to distinguish one regiment from another, to call for officers, sergeants, corporals, and then for important daily items such as assembly, the distribution of letters, Lights Out, Retreat and Reveille. All had to be learnt and responded to.

Private Anthony Nash, 1/6th The Gloucestershire Regiment

When the bugles sounded Cookhouse the men tumbled out of their tents, mess-tins in hand, and were marched by the Orderly Corporal to where the cooks were serving out breakfast. Each man received half a pint of tea, without milk but flavoured with onions, and an undercooked piece of bacon two inches square handed to him in the cook's fingers. That together with a hunk of bread furnished our breakfast. All meals had to be eaten in the tent in which we lived and slept.

Private Thomas Lyon, 2/9th The Highland Light Infantry (Glasgow Highlanders)

We drink our tea out of the bowls which held the porridge and milk, and which only ten minutes previously served as shaving mugs. And I am of the opinion now that tea out of an enamelled bowl that has porridge sticking to the rim, tastes quite as good – and especially after a morning running parade – as tea drunk from Crown Derby china. I did not always think so.

During my first few days in barracks I had foolishly fastidious notions of cleanliness. I believed it to be necessary to wash my bowl after the porridge course in order to prepare it for the tea. And I even took the trouble to descend three flights of stairs to the water tap to put my silly theory into practice. My fastidiousness even went the length of compelling me to wash my bowl after it had contained stew and potatoes in order to prepare it for canned pears or pineapple! How very ridiculous the idea seems now after six weeks of life in barracks!

SIMPLE BARE NECESSITIES

Waiting patiently for food with their D-type mess tins. Not all queues were so orderly or patient.

And what a lot of civilians, with their inane conceptions of cleanliness, have still to learn from us old soldiers in the matter of saving work and conserving energy!

Doubling up on knives and forks disgusted more refined recruits. '[I] thought it was bad for one's morale to pig it,' wrote Second Lieutenant Norman Dillon, reluctant to let standards drop.

I remember one day, my C.O. (Morley) when we were doing an exercise and a sort of picnic lunch was produced, laid down his knife and fork and handed them to me. He expected me to continue on the same plate and with the same implements. I was tactful enough (or too frightened) to say anything, but wandered off and managed to eat cleanly with my pocket knife and some paper. But this illustrates the general atmosphere. War is a mess-up and so you may as well let go all the decencies.

Second Lieutenant Norman Dillon, 14th The Northumberland Fusiliers

I was mess orderly, or 'orderly man' and had duties of drawing the day's rations for my section, attending to washing-up, cleansing the tent, etc. The 'table service' in possession of the inmates of our tent at this time

Private Sydney Fuller, 8th The Suffolk Regiment

consisted of 11 plates, 4 enamelled mugs, and an iron bowl for washing-up. Only four of the men in the tent possess knives and forks, and of these, two knives and two forks disappeared whilst I was away from the tent for a short time. Mice, I suppose.

We held out our plates while a soldier in a grimy uniform ladled cabbage, meat, and a greasy liquid on to them. We sat down on benches in front of a table that were littered with potato peel, bits of fat, and other refuse. We were packed so closely together that we could hardly move our elbows. The rowdy conversation, the foul language, and the smacking of lips and the loud noise of guzzling added to the horror of the meal. I was so repelled that I felt sick and could not eat. The man who sat opposite kept me under close observation. All at once he asked, 'Don't yer want it, mate?' I said 'No!' whereupon he exclaimed eagerly, 'Giss it.' A bestial, gloating look came into his face as he seized my plate and splashed the contents on to his own, so that the gravy over-flowed and ran along the table in a thin stream. He took the piece of meat between his thumb and his fork and, tearing off big shreds with his teeth, gobbled them greedily down.

Gunner Frederick Voigt, Royal Garrison Artillery

To avoid such sights and sounds, William Andrews and his newspaper colleagues banded together, preparing their own food or, if they could, leaving the camp to find someone to prepare it for them. It seemed like a good idea.

Private William Andrews, 2/4th The Black Watch (Royal Highlanders)

We did not draw our rations cooked, preferring to receive our meat raw and take it to a local pastry cook, who turned it into meat pies, and added vegetable and sweetmeats at some small expense. We clubbed together to buy respectable cutlery, and were astonished when Captain Boase told us it was bad taste for us to differentiate ourselves in that way from the rougher men. It was our duty to eat exactly what the others ate and in the same way. We listened with some indignation. Then one of us found ironic tongue. 'Very good, sir,' he said, 'and shall we modify our table manners, too?'

I forget how the discussion went on, but after that we drew our army stew like the rest and ate it from tins. Perhaps Captain Boase was right. It did not matter very much. We were soon to be beyond the reach of table refinements.

Opposite: A 'cook' with ladle in hand stands over steaming dixies full of food. Complaints about the quality and quantity of food were legion during the first weeks of training.

Those who felt compelled to clean mess tins used whatever they could find. In the 1/6th Gloucestershire Regiment the men had but one option; to head down to a muddy ditch and to clean their greasy tins with cold mud. Each man then wiped the tin with his handkerchief or face towel to remove any remaining sludge or grease. It was a gesture at civility.

The tedious task of preparing food was often awarded to men on 'jankers', punishment for mild indiscretions. The men, known as defaulters, were given unpleasant jobs, emptying latrine buckets or washing thousands of dirty plates. Attending to cookhouse chores would also keep them busy for hours. Thomas Lyon had done nothing wrong that he was aware of, but he was ordered with another man named Smith to undertake fatigues, including stirring vats of breakfast porridge and then, for dinner, potato peeling.

Seated on upturned pails, [we] began to peel potatoes for the day's dinner… I used my pocket knife then and discovered that the game was very like golf, for if you didn't keep your eye on the ball – or the potato – you were very liable to foozle your stroke and have to go about with your hand tied up on one of the cook's dumpling rags for the next few days. At the end of an hour's work I surveyed the result, and

Private Thomas Lyon, 2/9th The Highland Light Infantry (Glasgow Highlanders)

Spud-peeling was hardly an art though some men were left with little potato after their aggressive efforts.

somehow it didn't seem quite satisfactory. At the bottom of the dixie lay about two dozen round things of the colour of a rat; the largest was the size of a walnut, but most of them were no bigger than marbles. And at my side was a heap of parings that seemed quite prodigiously large. I looked at the potatoes and then at the parings, and wondered how the dickens such little fellows ever wore such large jackets. 'Greatest collection of misfits ever I saw,' I said to myself. 'These murphies must have got their tunics from an army tailor; there's more jackets than potato.'

Those who catered were cooks but not chefs and did not see their duty as being greater than that of achieving acceptable results with minimal effort. 'There were no such things as catering staff. Cooks merely volunteered. Sometimes I think they did so to avoid even more unpleasant jobs,' remembered Norman Dillon, while in Anthony Nash's company, 'the cooks were two of the roughest [men] I have seen… They had not been selected for their culinary skill, but because of their physical unfitness.'

Corporal Frederick Keeling, 6th The Duke of Cornwall's Light Infantry

[Cooking food] has mostly been relegated to old soldiers in order to enable recruits to be constantly on parade. The result has not been satisfactory; and this must be attributed in part to the slackness and dirtiness of the subordinate cooks, since making tea and the simple stewing and roasting of meat on camp fires or in field ovens requires no technical knowledge beyond what is supplied by the sergeant cook.

But I believe that probably the most important source of complaints about food in the New Army is due to an apparently trivial point which can scarcely be fully appreciated by any one who has not had some experience of camp life in the army. It is useless to supply good rations, to give technical instructions to cooks, and to make elaborate arrangements for the distribution of food if the camp kettles (so-called dixies) in which tea, cocoa, soup, potatoes, and stews are all cooked are not kept clean. In point of fact, in many camps it has been the rule rather than the exception to find each meal unpleasantly reminiscent of the last…

As it is, any tent has been liable to have its tea served in a kettle which has not been properly cleaned for days because the tent orderlies through whose hands it passed have preferred the luxury of a quiet smoke after dinner to the rather unpleasant task of scrubbing out a greasy kettle with probably inadequate materials – trusting to luck with regards to getting some one else's clean kettle for tea.

Food preparation was no better amongst the tents of the Suffolk Regiment, where contamination across dishes was rife and the resulting flavours described as 'peculiar'. There was bound to be trouble.

The cooks said the orderly men had not washed up the dixies after dinner (stew) and as <u>they</u> were not responsible for washing-up, which was the orderly men's job, we had to put up with the consequences. The general opinion was that the cooks had taken one of our clean dixies for their own tea, and had used their own unwashed dixies for ours. I know I cleaned mine well enough, scouring it with sand afterwards. However, no more tea being available, there was so much moaning that the news of the trouble got to Battalion Headquarters, and all orderly men of the affected tents were ordered to parade at the Orderly Room. On reaching there, we were brought before the Adjutant, Captain Silver, who was an old soldier perpetually red or purple of face, and with one of the vilest of tempers. No sooner did he catch sight of us than one man was placed under arrest for smiling and was escorted to the guardroom. The remainder of us thereafter tried to assume expressions befitting the solemn occasion. We were explosively informed that we were all prisoners and were to parade at the Orderly Room at 10.15 am next day.

Private Sydney Fuller, 8th The Suffolk Regiment

The 'prisoners' were given a lecture on the virtue of cleanliness and confined to camp for two days with an extra hour's drill late in the afternoon. Fuller recorded that the men had not been permitted to offer up a defence, which caused yet more grousing.

A seemingly better-organised cookhouse with cooks wearing unusually clean attire. These men were serving in the Royal Army Medical Corps, which might explain a more hygienic appearance.

Complaints did not necessarily lead to improvements. When Sydney Fuller's battalion was sent on a route march weeks later, the issue of food was raised yet again. After marching for nearly three hours, the men had halted in a field just as rain began to fall.

Private Sidney Fuller, 8th The Suffolk Regiment

Dinner was not yet ready as fires had to be started, the meat cut up, to say nothing of the cooking. We were hungry already. When the dinner was served, the meat was little more than half cooked and, as we had no plates, knives or forks with us, we were rather in a fix. We had to eat a la pig, grabbing the hot meat from the dixies with our fingers, and wolfing it. The meat was extra tough, too, which made things worse. Chaps with good teeth got some of it down, but the plight of those with bad teeth, or artificial ones, was worse than awful.

Frederick Keeling argued that the quality of food in his battalion was satisfactory and that there was 'no reasonable cause for complaint'. If food was inedible or where food was in short supply, it was to do with the manner in which it was served out and the desire by some men to take more than their fair share. The company orderly drew the company's rations and distributed them to each tent's orderly man, the distribution overseen by an officer to ensure fairness. 'Any irregularity in the routine is almost certain to result in some men being deprived of their fair share of food.' Yet, equitable portion size was not entirely the point. Some men *needed* more food than others.

The word calories as we know it today never existed in Aldershot. The Quartermaster-General never considered the needs of a growing body engaged in hard training, trench digging or route marching. The army clerk at his desk received the same amount of rations.

Private George Coppard, 6th The Queen's (Royal West Surrey Regiment)

Feelings of ravenous hunger disproportionately affected growing lads, as 16-year-old Ernest Parker knew well: on his first day at the regimental depot the fight for food had proved both determined and dominated mainly by older men. Those who had service behind them knew all the tricks.

During the whole of September rations were of the scantiest… At last when a crowd assembled outside the Quartermaster's Stores several officers hurried to the spot to listen tactfully to a long string of grievances that they immediately promised to put it right. From that day onwards there was a general improvement in the rations. What happened to our food during the previous month is a mystery that has never been solved.

Private Ernest Parker, 15th (The King's) Hussars

Before receiving his commission, George Butterworth recalled how easy it had been for cooks to abuse their position.

Every Friday evening the cooks of D Company are in the habit of sending the hat down the lines, the implication being that the quality of next week's rations will vary in proportion to the amount collected. On this occasion a strong-minded corporal set up an objection; there was a row, the Major was summoned, and grossly insulted by the

Private George Butterworth, 6th The Duke of Cornwall's Light Infantry cooks who were eventually marched off in a body to the guardroom. The incident is a good illustration of the kind of petty bribery which appears to be rampant in the army; I doubt whether even the sergeants are always above suspicion – at any rate they keep their eyes discreetly shut – and, as for these cooks, they are simply vagabond old soldiers who have re-enlisted on the chance of making a bit.

Private Douglas Butler was shocked by the food served up by his battalion's 'so-called cooks'. And like many men, he could not understand why officers had not intervened.

Private Douglas Butler, 1/4th The Gloucestershire Regiment

As it happened I was the cause of a dramatic change in the unsatisfactory state of affairs. Each evening some of us would forgather in a nice old pub on Danbury Green. I was relatively rich, for my mother used to send me a postal order for five shillings in her weekly letter to me. This was a great boon, as each night I would fill my empty stomach with a vast meal of beer, bread, and cheese. One night a quartermaster sergeant from one of the other companies sat and watched me in amazement. When I ordered my third lot of bread and cheese he said, 'Don't they feed you down at Warren Farm?' When I told him what we were getting he just said, 'Well, well,' then drank up his beer and sauntered away across the green. Three days later an NCO and another man from K Company vanished from the scene. It had been discovered that they had been selling our rations.

In addition to this crime, there were dark suspicions that private contractors were deliberately supplying substandard monotonous food in order to increase profits. Anthony Nash baulked at having the same 'dish' every night for five months. 'Something was wrong there. Army rations are good and varied. Somebody must have been doing pretty well out of the grub issued to us,' he speculated.

Insubordination was quite common in our early days, for we were unique in a way in so far that we were all new with the exception of a few old soldiers, and these were few. If our food did not suit, we would refuse it until our complaints were listened to. For this much we did know, that they were private caterers and exploitation was not too rare.

Private Tom Easton, 21st The Northumberland Fusiliers (2nd Tyneside Scottish)

Despite the best efforts of officers, improvements could not be guaranteed, regardless of protestations. In the Essex Regiment, the 10th Battalion's tented orderly room received a delegation described by one witness as being made up of 'the prettiest lot of ruffians that London was able to produce at a moment's notice'. The men aired their complaints and Captain Heppel, the adjutant, listened patiently, as he had done on many occasions. The War Office, he explained, 'had sent a thousand men down to where none were expected, and that he was doing his level best to get them food at the very earliest moment possible'. The men were hungry and tempers were fraying. In the end, the captain took the only course he felt open to him. 'Well, boys,' he is reputed to have said, 'if you don't believe that I'm doing my damnedest, I'm ready to fight each one of you in turn until you do.'

The mixture of guileless honesty and obvious exasperation saved the day and brought Heppel temporary respite as he sought to solve the recurring problem.

In regional cities, the provision of inadequate meals could prove to be as challenging an issue as it was in the countryside, but for slightly different reasons. Thousands of men living and eating in confined urban spaces made congestion at mealtimes unavoidable. Tom Easton and his comrades were accommodated in, of all places, a former restaurant in Newcastle upon Tyne's city centre.

Those must have been anxious days for the organisers for they were faced with housing and feeding about 1,100 men [all] passing through the one dining hall three times a day, which meant waiting hours in queues for each meal. We commenced at the basement of this fairly huge building, standing in our turns, then we moved up the stairs step by step up four or five floors to the dinner room at the top then our meal had to be swallowed in haste and then we had to get out to allow

Private Tom Easton, 21st The Northumberland Fusiliers (2nd Tyneside Scottish)

the others to get in. This performance occurring three times a day was sufficient to daunt the spirit of boys who for the most part had always been tended and waited on by mothers and sisters.

Food parcels sent by thoughtful relatives to fortunate recruits supplemented the army's efforts. Gunner Cecil Longley remembered that he and two friends were pretty well supplied with food parcels when others received nothing. 'One feels one can't gloat over delicacies when two (and for that matter three and four and several others) are splashing away in their tins of greasy broth,' he wrote. Longley received not only a parcel from home but another from a friend containing malt wheat bread and sardines. 'My meals lately have appeared to the others as a sort of glorified table d'hote.' Fruit, including pears and peaches, he shared with those less fortunate.

Just as it seemed unfair to pay a form of tithe to cooks to guarantee better food, so it seemed equally unfair that men were forced to supplement their diet by purchasing food in the camp canteens with whatever little money they had left.

Private George Butterworth, 6th The Duke of Cornwall's Light Infantry

We are supposed to be able to fill up deficiencies at the regimental canteens, of which there are three, one for beer only, and two for food, tobacco, etc. All of these are very unsatisfactory, being quite insufficiently equipped. The beer is simply not worth fighting for; and there is no other way of getting it. The 'dry' canteens are always running short of everything, and there is no way of getting the cup of hot coffee or cocoa which would be so acceptable at night. For our part, we have formed a habit of going into Farnborough every evening and getting a proper supper, but there are not many who can afford that regularly.

Private Ernest Parker, 15th (The King's) Hussars

Every evening while I was at Longmoor I paid a visit to the Soldiers' Home, where for fourpence, the price of twenty cigarettes, I could obtain a huge basin of porridge floating in milk. The old soldiers would have scorned such food, but for a teenager with a never-satisfied appetite this was just what was needed after a hard day's work.

Of course, it helped being closer to home, a strategic advantage traded upon by recruits in the Pals battalions. When on a route march, halting for a midday meal in the mining town of Seaton Burn, the men of Tom Easton's battalion of the Tyneside Scottish were none too bothered with army food when they were amongst their own people. 'Many of our number could be seen in the miners' cottages supping as fast as they could go at huge basins of good broth that these kindly folk had specially prepared.'

Indifferent provisions and tough but healthy exercise meant that many men spent much of their surplus wages in the camp canteen.

I cannot say that any man in my battalion has experienced any physical hardship for which a recruit ought not to be prepared under existing conditions. The food is excellent, if somewhat monotonous. I have lived on it without spending more than a few pence a day on luxuries as often as not consisting merely of a pennyworth or two of fruit. The only really serious criticisms which might be directed against the physical conditions under which we live relate to the sanitary

Corporal Frederick Keeling, 6th The Duke of Cornwall's Light Infantry

arrangements. The non-commissioned officers have a healthy terror of enteric [typhoid fever], but the lack of discipline in the battalion reflects itself in the failure to enforce the orders and instructions issued with a view to keep the camp healthy. One cannot help feeling that a little more zeal in the enforcement of sanitary rules and the provision of the means of enforcing them would be more to the point… The arrangements for washing are also miserably inadequate.

Personal hygiene, encouraged by the army (with lectures on the 'virtue of cleanliness'), was not always facilitated. The army issued toothbrushes, shaving kit, soap, cutlery, and towels, but supplies were not immediate and men might have to make do for days and even weeks before owning them all. The army did provide facilities for washing and bathing, but not for everyone all of the time. For soldiers whose camps were near the sea they had the advantage of bathing in the waves, at least in decent weather.

From Bristol, the men of the 1/6th Gloucestershire Regiment had been taken to a tented encampment near the Essex village of Great Totham. 'Great' was an exaggeration as there appeared to be four cottages and a pub. The camp had few facilities, with washing in the field's muddy ditch, the same watering hole in which the men cleaned their mess tins.

Private Anthony Nash, 1/6th The Gloucestershire Regiment

The approach to the ditch and its immediate surroundings were of liquid mud, like the much trodden watering place for cattle. I stole a bucket and washed in comfort but many of my comrades were too disheartened to wash at all.

Sergeant Frederick Keeling, 6th The Duke of Cornwall's Light Infantry

It was impossible to obtain a hot-water bath except by waiting for perhaps half the evening at a crowded Soldiers' Home. The weekly compulsory visit to a swimming bath, where the water was often very definitely opaque as the result of contact with several hundred previous bathers, was scarcely an adequate substitute for a hot bath, and the opportunities for a splash in a cold tub in camp were not frequent. Although one is grateful for the practical arrangements eventually made, it seems unfortunate that the new recruit should have been left

A fatigue party with items from the barracks: the pales with spouts were tea buckets. One man appears to be standing in the urine tub. The picture was probably taken in the morning when these men were cleaning and scrubbing hut contents.

for two months entirely dependent upon private and philanthropic enterprise for an elementary essential of cleanliness.

Morning came and then a mad scramble would commence to get a wash – queuing again. Many men paraded for breakfast without any wash and as time went on, we used to hop out and pay to be allowed to use the public lavatories and wash houses in Pilgrim Street.

Private Tom Easton, 21st The Northumberland Fusiliers (2nd Tyneside Scottish)

As part of its determination to reduce the risk from debilitating diseases, the army inoculated (or its synonym, vaccinated) the men against typhoid and smallpox. While inoculation was never made compulsory, each soldier was vigorously encouraged to submit himself to a short course of jabs. On the outbreak of war, Lieutenant Arthur Martin of the Royal Army Medical Corps had examined recruits, inoculating them as he passed them fit for service. Some had made conscientious objections and refused the injection, but in Martin's opinion, no recruits should have been permitted such 'liberty of conscience'. Inoculation should have been given on word of command.

The vast majority of recruits could not have been inoculated on or immediately after attestation for the facilities to do so did not exist. Most men discovered it would be weeks before the issue was raised. Sydney Fuller was in the army two months when the word went round that jabs were being offered.

Private Sydney Fuller, 8th The Suffolk Regiment

The Colonel appeared and 'requested' any man who did not wish to be inoculated to step forward a few paces. About half the company forthwith stepped forward. They were (also forthwith) marched round to the front of the Orderly Room and given a lecture on the horrors of typhoid fever, and the happy lot of the man who had the pleasure of having anti-typhoid fever serum in his blood. After a few minutes of this, most of the objectors decided to be 'done'. We were treated in alphabetical order and soon got it over. A dab of iodine on the upper part of the left arm, the needle of a hypodermic syringe jabbed about an inch into the arm in the middle of the patch of iodine, a few seconds while the stuff was being injected, then another dab of iodine and we were finished. The whole of the company (excepting a few who absolutely refused to be done) were treated in a very short time – Dab, jab, dab.

Paraded again at 5 pm on the square… We were informed that those men who had refused inoculation would parade on the morrow as usual, but the remainder not until further orders. All the officers were treated in full view of the men – shining examples. I felt no very bad effects of my dose – merely a similar sensation to that usually experienced when one has a bad cold coming on and of course, a stiff and sore arm.

For a minority of men inoculation could be extremely painful, with associated severe headaches, fever, and an alarmingly swollen arm: in one or two rare cases, even death was the result. No wonder some soldiers looked dubiously upon the injection. Army coercion took many forms, including the threat to permanently separate friends. 'The inoculation was not compulsory,' wrote one man, 'but we were warned that those refusing would almost certainly be sent down to the 7th Battalion [Duke of Cornwall's Light Infantry], which consists chiefly of undesirables, and will probably never be of much use.'

Second Lieutenant John Hay Beith, 10th Princess Louise's (Argyll & Sutherland Highlanders)

Last week we were all vaccinated, and we did not like it. Most of us have 'taken' very severely, which is a sign that we badly needed vaccinating, but makes the discomfort no easier to endure. It is no joke handling a rifle when your left arm is swelled to the full compass of your sleeve; and the personal contact of your neighbour in the ranks is sheer agony.

SIMPLE BARE NECESSITIES 219

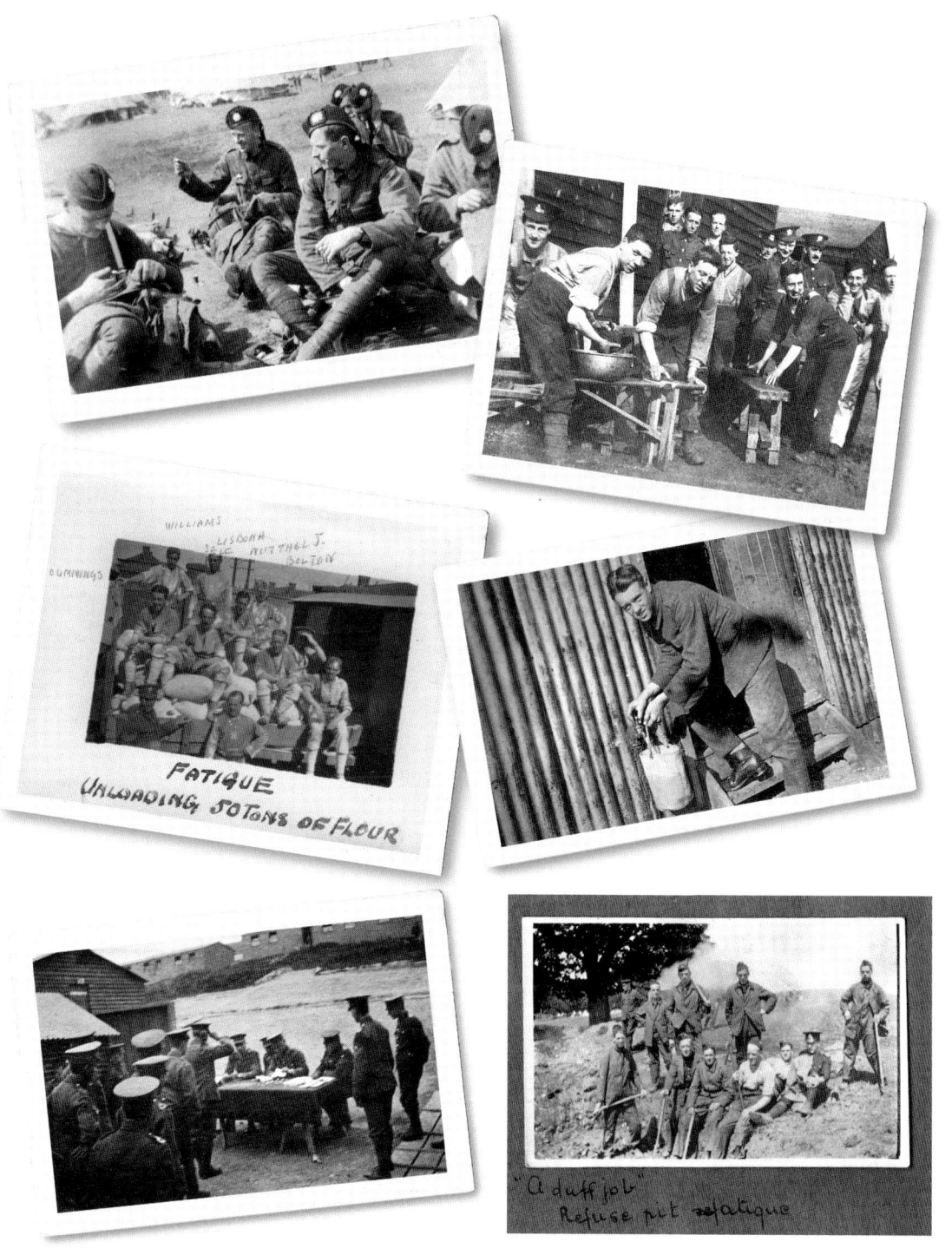

A montage of images showing daily chores undertaken in camp, including cleaning, sewing, and scrubbing. Bottom left shows men of the Birmingham Pals receiving their weekly pay.

However, officers are considerate, and the work is made as light as possible. The faint-hearted report themselves sick; but the Medical Officer, an unsentimental man of coarse mental fibre, who was on a panel before he heard his country calling, merely recommends them to get well as soon as possible, as they are going to be inoculated for enteric next week. So we grouse – and bear it.

Two weeks after his first vaccination, Sydney Fuller was paraded again for a second injection against typhoid.

Private Sydney Fuller, 8th The Suffolk Regiment

Same procedure as before, but it seemed a bit more painful this time, and the effects were more marked. No doubt the dose was larger. A few men fainted during the process, and a few more afterwards, when the stuff began to take effect. I had a bad night's rest, but did not feel it as much as many seemed to do. Had a very stiff and sore arm. No parades and free to leave the barracks.

Despite a minority of soldiers' resistance to all injections, the army's persistence (and coercion) paid off. In the end, around 97 per cent of all recruits were inoculated.

* * *

There was nothing like an absence of uniforms to make an enthusiastic recruit feel un-soldierly. The men craved anything representative of the business that they had joined, a tunic perhaps, or some khaki trousers; it did not really matter how tailored an item was, even what colour. Early on, armbands, badges or even cardboard discs were handed out with unit-identifying words, letters or insignia so that men at least felt some sort of affiliation to their clan: Sydney Fuller and his friends were issued with yellow cloth cut into the shape of a castle (the regimental badge) to sew onto the sleeves of their civilian coats.

Quartermaster stores in regimental depots had been rung empty in the first two or three weeks as Reservists were handed their uniforms to be followed by the early recruits to K1. *Some* battalions in the first New Army were fortunate, pre-war stocks were available and most of the men were given khaki uniforms straight away, but these battalions were the exception rather than the rule. By the time K2 arrived, there was precious little but odds and ends to hand out.

As a man would wish to be equipped: a private in the Royal Warwickshire Regiment (John Fairclough) in full kit. It could take nine months before a recruit had everything he needed for overseas service.

We declined to accept the responsibility for the seeming slowness of our progress. We threw it unhesitatingly upon the War Office, which had not equipped us in a manner befitting our new station in life. Although we were recruited immediately after the outbreak of war, less than half of our number had been provided with uniforms. Many still wore their old civilian clothing. Others were dressed in canvas fatigue suits, or the worn-out uniforms of policemen and tramcar conductors. Every old-clothes shop on Petticoat Lane must have contributed its allotment of cast-off apparel.

Our arms and equipment were of an equally nondescript character. We might easily have been mistaken for a mob of vagrants which had pillaged a seventeenth-century arsenal. With a few slight changes in costuming for the sake of historical fidelity, we would have served as a citizen army for a realistic motion-picture drama depicting an episode in the French Revolution.

We derived what comfort we could from the knowledge that we were but one of many battalions of Kitchener's first hundred thousand equipped in this same makeshift fashion. We did not need the repeated

Private James Hall, 9th The Royal Fusiliers (City of London Regiment)

assurances of cabinet ministers that England was not prepared for war. We were in a position to know that she was not. Otherwise, there had been an unpardonable lack of foresight in high places. Supplies came in driblets. Each night, when parades for the day were over, there was a rush for the orderly room bulletin board, which was scanned eagerly for news of an early issue of clothing. As likely as not we were disappointed, but occasionally jaded hopes revived.

Although War Office contracts were signed for vast quantities of equipment, manufacture was secured on a peacetime basis, delivered by a small number of experienced and 'trusted' companies. Even when supplier numbers expanded, these manufacturers would still need to procure the raw material to make greatcoats, shirts, jackets, puttees, and socks, and supplies were not guaranteed when so many people were chasing the same items. Delivery of contracted items, like much else, would take time.

Plates, cutlery, mugs, and toothbrushes could be purchased from general retailers. As organising committees (or generous benefactors) had free reign to supply their local Territorial or Pals battalions, they could move quickly to buy available stock. Elsewhere, civilians supplied gifts such as blankets to local men. More generally, charitable funds were established nationwide to provide additional comforts to recruits. This was a temporary fix for some of the army's less exacting problems, but none could address core problems: the supply of essential items, including the infantryman's web equipment.

The 1908 Web Equipment was the standard pattern used by British infantry. In August 1914, only two companies had the looms that could make the complicated web amunition pouches and the specialist tooling required was not easily replicable. Charged in peacetime to make 10,000 sets, it would be impossible for these two firms to meet wartime demand. In response, the British Army resorted to using leather, an easily accessible commodity to be used temporarily for everything except the pack and haversack. The new 1914 Pattern Infantry Equipment was developed and approved by early September and the vast majority of recruits would be issued with it as and when production permitted. Orders were placed in both the USA and Great Britain.

SIMPLE BARE NECESSITIES

In the meantime, older pattern leather equipment was issued to a number of New Army battalions. Whether this was welcomed is debatable. Private Ashley Gibson was biding his time before he received a commission. For five weeks, he played the role of 'other rank' with reluctance. 'Some people have told me that they liked it. I didn't. I absolutely hated it.' From his description it would appear the battalion was issued with antiquated leather equipment dating from the late 1880s that according to Gibson was liable to split fingernails every time it was buckled up.

Private, later Lance Sergeant, Rowland Banks, 20th Royal Fusiliers. Behind him are stacked several antiquated Lee-Metford rifles. Killed on the Somme in an attack on High Wood, his name is now on the Thiepval Memorial to the Missing.

Two lines in the [London] *Gazette* one morning [announcing Gibson's commission] took a load off my mind. Somebody else's aching fingers and thumbs could fumble with that accursed equipment of mine, of more or less obsolete leather pattern but as hard and unyielding as a board, which had to be unbuckled and rebuckled in its various degrees of 'order' at least a dozen times a day, in the last five minutes before parade.

Private Ashley Gibson, 20th The Royal Fusiliers (City of London Regiment) (3rd Public Schools)

All contractors were over head and ears in work, and much confusion and delay resulted. The men drilled in plain clothes for months, and wore their own civilian greatcoats and boots, receiving allowances for so doing. Owing to the fact that tartan could not be obtained for love nor money, we instituted the khaki kilt, and this made a very neat and workmanlike garb, and was quite popular with the men, as it did away with the necessity for wearing a khaki apron.

The receipt of clothing, boots, and equipment, which could not possibly be passed as up to standard, was the source of many fiery

Lieutenant Colonel J. Craig, 2/6th Princess Louise's (Argyll and Sutherland Highlanders)

disputes between the unit and the contractors concerned, and kept life from being altogether a bed of roses. Great was the envy of the first line battalion when it was known that we were to be supplied with the 1914 leather pattern equipment and canvas pack, as they were still wearing the old bandolier pattern at Bedford. They need not have concerned themselves so much about our so-called luck, as the material supplied to us at first was of a very shoddy description, and subsequently gave us much trouble.

Private Geoffrey Fildes, 2/28th The London Regiment (Artists Rifles)

With the passing weeks it was remarked that the Territorials far surpassed their rivals, the 'regular' volunteers, in matters of kit and equipment, though, even in the case of the former, supplies were still hopelessly inadequate. 'Getting into khaki' became with them less a figure of speech and more a matter of accomplishment. Occasionally a Territorial battalion would pass in the street one of the Kitchener units. Their respective manners were amusing, for criticism of the unsoldierly appearance on one side was met with good-humoured toleration of the 'irregular' branch of the Service on the other.

No one knew when items might arrive. Speculation that kit would be distributed imminently was usually based on nothing more than wishful thinking. 'Probably khaki uniform tomorrow,' wrote Royal Fusilier Andrew Buxton on 15 October. 'No uniforms yet except cap and puttees,' he was to write *two months* later, on 13 December, 'and a pair of boots, which seems to fit well in spite of simply "drawing" them by size only'. Only in January did he finally 'possess a uniform as an outward and visible sign of being a full "private!"', he wrote. 'I am told that my hat does not fit and I look like a bus driver!'

Private John McCauley, 2nd The Border Regiment

The authorities commandeered entire stocks of boots, shoes, and clothing from the local shops. Then the real burlesque commenced. Wagons loaded with all kinds of men's coats, trousers, boots, and shoes drove into the middle of the barrack square and shot their contents on to the ground. Hundreds of men assembled round the pile and the colonel and quartermaster stood in the middle of the ring.

'Who takes size nine?' the colonel would shout, holding high a pair of boots. A great roar of voices would be the answer, the boots would be tossed over and a scramble would ensue for possession. After the distribution, we looked funnier than ever. One chap, whose feet were so big that no ordinary-sized boot would fit him, walked round for nearly a month with the toes cut from one pair of boots tied with string to the heels of another pair. The town was searched in vain for a pair big enough to fit him and eventually a pair of boots had to be specially made. He certainly had a good grip of the earth.

Our first issue of service boots turned out to be very poor stuff. They could not stand up to ordinary wear and tear let alone the rough country we worked over. The boots were not made by a Leeds firm or the heels would have stayed on once they were put on instead of falling off as happened scores of times. Many a chap has lost his heel miles away from camp and had to make his own way back sometimes arriving in the early hours of the next morning.

Private Arthur Pearson, 15th The Prince of Wales's Own (West Yorkshire Regiment) (1st Leeds)

'Number 15 platoon will parade at 4 p.m. on Thursday, the 24th, for boots, puttees, braces, and service dress caps.' Number 15 is our platoon. Promptly at the hour set we halt and right-turn in front of the Quartermaster Stores marquee. The quartermaster is there with pencil and notebook, and immediately takes charge of the proceedings. 'All men needing boots, one pace step forward, march!'

The platoon, sixty-five strong, steps forward as one man. 'All men needing braces, one pace step back, march!'

Again we move as a unit. The quartermaster hesitates for a moment; but he is a resourceful man and has been through this many times before. We all need boots, quite right! But the question is. Who needs them most? Undoubtedly those whose feet are most in evidence through worn soles and tattered uppers. Adopting this sight test, he eliminates more than half the platoon, whereupon, by a further process of elimination, due to the fact that he has only sizes 7 and 8, he selects the fortunate twelve who are to walk dry shod.

Private James Hall, 9th The Royal Fusiliers (City of London Regiment)

The same method is carried out in selecting the braces. Private Reynolds, whose trousers are held in place by a wonderful mechanism composed of shoelaces and bits of string, receives a pair; likewise Private Stenebras, who, with the aid of safety pins, has fashioned coat and trousers into an ingenious one-piece garment. Caps and puttees are distributed with like impartiality, and we dismiss, the unfortunate ones growling and grumbling in discreet undertones until the platoon commander is out of hearing, whereupon the murmurs of discontent become loudly articulate.

In the competition for uniforms the assumption was often made that others were doing better, the grass always being greener elsewhere.

Gunner Cecil Longley, 1st South Midland Brigade, Royal Field Artillery

We feel rather sore that Kitchener's Army is being better equipped than our own. We have no uniform yet, and we are told we should be outfitted directly on arrival and therefore not to take anything but old things; consequently we have no change of clothes and are still in thin summer flannels, and frequently get wet through and have to let them dry on our bodies. This is not grousing but just airing facts of very poor management. Either our officers are hopelessly incompetent as regards organisation, or else the County Association; it lies between them.

Private James Hall, 9th The Royal Fusiliers (City of London Regiment)

'Kitchener's Rag-Time Army I calls it!' growls the veteran of South African fame.

'Ain't we a 'andsome lot o' pozzie wallopers? Service? We ain't never a-go'n' to see service! You blokes won't, but watch me! I'm a-go'n' to grease off out o' this mob!'

No one remonstrated with this deservedly unpopular reservist when he grumbled about the shortage of supplies. He voiced the general sentiment. We all felt that we would like to 'grease off' out of it. Our deficiencies in clothing and equipment were met by the government with what seemed to us amazing slowness. However, Tommy is a sensible man. He realised that England had a big contract to fulfil and that the first duty was to provide for the armies in the field. France, Russia, Belgium, all were looking to England for supplies. Kitchener's Mob must wait, trusting to the genius for organisation, the faculty for getting things done, of its great and worthy chief, K. of K.

Sydney Fuller's diary kept up a running commentary on the issue of kit and the dates by which items were handed out. Collated into a short narrative, the picture is produced of men waiting weeks and months for items:

> 10 September: a towel, a knife and fork, and a pair of socks. 24th September: a limited number of civilian overcoats and service caps issued. 25 September: hairbrushes and toothbrushes. 27 September: four rifles for each tent. All were worn-out Long Lee-Enfields. Also issued were two shirts, two pairs of pants, two pairs of socks, a pair of braces and a 'housewife' (a small cloth roll containing needles, thread and a thimble). 12 October: old Long Lee-Enfield rifles handed to each man. 5 November: razors issued. 20 November: khaki puttees. 24 November: a khaki service dress cap and a tin water bottle. 17 January: belts, bayonet frogs, and ammunition pouches. Two straps for overcoats.

The men continued to wear civilian clothes until 13 October. On that day, they received a uniform, though not one coloured khaki.

Received my first 'uniform' – one of the blue serge suits – about two sizes too large. I measured 36 inches round the chest – the coat was 42 inches. This allowed for quite a lot of future expansion, and it was difficult to get clothes altered, the only thing for it was to fill them out. I must admit I never did manage this.

Private Sydney Fuller, 8th The Suffolk Regiment

Blue serge uniform, quickly dubbed 'Kitchener Blue', was the army's response to a critical shortage of khaki. Five hundred thousand blue-coloured suits had

After being kitted out with odds and ends of khaki uniform, the men of the 7th Royal West Kent Regiment were handed so-called Kitchener Blue uniforms as an interim measure. Below: Vic Cole, pipe in mouth, wearing his blue uniform.

been purchased, many from Post Office stores and distributed nationwide. Where men at regimental depots had been issued with odd items of khaki uniform, these were exchanged for the blue outfit to present some semblance of continuity, Kitchener himself being more concerned that the men look alike than being wedded to the orthodox. Recruits chided at having to wear the pocketless, cheap-looking and shapeless suits, with blue side-cap, but they were at least in uniform.

Rifleman Bill Worrell, 12th The Rifle Brigade

The new uniform – Kitchener Blue. The model for it must have been a City Policeman. Dicky and I had about the same vital statistics, 32–22–28. We both finished with a modish 8-inch turn-up and double-breasted trousers. Having once done up the buttons of our tunics we never undid them again as we were able to pull them on like jerseys. The natty ensemble was crowned with a forage cap of the same material.

Men felt they had been made to look like postmen, tram guards or even convicts and were embarrassed to be seen in public, especially by friends and relatives. Sydney Fuller had to make do with the blue serge for two months but interestingly, in the first days of January, he treated himself, by buying his own khaki uniform; he was not the first to do so.

> I had purchased [it] in a second-hand clothes shop in town. These shops did quite a brisk trade in khaki clothing, the clothing being, presumably, some that they had bought in peace time from 'Regulars' stationed in the town [Colchester]. They naturally made a good price of this stuff owing to the great demand. My tunic, for instance, cost me 16/-. However, one had a natural desire to look like a <u>real</u> soldier when on leave, so the large prices were gladly paid.

Private Sydney Fuller, 8th The Suffolk Regiment

Not until March was the battalion issued with a complete suit of khaki for every man and 'at last [we] began to look like business,' wrote Fuller, the blue serge uniform being relegated for fatigues only. Soon after, the men were issued with American-made leather equipment, followed on 10 April by all being given the rifle that they would take to France.

Only in spring 1915 did all the men in Fuller's battalion look like the professional soldiers they had aspired to be and even then they were short of a bayonet and a waterproof groundsheet; these items were finally distributed at the end of the month.

In Newcastle, George Harbottle was serving with the 1/6th Northumberland Fusiliers, a first-line Territorial unit. In August 1914, he had been delighted on enlistment to receive not only a khaki uniform from stores but also a rifle soon afterwards, a perfectly serviceable Long Lee-Metford, albeit twenty years out of production.

> We often saw some of the early Kitchener's army units route marching with hardly any rifles and dressed in denims, which made us realise how fortunate we were to have joined a properly equipped unit with trained officers and NCOs.

The Royal Ordnance Factories produced the bulk of rifles for the British Army, and would be prepared to supply the Regular Army and those of a small British Expeditionary Force in a short war. These factories annually manufactured just over 47,000 examples of the British Army's standard infantry weapon of 1914, the Short Magazine Lee-Enfield Mark III.

At the outbreak of war there were barely enough rifles to meet the demand of the mobilised Regular Army when additional battlefield wastage was adjusted for. There were almost no new rifles for Kitchener's First New Army, never mind K2 and K3, and only a small supply of antiquated rifles that could be brought out of storage.

In the first instance, a lack of rifles was not too serious. Wooden rifles and even broomsticks were substitutes to teach recruits the rudimentary skills of drill, but broomsticks were still demeaning so that when a handful of antiquated rifles appeared they were greeted with almost boyish excitement.

Private Albert Simpson, 2/6th The Duke of Wellington's Regiment (West Riding Regiment)

The whole battalion had only six rifles, and they were for drill purposes only. It's very doubtful whether any one of them would have fired, even if there had been any ammunition, but there was always a rush by men of the leading company of the day to fill the first four places and the two outside places of the next four, and so have the honour of bearing the precious arms when we went on our afternoon route march.

Lieutenant & Quartermaster Joseph Goss, 8th The King's Own Scottish Borderers

At length, we received a few D.P. [drill purpose] rifles, life seemed to become a little rosier and our prospects more hopeful. These few rifles were passed round on parade from squad to squad, each in turn receiving instruction in handling arms. To carry the rifles at a correct angle at the slope seemed to be the most important movement in exercises with arms. Sergeant-majors would roar at the men to press on their butts, or to get the heel of the butting line with the centre of the thigh. A well-meaning subaltern, not liking to be as stern as the sergeant-major, would cajole his men by offering them chocolate if they carried their rifles in the right way.

Lieutenant Colonel J. Craig, 2/6th Princess Louise's (Argyll & Sutherland Highlanders)

We possessed a guardroom, and we mounted a Headquarters Guard at the Drill Hall, and its solitary sentry was armed with the only rifle and bayonet we possessed at the commencement of our career. The changing of the sentry and the handing over of the lonely rifle and bayonet was a never-ending source of entertainment for the crowd that watched from the street below.

Rifles may have been prized for show, but they did not have a dedicated owner, posing an unforeseen problem of care and maintenance. 'With 167 rifles among 250 men, each rifle belonged to no one in particular,' wrote one officer of the 16th Sherwood Foresters. 'It had no guardian, no one wanted to clean it, no one wanted to take a pride in it, no one wanted to father it – the proprietary principle had given way to communism.'

The effort to ramp up production was hampered in part by a lack of skilled labour, a shortage caused by summer's recruitment. To help alleviate the problem, orders were placed with companies in the USA and Canada. Additional rifles were bought from India and Japan for training purposes, including the Japanese Arisaka, a rifle with a hopelessly complicated mechanism: 'beautiful toys, but quite useless under war conditions', as one frustrated recipient wrote.

As always, equipment was sent to where demand was greatest. By June 1915, 1.15 million new rifles had been supplied to the army, of which just 15 per cent were issued to the New Armies. Half a million new rifles had rightly gone with the expeditionary forces to the Western Front and to the recently opened campaign in the Turkish Dardanelles. This included a number of Territorial divisions sent before any New Army divisions could be spared for this significant but secondary operation, secondary to the main task of defeating Germany on the Western Front.

Below: *With the weather closing in, the men of the 2/6th Gloucestershire Regiment are issued with non-military oilskins and sou'westers. The men are armed with the Japanese Arisaka Type 38 Carbine, imported primarily for use by the Royal Navy, but also for use by the army for drill purposes.*

Overleaf: *A team from the South Wales Borderers helping to construct a camp in the early autumn of 1914. They are sitting on sheets of corrugated iron, material withdrawn from hut construction before the end of the year, as it was required for the war effort.*

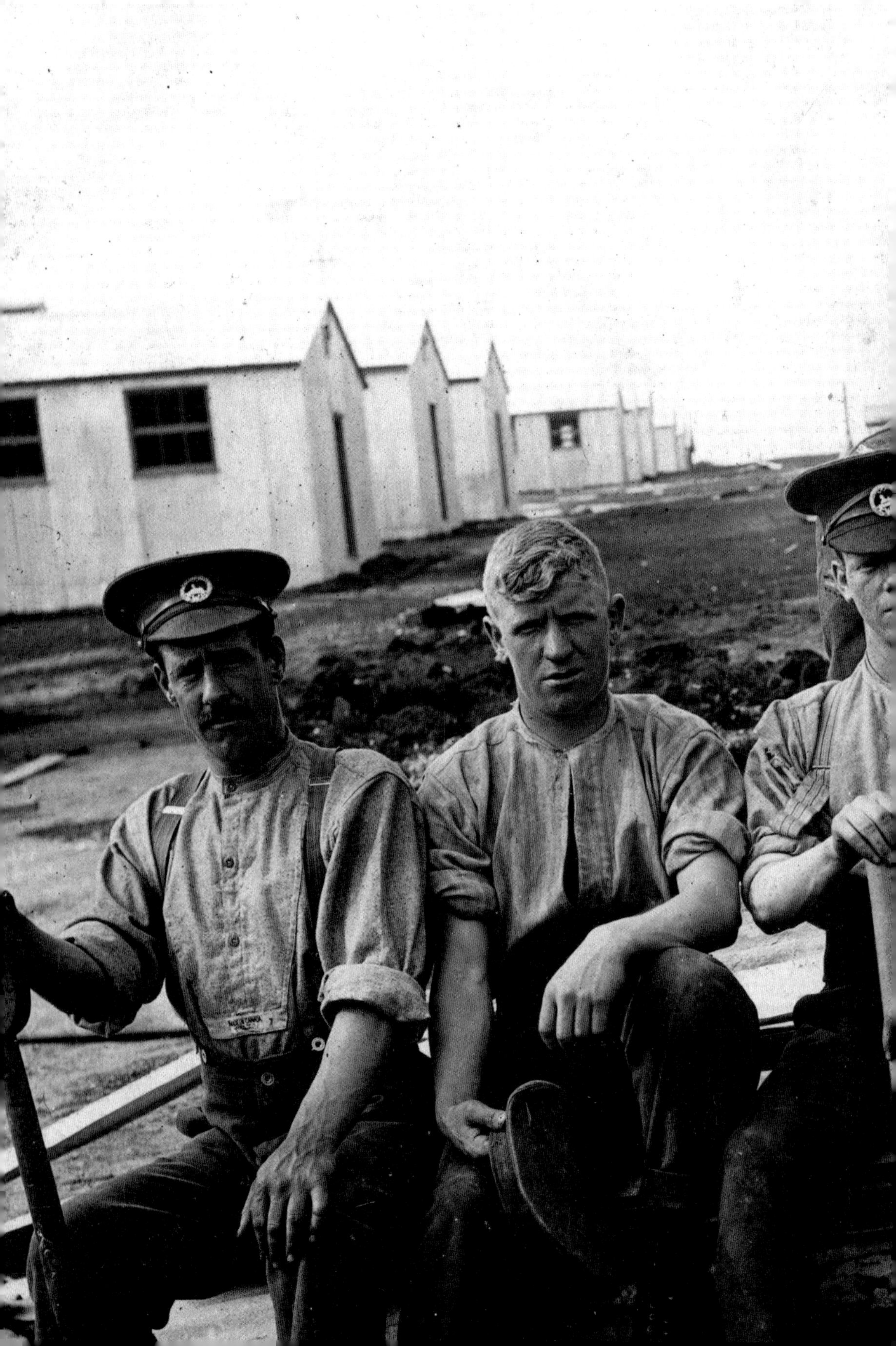

8 Living the Dream

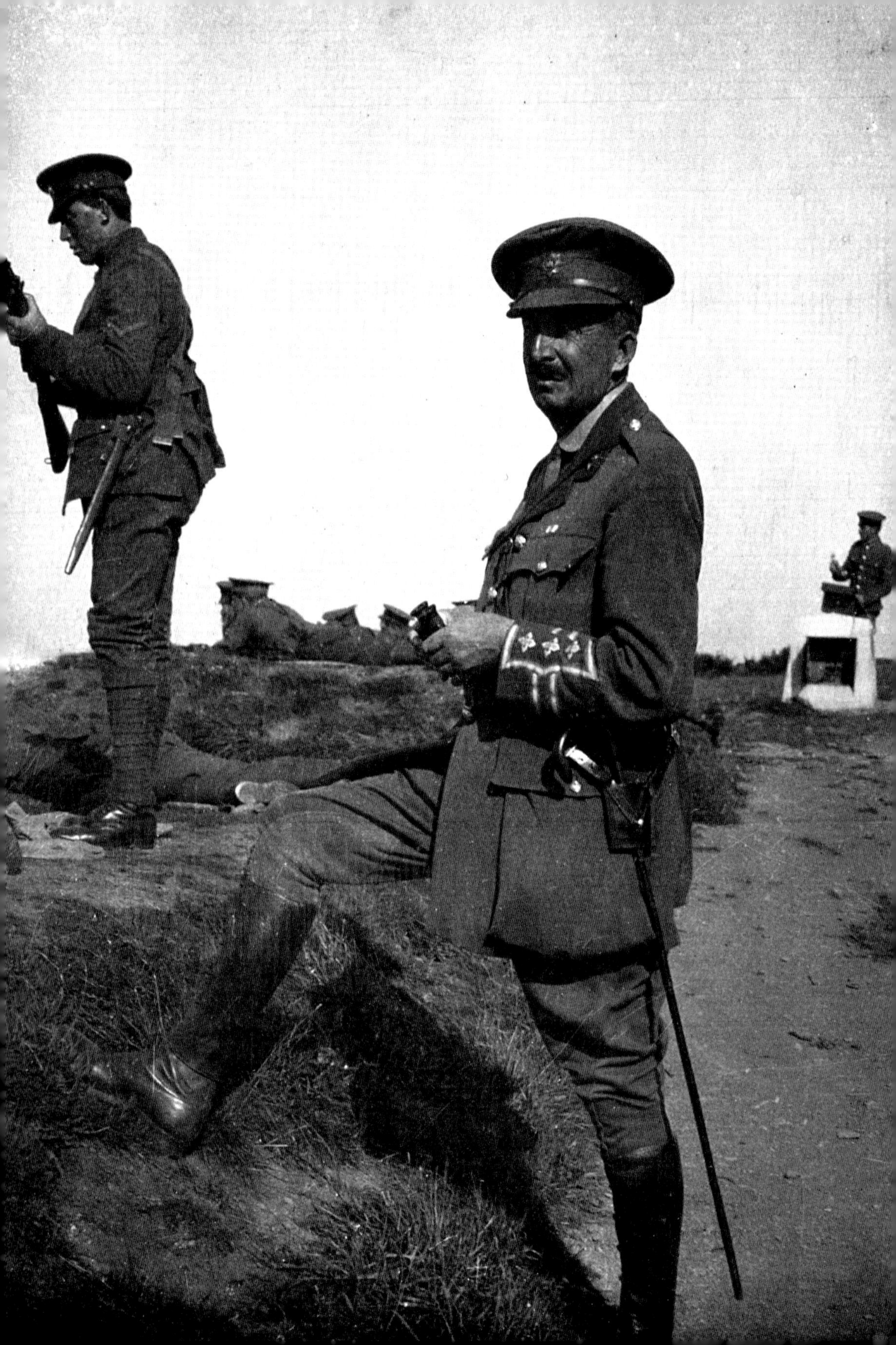

'From the mysteries of forming fours when turned about we were now initiated into the higher arts of war. Fieldwork and musketry on the miniature range came as a relief after the tortures of "frog marching" and other sundry inflictions beloved of the instructor in physical training.'

Private Geoffrey Fildes, 2/28th London Regiment (Artists Rifles)

———

For the last fortnight [the men] have been engaged in imbibing the science of musketry. They have learned to hold their rifles correctly, sitting, kneeling, standing, or lying; to bring their backsights and foresights into an undeviating straight line with the base of the bull's-eye; and to press the trigger in the manner laid down in the Musketry Regulations – without wriggling the body or 'pulling off'. They have also learned to adjust their sights, to perform the loading motions rapidly and correctly, and to obey simple commands.

But as yet they have discharged no shots from their rifles. It has all been make-believe, with dummy cartridges and fictitious ranges, and snapping triggers. To be quite frank, they are getting just a little tired of musketry training – forgetting for the moment that a soldier who cannot use his rifle is merely an expense to his country and a free gift to the enemy.

Second Lieutenant John Hay Beith, 10th Princess Louise's (Argyll & Sutherland Highlanders)

Pre-war, musketry drill and the accuracy of rifle fire were, unsurprisingly, deemed of high importance to the Regular Army. Annually, all infantrymen completed a course at one of the many ranges, men firing over an assortment of distances from 100 to 600 yards, kneeling and lying down, and being carefully marked on their performance. A 'mad minute' followed, in which the infantryman discharged fifteen rounds (reloading the ten-round magazine) at a target 300 yards away, though most infantrymen worth their salt could achieve noticeably better results than this.

Opposite: *Men of the 8th Devonshire Regiment on the rifle range, their efforts overseen by a senior officer of the battalion. To the rear is a man on a field telephone, in constant contact with those working the targets.*

Below: *Shooting at targets on the rifle range at Clipstone Camp, Nottinghamshire. The men of the 20th Royal Fusiliers were amongst the first to occupy the wooden city built to accommodate up to 30,000 men.*

Private James Hall, 9th The Royal Fusiliers (City of London Regiment)

During training each man was taught to judge distance, how to adjust for wind direction or for a moving target, and they were taught too to adjust to the tiniest variations or small idiosyncratic biases their rifle might have. Furthermore, 'we were instructed in the description and recognition of targets, the use of cover, but chiefly in the use of our rifles. Through constant handling they became a part of us, a third arm which we grew to use quite instinctively,' wrote Private James Hall.

The army awarded proficiency payments for those who proved to be good shots and an additional six pence a day for those who were marksmen, these men securing the coveted crossed rifle badges on the tunic sleeve.

We fired the recruits', and later, the trained soldiers' course in musketry on the rifle ranges at Hythe and Aldershot, gradually improving our technique, until we were able to fire with some accuracy fifteen rounds per minute. When we had achieved this difficult feat, we ceased to be recruits. We were skilled soldiers of the proud and illustrious order known as 'England's Mad-Minute Men'.

LIVING THE DREAM

The pre-war marksmanship of the army was exceptionally high, but with the New Army such standards were never going to be maintained, not least owing to the paucity of rifles with the result that many men were not introduced to one until relatively late in training. Private James Hall appears to have been more fortunate than many others. He was able to hone his skills, whereas others bemoaned their lack of practice for there was never the abundance of ammunition necessary to permit all men to spend enough time on the ranges, let alone completing the recruits' musketry course.

At Caterham, Guardsman Norman Cliff and his comrades had to wait for 'their' rifles to be passed down from a prior squad of recruits. With inherited rifles, the men were taught the first 'important lesson to winning the war', Cliff recalled. 'Oh, no, not to shoot straight, but how to strike the rifle in the mechanical motions of sloping and presenting arms.'

As in all drill exercises, the volume of noise produced was the main measure of success. The louder the noise of feet stamping, the greater the drill-sergeant's content, but the butts of rifles could never be struck noisily enough to satisfy his hearing. Hands might sting or be bruised, the weapon might be smacked almost to pieces, but 'Don't tickle it – hit it!' the sergeant would scream, flushed with anger... And the rifle was supposed to be the soldier's best friend.

Guardsman Norman Cliff, 1st Grenadier Guards

Rifle drill was tedious. We sloped, trailed, presented, ordered, reversed, wheeled, and piled. We did it for hours until we were totally exhausted. Then we did some more. We all wondered how it would help us when we faced the Germans.

Private Ewart Hale, 12th The Gloucestershire Regiment (Bristol)

A private in the Devonshire Regiment under instruction on an unknown range.

It might be months before recruits reached the butts and even then range discipline or etiquette, though taught, were often found lacking.

Second Lieutenant John Hay Beith, 10th Princess Louise's (Argyll & Sutherland Highlanders)

Upon a long row of waterproof sheets – some thirty in all – lie the firers. Beside each is extended the form of a sergeant or officer, tickling his charge's ear with incoherent counsel, and imploring him, almost tearfully, not to get excited.

Suddenly thirty targets spring out of the earth in front of us, only to disappear again just as we have got over our surprise. They are not of the usual bull's-eye pattern, but are what is known as 'figure' targets. The lower half is sea-green, the upper white. In the centre, half on the green and half on the white is a curious brown smudge and is intended to represent the head and shoulders of a man in khaki lying on grass and aiming at us. However, the British private, with his usual genius for misapprehension, has christened this effigy 'the beggar in the boat'.

With equal suddenness the targets swing up again. Crack! An uncontrolled spirit has loosed off his rifle before it has reached his shoulder. Blistering reproof follows. Then, after three or four seconds, comes a perfect salvo all down the line.

There was nothing 'perfect' about the musketry of gunners belonging to the Royal Field Artillery. Their normal position on a battlefield, some distance from the trenches, meant there was little chance they would ever need to shoot, never mind shoot accurately. 'Instruction in the use of the rifle [was] not of great importance in an arm where only ten rifles are allowed per battery,' wrote Cecil Street, though it was still a part of a gunner's training that he knew how to hit a target.

Captain Cecil Street, 23rd Siege Battery, Royal Garrison Artillery

The great idea is to get the business over: it is so much time wasted that might be devoted to more useful things. Consequently from the word go the air is full of flying bullets, some few of which, guided by a pitiful providence, contrive to find their way through the targets.

Bored with the whole proceeding, I once walked up behind the lines of men, [who were] dutifully pulling triggers because they had been told so. One of the most industrious was holding the gun upside down, a method that resulted in rather wild shooting. Approaching him with care, I remonstrated with him and received the reply: 'I don't hardly know how to use 'eee, I never had 'ee in my hands before.' Why should he have?

So little did artillerymen think of musketry that according to Julian Tyndale-Biscoe, the men of his battery first saw a rifle range two weeks before overseas embarkation.

We had a most exciting time at the rifle range. Most of the men had never seen a rifle. When we got to the range, it was quite chaotic. No one seemed to know what to do. Men started to fire before orders were given and were not particular as to what they fired at. Some bullets hit the ground a yard or two off and whizzed off with a whine, while many more cleared the butts completely. Different people were shouting different orders, and, then, some soldiers from another division started walking along the butts in front of the targets! This resulted in yells of 'Cease fire!' from behind us, which seemed to have little effect. I do not think many knew what the sights of their rifles were for.

<small>Second Lieutenant Julian Tyndale-Biscoe, Royal Field Artillery, 14th Division</small>

For those undertaking the recruits' musketry course, there was always a chance for some fun.

My pal told me, 'If you fail your rifle practice, know what they say? You go back the next day. But if you pass your rifle practice you're on a five mile run.' So I made it my duty to fail my rifle practice, to miss the target. So I went back to the ranges, while those who passed had to go for a long run.

<small>Private Robert Burns, 7th The Queen's Own Cameron Highlanders</small>

By the time men got to the ranges there were a few recruits who had changed their minds entirely about the army and rather fancied a return to civil life. Atrocious shooting on the range might lead to an early discharge: it was an opportune moment to feign poor vision.

Second Lieutenant John Hay Beith, 10th Princess Louise's (Argyll & Sutherland Highlanders)

'Eyesight wrong?'

'So he says, sir.'

'Been a long time finding out hasn't he?'

The Private [is] led off to the lair of that hardened cynic, the Medical Officer. Here he is put through some simple visual tests. He soon finds himself out of his depth. It is extremely difficult to feign either myopia, hypermetria, or astigmatism if you are not acquainted with the necessary symptoms, and have not decided beforehand which (if any) of these diseases you are suffering from. In five minutes the afflicted [man] is informed, to his unutterable indignation, that he has passed a severe ocular examination with flying colours, and is forthwith marched back to his squad, with instructions to recognise all targets in future.

While recruits commenced their tuition, there were others placed at the far end of the range, beneath the butts. Their job would be to signal the accuracy (or inaccuracy) of a man's shooting and then to paste over the hole so that the target could be used again. Theirs was a relatively easy job with time enough for experienced men to gamble, betting on a recruit's accuracy with pennies being exchanged back and forth between adjacent targets as each set of five shots was scored.

Private George Coppard, 6th The Queen's Own (Royal West Surrey Regiment)

During the course I took my turn at the butts, an alarming experience at first. Quite often the bullets would strike something hard and make a fearsome howl. Once, a bullet ended its flight spinning like a top on the concrete floor beside me. Duly warned of the danger, I kept well back under the canopy during the firing.

LIVING THE DREAM

The butts were their own small world: safe, but unnerving at first. The men known as markers worked the intricate system of metal frames and canvas targets, growing accustomed to their subterranean habitat and the strange noises as a bullet terminated its flight.

The interior of the butts is an unexpectedly spacious place. From the nearest firing-point you would not suspect their existence, except when the targets are up. Imagine a sort of miniature railway station – or rather, half a railway station – sunk into the ground, with a very long platform and a very low roof eight feet high at the most. Upon the opposite side of this station, instead of the other platform, rises the sandy ridge previously mentioned, the stop-butt, crowned with its row of number-boards. Along the permanent way, in place of sleepers and metals, runs a long and narrow trough, in which, instead of railway carriages, some thirty great iron frames are standing side by side. These frames are double, and hold the targets. They are so arranged that if one is pushed up, the other comes down. The markers stand along the platform, like railway porters.

Opposite: *'Eyesight wrong?'*

Second Lieutenant John Hay Beith, 10th Princess Louise's (Argyll & Sutherland Highlanders)

Men, known as 'markers', work the butts on a rifle range, lowering and raising each target, signalling scores and then pasting over the holes. It was possible to gamble on the accuracy of shots fired, pennies moving backwards and forwards between the markers.

There are two markers to each target. They stand with their backs to the firers, comfortably conscious of several feet of earth and a stout brick wall between them and low shooters. Number one squats down, paste-pot in hand, and repairs the bullet-holes in the unemployed target with patches of black or white paper. Number two, brandishing a pole to which is attached a disc, black on one side and white on the other, is acquiring a permanent crick in the neck through gaping upwards at the target in search of hits. He has to be sharp-eyed, for the bullet-hole is a small one, and springs into existence without any other intimation than a spurt of sand on the bank twenty yards behind. He must be alert, too, and signal the shots as they are made; otherwise the telephone will begin to interest itself on his behalf.

The art of bayonet fighting undertaken with the aid of padded clothing and facemasks worn to negate the danger of accidental 'prods'.

There was a largely dispassionate reaction to shooting at human-shaped targets and from hundreds of yards away. Bayonet practice was different. Even if the 'body' was a stuffed sack of straw, a man did not have to feign squeamishness about running it through. But first a recruit had to learn how to handle a rifle with steel bayonet attached and to how to avoid inadvertently prodding a comrade.

Bayonet fighting is a highly amusing pastime – if you stand by and watch other men doing it. It is a very breathless form of exercise, and a very dangerous one – more especially when, as sometimes happens, a large squad of men receive instruction in it in a small hall. The consciousness that all around you and within a few feet of you are men brandishing heavy rifles, and not very certain of what these weapons will do in their not too dexterous hands – the sudden exclamation of a man adjacent to you as the butt of a rifle gets him a wallop on the posterior, the half-smothered expletive of another as he gets a violent prod in the ribs, the crash of glass as the shade of an electric light falls to the floor – all these things do not conduce to your ease of mind, and they take much of the pleasure and 'pith' from your own efforts. And even the Sergeant's assurances that all these lunges and points and parries wouldn't hurt a fly in mid-air, let alone kill or disable an enemy, don't help you much.

Private Thomas Lyon, 2/9th The Highland Light Infantry (Glasgow Highlanders)

Close-quarters fighting using the butt of the rifle as well as the bayonet to subdue the enemy. On the left, Private John Burnside, 14th Royal Warwickshire Regiment, 1st Birmingham Pals, who was killed fewer than six weeks after arriving in France. His brother, William, fell the following year.

Anonymous, 10th The East Yorkshire Regiment (1st Hull)

In the elementary stage the recruit is taught how to handle his rifle quickly and easily without strain. He is shown how to adopt the 'On guard' position, pointing and parrying in any direction and also the method of shortening arms, which is used to extract the bayonet cleanly after a point has been made. The instructor impresses upon recruits the vital importance of quickness of movement both in dealing with an opponent and at the same time guarding oneself. After thoroughly mastering the art of bayonet fighting, instruction is given in using the butt, knee, trip etc., and in order to demonstrate more clearly the reality of the business recruits are paired off, and, after donning protective gear [wire head and face guards, and body pads] for the head and body, fight each other with spring bayonets, under the guidance of an instructor, who points out to the class the varied faults of the combatants.

Lance Corporal David Philip, 16th The Royal Scots (Lothian Regiment)

Now we were mostly intelligent lads. My own imagination was no more and no less vivid than the average. Shooting a man several hundred yards away, or tossing a bomb in his direction, were remote acts. Thrusting a bayonet into his body necessarily took a bit of contemplation, especially if, as expected, he was trying to do the same to you.

I surveyed my companions and saw only a small handful of men who were comfortable in the drill, a smaller number still, moreover, who I thought would be likely to carry their skill and enthusiasm into the real fight.

Guardsman Norman Cliff, 1st Grenadier Guards

Faced with suspended sacks, with the vital parts of the body labelled, we were ordered to howl blood-curdling cries as we rushed forward with bayonets fixed. Then: 'Shove the bayonet straight in his stomach. And pull it out at the same angle or it will get entangled in all sorts of guts and snot and gristle. Then jab it in his throat, kick him in the balls, and bash his brains out with the butt. Your job is not to tickle the Hun. You have to kill him. The whole idea is to make new faces in Hell and more widows in Germany.'

Men of the 8th The King's Own Scottish Borderers in 'action'.

The prospect of fighting at the point of the bayonet gave most infantryman pause for thought. Could they themselves face the bayonet? Could they deliver cold steel to end another's life? It was a sobering thought for even the most unemotional, though mercifully few men would ever have to engage in hand-to-hand combat.

Reckoning that any enemy force with which we came into contact would boast much the same thin sprinkling of potential 'killers', I drew much consolation. Unless I was dreadfully unlucky, I consoled myself, I was quite likely to find myself facing an adversary every bit as squeamish as myself. If I could only keep my nerve, therefore, I felt I would prevail. I imparted these thoughts to my friends only to be roundly mocked for my foolishness. Privately, however, in days to come, a number of them asked me did I really believe I was right. Oh yes, the bayonet got us thinking, I must say.

Lance Corporal David Philip, 16th The Royal Scots (Lothian Regiment)

Private James Hall, 9th The Royal Fusiliers (City of London Regiment)

Plenty of hard work in the open air brought great and welcome changes. The men talked of their food, anticipated it with a zest that came from realising for the first time the joy of being genuinely hungry. They watched their muscles harden with the satisfaction known to every normal man when he is becoming physically efficient. Food, exercise, and rest, taken in wholesome quantities and at regular intervals, were having the usual excellent results. For my own part, I had never before been in such splendid health… My fellow Tommies were living, really living, for the first time. They had never before known what it means to be radiantly, buoyantly healthy.

Lance Corporal Vic Cole, 7th The Queen's Own (Royal West Kent Regiment)

At Purfleet there were lots of other battalions. The Queen's Own (Royal West Surrey Regiment), they were next to us, and then the East Kent Regiment, with the 'Buffs' on their shoulder titles or 'Buggered up for foreign service' as we would call them. On our shoulders was 'RWKent', or 'Remember we kiss every nice tart', but the officers said, 'no it means "remember we keep every nation tame"'.

Around the camp we practised morse code using flags. We'd go out with the section and form a square and signal to each other. I had messages all written out, 'Enemy attacking such and such, send reinforcements' and this would be signalled round the square and we would see if the same message came back. The blokes were pretty good and it was better than company drilling, marching up and down all day.

As the training progressed the telephones came in, and morse became morse by sound instead of sight. The telephone came with thin copper wire, number 18 size, just japanned over black. On manoeuvres it used to get entangled in everything and the infantry used to curse us as they frequently got enmeshed in the stuff.

Later we got D3 cable and a dry cell battery to which you added water to make it active, and they lasted about two or three weeks.

On my suggestion we went out for a bit of a march with the signals section around Purfleet. It was an agricultural area, fields bounded by dirt road tracks and telephone poles, plenty of room to muck about. We had two sets of climbing irons so we could scale the telegraph poles. There were two terminals on the D3 telephone, and we put wire round one terminal on the phone. One terminal went to the line and the other went to earth or was clipped onto some railings. Then one man would scale the telegraph pole and clip onto one of the wires and the rest of the section would go up the road a couple of hundred yards and clip to see if we could get through.

There was a permanent current on the wire and when we tuned in we could listen to civilians talking on the telephone. It was great fun.

We had call signs: 'Is that AK1?' and we would hear:

'I say Gladys, whatever's that terrible noise on the wire?'

'I don't know, it must be the soldiers, dear.'

'Er, sorry, madam, um, troops on manoeuvres.'

Opposite below: 1915: signallers of the 2/5th East Kent Regiment use lightweight silk blue and white flags to send messages by semaphore. Daylight and good visibility were required and signals could be read by the enemy. The use of flags declined rapidly with advances in technology, such as wireless telegraphy.

Punctually at 9.30 the Colonel appears and takes command of the battalion. 'Quick – march.' The drums beat, the pipes skirl, there is the steady ramp of marching feet, and the business proper of the day has begun.

We are on a route march, and as we climb the long hill that leads from the town jaunty is our step, and saucy is the swing of our kilts with their buff apron coverings. The shrilling of the pipes stimulates the blood and makes it flow faster, faster, and there is exhilaration in every forward step…

Fifeshire is a kingdom of stey braes [steep hills], the country being extremely undulating and the highways hilly and tortuous. But what matters the climbing of a brae when, its summit reached, the eyes are refreshed with the glorious vision of the little, friendly looking Roscobie Hills, now draped like a bride in a garment of snow, spangled with the diamonds of the sun? Or, turning one's head, one sees, beyond a stretch of rolling and variegated meadow lands a riband of gleaming

Private Thomas Lyon, 2/9th The Highland Light Infantry (Glasgow Highlanders)

silver that is the Firth of Forth and the darkly sinister spots upon its brightness one knows to be battleships at anchor off the naval base. Or again there expands before the eyes a charming vista of field and wood, of brown ploughed lands and grassy knolls, with here and there the contrast of a vivid patch of warm colour afforded by a red-roofed house. One does not weary readily when scenes so pleasing as these are constantly meeting the gaze.

Private Clifford Hollingworth, 15th The Prince of Wales's Own (West Yorkshire Regiment)

We said we'd have a walk over the moors [at Colsterdale] and this would be perhaps beginning of November. We walked on and we came across a little croft, a little farm – a shepherd's place, and that chap didn't know the war had broken out! He didn't know anything about the war! But you see parts of the country were like that, they go to town twice or three times a year. They buy the bulk of their food for the year because they live off the land normally. He'd only been the week before the war broke out, down to town, him and his three children and his wife.

For a month after enlisting I scarcely spoke to a civilian except occasionally to shop assistants or hawkers in the course of making small purchases. I have only once been away from camp for a night and slept in a bed. In so far as I think of the future at all it is on my possible experiences as a soldier that I reflect. But I have been too exhilarated to think. I have certainly never in my life experienced more continuous cheerfulness and in the truest sense of the word more happiness than in these three months. The sense of physical fitness; the exhilaration of a collective regimental life; the constant opportunities for the formation of new friendships with men of widely varying experiences; the congeniality of a life which is communistic in just the aspects in which communism is convenient and stimulating; the variety of the work (which does not seem to me personally to lose its sense of freshness and novelty to any extent), and last but not least, the humorous aspects of one's own and one's comrades' activities, all combine to expel the baneful elements of existence. I may possibly live to think differently; but at the present moment, assuming this war had to come, I feel nothing but gratitude to the gods for sending it in my time.

Sergeant Frederick Keeling, 6th The Duke of Cornwall's Light Infantry

At the beginning of their training, the men of the new armies were gently dealt with. Allowances were made for civilian frailties and shortcomings. But as they adapted themselves to changed conditions, restrictions became increasingly severe. Old privileges disappeared one by one. Individual liberty became a thing of the past. The men resented this bitterly for a time. Fierce hatreds of officers and NCOs were engendered and there was much talk of revenge when we should get to the front. I used to look forward with misgiving to that day. It seemed probable that one night in the trenches would suffice for a wholesale slaughtering of officers. Old scores were to be paid off, old grudges wiped out with our first issue of ball ammunition.

All these threats were forgotten months before the time came for carrying them out. Once Tommy understood the reasonableness of severe discipline, he took his punishment for his offences without complaint. He realised, too, the futility of kicking against the pricks.

Private James Hall, 9th The Royal Fusiliers (City of London Regiment)

Opposite: *Rural poverty: an infantry officer photographs a child in the countryside near Invergordon. Some isolated farming families would remain almost entirely ignorant of the war.*

In the army he belonged to the government, body and soul. He might resent its treatment of him. He might behave like a sulky schoolboy, disobey order after order, and break rule after rule. In that case he found himself check-mated at every turn. No one was at all concerned about his grievances. He might become a habitual offender from sheer stupidity, but in doing so, he injured no one but himself.

Second Lieutenant John Bellerby, 1/8th The Prince of Wales's Own (West Yorkshire Regiment)

The responsibility for discipline and for minor punishments fell upon the youngest officers, with the consequence that there was much inequality in the penalties for similar 'crimes'. My own principle was never to give any punishment whatever except for something really heinous, for which I should have proposed to give the maximum. I fell-in the platoon and told them my principle, and said that I should do my utmost to cause the ejection from the army of any member of the platoon who might be caught taking the property of another. I did not realise how empty such a threat was at the time, but it worked.

The only subsequent offender was Busby, the cook, who had the misfortune not to be present when my remarks were made. Some weeks later I discovered, by a piece of detection simplified by Busby's largeness of foot, that he had stolen the slippers of another member of the platoon similarly distinguished, and I induced the Colonel to give him a stiff dose of detention. For some odd reason, this raised me in his estimation. One hears stories of irate other ranks threatening to shoot dastardly officers in the back once they had them in No Man's Land. I doubt whether much of that ever existed in the British Voluntary Army. At all events Busby, released from detention, was the first to volunteer when I asked for aid in a somewhat sticky task during our first days in the trenches, and I felt no apprehension as to his motive.

Private James Hall, 9th The Royal Fusiliers (City of London Regiment)

If the standard of conduct in my battalion is any criterion, then I can say truthfully that there is very little crime in Lord Kitchener's armies… The 'jankers' or defaulters' squad was always rather large; but the 'jankers men' were offenders against minor points in discipline. Their crimes were untidy appearance on parade, inattention in the ranks, tardiness at roll-call, and others of the sort, all within the jurisdiction of the company officer. The punishment meted out varied according to the seriousness of the offence, and the past-conduct record of the offender. It usually consisted of from one to ten days, 'C.B.' – confined to barracks. During the period of his sentence the offender was forbidden to leave camp after the parades for the day were ended. And in order that he might have no opportunity to do so, he was compelled to answer his name at the guardroom whenever it [his name] should be sounded.

Soon after 9 am, the battalion is drawn up in double rank… and the officers in charge of the various platoons make a rapid but nonetheless thorough inspection of the men's personal appearance and equipment.

    The officer takes between his two fingers one of the buttons on Private John McBull's tunic – very gingerly, as though it were an unclean thing. 'Filthy,' he says, 'simply filthy. If you ever come on parade again with your buttons in this appalling condition, you'll be crimed.'

    The next man – or boy, rather – had a faint, fair down upon his chin. 'Did you shave this morning?' asks the officer. 'No sir, I've never shaved yet in my life. I didn't think I needed to.' 'Don't need to! Good heavens, man, your face is like a gooseberry. You'll be moulting soon. Get shaved at once.'

Private Thomas Lyon, 2/9th The Highland Light Infantry (Glasgow Highlanders)

Looking more like soldiers: men of the 2/6th Gloucestershire Regiment present arms.

At the next man the officer stares aghast, and there is horror in his voice when he speaks. 'Good gracious, sir! You're almost wholly undressed. You're positively indecent. Disgraceful!' The men adjacent squint along to see for themselves the enormity that their comrade has committed in the matter of undress, and discover – that the button on one of his shoulder straps has become unfastened!

Humorous anecdotes aside, there were routine issues of drunkenness and ill discipline amongst old soldiers recalled to the army or amongst those who had chosen to re-enlist. Frederick Keeling came to the conclusion that Reservists in particular should not have been mixed in with inexperienced recruits.

Sergeant Frederick Keeling, 6th The Duke of Cornwall's Light Infantry

It is natural to assume that a sprinkling of veterans will stiffen the quality of a recently recruited fighting force on active service. And on paper it seems an excellent plan to keep a certain number of trained veterans in a new battalion for the purpose of undertaking the work of cooks, pioneers, sanitary squad, etc., and thus enabling the untrained men to be constantly on parade. But in practice these advantages prove to be very doubtful, and, in any case, are counterbalanced by the constant trouble caused by the old soldiers from the disciplinary point of view…

It is not easy for an average young lance-corporal, acting as a section leader after perhaps two months' service, to control effectively two or three rough old soldiers who have come back after five or more years in civil life.

One Reservist and Boer War veteran well known to Private James Hall had never stopped moaning. This individual had grown increasingly tired of army life and of the way the men were ill equipped. In any case, as he often postulated, he was certain it was all for nothing: the battalion would never see action. He had on many occasions threatened to disappear.

A few of these incorrigibles were discharged in disgrace. A few followed the lead of the Boer warrior. After many threats, which we despaired of his ever carrying out, he finally 'greased off'. He was immediately posted as a deserter, but to our great joy was never captured. With the disappearance of the malcontents and incorrigibles the battalion soon reached a high grade of efficiency.

Private James Hall, 9th The Royal Fusiliers (City of London Regiment)

Without the 'incorrigibles' to cause trouble, Sergeant Frederick Keeling was in his element amongst recruits he knew well and, more importantly, understood.

I have had the devil of a week of it as Company Orderly Sergeant. Up any time after 5 am, and tearing about the camp in rain and swamps of mud, warning fatigues and musketry parties, compiling endless rolls and absentee reports, calling rolls, acting as a sort of magistrate's clerk, jailer, and usher rolled into one when men come up for trial at orderly room, etc., in addition to attending orderly parades and being in charge of half a platoon for musketry. You can imagine that I have enjoyed myself. On Friday night we suddenly had field firing put on our company at twelve hours' notice, so I had to rout all our lines out of bed at five o'clock. As a lot of them had been frozen to death pretty well on a motor-lorry when on fatigue at Witley, and had missed most of their grub, they were inclined to grumble, but I am learning how to mix discipline and persuasion, and flatter myself that I got them on parade smarter than the company sergeant-major would have done.

Sergeant Frederick Keeling, 6th The Duke of Cornwall's Light Infantry

I have got to know the roughs in our platoon pretty well, fellows who are in and out of clink regularly for drunkenness and answering back to NCOs, and am rather proud of the fact that I have managed to get on good terms with them and at the same time got some control over them. It's easy enough to deal with the cheekiness of young clerks and mechanics, or relatively easy, but these fellows lie and thieve and fight as part of their everyday life. You never get to the stage of really trusting them, but you can establish working relations with them by expedients which seem almost childish, silly jokes and a kind of assumed (for me) music-hall, pub-loafing heartiness. It's acting, of course, but I have come to feel more and more that all leadership is in a way acting, conscious or unconscious… After a time you become the character you act, whether it is a sergeant in the DCLI, or a popular politician, or a music-hall character, or a barrister. There is very little difference in the quality of any of the parts.

Not every battalion could hope to be efficient or as content, for reasons that became all too transparent to Second Lieutenant Guy Chapman. He had joined the 13th Royal Fusiliers, part of K3, just after Christmas and was deeply unimpressed with what he found. His was a battalion seemingly unloved and in disarray. Here, the malcontents and incorrigibles were not the other ranks, but the officers.

Second Lieutenant Guy Chapman, 13th The Royal Fusiliers

I was shocked with my first contact with the New Army… It was not the men in shabby blue clothes and forage caps with their equipment girt about them with bits of string; it was the obvious incapacity and amateurishness of the whole outfit which depressed. The 13th had been broken off from a swarm of men at the depot some three months earlier, and from then left almost completely to its own devices. It never had more than three regular officers, and those very senior and very retired, two from the Indian Army and not one from the regiment… Below these seniors lay a heterogeneous mass of majors, captains, and subalterns from every walk of life… Many displayed only too patently their intention of getting through the war as quietly, comfortably, and as profitably as they could manage. They effectively discouraged the juniors from demonstrations of excessive zeal and by sheer negation tried to stifle our hunger for information.

Established in the first half of September, the battalion had had plenty of time to build cohesion. Instead, it was undermined by acts of petty jealousy, bickering, and intrigue amongst officers from wildly different backgrounds. As far as Chapman could see, not one officer had any link to the regiment and no sense of its grand historical narrative or exploits of the regiment's Regular battalions had been imparted to build esprit de corps.

Discipline, of course, varies a good deal from one battalion to another in Kitchener's Army as it does, by the way, in the Regular Army, where the differences between English and Irish regiments or between Guards and some of the line regiments are particularly striking. The differences in the New Army are largely due to the personal idiosyncrasies of officers commanding companies and battalions. But they are also attributable to the varying extent to which old Army NCOs are scattered through the new units.

From accounts which I have heard of the more recently formed battalions of Kitchener's Army, I should say that in some respects there is at the present moment less difference from the point of view of discipline and military spirit between the old Regular Army and the First New Army than there is between the First New Army and these new battalions of the later New Armies.

Sergeant Frederick Keeling, 6th The Duke of Cornwall's Light Infantry

Keeling believed that the NCOs in K1 were the pick of the autumn recruits. 'They [were] selected purely on merit, and the field of selection was exceptional in quality and quantity alike.' While admitting he could be regarded as a prejudiced witness, he believed these NCOs would make excellent officers if offered commissions.

A welcome ten-minute rest by the roadside.

In the Royal Fusiliers, Chapman described his fellow officers as a mixture of 'colonial policemen, solicitors, ex-irregulars, planters, ex-rankers, and in three cases pure *chevaliers d'industrie*'. It was unlikely any of these men had known each other pre-war and ironing out differences between them would be slow and painful.

'The new army will be officered with the queerest collection of people outside a menagerie,' wrote 39-year-old Thomas Butler-Stoney after becoming acquainted with officers in the 7th Leinster Regiment in Fermoy, Ireland.

Butler-Stoney was sent to join his battalion, part of K2, discovering that it had struggled to attract recruits. In a letter, he painted a dreary picture of a unit working hard for an identity. 'I am in two rooms at a corner of a great bleak square and there are eight of us. We have a table but no chair and sleep on immense sausages filled with straw.' He did at least know one officer from home, Second Lieutenant Lancelot Studholme.

Second Lieutenant Thomas Butler-Stoney, 7th The Prince of Wales's Leinster Regiment

I found poor Studholme looking most miserable sitting up in bed in a little crowded room that was horribly untidy. He was holding an end of candle in one hand and writing out lists of parades and names. He and his companions were inoculated on Monday against enteric and were all very miserable yesterday. As far as I can see he is the only man in the whole crowd (60 or so) that you'd be likely to mistake for a gentleman.

The battalion had just received several hundred volunteers from Belfast, 'an extraordinary crowd', Butler-Stoney noted, none of whom had yet made it onto a muster roll. Being in effect incognito, they regularly broke out of camp, climbing over a wall and disappearing off into town.

Second Lieutenant Thomas Butler-Stoney, 7th The Prince of Wales's Leinster Regiment

Apparently the Nationalists had promised a certain number and had to send every man they could scrape up – in one room there's a father and son – the son has children married in America – the father is a widower and has his separation allowance sent to his sister one-and-a-half years older than himself, who has been drawing the old age pension for two years. There were two or three cripples too – two enormously fat brothers and a boy of sixteen, all of whom had to be sent home.

Winter weather blew down or flooded bell tents, making rural living not just difficult but untenable. These men of the 2/6th Gloucestershire Regiment have just weathered a typical December storm.

There were cautious reasons for hope. The 'old sergeant' was 'a most pleasant fellow', and an officer, a solicitor from Fermoy, proved 'most respectable and quiet'. Studholme's mood improved too.

'I shall be quite happy,' decided Butler-Stoney on reflection, though in the end he did not remain with the battalion, serving overseas in the Irish Guards. Neither Butler-Stoney nor Studholme survived the war.

Less happy was Guy Chapman. His battalion was in a state of slumber and it would take the enthusiasm of junior officers to wake it up.

Second Lieutenant Guy Chapman, 13th The Royal Fusiliers

Even now I am amazed at the zeal which induced some of us after dinner to push matches representing platoons about the table uttering words of command in hoarse whispers, or on Sunday mornings climb the frosty, wind-cropped downs to practise map-reading and marching by the compass. We had no one to explain things to us. We had to get our textbooks by heart before we could impart a crumb of information to our platoons. We seized on and devoured every fragment of practical experience which came our way, gobbled whole the advice contained in those little buff pamphlets entitled *Notes from the Front*, advice, alas, out of date before it was published. We listened to the lectures of general officers who seemed happier talking of Jubbulpore than of Ypres. We pondered the jargon of experts, each convinced that his peculiar weapon, machine gun, rifle, bayonet, or bomb, was the one designed to bring the war to a satisfactory conclusion. We were inclined to resist their pedantry, suspecting that in truth they knew little more than ourselves; and we – we knew nothing. We were in fact amateurs, and though we should stoutly have denied it, in our hearts amateurs we knew ourselves to be, pathetically anxious to achieve the status of the professional.

* * *

With late autumn, there was a faster, prolonged deterioration in the weather. Living in bell tents turned from fun to forlorn and then quickly to miserable. The 'swamps of mud' Keeling described, the incessant rain and falling temperatures threatened not only morale but also good discipline.

LIVING THE DREAM

It isn't pleasant to awaken from a dream of peace and home and discover that your shoulders are cold and clammy and your blankets sodden. Drip-drip-drip! You move your head slightly and a big drop of water hits you – splosh! – in the eye – and then another – and another. That refreshes you and thoroughly awakens you, and you sit up amid your blankets, and your head strikes the canvas of the tent, and immediately the dripping of rain increases in volume. You put up your hand to the spot where the water is coming through and run it down the canvas so that the water may find a channel to the foot of the tent instead of creating a miniature Niagara just over you. And in doing this you discover that the rain has caused the canvas to tighten considerably.

You wonder if you should bother to rise and go outside and slacken the guy ropes. This course calls for a good deal of courage, for the night air is chilly. You cannot summon up the necessary courage, so you lie still in the hope that somebody else will do the needful. Nobody moves. At last you mutter, 'The selfish pigs! Won't do a thing to help themselves. They'd lie and sleep even if the tent went on fire. Always me that gets the dirty work!' And you rise and stumble over the inanimate forms of your comrades towards the tent flap. It takes you ten minutes to undo this, and you inwardly curse the man who tied it – then suddenly remember that it was yourself, and start to curse the others for lazy, useless dogs.

Immediately you step outside, a sheet of water is shaken from the flap, and gets you on the neck, and it trickles down your spine and you feel mad. A moment later you stub your big toe violently against a tent peg and you feel madder still. Then you trip over a guy-rope and fall heavily against the wet canvas, and immediately there is a loud 'ouch!' from the interior of the tent, and an angry voice asks who the blinkety-blank is playing fool tricks outside. The tent is leaking like a sieve, and the owner of the angry voice is half-drowned and he'll punch your fat head when he gets hold of you, etc., etc. And as you slacken the guy-ropes you think thoughts about man's inhumanity to man, and you are the chief mourner among all the countless thousands who man's inhumanity makes to mourn.

Private Thomas Lyon, 2/9th The Highland Light Infantry (Glasgow Highlanders)

You are cold and wet and miserable, and sleep has forsaken you; yet when you re-enter the tent and awaken your messmates to tell them of your altruism and of the service you have rendered them, they don't seem a bit grateful. And when you descant on your miserable wet condition the only consolation you have thrown at you is, 'Serves ye right. Ye should never hae jined!'

It's a terrible war, this!

The ground around tents, long stripped of grass, changed from delivering up invasive dust clouds in August and September to hosting glutinous cloying mud. In mid-October, the weather broke and while it was not particularly cold, rain came down in torrents and for days on end. By mid-November, the climate was not so much wet as freezing.

After the offer of a commission, and after much prevarication by his commanding officer, George Butterworth was released in November to join the Durham Light Infantry in the 68th Infantry Brigade, arriving at Bullswater camp near Pirbright.

Second Lieutenant George Butterworth, 13th The Durham Light Infantry

The last fortnight has been extremely trying for us all owing to the complete break-up of the weather; one realises now how extremely lucky we have been in this respect. The autumn being exceptionally fine, we have begun to think that after all a winter camp would be quite tolerable, but we do not think so now. Our first catastrophe occurred one very squally evening when a sudden gust of wind carried away four of the largest marquees, burying several men beneath them. The alarm was sounded and we swarmed on to the parade ground, but fortunately no one was hurt.

Soon after this we had a week's cold snap – unusually severe for the time of year, 20 degrees of frost being reported one night. Luckily we escaped snow, but of course hard frost under canvas is no joke.

The battalion was due to move to dry accommodation in Malplaquet Barracks, Aldershot, but the order was delayed.

A rare image taken inside a bell tent in late autumn. The tent looks reasonably full with seven men but occasionally, double this number were squeezed in.

After several false alarms our long-overdue exodus took place on the very last day of November. This was probably just in time to prevent disaster; the last few days were desperate; after the frost broke we had a bad spell of wet, which not only swamped the camp, but penetrated everything inside the tents. For several nights there was hardly a dry blanket to be had, and it is clearly impossible to carry on with that sort of thing indefinitely.

Second Lieutenant George Butterworth, 13th The Durham Light Infantry

Private James Hall, 9th The Royal Fusiliers (City of London Regiment)

Mud was the great reality of our lives, the malignant deity which we fell down [in] and propitiated with profane rites. It was a thin, watery mud or a thick, viscous mud, as the steady downpour increased or diminished. Late in November we were moved to a city of wooden huts at Sandling Junction, to make room for newly recruited units. The dwellings were but half-finished, the drains were open ditches, and the rains descended and the floods came as usual.

Over the autumn, an ambitious programme to erect hundreds of wooden huts had fallen behind schedule. In part, the weather was to blame. Incessant rain led to churned-up construction sites and impassable, unmetalled rural roads, along which materials were ferried. Building supplies were often of inferior quality; seasoned timber was in short supply as were the sheets of galvanised zinc used for roofs. Demand outstripped supply as with everything else, encouraging unscrupulous contractors to cut corners to meet contractual obligations whilst coincidentally improving profits.

Second Lieutenant Arthur Heath, 6th The Queen's Own (Royal West Kent Regiment)

The huts were badly built and not half finished. The rain comes in through the roof and the windows, and the leaks have become worse and worse, till now it rains as fast inside as out in some places, and drips everywhere. Also, it does this every day now for a fortnight. It is a dreadful waste of money over the huts, which we probably shan't be able to occupy till February now – about a month or six weeks before we are sent off to France. But there's really nothing for it. Neither the health nor the morale of the troops can stand against winter in wooden shower baths sunk in a quagmire of mud.

Aggressive recruitment had resulted in a shortage of skilled workers, with the War Office turning to labour exchanges for manpower. The men sent were frequently semi-skilled and liable to down tools in poor weather; shoddy workmanship exacerbated the problems.

On Salisbury Plain, Cecil Langley found a scene of near carnage as workmen frantically tried to assemble accommodation that lacked even basic infrastructure.

Salisbury Plain is a weird sight: no plain at all, but folds and waves of ground for miles, with an occasional square of firs; everywhere are towns of hutments, tents and other buildings on every point of the horizon. Heaven and the War Office only know what countless hosts of soldiers are here. We continually met marching parties and saw others skirmishing and generally 'messing about'.

We finally got to our hutments; wooden buildings about fifty feet long and twenty wide, with thick cardboard for ceiling and wallpaper, and three boards stretched across two low trestles four inches high for each man's bed. Outside is a sea of black toffee, piles of timber, rusting galvanised iron, hundreds of stoves, pipes, and fittings, rotting and rusting, breaking and cracking in a vast filthy welter, hordes of workmen putting up hutments so fast that one turns round to blow one's nose and on facing front again sees another building up! As yet only two taps laid on, and they spring up out of the ground like stuffed snakes erect, covered with frost-proof; but we many only drink thereat, so no one had a wash for two days.

Gunner Cecil Longley, 1st South Midland Brigade, Royal Field Artillery

There was no mud, of course, before the camp was constructed – only dry turf, and wild yellow gorse, and fragrant heather. But the Practical Jokes Department was not to be discouraged by the superficial beauties

Second Lieutenant John Hay Beith, 10th Princess Louise's (Argyll & Sutherland Highlanders)

Winter 1914: a hut under construction. Too many were hastily built using poor quality materials and indifferently skilled labour.

A muddy morass surrounds these huts at an unknown camp. The pressure to rehouse recruits in civilian homes became irresistible by the New Year of 1915.

of nature. They knew that if you crowd a large number of human dwellings close together, and refrain from constructing any roads or drains as a preliminary, and fill these buildings with troops in the rainy season, you will soon have as much mud as ever you require. And they were quite right. The depth varies from a few inches to about a foot. On the outskirts of the camp, however, especially by the horse lines or going through a gate, you may find yourself up to your knees. But, after all, what is mud! Most of the officers have gum-boots, and the men will probably get used to it. Life in K1 is largely composed of getting used to things.

In the more exclusive and fashionable districts – round about the Orderly-room, and the Canteen, and the Guardroom – elevated 'duck-walks' are laid down, along which we delicately pick our way. It would warm the heart of a democrat to observe the ready, nay, hasty, courtesy with which an officer, on meeting a private carrying two overflowing buckets of kitchen refuse, steps down into the mud to let his humble brother-in-arms pass. Where there are no duck-walks, we employ planks laid across the mud. In comparatively dry weather these planks lie some two or three inches below the mud, and much innocent amusement may be derived from trying to locate them. In wet weather, however, the planks float to the surface, and then of course everything is plain sailing. When it snows, we feel for the planks with our feet…

Our parade-ground is a mud-flat in front of the huts. Here we take our stand each morning, sinking steadily deeper until the order is given to move off. Then the battalion extricates itself with one tremendous squelch, and we proceed to the labours of the day.

Matters deteriorated to such an extent that one solution only presented itself to the War Office: move large numbers of men into private billets. Over the winter of 1914/15, around 800,000 men of both the Territorial Force and New Army were shifted to hotels, municipal buildings, and private homes: homeowners were rewarded with generous allowances.

In Hythe on the Sussex coast, George Coppard and his comrades struck lucky in a comfortable private home.

Our landlady, although very old, was a first-rate cook and did all our washing and mending. Having no visitors to attend to, she looked after us as if we were her own sons. I believe she received twenty-six shillings per week for the privates, which was good money then. Christmas Day in the billet was a day to be remembered, with lashings of good food and beer.

Private George Coppard, 6th The Queen's Own (Royal West Surrey Regiment)

In Folkestone, the men of the Royal Fusiliers savoured life in one of the town's most fashionable hotels, the Metropole. The beds were gone but that hardly mattered. It was luxury in comparison with what went before.

To be sure, we slept on bare floors, but the roof was rainproof, which was the essential thing. The aesthetically inclined could lie in their blankets at night, gazing at richly gilded mirrors over the mantelpieces and beautifully frescoed ceilings, refurnishing our apartments in all their former splendour. Private Henry Morgan was not of this type. Henry came in one evening rather the worse for liquor and with clubbed musket assaulted his unlovely reflection in an expensive mirror. I believe he is still paying for his lack of restraint at the rate of a sixpence per day, and will have cancelled his obligation by January 1921.

Private James Hall, 9th The Royal Fusiliers (City of London Regiment)

The men of the Argyll & Sutherland Highlanders arrived in their billeting village 'with kilts swinging, bonnets cocked, and pipes skirling'. They caused something of a sensation amongst the Hampshire residents used to seeing servicemen but not an entire battalion.

Second Lieutenant John Hay Beith, 10th Princess Louise's (Argyll & Sutherland Highlanders)

It was impossible to get the children into school, or the maids to come in and make the beds. Whenever a small boy spied an officer, he stood in his way and saluted him. Dogs enlisted in large numbers, sitting down with an air of pleased expectancy in the supernumerary ranks… When we marched out to our training area later in the day infant schools were decanted on to the road under a beaming vicar, to utter what we took to be patriotic sounds and wave handkerchiefs.

The men quickly settled in, establishing a routine.

Second Lieutenant John Hay Beith, 10th Princess Louise's (Argyll & Sutherland Highlanders)

It is a quarter to nine in the morning. All down the street doors are opening, and men appear, tugging at their equipment. Most of B Company live in this street. They are fortunate, for only two or three are billeted in each little house, where they are quite domestic pets by this time. Their billeting includes 'subsistence', which means that they are catered for by an experienced female instead of a male cooking-class still in the elementary stages of its art.

'A' [Company] are not so fortunate. They are living in barns or hay-lofts, sleeping on the floor, eating on the floor, existing on the floor generally. Their food is cooked in open-air camp-kitchens; and in this weather it is sometimes difficult to keep fires alight, and not always possible to kindle them.

'D' are a shade better off. They occupy a large empty mansion at the end of the street. It does not contain a stick of furniture; but there are fireplaces, and the one thing of which the War Office never seems to stint us is coal. So 'D' are warm, anyhow. Thirty men live in the drawing-room. Its late tenant would probably be impressed with its new upholstery.

The new upholstery was nothing more than scores of straw palliasses. Above, strung across the room were improvised clotheslines on which hung washed clothing. It was private accommodation, better than leaky huts or tents, though not quite the sought-after private home.

Men of the Territorial Force arriving in Hoddesdon, Hertfordshire, to be housed with civilian families.

5th Notts & Derby going into billets, Feb 1915.

Many householders laid down strict ground rules before offering a bed. William Andrews' only experience of billeting came shortly before he went overseas, being housed in one of the wealthier villages on the edge of Dundee. Indoors, it was left to a member of staff to ensure all knew where they stood.

I was exceptionally fortunate, being treated as an honoured guest by a most gracious hostess, but I had a jolt from the start. A sharply-spoken maid said: 'if you're coming in here, soldier, you've got to be clean. You can have as many baths as you like, but if we find you dirty, out you go.' Happily, I passed Minnie's test of cleanliness, and within a day or two the good girl was insisting on cleaning my rifle and equipment for me.

Private William Andrews, 2/4th The Black Watch (Royal Highlanders)

The Specials [policemen] with an officer, took men from each platoon off to billets. Sixteen, including my friend Private Place, went to a large boarding house, they were lucky there. The owners had a lovely daughter! (Later, I used to call to see if the lads were going out, but I couldn't get them away from the place!) Private McGoughlin and myself went two doors away to the finest confectioners in Caernarvon. We were lucky as well. To get to our room we went through the shop, past trays of pies and cakes. We could just put our hands in and help ourselves. It was marvellous!

Private George Pollard, 11th The East Lancashire Regiment (Accrington)

Not everyone was so generous. Norman Ellison joined a Territorial battalion of the King's Liverpool Regiment and was sent to Canterbury. Ellison with one other was pointed to the house of a woman whose husband was serving in Egypt.

Rifleman Norman Ellison, 1/6th The King's (Liverpool Regiment)

She did not want anybody billeted on her and we were not welcome. A series of incidents brought matters to a head when we found the bolts of our rifles were full of jam. She said her child had done it. We wondered but were moved to the house of [an] old cobbler.

Ellison's reception was not untypical as soldiers found front doors were slammed in their faces. In leafy Epsom, two privates met a landlady with folded arms and a firm invitation to go away. 'I don't want you,' she had said. Tired and hungry, the men barged their way into the house regardless.

> [We] installed ourselves in the kitchen, where the hostess reluctantly produced bread and onions. My companion and I, ignoring her, talked together for five minutes, when the lady, who had been regarding us with suspicion and hostility changing to bewilderment, suddenly broke in with 'Are you volunteers?' We agreed. 'Oh,' (with intense relief), I thought you were common soldiers!'

Pre-war suspicion of soldiers persisted, a view that only eased with all-class mass voluntary enlistment. Tellingly, old soldiers could be amongst the most hesitant to help, as Norman Ellison discovered in Whitstable.

Rifleman Norman Ellison, 1/6th The King's (Liverpool Regiment)

Patriotism undergoes an acid test when there comes a knock on your door and without warning, you are asked to provide a billet for two strange soldiers. We waited in the road whilst Captain Wainwright, O/C 'B' Company, and the billeting sergeant knocked at each door and allocated one or two men there. When it came to our turn a grey bearded man with the South African campaign medals pinned to his dressing gown, an ex-army surgeon, replied to the billeting officer's request. 'I shall be proud to have soldiers in my house, Captain, provided they are clean men who will not spit upon the wallpaper.' The soldiers he knew of old were regular 'swaddies' of Rudyard Kipling fame; fine tough fighting men but unvarnished. The war was still young and the idea of educated civilian soldiers unknown to him.

Ellison's battalion had arrived at very short notice after being 'whisked out of bed about midnight', packed into a train and sent to dig defensive trenches outside the town by lantern-light. There were warnings that a seaborne invasion was likely, and men were needed to prepare for the worst. By the morning, there was an urgent need for accommodation and Whitstable's residents were challenged to meet the demand.

There were inevitable frictions between soldiers and their civilian hosts, but billeting usually worked extremely well. An officer of the 8th The King's Own Scottish Borderers enjoys the comforts of his temporary home.

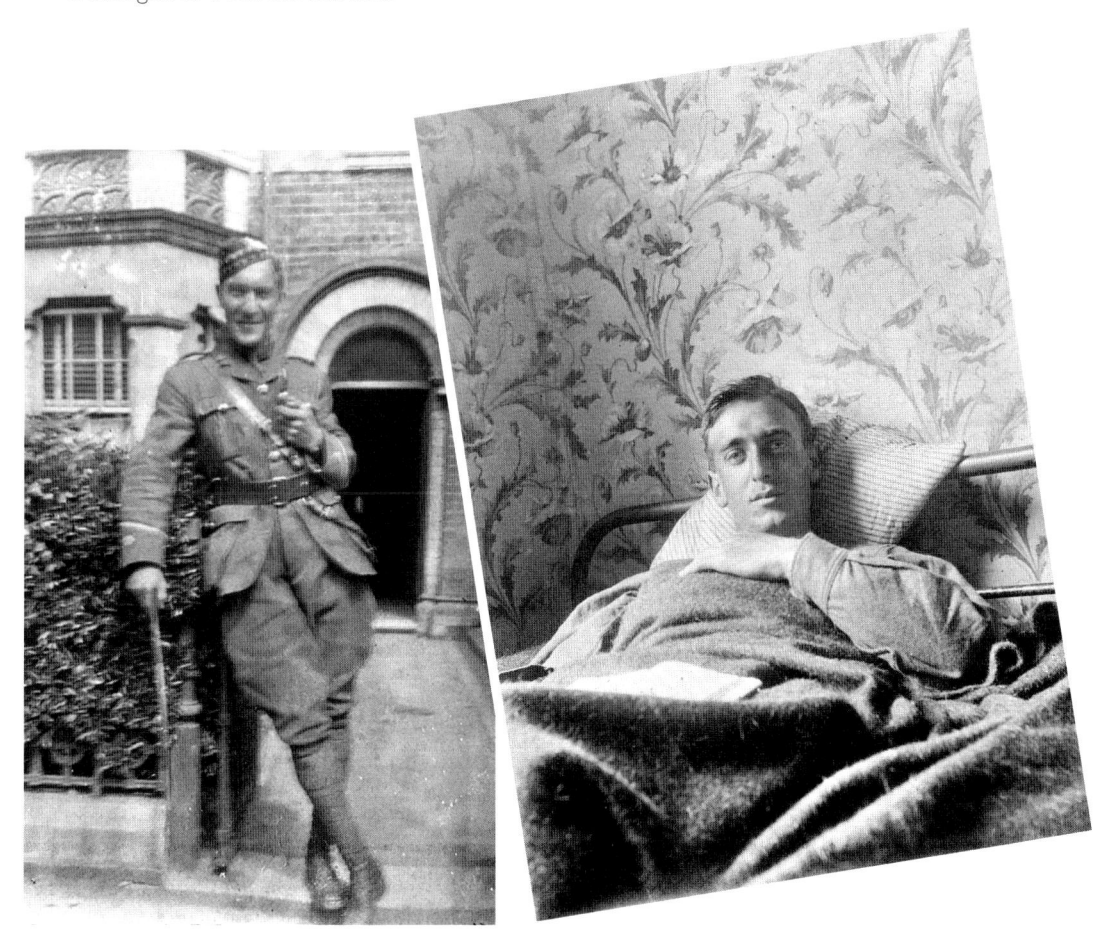

Rifleman Norman Ellison, 1/6th The King's (Liverpool Regiment)

Dr C. was an eccentric who thought teetotalism a vice. On his sideboard was a large jug of whisky and milk, frequently emptied but as quickly replenished. We stayed there several days to complete the defence works on the front. On the night before we left, he asked us to invite a few of our friends to an oyster feast. Ten crowded round a table on which was a mammoth meat platter heaped high with oysters. 'There's just one thing boys, before we start,' he said, 'all the empty shells must be thrown in the firegrate.' With ten fellows pitching empty shells into the fireplace, the picture of the shambles that ensued I leave to your imagination.

In Sussex and in Hampshire, George Coppard and John Hay Beith were fortunate to find landladies happy to look after soldiers and cook their meals. Whether the food was the landladies' own for which they were reimbursed, or the army's rations taken by the men to their billets is not clear, for it could have been either.

Rifleman Norman Ellison, 1/6th The King's (Liverpool Regiment)

The daily distribution of rations to hundreds of men billeted, rarely more than two in a house, amongst dozens of streets became one of those knotty problems to which no satisfactory solution was ever discovered. 'Raw' rations were issued to each man, so many ounces of this, so many ounces of that. Any fine day the same scene was enacted in a dozen streets; a handcart laden with rations, and on the pavement a worried corporal and two men subdividing the meat, the butter, the bread, and even the pepper and salt, into a number of small heaps, each for a particular house. To apportion one tin of jam between five men living in three houses was a puzzle usually solved by the spinning of a coin.

There was another alternative and that was for all men to eat at a cookhouse rather than in billets. No system was perfect, though the cookhouse avoided confusion over distribution or unequal portions. Nevertheless, it was usually the least popular option for soldiers living in private accommodation.

There were obvious downsides to dispersing men amongst a civilian population, away from the hub of a barracks or camp. In the artillery, Captain Street noted the loss of time as men went to and fro between billet and depot, and that lax discipline became commonplace. Recruits were late for training and some men could not be bothered to turn up at all. In poor weather and with a long walk to the depot, anyone still in civilian clothes could hardly escape a soaking and had no opportunity to change at the end of this journey.

There was practically only one offence, that of absence without leave and it became an acute problem as to how to deal with it. Obviously an extremely serious military crime, it had in the previous experience of the recruits been no offence at all, merely an indulgence involving a shortage of pay at the end of the week. Naturally, it was almost impossible to convey to their minds this sudden change of their conditions, and the infliction of 'Field Punishment', which corresponds to imprisonment, was undoubtedly too severe a penalty for a New Army recruit. Yet some deterrent had to be found. Confinement to barracks, when three-quarters of the offenders were in billets a mile or so away, was obviously a farce. The best solution of the difficulty appeared to be deprivation of pay and a warning that a second offence would involve a term of Field Punishment.

Captain Cecil Street, Royal Garrison Artillery

The humour of the defaulters' hour lay in the amazing excuses offered to account for the absence, in all fervent earnestness. The average recruit was so appalled by the unwanted experience of being marched in before the CO under the protection of an escort that he was utterly tongue-tied, and only after much persuasion could he be induced to stammer out a few words of exculpation. Under these circumstances there could be no doubt of the genuineness of his excuses, and I have heard men state perfectly seriously that they had stopped to help their landlady in her washing, that it was too wet to come on parade, that they had felt tired, or that they had an appointment to keep.

But the darkest days of all were those upon which were held periodical muster parades… It often happened that the number of men on parade and the number of attestation papers in the office failed to tally. Then a muster parade was decided upon, a party was sent to hunt in every nook and corner to round up the last laggard, and the whole Depot in its unwieldiness would be assembled on parade. Then would begin the search for No. 44272 Gunner John Smith, whose papers lay in the office, but of whose body no trace could be found. After much investigation it would transpire that No. 44272 Gunner John Smith had gone on a draft to Bantry Bay a fortnight ago in the place of No. 42857 Gunner John Smith, both of them having blissfully forgotten their numbers. Then ensued much recrimination, and frantic correspondence with Bantry Bay.

Whenever large numbers of soldiers descended on a district, curiosity amongst the host population was piqued – for a while. Heavy regional accents could be startling and in leafy Hampshire, Scottish soldiers may as well have come from another continent.

Second Lieutenant John Hay Beith, 10th Princess Louise's (Argyll & Sutherland Highlanders)

The language was a difficulty, of course; but a great deal can be done by mutual goodwill and a few gestures. It would have warmed the heart of a philologist to note the success with which a couple of kilted heroes from the banks of Loch Lomond would sidle up to the giggling damosels of Hampshire at the corner of the High Street by the post office and invite them to come for a walk. Though it was obvious that neither party could understand a single word that the other was saying, they never failed to arrive at an understanding.

Second Lieutenant John Hay Beith had placed a positive sheen on differences between soldiers and civilians. In Bedford, Private Alex Runcie, serving with the Gordon Highlanders, recalled a slightly different atmosphere.

Private Alex Runcie, 1/6th The Gordon Highlanders

When we got to know folks well, they told us they were a bit alarmed when they heard that a kilted army was to be quartered on them. They had visions of all kinds of savages armed with claymores descending on them. One girl of my acquaintance, who worked as a manageress in a laundry, told me her boss had called together all the employees and painted a truly bloodthirsty picture of us, and a warning not to mix. We hadn't been there long before they realised we were quite law-abiding people like themselves. One girl asked me if I didn't feel the cold at night on the hills with only my plaid to cover me while sleeping. Another, knowing the house we were quartered in, remarked that the bath in it would be a great surprise for us never having seen one before.

Until trust was established, it was wise for homeowners to be prudent, especially those who had daughters. Yet on the whole, Kitchener's men, so recently civilians themselves, much preferred fun to confrontation.

The River Exe was quite near the town and a great meeting place for the public who liked yatching or rowing and even skiffs and canoes.

Frank and I had many a good time on the river: we would tie our rowing boat to the bank near a farmhouse where we could have our

Two privates belonging to the 1/4th The Essex Regiment leaving their billet, possibly in Norwich. The chalk inscription to the right of the door shows that this house would be willing to take three soldiers from the battalion's D Company.

Private Albert Knight, 87 Brigade, Royal Field Artillery

Men of the Royal Army Medical Corps attempt some impromptu fishing.

tea, and there was always apple jelly and thick Devonshire cream to follow. I have never tasted anything like it since and the best of it was they would rarely take any money for it.

[One time] we took two girls in a rowing boat up the river when a large salmon leapt out of the water and dropped into the rear of our boat. The two girls were terrified as the salmon swayed the boat with his struggles to get back into the water. The girls stood up on the seat which did not improve matters, and while I was trying to beat the salmon with my oar, one of the girls fell overboard. Eventually I managed to beat the salmon insensible while Frank got the girl back into the boat.

We were just going to pull in to the bank when a man ran along the bank opposite and shouted to us to throw the fish back into the water and that he was a river attendant and that we must not take the salmon away. I was for doing what the man said, but Frank had different ideas and told me to row as hard as we could up the river. The man followed, running along the river bank shouting all the time, when Frank guided the boat to the opposite side to the man and jumped out, telling the girls to run through a nearby wood and told me to grab the salmon and between us we hurried after the girls, leaving the boat drifting on the river. We managed to lose ourselves in the wood and so did the girls as well, for we did not see them again, and probably they were glad to see the back of us. Frank suggested that we hide the salmon in some green leaves under a tree and come back later with something to carry it in so that it would not be seen by anyone.

In Canterbury, Norman Ellison found his next accommodation more to his satisfaction and his housekeeper, an old cobbler by the name of Cooper, extremely genial as well as a consummate poacher.

He was a character in every sense of the word. He had a dog, a lurcher, with more brains than many a human being. Very early on a Sunday morning, Cooper, the dog, and I would go out poaching. I knew nothing about the game, but that dog needed no instructing. Cooper would set a net at some gap in a hedge or under a gate across the regular path of a hare, and the dog would go into the field and drive the hare into it. Then back in the keen autumn air to breakfast followed by a thorough spruce-up for church parade at the Cathedral.

<small>Rifleman Norman Ellison, 1/6th The King's (Liverpool Regiment)</small>

Any novelty would wear off. Over time, civilians got used to soldiers and the gratifying attention of parents and children dwindled. Soldiering was a chore of endless repetition in the main, soldiers knew it and so in the end did civilians.

We fall in for our labours in comparative solitude, usually in heavy rain and without pomp. We have been worked desperately hard for more than four months; we are grunting doggedly away at our job, not because we like it, but because we know it is the only thing to do. To march, to dig, to extend, to close; to practise advance-guards and rear-guards and pickets, in fair weather or foul, often with empty stomachs – that is our daily and sometimes our nightly programme. We are growing more and more efficient, and our powers of endurance are increasing. But as already stated, we no longer go about our task like singing birds.

<small>Second Lieutenant John Hay Beith, 10th Princess Louise's (Argyll & Sutherland Highlanders)</small>

<small>Overleaf: *An unknown infantry battalion on the march across snow-covered hills.*</small>

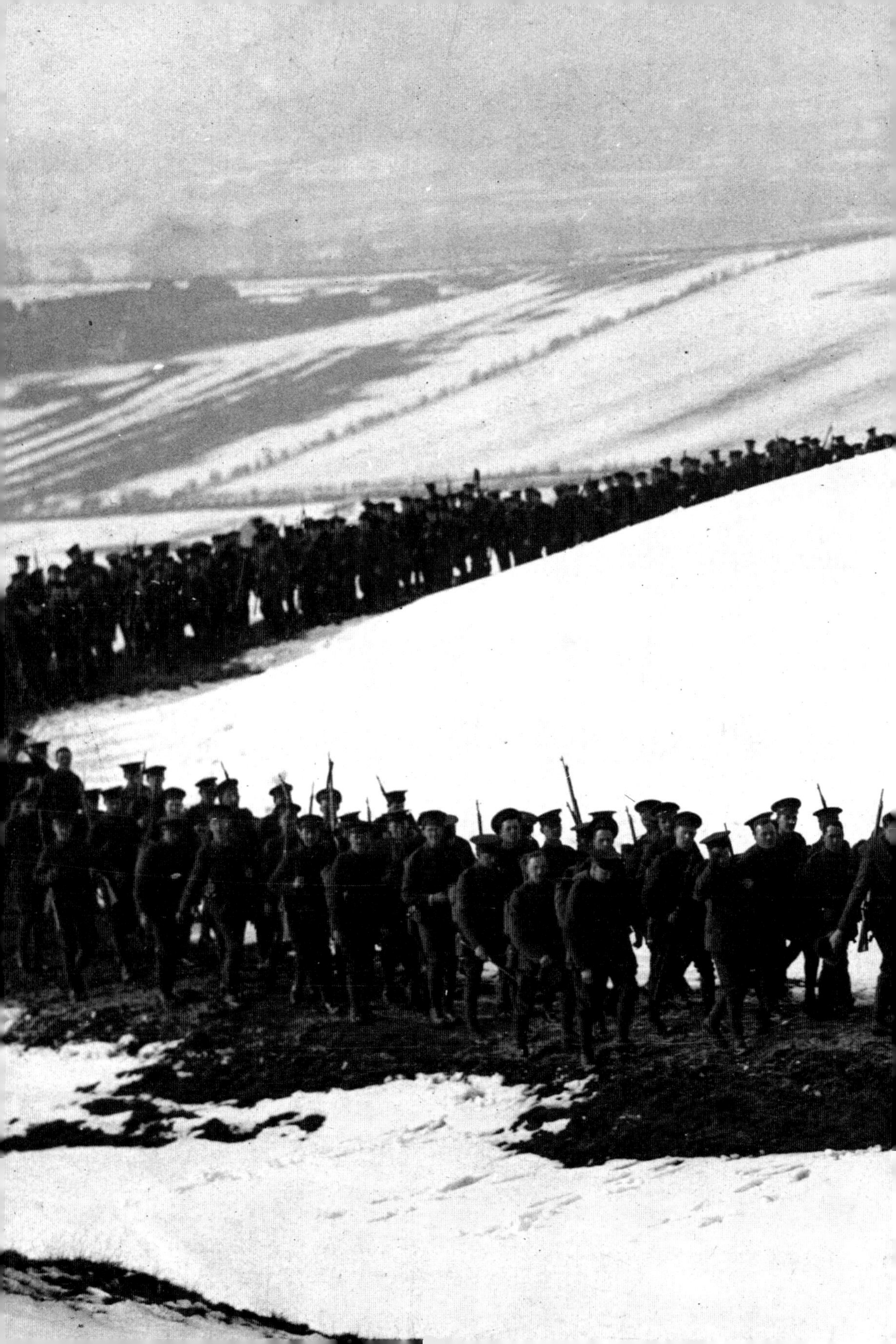

9 Winter Blues

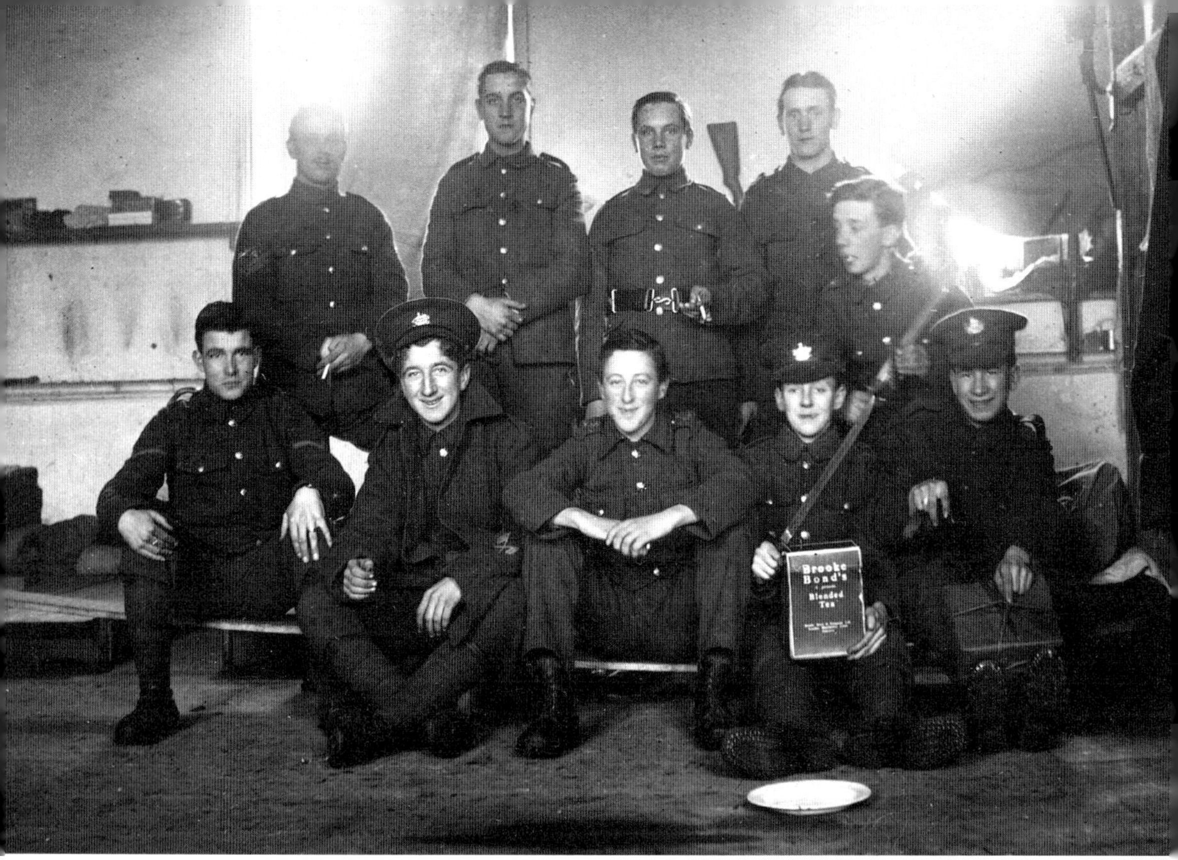
Brooke Bond's
Blended Tea

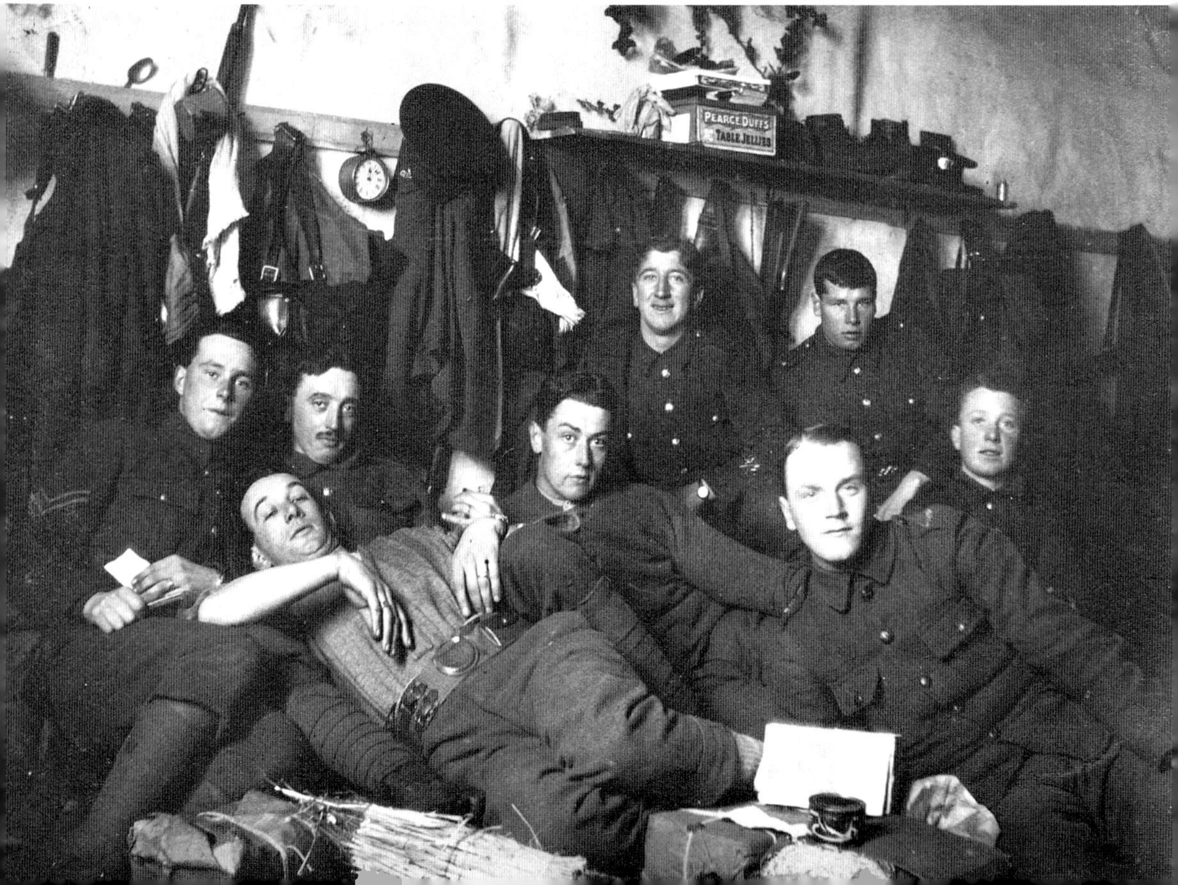
PEARCE DUFF'S
TABLE JELLIES

> 'The glorious splash of patriotic fervour which launched us on our way has subsided; we have reached mid-channel, and the haven where we would be is still afar off.'
>
> Second Lieutenant John Hay Beith, 10th Princess Louise's
> (Argyll & Sutherland Highlanders)

The first Christmas of the War and its companion Scots festival, Hogmanay, brought us much hospitality. Our company had its Christmas dinner at Carolina Port, on the Tay. It was the usual stew, but an English officer Lieutenant Gladstone, a kinsman of the great statesman, provided Christmas pudding. Our real feasting was on Hogmanay, which we had turkey bridies (Scots for pies), Christmas pudding, and beer. It was all very well, but the effect of goodwill was spoiled by the fact that armed sentries were placed at the doors to keep us in. Hogmanay was celebrated with much drinking by many Scots people in those days…

Soon after this I was given a long weekend leave, which I spent in Glasgow seeing old Yorkshire friends. I went off very early in the morning and had breakfast on the train. When I was halfway through my bacon and eggs a naval officer came in. He said nothing to me, but told the attendant that he must turn me out, since an officer could not have breakfast in the same dining-car as a lance-corporal. The attendant was a little sarcastic. 'Couldn't he really, sir?' he said. Thereupon he came over to me and said: 'Come into the kitchen, Jock. I'll give you the finest breakfast there you ever had.' Nor would he let me pay for it.

Lance Corporal William Andrews, 2/4th The Black Watch (Royal Highlanders)

Opposite: Two photographs taken on Christmas Day capture men of the 2/6th Gloucestershire Regiment cradling presents sent from home. They are billeted in a requisitioned tower at St Osyth Priory, Essex.

Gunner Cecil Longley, 1st South Midland Brigade, Royal Field Artillery, 1 January 1915

Last Saturday I gave myself an afternoon and evening holiday with some congenial souls – in London. And what a delight it was to get into life once more, to go to a theatre and sit in a decent seat amongst ladies and gentlemen in evening dress and imagine I had mine on too! I wondered what horror would have been depicted on their faces had they seen us a few hours before, or better still a few hours after on 'The Plain' legs, boots, and overcoat indistinguishable in mud, splashes of mud on faces, hands, and hats, and generally very dishevelled-looking and dirty. I wonder if any of them we saw that night happened by chance to be motoring on Salisbury Plain three days afterwards and saw a lot of revoltingly dirty Tommies; if so I should have loved to call out, 'Hi, I sat next to you in the orchestra stalls at the Aldwych on Saturday night.' Tableau vivant in expressions.

One seems to live two lives: one that of a flounderer in mud and rain with the ever-present aroma of horse 'temporarily-attached'; the other, occasional squirmings out of the mud like a worm on to the green grass of life again, when self-respect asserts itself with a feeling of I'm-as-good-as-you-and-be-blowed-to-you sort of feeling when you see a clean collar and white spats.

Step into the train again and gradually the old feeling comes on… it is quite a pleasure to feel a soldier again. And after all you cannot get far away from the soldier in London. In the daytime your hand aches with saluting officers, and at night khaki is sprinkled pretty freely over the theatres and foodmongers' and drinkwrights' establishments, to remind you of the steel and khaki ring which encloses London, with its radius of thirty miles and circumference of – well, work it out yourselves (3.14 by 30*)!

It looks strange to see a peaceful [London] park with a huge gun emplacement thirty feet high in the middle of it, and with a grey anti-aircraft gun craning its neck up at the skies therefrom, and at nighttime from the same place, and from the top of the gates and other points, moving shafts of light keep stabbing the darkness in all directions, watching over the seven millions who grope in semi-obscurity beneath, cursing – with the quick forgetfulness and wholly self-centred priggishness of the British man-in-the-street – the War

Office that restricts the lighting and illumination of shop windows. I'd love to take such a man for a midnight tramp on Salisbury Plain, where you positively push against the darkness, and certainly stub your toes on a hillock or jar your knees in a hole sixty times to the hour.

* * *

With a million and more men under arms, unintentional injuries and deaths were inevitable. As men drew bayonets, threw bombs, or undertook live firing on the ranges, there were bound to be accidents. And with hitherto out of shape men challenged to exert themselves in the search for fitness, there would be deaths from heat exhaustion or over-exertion. Sadly, not all fatalities were through misfortune: occasionally, rank neglect took more. On 22 January, the 9th, 14th, 15th, 20th and 23rd Divisions gathered on Epsom Downs to be reviewed by Lord Kitchener, accompanied by the French Minister of War, Alexandre Millerand. Hours before these two men arrived, the soldiers were taken from their camps to stand and wait in sub-zero, blizzard conditions.

22 January 1915: thousands of men wait for Lord Kitchener's inspection on a day of appalling weather.

Second Lieutenant Ian Melhuish, 7th Prince Albert's (Somerset Light Infantry), 23rd Division

The official cars arrive but already men were succumbing to the bitter weather, with scores passing out. The men remembered the day as one of unmitigated misery.

Of course the roads were awful, thick slush and mud, and naturally everyone had their boots full of water. Long before we had completed the seven miles to the [parade] ground most of us were wet to the skin in spite of macks and coats. Well, we got to the parade ground at 1.20 pm. Kitchener did not turn up till 4 pm and then he only went by in a closed car and we did not see him. Those two and a half hours standing in water and slush over our ankles, wet through with a biting wind, driving sleet, and heavy rain against you all the time, was about the nearest attempt at hell I have so far experienced. We could not move about much as we were in review order. The only recreation and amusement we had was to count the people who fainted and had to be carried out. The engineers won with thirty-two, our company had eight only.

The scandal was that [thousands of] men had been brought out seven miles from home with one small ambulance wagon to hold six.

The remainder had to lie in the slush, some almost covered, until help arrived. Of course, some suffered from exposure, fortunately only two died.

Our horses kept slipping and several fell. No one was allowed overcoats. Out hats looked like iced cakes. When we arrived, thousands of infantry were already forming up. Our four brigades of artillery formed up in front with us subalterns in front of our sections. There we sat with swords drawn for one and three quarter hours. The snow melted down our necks into our breeches, and out of our knees. The horses got very cold. Mine was shivering so I kept banging my legs against his sides in an attempt to warm both him and my legs. At last, two cars swept past in front of us with Kitchener and company. They did not stop and the parade was over. We shoved off, stiff with cold and rather deflated… We received a general order yesterday congratulating the Division on its turn out and steadiness in the adverse conditions, and that it had made a favourable impression on some big pot of a French General whom Kitchener had brought to see the New Army in training.

Second Lieutenant Julian Tyndale-Biscoe, Royal Horse Artillery, 14th Division

Those camped nearest the review marched 3 miles to the rendezvous, Julian Tyndale-Biscoe rode 7 miles. Private John Jackson of the Cameron Highlanders recorded that his battalion covered 9 miles from Bramshott Camp, not forgetting the 9 they marched back.

We marched in the fiercest of winter weather. We carried no greatcoats, although snow fell all day, and for three hours we stood waiting, numb and cold, for our visitors. Many a poor beggar fainted under the trying ordeal, and was carried off on a stretcher. Through the stampeding of an officer's charger, we were treated to a fine exhibition of horsemanship on the part of our transport officer, an ex-Canadian rancher, who succeeded in rounding up the runaway in true cowboy fashion, after an exciting chase on the common, to the cheers of 20,000 onlookers. Our struggle back to Bramshott through a foot of snow comes back to my memory as clearly as if it happened yesterday.

Private John Jackson, 6th The Queen's Own Cameron Highlanders, 15th Division

In Scotland, a similar inspection played out with thousands of men parading before their divisional general.

Colonel J. Craig, 2/6th Princess Louise's (Argyll & Sutherland Highlanders)

We were inspected and minutely overhauled by the General Officer Commanding the 2/1st Highland Division, and I don't think that any of us enjoyed this function. We paraded at Ferguslie Park amidst deep snow, and were kept shivering for two hours after the appointed time of assembly owing to the General having been taken by his staff to the wrong destination. The result was that the men naturally did not appear to the best advantage, and the Inspecting Officer, irritated by his lengthy tour in search of us, was not in a temper sufficiently good to overlook minor deficiencies. One looks back on these little troubles now with mild amusement and sympathy for the mental attitude of General Officers who objected to the khaki greatcoats being slightly different in shade; were annoyed at the men when halted shivering in the icy blast; and who expressed themselves in tones of strong disapproval when a long-suffering adjutant failed to quite close his heels while standing at attention in snow a foot deep. Colonel Douglas Dick did his best for us on this, as on other occasions, but these fiery Divisional veterans of the old school of spit and polish often failed, I think, to realise what the training of modern armies really involved.

* * *

Of all the army's repetitive tasks perhaps the dullest was guard duty, and guard duty at night was especially grim, above all in winter.

Private Thomas Lyon, 2/9th The Highland Light Infantry (Glasgow Highlanders)

As a child I had a profound veneration for a military sentry. I admired him and longed to change places with him… He seemed such a romantic and picturesque figure – keeping watch and ward over others while they slept, and all that.

Then, between two and four o'clock on one bitterly cold winter's morning, I found myself carrying a loaded rifle with fixed bayonet, marching up and down a deserted stretch of railroad track that runs alongside the local gasworks, and somehow the romance and quixotic picturesqueness of the job didn't just strike me very hard. I was principally impressed by the fact that my occupation was a very cold and cheerless one.

Rain, rain, and wind, and yet more rain. Water lying in large sheets all over the horse lines two inches deep alternated with mud banks, where the feet slip in over the ankles. Rain running down the rifle, and trickling along the forearm; rain trickling from your cap down your neck and spine; rain sopping through your overcoat, tunic, and shirt, till your body is a wet pack; rain swishing off the trees in broad sheets, and then – the irony of it – a sharp voice breaks in through the everlasting swish and slush of water. 'Guard at the water trough, is all well?'

You advance swampily into the dark impenetrable wall of night, and answer, perhaps with an inward sardonic laugh, 'All's well.' Silence again, broken only by the eternal swishing sound. Would that a German would only come and try to poison the water! It would be a welcome relief to challenge and shoot at something, and hear the tinkle of glass as his spectacles caved in!

After an hour or so of walking up and down in the darkness I prayed that somebody, anybody, would come along, so that I might voice a challenge and break the silent monotony of my vigil. A sleety drizzle added to my discomfort, which was further accentuated by contrast with the cheery, inviting blink of a few scattered lights that still relieved the blackness of the sleeping town.

Freezing weather made life in huts miserable. Over 800,000 recruits were eventually billeted on civilians over the winter of 1914/15.

Gunner Cecil Longley, 1st South Midland Brigade, Royal Field Artillery

Private Thomas Lyon, 2/9th The Highland Light Infantry (Glasgow Highlanders)

Occasionally an unusual sound fell on my ears and made me all alertness and attention, but it proved to be merely arising from the operations in progress within the gasworks. I resumed my pacing to and fro.

A few minutes later a splash of light was visible in the gloom far down the railroad track. It drew nearer with a slightly swinging motion, and footsteps were heard. – 'Halt! Who come there?' – The sound of footsteps ceased, and a voice came, 'Corporal of the Guard with relief.' – 'Advance one and be recognised.' – The figure with the lanthorn [lamp] approached, and when I had satisfied myself that it was indeed the Corporal, the others were allowed to advance. I detailed the duties of the post to the relief sentry, and, having fallen in behind the other sentries who had similarly been relieved, we were marched back to the guardroom. This was a large room ordinarily used as a cloakroom and washroom by the employees of the gasworks, and it boasted a big open fireplace that was now heaped high with red, glowing coals. Two benches and a table comprised the sole furniture of the room, and the former were drawn up close to the fire, and thereon the members of the guard, still harnessed with their full equipment, sat and toasted themselves.

Each member of a guard usually has two hours on sentry duty and four off, but during the time that he is off he must retain his full equipment and have his rifle at hand, and be ready to turn out the moment an alarm is given by any of the sentries, the guard is not supposed to sleep while in the guardroom, but the rule is somewhat relaxed, and while at least one man must necessarily remain awake and alert, the others are usually permitted by the Sergeant in charge to lie down and snatch a few hours' sleep between their spells of sentry duty.

Gunner Cecil Longley, 1st South Midland Brigade, Royal Field Artillery

'Two o'clock! Come on, next relief, gerrup. You lazy blighter' – thus the Corporal of the guard addressed a recumbent figure, one of four that lay huddled, but fully dressed with overcoat, bandolier, and spurs on; three rustled themselves sleepily into more comfortable positions in the straw, while the fourth, with a wide-awakeness that comes only with practice, snatched up his rifle and cap, and prepared to be escorted to his post by the Corporal, who would return with the relieved sentry.

'Gosh! What a filthy night,' said the gunner, as they slashed their way along in the snow-covered mud. Snow was falling fast and steadily in big crown-piece flakes, so thickly that the two groping blindly almost bumped into the sentry.

'Anything to report?' 'Nothing, Corporal.' 'Right then, sentries pass, about turn, quick march!' and off went the Corporal and the old sentry to the primitive but blessed shelter of the guard hut, leaving the new one 'packing' his upturned collar with his handkerchief to prevent the snow from melting down his neck. 'Rotten game this,' he had been saying only a few hours before to a fellow-guard, 'Why don't they send us abroad if we *are* going, and not keep us messing about a wretched little English hamlet? We're doing no good here.'

Snow was still falling, till the sentries' own footsteps of a minute before were obliterated. Three o'clock had just sounded thickly from the little church, followed by a quite audible Ting-ting-ting from some clock in a cottage nearby, when the sentry thought he saw something move along the dark line of hedge in front of him; but then on night duty you so often do see things move when staring fixedly at them – even a two-ton gun will change its shape, or a bush turn into the similitude of a man that you could swear is moving. The only way to tell is to turn your eyes elsewhere for a moment, and then suddenly flick them back on the object.

Not all the guards are so lonely as that of the gasworks. For instance, the man doing sentry-go before the Post Office in the early hours of the evening has quite a lively time. Friends and acquaintances are constantly passing, and, though he may not speak to them, the mere sight of their

Standing guard in the snow.

Private Thomas Lyon, 2/9th The Highland Light Infantry (Glasgow Highlanders)

faces does him good. And in any case much may happen without a word being spoken. It is credibly reported that Jimmy Shaughnessy, while on guard at the Post Office one night, introduced himself to a young lady, and arranged a date – hour, and place of meeting with her – and all without uttering a syllable; simply by expressive movements of his lower eyelid. You may not believe the story: you don't need to, unless you care. But I myself believe it – because I know Shaughnessy.

Lieutenant Andrew Buxton, 6th The Rifle Brigade

I wrote you a card yesterday and told you that I was on Orderly duty, or rather supernumerary for the purpose of learning the job. The day was extremely strenuous as I did not get to bed till 6 am (so till 11.30 today I have slept). The Orderly duty consisted of at 12 (noon) attending Commanding Officer's orders, i.e. Col. D. for seeing defaulters, after which going round to the three hospitals and seeing all 6th R.B. in the wards had all they wanted, then to the prison. After lunch I saw the start of a football match of the 6th v. Crew of HMS *Albermarle*, then to the parade square to see drills were all right. At 4 to mounting the Guard on Alma Road and sending them to their different stations; at 5.30 a tour round to the six kitchens – one to each Company – to see everything was clean and in order. The men, or as they are called 'Riflemen', are billeted and fetch their meals from the kitchens. From these to the QMS store to supervise the giving out of rations for 24 hours. Everything of course is exact measurement… At 9.30 pm dismissing the Orderly Sergeants, at 10 dismissing the billet patrol. The billet patrol goes to all billets and sees the men are in. At 12.15 a long trudge round till 2.15 to the three guard pickets outside the town – a very muddy and difficult walk and extremely dark night, challenged of course by all sentries en route. Turned out and inspected each guard and questioned sentries on their duties. They are all instructed to look out for pigeons – one described looking out for 'pigeon-carriers'! He may or may not have known what was meant! Probably the authorities do not know what it means to see a pigeon in the dark! At 4.15 am a similar inspection of the three guards in the town, then to bed at 6 am.

The sentries are on all day but are doubled at night. It is divided into three watches, one per officer, 9–12 the nicest, then 12–3, then 3–6. I had 3 till 6 last night. The other officer on duty just before me woke me up at 3 0'clock in the morning and I sallied forth into an absolutely deserted Chelmsford about 3.30 in pouring rain.

I visited the nine sentries on duty at the main station where we are quartered and had great difficulty in finishing them all. Then I went off on a bicycle to another station about a quarter of a mile away at the other end of town, and inspected the sentries there: from there I went to another station at Broomfield, about a mile away: then home again at about a quarter to five.

I went to sleep again at 5.30, but I kept most of my clothes on and had to sleep on the floor in my Wolseley valise, which had no mattress, rug or anything. Luckily I had my greatcoat, but it was very cold.

Second Lieutenant Graham Greenwell, 1/4th The Oxford and Buckinghamshire Light Infantry

Wednesdays and Saturdays were half-holidays, but in case we should be pining for something to do on these afternoons, we had to set to immediately after dinner and wet-scrub all the tables and benches, although all that had already been done the same morning, as it was every day. The room orderlies (known as 'swabs') were appointed daily in rotation, four at a time, and in addition to all the duties already mentioned they had to fetch the food from the cookhouse, clean and wash down the tables after meals, wash up the dishes, etc. They also had to carry all meals to any sport belonging to the squad who happened to be languishing in the guardroom at the time, and generally act as hewers of wood and drawers of water to all the others. I must say though that any man who had a moment to spare always gave the swabs a hand. These poor swabs on their day at that duty had to turn out to all parades with the rest of the squad. I had several shots at it myself, and I know it's not easy.

Guardsman Douglas Cuddeford, Scots Guards

The men might feel ready to deploy overseas, but whilst the basics had been embedded, chores learnt to an art, fine-tuning was still needed. Work might seem repetitive and infinitely dull, but only continuous acts of preparation would bring men to a state of combat readiness.

Second Lieutenant John Hay Beith, 10th Princess Louise's (Argyll & Sutherland Highlanders)

Today the pickless squad are lined up a short distance away by the relentless Captain Wagstaffe, and informed – 'You are under fire from that wood. Dig yourselves in!'

Digging oneself in is another highly unpopular fatigue. First of all you produce your portable entrenching-tool – it looks like a combination of a modern tack-hammer and a medieval back-scratcher – and fit it to its haft. Then you lie flat upon your face on the wet grass, and having scratched up some small lumps of turf, proceed to build these into a parapet. Into the hole formed by the excavation of the turf you then put your head, and in this ostrich-like posture await further instructions.

After Captain Wagstaffe has criticised the preliminary parapets – most of them are condemned as not being bullet-proof – the work is continued. It is not easy, and never comfortable, to dig lying down; but we must all learn to do it, so we proceed painfully to construct a shallow trough for our bodies and an annexe for our boots. Gradually we sink out of sight, and Captain Wagstaffe, standing fifty yards to our front, is able to assure us that he can now see nothing.

Breastworks of snow.

By this time the rain has returned for good, and the short winter day is drawing to a gloomy close. It is after three, and we have been working, with one brief interval, for nearly five hours. The signal is given to take shelter. We huddle together under the leaf-less trees, and get wetter.

Next comes the order to unroll greatcoats. Five minutes later comes another – to fall in. Tools are counted; there is the usual maddening wait while search is made for a missing pick. But at last the final word of command rings out, and the sodden, leaden-footed procession sets out on its four-mile tramp home.

We are not in good spirits. One's frame of mind at all times depends largely upon what the immediate future has to offer; and, frankly, we have little to inspire us in that direction at present. When we joined, four long months ago, there loomed largely and splendidly before our eyes only two alternatives – victory in battle or death with honour. We might live, or we might die; but life, while it lasted, would not lack great moments. In our haste we had over-looked the long dreary waste which lay – which always lies – between dream and fulfilment. The glorious splash of patriotic fervour which launched us on our way has subsided; we have reached mid-channel; and the haven where we would be is still afar off. The brave future of which we dreamed in our dour and uncommunicative souls seems as remote as ever, and the present has settled down into a permanency.

Today, for instance, we have tramped a certain number of miles; we have worked for a certain number of hours; and we have got wet through for the hundredth time. We are now tramping home to a dinner which will probably not be ready, because, as yesterday, it has been cooked in the open air under weeping skies. While waiting for it, we shall clean the same old rifle. When night falls, we shall sleep uneasily upon a comfortless floor, in an atmosphere of stale food and damp humanity. In the morning we shall rise up reluctantly, and go forth, probably in heavy rain, to our labour until the evening – the same labour and the same evening. We admit that it can't be helped: the officers and the authorities do their best for us under discouraging circumstances: but there it is.

Private Thomas Lyon, 2/9th The Highland Light Infantry (Glasgow Highlanders)

In a lengthening list of onerous tasks, nighttime training exercises had the greatest risk of falling apart. Men were marched off into the stygian darkness unclear either of where they were going or of the task to be undertaken.

You have had a tiring day; perhaps even a tiresome one – for the charms of platoon drill or musketry practice are apt to wear thin through eternal repetition. And you desire nothing more than to seek dreams of peace on the three planks that are your bed. But there are to be night operations – events which occur sometimes twice sometimes three times a week… You pray for a deluge of rain, an avalanche of snow, a fusillade of hail, an earthquake – anything at all that will make the roads impassable and the officers uncomfortable, and that will thus lead to the postponement of the night operations. But at 7.30 pm the atmosphere is clear and frosty and bracing, whereupon you say 'hang!' and 'dash!' and 'blow!' or other words to that effect, and proceed to put on your equipment, stuffing your greatcoat and slacks into your pack, and to harness yourself with the whole. At 8 o'clock the company leaves the billet for the parade ground.

As you 'stand easy' in an uneasy silence and glance along the dimly lit side street in which the battalion assembles you see two endless rows of dark figures stretching into the gloom on either side.

Getting warm after a night in the open. Working in the freezing cold tested the morale of all soldiers, but was the routine once these men reached the Western Front.

To replicate night operations on the Western Front, 'silence was the order of the day', wrote Lyon. There was a whisper to fix bayonets, and with minimum of noise they are clicked into place, each man taking his cue to 'fix' from the action of the soldier to his left. The men then shuffled into fours and the battalion moved off into the countryside.

WINTER BLUES

The hard road rings to the measured tread of a thousand pairs of feet. There is a creaking sound made by the leather equipment and the constant jug-juggling of water in water bottles. As time passes and in the absence of all other sounds, these noises seem to grow louder; your attention is riveted by them, and you are hardly conscious of anything else. You feel confident that they must be audible a mile away, and think it funny that the water in your bottle should splash so noisily at night, since it is never heard on day marches. It occurs to you that similarly you have noticed that the music of a stream seems to deepen with the coming of darkness, and you fall to marvelling on the tricks one's senses play – when suddenly you are pulled up short in your musings and marchings. You walk slap-bang into the pack of the man immediately in front of you, and almost instantaneously the man behind prods you with his rifle.

The unexpected halt indicates that the leading files have entered upon a stretch of bad road, and the consequent slowing down of the pace leads to numerous collisions among the rear files. At last there is a real halt, of which you learn by bumping again into the man in front. The ranks are not allowed to fall out, but the whispered command 'Stand easy!' is passed along the column. You whisper to a comrade – you can't see who he is – 'By Jove! I'm dying for a smoke,' – and immediately the Sergeant's voice comes out of the surrounding blackness, 'Shut up there! Any man I hear talking will be reported.' And though his voice is muffled to a whisper, there is so much of gruffness in it and such a tone of conviction that you desist from your effort to make conversation.

You can think of nothing now but your old pipe. The fragrance of tobacco smoke makes your nostrils twitch, and you look to right and left to see if somebody has dared the wrath of the powers that be and is enjoying a whiff on the quiet. But there is no one so foolhardy; your imagination is playing pranks with you. Never have you wanted to smoke so badly now when it is forbidden, and you wonder how you're going to stick the march to the end without the consolation and comfort of a 'draw'.

Private Thomas Lyon, 2/9th The Highland Light Infantry (Glasgow Highlanders)

The night continues with endless halts and collisions. Silence is maintained and the battalion, by companies, leaves the road and enters a coarse and tufted heath that lays traps for unwary feet.

Private Thomas Lyon, 2/9th The Highland Light Infantry (Glasgow Highlanders)

There are unexpected little knolls and dips that jar your body and your nerves unpleasantly when you step on or in them, and your water bottle, your entrenching tool carrier and your haversack splash and rattle and bang against you with a noise that might awaken the seven sleepers. Or so it seems to you. Tripping, falling, sprawling, the battalion moved across the dark moorland, jumping ditches, scaling dykes, creeping through wire fences, plunging through drifts of snow lying in the hollows. 'I wonder where the deuce we are,' somebody whispers…

After a little while the whispered command is given 'Platoons – right form!' and you right form and wonder what the officers are playing at. You hear the company on the right moving forward, and you judge that there is some kind of muddle, for their progress is very slow. Then your company gets the order to move, but again something impedes their progress; you wonder why the dickens those in front don't step out. But you learn the reason when you see the men immediately in front of you suddenly disappear into a strip of blackness that yawns beneath your feet. It is a trench – dug by another company earlier in the week – and the order has been given for your company to enter it. You jump in – into a puddle of mud and water reaching nearly to the top of you spats – and scramble forward. The trench is very narrow – only about 18 inches across – and about 3½ feet deep. As you feel the buff apron that covers your kilt rubbing against the claying sides you inwardly curse your luck, for had you not spent a half-hour and more in washing it only the previous evening? Constantly you bump up against projections of earth, for the trench had been dug with transverse sections and seems one interminable zigzag…

Your feet are horribly cold and wet and heavy; there appears to be half an acre of claying soil adhering to each boot; you make a horrid, squelching sound that is echoed many times both in front and in rear.

An NCO rushes along the parapet of the trench. 'Halt!' he whispers as he goes. 'Stay where you are, you fellows!' – Stay where you are! – and you are standing in six inches of water. Then another company heaves out of the blackness alongside the trench. The man immediately above you whispers, 'Give me your rifle. You're to take this.' 'This' is a spade. And again the whispered order passes down that you are to begin digging – the trench is to be deepened. Some one beside you murmurs a muddy oath appropriate to the occasion.

For half-an-hour or so you toil and moil in the trench – throwing up shovelfuls of mud and water. By reason of your necessarily cramped position your back aches, and while your brow is beaded with drops of muddy perspiration your feet are like lumps of ice. And even the thought that your King and Country need you to do this while it may give you mental consolation does not tend to allay your physical discomfort. You repeat over and over again, 'My feet are not cold and my back doesn't ache and my arms aren't tired; I am warm and cosy and comfortable; I am very happy; I am doing this merely for pleasurable recreation; also because my King, etc.' But somehow the formula doesn't work; you are as uncomfortable as ever.

Eventually the order to quit the trench is received, and the homeward march is begun. Your thoughts revert to your old pipe and you promise yourself the greatest smoke of a lifetime the moment the billet is reached. Then the thought of bed possesses you, and it is inexpressively sweet. The steady rhythm of the tread and ju-juggoling of the water bottles exercises a somnolent influence upon you. Walking has become purely mechanical, and you are quite unconscious of exerting any will to move. The man whom you are covering off has become merely a dark blur, with no distinctive shape. The stars are frisking about in the sky in a most amazing manner; you see the Seven Sisters sporting with Orion's Belt, and the North Star skipping from side to side and end to end of The Plough, but it causes you no surprise. Even the thought of your old, sweet pipe doesn't awake any enthusiasm in you now.

Then – suddenly crash into the man in front, and the man behind bangs into you, and you pull yourself together and look around, and

'This photograph was taken early one morning in a fog after we had been out all night on listening post.'

Second Lieutenant John Hay Beith, 10th Princess Louise's (Argyll & Sutherland Highlanders)

find that all things – even the stars are as they should be. 'Great Scot!' whispers your left hand neighbour, 'I've been asleep.' And you think, 'I believe I've been asleep too' – and it occurs to you that mere civilians wouldn't believe you if you told them that you had been asleep while doing a march.

The rain has ceased for a brief space – it always does about parade time – and we accordingly fall in. The men are carrying picks and shovels, and make no attempt to look pleased at the circumstance. They realise that they are in for a morning's hard digging, and very likely for an evening's field operations as well. When we began company training a few weeks ago, entrenching was rather popular. More than half of us are miners or tillers of the soil, and the pick and shovel gave us a home-like sensation. Here was a chance too, of showing regular soldiers how a job should be properly accomplished. So we dug with great enthusiasm.

But A Company have got over that now. They have developed into sufficiently old soldiers to have acquired the correct military attitude towards manual labour. Trench-digging is a 'fatigue', to be classed with coal-carrying, floor-scrubbing, and other civilian pursuits. The word 'fatigue' is a shibboleth with the British private. Persuade him that a task is part of his duty as a soldier, and he will perform it with tolerable cheerfulness; but once allow him to regard that task as a 'fatigue', and he will shirk it whenever possible, and regard himself as a deeply injured individual when called upon to undertake it.

Our training was intensified, but it could not be claimed at the end that we were really versed in the art of war. We had dug one trench and that took us three days to complete, working in relays and with the assistance of picks and shovels: precious little practice for men who were to hack desperately with entrenching tools and bare hands to get cover from fire! We had let off twenty rounds of ammunition from obsolete rifles and some of us had not even hit the targets. We had marched a few miles at a time without equipment with the aid of a band, refreshed by frequent halts and fortified by an abundance of good food. These feats, together with a real proficiency in presenting arms and saluting, comprised the sum total of our military achievements when we set sail for France. What we really needed was practice in carrying weights over slippery ground, filling sandbags, laying wire and throwing bombs, and instruction in the gentle art of cooking.

Rifleman Aubrey Smith, 2/5th (City of London) Battalion (London Rifle Brigade)

The art of trench digging undertaken near Invergordon with the men using wood to shore up or revert the trench. The work was physically demanding and disliked, especially when the ground was hard and the weather cold, but it was a skill that saved lives.

Men of the Gloucestershire Regiment guarding England's east coast, where the authorities perpetually feared an enemy invasion. These men are in trenches near the Essex marshes.

With the benefit of hindsight, many additional things might have been adapted during training to better represent the world into which these men were to be plunged. Yet, no hindsight was needed to see that too few men were given the opportunity to become anything like proficient in musketry. With a nationwide shortage of ammunition, it was inevitable that many recruits complained that they had fired too few rounds, as Aubrey Smith ruefully acknowledged. As was so often the case, resources flowed to where they were most urgently needed. Lance Corporal George Harbottle remembered musketry as 'something of a red letter day', that rare occasion when his company visited a rifle range at Ponteland to fire live ammunition.

When the men of the 10th East Yorkshire Regiment were sent to the east coast amid swirling rumours of a year-end invasion, the recruits were armed with antiquated rifles and precious ammunition: none was to be used unless against a German. It had to be pointed out to the War Office that these men on whom Britain's defence relied had yet to fire any rifles. Only after pressure was applied were the men permitted to fire a few practice rounds.

The colonel who had made the urgent request subsequently received a telegram from the War Office asking him to report on how the antiquated rifles had performed. He replied in good humour: 'Reference your Telegram… Rifles will certainly go off, doubtful which end.'

* * *

We are more or less in possession of our proper equipment now. That is to say, our wearing apparel and the appurtenances thereof are no longer held in position with string. The men have belts, pouches, and slings in which to carry their greatcoats. The greatcoats were the last to materialise. Since their arrival we have lost in decorative effect what we have gained in martial appearance…

But now the khaki-mills have ground out another million yards or so, and we have regulation greatcoats. Water bottles, haversacks, mess-tins, and waterproof sheets have been slowly filtering into our possession; and whenever we 'mobilise', which we do as a rule about once a fortnight – whether owing to invasion scares or as a test of efficiency we do not know – we fall in on our alarm-posts in something distinctly resembling the full 'Christmas-tree' rig. Sam Browne belts have been wisely discarded by the officers in favour of web-equipment; and although Bobby Little's shoulders ache with the weight of his pack, he is comfortably conscious of two things – firstly, that even when separated from his baggage he can still subsist in fair comfort on what he carries upon his person; and secondly, that his 'expectation of life', as the insurance offices say, has increased about a hundred per cent now that the German sharpshooters will no longer be able to pick him out from his men.

Second Lieutenant John Hay Beith, 10th Princess Louise's (Argyll & Sutherland Highlanders)

We've got the new equipment – leather instead of webbing. Equipment, by the way, means belt, ammunition pouches, water bottle, entrenching tool, and haversack in which greatcoat and a change of underclothing

Second Lieutenant Arthur Heath, 6th The Queen's Own (Royal West Kent Regiment)

are carried. The total weight carried in this way is about 50 lbs. What concerns me more nearly is that the officers carry it as well as the men now, under the new regulations, and there's no doubt that it adds very greatly to the burden of marching. In fact, yesterday was the first day I have been knocked up since joining. We went out seven or eight miles, and then did a 'brigade exercise', during which I was what is called a 'liaison officer', keeping up communication between the Battalion and the Brigade. That involved a certain amount of running about, and, what was more important, I didn't manage to get anything to eat till three o'clock, and then only one sandwich. As we started at 8.15 and got back at 4.15, I was driven a bit too hard, and the last hour I suffered agonies, feeling faint and sick and sweating all over. I couldn't fall out because we make it a point of honour not to.

Private James Hall, 9th The Royal Fusiliers (City of London Regiment)

The character of our training changed as we progressed. We were done with squad, platoon, and company drill. Then came field manoeuvres, attacks in open formation upon entrenched positions, finishing always with terrific bayonet charges. There were mimic battles lasting all day, with from ten to twenty thousand men on each side. Artillery, infantry, cavalry, aircraft – every branch of army service, in fact – had a share in these exciting field days when we gained bloodless victories or died painless and easy deaths at the command of red-capped field judges.

We rushed boldly to the charge, shouting lustily, each man striving to be first at the enemy's position, only to be intercepted by a staff officer on horseback staying the tide of battle with uplifted hand.

'March your men back, officer! You're out of action! My word! You've made a beastly mess of it! You're not on church parade, you know! You advanced across the open for three quarters of a mile in close column of platoons! Three batteries of field artillery and four machine guns have blown you to blazes! You haven't a man left!'

Sometimes we reached our objective with less fearful slaughter, but at the moment when there should have been the sharp clash and clang of steel on steel, the cries and groans of men fighting for their lives, we heard the bugles from far and near sounding the 'stand by', and friend and enemy dropped wearily to the ground for a rest while our officers assembled in conference around the motor of the divisional general.

'C' Coy. Resting after an attack Sailsbury Plain

A Walker — Self — A S. Williams

On Monday we attacked a small village called Shrewton about seven miles from camp and on Tuesday marched a few miles further for another attack. On Wednesday we went further still and attacked again. It rained very hard this day and our Battalion fought a rearguard action for two miles, covering the Division as it was retiring. Thursday was the same again and by Friday morning we were all feeling the after effects of this hard work with full pack and rifle all the time; some of the fellows were hardly able to put their feet to the floor. It was raining, and we all hoped it would keep on so as to give us a bit of a rest, but we were out of luck, we had to turn out. I think about 100 men fell out in the first seven miles, unable to stick it any longer. I myself, never having fallen out of a march, kept on. On Saturday we did not go far and after this attack the Brigadier formed us up and spoke to us. He said we had had a very hard week of it. Marching alone we had covered

Private Albert Andrews, 19th The Manchester Regiment (4th City)

Above: *Men of the 20th Royal Fusiliers rest after their strenuous day simulating a brigade attack against an entrenched 'enemy'.*

136 miles and over rough ground, but at the front we would have to do much more. He said, one Brigade in the retreat from Mons covered 224 miles in the same time.

Private Sydney Fuller, 8th The Suffolk Regiment

Paraded with the Companies at 8 am for trench warfare at Yarnbury Castle [Wiltshire]. The Suffolks were the reserve Battalion of the 53rd Brigade. We attacked a trench system, supported by a few 18-pounders, which 'shelled' the trenches before we attacked by firing several rounds of blank [ammunition]. The attack commenced at 11 am, and I was, shortly afterwards, told by a Staff Officer that I was a casualty – bayonet wound through the left arm. I was given a piece of paper on which was written the nature of my injury and sent back to the Dressing Station which was represented by the Brigade Office, near our camp. Here each casualty was noted as he arrived, and sent to his camp.

Second Lieutenant John Hay Beith, 10th Princess Louise's (Argyll & Sutherland Highlanders)

Commands are no longer preceded by cautions and explanations. A note on a whistle, followed by a brusque word or gesture, is sufficient to set us smartly on the move.

Suddenly we are called upon to give a test of our quality. A rotund figure upon horseback appears at a bend in the road. Captain Blaikie recognises General Freeman.

(We may note that the General's name is not really Freeman. We are much harried by generals at present. They roam about the country on horseback and ask company commanders what they are doing; and no company commander has ever yet succeeded in framing an answer that sounds in the least degree credible. There are three generals; we call them Freeman, Hardy, and Willis, because we suspect that they are all – to judge from their fondness for keeping us on the run – financially interested in the consumption of shoe-leather. In other respects they differ, and a wise company commander will carefully bear their idiosyncrasies in mind and act accordingly, if he wishes to be regarded as an intelligent officer.)

Freeman is a man of action. He likes to see people running about. When he appears upon the horizon whole battalions break into a double.

Hardy is one of the old school: he likes things done decently and in order. He worships bright buttons and exact words of command, and a perfectly wheeling line. He mistrusts unconventional movements and individual tactics. 'No use trying to run', he says, 'before you can walk.' When we see him, we dress the company and advance in review order.

Willis gives little trouble. He seldom criticises, but when he does his criticism is always of a valuable nature; and he is particularly courteous and helpful to young officers. But, like lesser men, he has his fads. These are two – feet and cookery. He has been known to call a private out of the ranks on a route-march and request him to take his boots off for purposes of public display. 'A soldier marches on two things,' he announces – 'his feet and his stomach.' Then he calls up another man and asks him if he knows how to make a sea-pie. The man never does know, which is fortunate, for otherwise General Willis would not be able to tell him. After that he trots happily away to ask someone else.

However, here we are face to face with General Freeman. Immediate action is called for. Captain Blaikie flings an order over his shoulder to the subaltern in command of the leading platoon:

'Pass back word that this road is under shell fire. Move!' and rides forward to meet the General.

Opposite: February 1915 at Epsom: 'wounded' men patched up after mock attacks during infantry training. The lucky ones were designated casualties and could rely on being carried from the battlefield by their comrades. All these men, and those standing behind them, are from the University and Public Schools Battalions of the Royal Fusiliers.

In ten seconds the road behind him is absolutely clear and the men are streaming out to right and left in half-platoons. Waddell's platoon has the hardest time, for they were passing a quickset hedge when the order came. However, they hurl themselves blasphemously through, and double on, scratched and panting.

'Good morning, sir!' says Captain Blaikie, saluting.

'Good morning!' says General Freeman. 'What was that last movement?'

'The men are taking "artillery" formation, sir. I have just passed the word down that the road is under shell fire.'

'Quite so. But don't you think you ought to keep some of your company in rear, as a supporting line? I see you have got them all up on one front.'

By this time A Company is advancing in its original direction, but split up into eight half-platoons in single file – one on each side of the road, at intervals of thirty yards. The movement has been quite smartly carried out. Still, a critic must criticise or go out of business. However, Captain Blaikie is an old hand.

'I was assuming that my company formed part of a battalion, sir,' he explained. 'There are supposed to be three other companies in rear of mine.'

'I see. Still, tell two of your sections to fall back and form a supporting line.'

Captain Blaikie, remembering that generals have little time for study of such works as the new drill-book, and that when General Freeman says 'section' he probably means 'platoon', orders Numbers Two and Four to fall back. This manoeuvre is safely accomplished.

'Now, let me see them close on the road.'

Captain Blaikie blows a whistle, and slaps himself on the top of the head. In three minutes the long-suffering platoons are back on the road, extracting thorns from their flesh and assuaging the agony of their abrasions by clandestine massage.

General Freeman rides away, and the column moves on. Two minutes later Captain Wagstaffe doubles up from the rear to announce that General Hardy is only two hundred yards behind.

'Pass back word to the men,' groans Captain Blaikie, 'to march at attention, put their caps straight, and slope their shovels properly. And send an orderly to that hill-top to look out for General Willis. Tell him to unlace his boots when he gets there, and on no account to admit that he knows how to make a sea-pie!'

Overleaf: 'This photo was taken on Thursday [24 June], when the King reviewed the 20th Division. It was a fine sight,' wrote an onlooker serving with the 9th Northumberland Fusiliers. The 20th Light Division would embark for France in late July 1915.

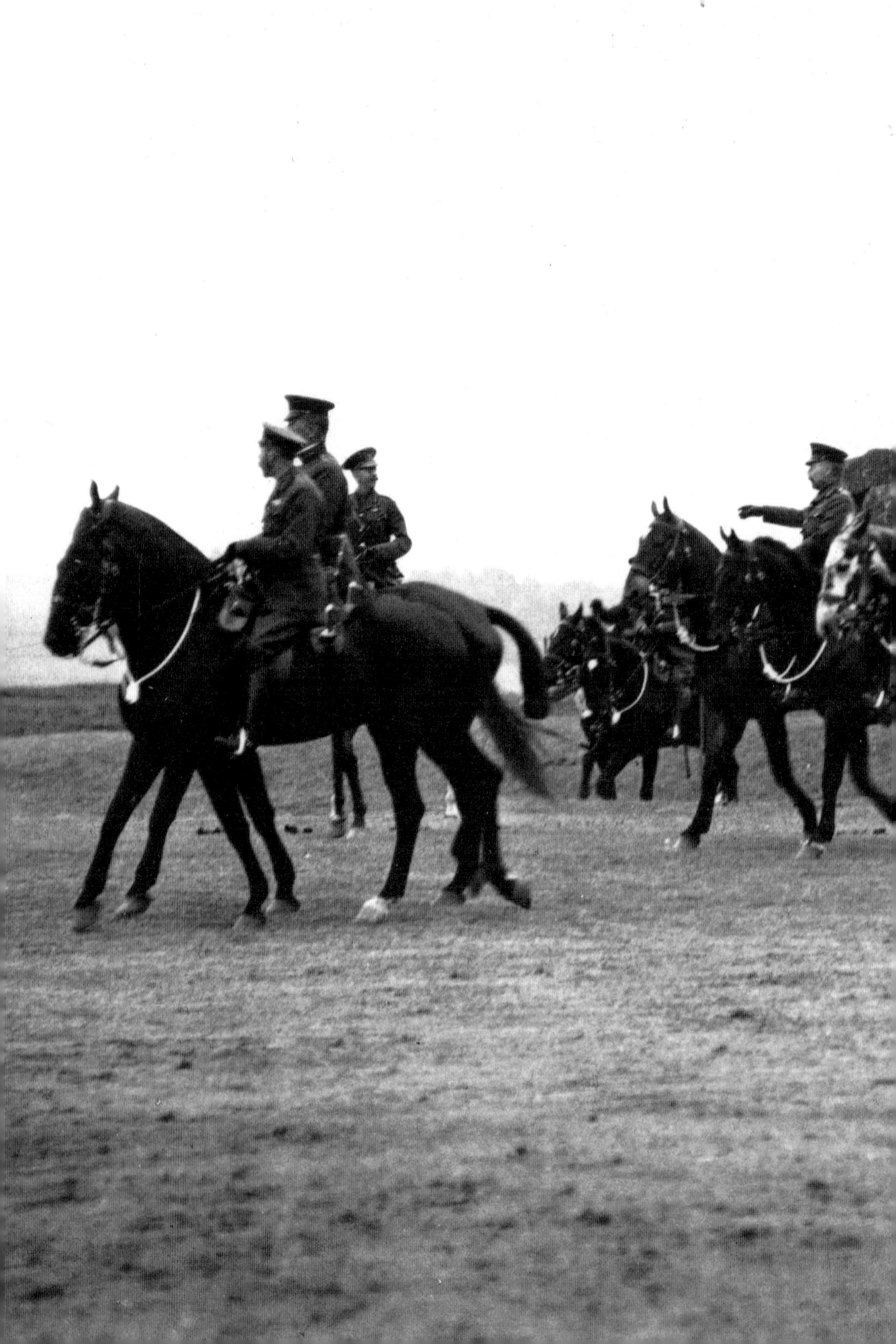

10 Fiddling About

TRENCHES. BEDLAM BUILDINGS SAILSBURY PLAIN.

> 'One thing we all know: that is, we shall be glad when we get to the front, for although we are not sick of the Royal Field Artillery, we are heartily sick of this Rotten Fiddling About.'
>
> Gunner Cecil Longley, 1st South Midland Brigade,
Royal Field Artillery

Recently generals and staff officers have been coming home from the front and giving us lectures. We regard most lectures as a 'fatigue' – but not these. We have learned more from these quiet-mannered, tired-looking men in a brief hour than from all the manuals that ever came out of Gale and Polden's. We have heard the history of the 'War from the inside'. We know why our Army retreated from Mons; we know what prevented the relief of Antwerp. But above all, we have learned to revise some of our most cherished theories.

Briefly, the amended version of the law and the prophets comes to this:

> Never, under any circumstances, place your trenches where you can see the enemy a long way off. If you do, he will inevitably see you too, and will shell you out of them in no time. You need not be afraid of being rushed; a field of fire of two hundred yards or so will be sufficient to wipe him off the face of the earth.
>
> Never, under any circumstances, take cover in farm buildings, or plantations, or behind railway embankments, or in any place likely to be marked on a large-scale map. Their position and range are known to a yard. Your safest place is the middle of an open plain or ploughed field. There it will be more difficult for the enemy's range-takers to gauge your exact distance.

Second Lieutenant John Hay Beith, 10th Princess Louise's (Argyll and Sutherland Highlanders)

Opposite: Intricate front line and support trenches dug on Salisbury Plain and occupied by the men of the 20th Royal Fusiliers as they undertook the final stages of training.

> In musketry, concentrate all your energies on taking care of your rifle and practising 'rapid'. You will seldom have to fire over a greater distance than two hundred yards; and at that range British rapid fire is the most dreadful medium of destruction yet devised in warfare.

All this scraps a good deal of laboriously acquired learning, but it rings true. So we site our trenches now according to the lessons taught us by the bitter experience of others.

Second Lieutenant Arthur Heath, 6th The Queen's Own (Royal West Kent Regiment)

We are all really very proud of ourselves. Here are our regular officers, who have been jeering at us for months and boring us to death by stories of what the first battalion did [in 1914]. Then a week or two ago a sergeant arrived who had fought with the first in France and come back wounded. Almost his first remarks were about the awful difficulties they had there. And he actually went on 'Of course it will be quite different with these men – you can see that. They joined because they wanted to help, but over there they were all unwilling.' No doubt he meant the reservists – still these men were praised to the skies… and generally placarded all over Kent as the heroes of the twentieth century.

Private James Hall, 9th The Royal Fusiliers (City of London Regiment)

Frequent changes were made in methods of training in England to correspond with changing conditions of modern warfare as exemplified in the trenches. Textbooks on military tactics and strategy, which were the inspired gospel of the last generation of soldiers, became obsolete overnight. Experience gained in Indian Mutiny wars or on the veldt in South Africa was of little value in the trenches in Flanders. The emphasis shifted from open fighting to trench warfare, and the textbook which our officers studied was a typewritten serial issued semiweekly by the War Office, and which was based on the dearly bought experience of officers at the front.

The men who had gone to war were taught infantry tactics as laid down in the army's 1914 manual *Infantry Training* and based on lessons learnt during the most recent conflicts. Owing to the warfare's evolutionary dynamic, with the withering effects of concentrated artillery fire on infantrymen in the open and the capacity for machine-gun fire to dominate the ground, changes were necessary in how men were instructed.

Hitherto, reinforcing front-line trenches meant sending in infantrymen and increasing firepower, but also congestion and packing trenches made men vulnerable to ever more accurate artillery fire. The firepower of machine guns helped alleviate that conundrum; fewer men would be needed. The army constantly adapted to changing circumstances, selecting men to attend specialist courses in bombing, signalling, and musketry, and critically, in the use and maintenance of machine guns.

Below: *The perfect pose: a demonstration of how to throw a bomb.*

> Our machine gunners at last obtained guns. Our bombing experts taught us about fuses and detonators. Even the C.O. bobbed his head in the narrow trench as the jam tins exploded. Range-finders made their appearance, and we lay prone on our 'tummies' to gaze wistfully at the retreating army when it reached the Rhine.

Lieutenant & Quartermaster Joseph Goss, 8th The King's Own Scottish Borderers

> Last, but not least, we dug furiously at trenches toiling amid obstinate chalk and flint. There was another plot of ground hard by the camp, at which our hands had not toiled, but over which our legs carried us time after time as we strove to render a complete account, before the C.O., of our prowess in trench-clearing.

> Bomb-throwing squads were formed, and the best shots in the battalion, the men who had made marksmen's scores on the rifle ranges, were given daily instruction in the important business of sniping. More generous provision

Private James Hall, 9th The Royal Fusiliers (City of London Regiment) for the training of machine-gun teams was made, but so great was the lack in England of these important weapons, that for many weeks we drilled with wooden substitutes, gaining such knowledge of machine gunnery as we could from the study of our M.G. manuals.

These new duties, coming as an addition to our other work, meant an increased period of training. We were impatient to be at the front, but we realised by this time that Lord Kitchener was serious in his demand that the men of the new armies be efficiently trained.

Lance Corporal Ralph Smith, 12th The Gloucestershire Regiment (Bristol)

I went on a bombing course. At that time the bombs or hand grenades that were available were very primitive. A bomb consisted of a tin filled with explosive which we filled through a small hole in the top, then cut a length of fuse five inches long and inserted it to a certain depth allowing a five seconds explosion. Off then to some trench to test. Someone would light the fuse while we held the bombs at arm's length. We then had to count to three before throwing it. I was pleased a few days later to hear I had passed and was entitled to wear a grenade [badge] on my sleeve.

Two officers undergoing specialist training on machine guns. On the far left sits Lieutenant Henry Bennett, 11th King's Liverpool Regiment. He went to France in 1915 and was killed three years later, in March 1918.

I have been put on a machine-gun course, which has lasted now nearly a fortnight and still has a week or so to run. I've enjoyed it and only fear that I may have to teach one of the machine-gun sections, which, on the whole, would be rather boring work. There isn't much probability of my handling machine-guns in battle for we've got a regular M.-G. [Machine Gun] officer and I should only be 3rd or 4th reserve. Still you never know, and I believe M.-G. officers only last about a month…

Our training is pretty well over, and, though I can't give exact dates, it is pretty certain that we shall be abroad within a month. A good thing too. There's lots more they could teach us officers, but any increase to our efficiency would be more than counterbalanced by the growing staleness the men will suffer from if we are kept back much longer. They have done in eight months what the ordinary regulars take three years for, and nothing could keep them going but the expectation of battle soon. I feel something of the same. The prospect of three more months training at the same pace as the last three makes me grow pale, and, though I don't expect to enjoy the real thing much, I feel it is about time to get on to it. The only thing that troubles me much is my mother. I'm afraid she thinks that I am certain to become a casualty, and though, of course, she has not talked much about it, it is pitiful to see how much she shrinks from my going. The thought of the vast amount of similar suffering all through Europe makes me more indignant against war than anything else. I find that, although my first Battalion has lost practically all its first set of officers and half its second, one assumes the chances of not being killed or disabled to be greater than they really are…

What I want is a life when you need not keep looking at your watch, where there are no parades, no absentees, no lost boots, no new issues of socks, no generals, no field days, but you can read a book when you want to read it and dawdle over your tea. That is what I want – laziness in some place like Heyford Rectory garden. But meanwhile, on the whole I'm quite happy and it doesn't matter a scrap whether I am or not because we shall get away in anything from three to six weeks unless the signs are deceiving us; and, once away, in my own opinion we shall all be casualties before very long. When we are all dead they

Second Lieutenant Arthur Heath, 6th The Queen's Own (Royal West Kent Regiment)

will make peace and the only thing that annoys me is that I shan't be alive to grumble at the terms.

Private James Hall, 9th The Royal Fusiliers (City of London Regiment)

All this was playing at war, and Tommy was 'fed up' with play. As we marched back to barracks after a long day of monotonous field manoeuvres, he eased his mind by making sarcastic comments upon this inconclusive kind of warfare. He began to doubt the good faith of the War Office in calling ours a 'Service' battalion. As likely as not we were for home defence and would never be sent abroad… And so he groused and grumbled after the manner of Tommies the world over. And in the meantime he was daily approaching more nearly the standard of efficiency set by England's inexorable War Lord.

Second Lieutenant John Bellerby, 8th The Prince of Wales's Own (West Yorkshire Regiment)

In the early months there was a tension and a zest in life imparted entirely by anticipation of what was to follow. It is impossible to continue for months training with one specific aim in view, to which all have implicitly committed their whole being, without becoming seized with eagerness to put the training to the final test.

It was probably this sort of feeling which led me to say 'Yes' when, after three weeks of training with the first battalion at Strensall, the Adjutant asked me if I would fill a vacancy in it. I think I rationalised my decision by saying to myself that if I was prepared to shoot Germans in the event of their landing in the UK, it was obviously more sensible to meet them on the other side.

Alleviating the frustration was sport, an integral part of soldiers' recreation with, wherever possible, goalposts or other sporting facilities erected in fields adjacent to camps.

Organised sport featured highly competitive inter-platoon football and rugby matches culminating typically in the award of enamelled medals to winners and runners-up. Boxing was popular, as was wrestling, while within battalions there were inter-company athletics and regimental sports days, with traditional track and field events as well as additional games such as the tug of war or obstacle races. Prizes including cups were presented by senior officers

FIDDLING ABOUT 315

Sports days and prize-giving: it is surprising how few memoirs make even passing references to these generally popular events, that is unless the author won! Bottom: 'The Royal and Ancient Game' of golf as played by men of the Royal Army Medical Corps at the Rhos-on-Sea golf club.

or invited dignitaries. As training expanded, so sports days developed into inter-brigade level competitions with teams from the infantry, artillery, and other ancillary services represented. Cross-country races and for the athletically elite, marathons, were held on the vastness of Salisbury Plain.

Private John Jackson, 6th The Queen's Own Cameron Highlanders

On May 19th we began our preparation for brigade sports. In the eliminating contests for the battalion I represented C Company in the 100 yards, but was beaten for a place in the final by Sergeant McAllister, a really fine runner. In the half mile I was second to a Scottish ex-amateur champion, both of us qualifying for the brigade final. The brigade sports were held in a field near camp on May 22nd, which was in the nature of a gala day for us. The Brigadier General had promised a silver cup for the regiment with the highest number of points. This added to the interest of the competition, and we Camerons vowed to make a bold attempt to win the trophy.

Although large numbers of men took part in these frequent, multi-level competitions or stood as spectators to cheer competitors on, few men mention them in memoirs or diaries, other than in passing. This is because sporting events were to be enjoyed but not necessarily remembered as noteworthy. That is, of course, unless a man won.

Private John Jackson, 6th The Queen's Own (Cameron Highlanders)

The first item was the final of the half-mile, each of the regiments having two representatives. I had been suffering from the effects of a strained leg and was in fact very lame. My pals wanted me to draw out of the race, but I wasn't giving in and so I lined up with the rest. The result of that race surprised even myself. At the half-distance I went to the front with a burst that surprised the other runners, and remained there to win by a couple of yards. I dropped as I broke the tape, and had to be carried off suffering terribly from my damaged leg, but I was proud to have scored the first three points for the Camerons; and I'm afraid I was treated like a hero for my share. Sergeant McAllister won the 100 yards and ¼ mile in fine style, and the silver cup was eventually won by the Camerons with a total of forty-seven points against the

Fusiliers, second with twenty-three. At the conclusion of the sports the prizes were presented by the Brigadier's wife, and I had the honour of receiving the cup on behalf of the regiment.

Brigade sports were weather-dependent events, put on necessarily from springtime onwards. Dozens of events were held across the country in May or in early June, often patriotically planned to coincide with Empire Day, or the king's birthday. All competitors were in near enough peak fitness, a tribute to the men themselves and the intensive training the army had given them.

We had staggered into [Parkhouse] camp weary and worn: when we came to quit it, no finer body of men ever swung along the King's Highroad. We all enjoyed Parkhouse. Away from town and temptations, we were brought nearer to the meaning of soldiering than ever before. We began to feel that we were not merely ourselves, not merely a battalion, but were part of one great whole – the 15th Division

Our bodies, hardening to the work, thought less of the pleasures of town life. When the time came to take our departure, we felt more like soldiers than ever before. Three weeks' hard training had oiled our joints and hardened our muscles. We were rapidly approaching the perfection of ideal 'cannon fodder'. The final touches were about to be administered. Our civilian minds accepted without too audible comment the wonderful manoeuvres we were called upon to perform. Blindly, at the bidding of the Brigadier, we were prepared to charge anywhere. Colossal triumph for the 'Manual of Infantry Training'.

Lieutenant & Quartermaster Joseph Goss, 8th The King's Own Scottish Borderers

Officers of the 8th King's Own Scottish Borderers ready to go overseas. Within a short time, these men were launched into the onerous Battle of Loos, suffering heavy casualties.

Second Lieutenant John Hay Beith, 10th Princess Louise's (Argyll & Sutherland Highlanders)

Whatever our ultimate destination and fate may be, the fact remains that we are now fit for active service as seven months' relentless schooling under make-believe conditions can render us. We shall have to begin all over again, we know, when we find ourselves up against the real thing, but we have at least been thoroughly grounded in the rudiments of our profession. We can endure hail, rain, snow, and vapour; we can march and dig with the best; we have mastered the first principles of musketry; we can advance in an extended line without losing touch or bunching; and we have ceased to regard an order as an insult, or obedience as a degradation. We eat when we can and what we get, and we sleep wherever we happen to find ourselves lying. That is something. But there are certain military accomplishments which can only be taught us by the enemy. Taking cover for instance. When the thin, intermittent crackle of blank ammunition shall have been replaced by the whistle of real bullets, we shall get over our predilection for sitting up and taking notice.

Close to the ancient earthworks of Yarnbury Castle, Sydney Fuller spent a day with his battalion digging trenches.

Private Sydney Fuller, 8th The Suffolk Regiment

Each man had to dig a little trench for himself. During this operation, I overheard the Brigadier tell Captain Catchpole (OC 'B' Company) that he thought this was our last day's digging – 'on this side of the Channel'.

Battalions were being readied for overseas service. The old blue serge uniforms (now used only for fatigues) were handed in, inspections were made, during which any damages to equipment such as broken straps were noted, and the man ordered to ensure the item was repaired.

Rifleman Aubrey Smith, 2/5th (City of London) Battalion (London Rifle Brigade)

The preparations for the departure of our draft were pushed on with all possible speed… All manner of equipment issued out in driblets, from packs and mess-tins to entrenching tools (which we had not handled before). Our uniforms, though clean, had to be handed in and brand new ones were issued, presumably because we were shortly going to plunge into Flanders mud! Our badges were blackened, lest the Hun should find good targets. All these things took many days to complete and our impatience to be off increased with every delay.

The public is concerned to know not what Kitchener's Army feels like and thinks of itself, but what is its real military quality as a disciplined force. What can the 120,000 men of the First New Army do that they could not do nine months ago?

    To begin with, they are capable of infinitely greater physical endurance. There is little doubt that in this respect they would prove superior even to the original Expeditionary Force which fought at Mons for two reasons. In the first place, the New Army is more sober than the old. And in the second, the original Expeditionary Force included large numbers of Reservists who were called straight up from civilian life. These were the men whose feet went to pieces in the retreat from Mons, it is extraordinary that most of them lasted as well as they did.

Sergeant Frederick Keeling, 6th The Duke of Cornwall's Light Infantry

The restraints of discipline and the very exacting character of military life and training gave them [the men of Kitchener's Army] self-control and mental alertness. At the beginning, they were individuals, no more cohesive than so many grains of wet sand. After nine months of training they acted as a unit, obeying orders with that instinctive promptness of action which is so essential on the field of battle when men think scarcely at all. But it is true that what was their gain as soldiers was, to a certain extent, their loss as individuals.

Private James Hall, 9th The Royal Fusiliers (City of London Regiment)

These fellows of ours are unlike any soldiers that ever set sail to make war in a foreign land at any previous time. In days past the men who did our fighting might have been classed as professional adventurers – they were men with the instinct for adventure in their blood; for them the dangers of war but added a spice to existence. But the men of the new army are, for the greatest part, of a different type – men having led sheltered lives and appreciating and enjoying the privileges of a

Private Thomas Lyon, 2/9th The Highland Light Infantry (Glasgow Highlanders)

Junior and senior officers of the 11th Royal Fusiliers. To the rear right sits the battalion adjutant, and next to him, to his left, Brigadier General William Heneker. Commanding 54th Infantry Brigade, Heneker was severely wounded in action but returned to service.

peaceful existence. To many of us fighting and militarism generally are alien if not actually repulsive to our natures. We are not soldiers by temperament, and consequently we have to steel ourselves to the ordeal before us.

Sergeant Frederick Keeling, 6th The Duke of Cornwall's Light Infantry

We shall never be fitter than we are. We have learned to march, to bivouac, to cook our own dinners in mess-tins over a fire of a few sticks, and, last but not least, to wait for hours in every variety of weather by day or night. We have had experience of life under canvas, in huts, and in billets. Our musketry is good, but not on the average as good as that of the old Regular Army, though we have plenty of crack shots. Our specialists, such as signallers and machine-gunners, are thoroughly trained and keen. Our drill on the barrack square is not generally up to the standard of the Old Army, but when we turn out for an inspection and really put our minds to the job, I think we can do a march-past or a rifle movement as well as a line battalion. A plethora of mimic warfare has made us perhaps rather more careless in such matters as taking cover than we were six months ago; but a breath of reality will alter that.

There were well-worn reasons as to why the musketry might not be as good 'on the average' as those Regular soldiers who had gone before.

> They suddenly realised our draft hadn't fired the musketry course, so we were rushed off to Larkhill. We knew we had to pass to go on active service. We fired our course in the most dreadful wind and rain imaginable. It was a farce. We couldn't see the targets, let alone hit them. By a miracle – or a fiddle – we all passed with good marks.

Private James Snailham, 11th The East Lancashire Regiment (Accrington)

It was a necessary 'fiddle'.

A clear sign that training days were nearly over was when senior officers appeared to inspect a brigade or division. In the late spring and early summer there was a flurry of impressive parades as the 9th (Scottish) Division assembled prior to deployment, followed by the 14th (Light) Division, including Frederick Keeling's brigade.

> Kitchener inspected the 43rd Brigade a few days ago. We marched past in column of platoons. I never felt so mad with emotion in all my life. The ritual of the Army beats that of the Christian Church any day. In fact, the ritual of soldiering comes nearer a decent civic religion than anything else I know. It is a queer thing that I should have found the social and emotional environment that suits me best in the Army. I wonder if I could ever find a family an adequate substitute for a regiment. If I do come back from the war I shall want to keep up a bit of soldiering as long as I can. I feel as if I couldn't live for evermore without bugle calls. They have eaten into my soul.

Sergeant Frederick Keeling, 6th The Duke of Cornwall's Light Infantry

The inspections increased in number. A month later and it was the turn of the 18th Division and Vic Cole's 55th Brigade.

> As a final gesture the whole 18th Division formed up in column of battalions (within sight of Stonehenge) flanked by attached sections of Royal Engineers, the Royal Army Medical Corps, Royal Field Artillery,

Lance Corporal Vic Cole, 7th The Queen's Own (Royal West Kent Regiment)

A group of officers of the 8th Devonshire Regiment shortly before going overseas in July 1915.

etc. For this parade all men with worn out clothing had been issued with new tunics, trousers and puttees, and we were ordered to carry rags or brushes in our haversacks to clean the dust off our boots.

Out in front of this vast array of men rode a solitary horseman. It was our Brigadier. Reining his horse he turned towards us, stood in his stirrups and gave, in a mighty voice, the order for the whole brigade ''Shun', then 'Slope Arms' and 'present Arms' – the whole thing went like clockwork.

For this parade Signallers had fallen in with their companies and I was at the extreme right of B Company, front platoon. As I stood there at the 'Present' wondering how long I would have to endure this most tiring position, I saw, from the corner of my eye, a small body of horsemen approaching. It was some moments before they drew near. It was King George and his Staff. A General said, 'West Kents, Sir.' And then I heard a deep voice say, 'Aha, my mother's favourite regiment,' but I reckon he said it to every battalion he passed.

I suppose I could take root somewhere else in the Army if I *had* to, but to part from my battalion would be to break one of the strongest ties I have ever known. The feeling has taken many months to grow up. At first one knew and felt little beyond the restricted circle of one's platoon. Gradually first one's company, then one's battalion, and finally one's brigade and division become living realities. Nine months ago I enlisted from a number of motives – general patriotism, indignation at the invasion of Belgium, enthusiasm for the principle of nationality, and sheer egotistical adventurousness. But now all my feelings about my own country and the rights and wrongs of this war seem to have been, as far as my everyday emotional life is concerned, absorbed in the sentiment of attachment to my own battalion and brigade. I don't personally bother about hating Germans; and patriotic and humanitarian sentiment only stirs me consciously at distant intervals. The thoughts that habitually rouse me to a desire of coming through this job tolerably creditable are the honour of my own battalion and its opinion of me.

Sergeant Frederick Keeling, 6th The Duke of Cornwall's Light Infantry

We have only two topics of conversation now – the date of our departure and our destination. Both are wrapped in mystery so profound that our range of speculation is practically unlimited.

Conjecture rages most fiercely in the Officers' Mess, which is in touch with sources of unreliable information not accessible to the rank and file. The humblest subaltern appears to be possessed of a friend at court, or a cousin in the Foreign Office, or an aunt in the Intelligence Department, from whom he can derive fresh and entirely different information each weekend leave. Master Cockerell, for instance, has it straight from the Horse Guards that we are going out next week – as a single unit, to be brigaded with two seasoned regiments in Flanders. He has a considerable following.

Then comes Waddell, who has been informed by the assistant sub-editor of an evening journal widely read in his native Dundee, that The First Hundred Thousand are to sit here, eating the bread of impatience, until The First Half Million are ready. Thereupon we shall break through our foeman's line at a point hitherto unassailed

Second Lieutenant John Hay Beith, 10th Princess Louise's (Argyll and Sutherland Highlanders)

and known only to the scribe of Dundee, and proceed to roll up the German Empire as if it were a carpet.

Captain Wagstaffe offers no opinion, but darkly recommends us to order pith helmets. However, we are rather suspicious of Captain Wagstaffe these days. He suffers from an over-developed sense of humour.

The rank and file keep closer to earth in their prognostications. In fact, some of them cleave to the dust. With them it is a case of hope deferred. Quite half of them enlisted under the firm belief that they would forthwith be furnished with a rifle and ammunition and despatched to a vague place called 'the front', there to take pot-shots at the Kaiser. That was in early August. It is now early April, and they are still here, performing monotonous evolutions and chafing under the bonds of discipline. Small wonder that they have begun to doubt, these simple souls, if they are ever going out at all.

Lieutenant Eliot Crawshay-Williams, 110th Battery, Royal Field Artillery

My chance of seeing active service has come. It has arrived in the shape of a memorandum asking for one officer to 'proceed overseas' for a fortnight's attachment to a Battery at the Front. The memorandum has considerably excited the officers in the Battery, quite needlessly, for I am selfishly sending in my own name.

Final words of encouragement to the men.

On the frieze round my bedroom there is a pattern of flowers which looks strangely like a sort of rough writing. Whilst in bed after inoculation the other day I kept gazing at this, trying to fashion it into some sense. At length the words appeared: 'Go June.' And a few days after came the memorandum. I feel quite proud of my prophetic powers!

Below: The 20th Royal Fusiliers in the trenches on Salisbury Plain at the height of summer. They would depart for France less than three months later.

For all the jocularity, every man harboured fears about his future. Keeling believed he was more conscious of them than most: he was not.

Rupert Brooke's death seems a peculiarly tragic episode. I have felt it the more as we started soldiering together when the war broke out. It has intensified my conviction that I shall not come back or rather my expectation for the feeling has no rational basis and I can imagine myself analysing it with interest after the war. Still, it is there. I wonder if most men who think and have not been accustomed to face Death before have it when they go on active service.

Many thanks for writing to stir me up about the will. I have now completed it, and enclose it herewith along with all the relevant

Sergeant Frederick Keeling, 6th The Duke of Cornwall's Light Infantry

papers… I hope to have many more jovial meals with you in the future; and if there is a Valhalla by any chance and I find my way there before you, I will keep a place for you at the festive board and sample the brews for you in advance.

Despite the army's innumerable hiccups and logistical problems, the camaraderie amongst the men was as good as anyone could have hoped for. *Esprit de corps* had been built in the face of adversity; it had been nurtured in muddy tents and freezing barracks, in the dining rooms serving indifferent food and insufficient portions. It had been built amidst parade ground toil and draining route marches. Once established, camaraderie had been preserved owing to the volunteers' innate sense of social cohesion.

Second Lieutenant John Hay Beith, 10th Princess Louise's (Argyll and Sutherland Highlanders)

No sergeant in a Highland regiment of the line would ever refer to a Cockney private with all humility as 'a young English gentleman'; neither would an ordinary soldier salute an officer quite correctly with one hand while employing the other to light his pipe. In 'K(l)' we do these things and many others, which give us a cachet of our own of which we are very rightly and properly proud.

So we pin our faith to the man who has been at once our despair and our joy since the month of August. He has character, he has grit; and now that he is getting discipline as well he is going to be an everlasting credit to the cause which roused his manhood and the land which gave him birth.

The officers and NCOs knew and understood their men and the respect was generally mutual. After a gentle start, stricter discipline had been imposed and accepted, but it was the fear of letting mates down that sobered most men to the demanding work that lay ahead and no one knew how he would hold up under the pressure of front-line life.

So far everything has been purely suppositious. We have no knowledge as to what our real strength or weakness may be. We have run our trial trips over a landlocked stretch of smooth water. When we steam out to face the tempest which is shaking the foundations of the world, we shall see what we shall see. Some of us, who at present are exalted for our smartness and efficiency, will indubitably be found wanting – wanting in stamina of body or soul – while others, hitherto undistinguished, will come to their own. Only War itself can discover the qualities which count in War. But we silently pray, in our dour and inarticulate hearts, that the supreme British virtue – the virtue of holding on, and holding on, and holding on, until our end is accomplished – may not be found wanting in a single one of us.

Second Lieutenant John Hay Beith, 10th Princess Louise's (Argyll and Sutherland Highlanders)

I can't help thinking more than most men about the first near screech of the shells while one is lying in the bloody mud, or the first near glimpse of a German uniform perhaps through the trees when one is scouting, and it's all a matter of touch and go whether you or he shoot first, or (remembering the textbook maxims) try to hide so as not reveal yourself, your heart beating like a bloody engine all the time (it does even when one is on manoeuvres). I think I have more than the average amount of cowardice in me. But, by God, what a thing to have lived through, if one does live through it!

Sergeant Frederick Keeling, 6th The Duke of Cornwall's Light Infantry

I suppose no one can go to a place at a time of peril with absolute equanimity. It is not exactly a question of fear. It is the sensation, partly excited anticipation, partly nervous apprehension, which always possesses one when about to play an important match, make an important speech, sing at a concert, act. Only, of course, it is more long-drawn-out. Briefly, one will be glad when it is all creditably over, but one would not forgo it for anything.

    I fancy that is how most people regard 'going out'. Of course there are some who do actually look forward to carnage and hardship with eagerness; but even with them, I fancy, it is more the adventure of it all that appeals than any desire to kill. What happens out there, what modifications of spirit take place, I suppose I shall find out. But I do

Lieutenant Eliot Crawshay-Williams, 110th Battery, Royal Field Artillery

not imagine I shall either enjoy it all or get used to it all. I do not think my opinion that war is a futile and barbarous business will be changed.

And I have no doubt I shall be in a blue funk!

Alan Thomas would leave for France with a draft of officers, two of whom stood out in Thomas's memory for their contrasting attitudes to war and their forthcoming role in it.

Second Lieutenant Alan Thomas, 6th The Queen's Own (Royal West Kent Regiment)

Young [Herbert] Mitchell was a high-spirited boy, of no particular gifts but desperately keen to take his share of duty: keen to be where the danger was greatest: keen, if need be, to die leading his men in battle. (One knew somehow that 'Young Mitch' would be taken. Less than a year later he died in the way he would have wished.)

Martin Hay was a quiet fellow… He was indeed an exception to most of us, because he had no desire to go to France at all. In civil life he was a solicitor and his home was in Sydenham. This latter fact was known to everyone, because Hay never tired of mentioning it. 'I'm a home bird, you know,' he would say to anyone who would listen. 'I live in Sydenham: lived there all my life, you know. Wish I was there now.'

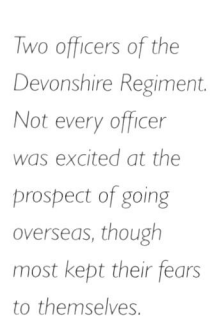

Two officers of the Devonshire Regiment. Not every officer was excited at the prospect of going overseas, though most kept their fears to themselves.

Who shall reveal the dazzling hopes and the wormy fears hidden in each man's heart? At times, as I walked alone, kilt swinging gaily, there came upon me a dread of what was to come. How could I take the life of another man, some decent, honest man, and leave him torn flesh like railway smash victims I had seen in my reporting days?

A bronzed old Regular sergeant, good old Callary, was a great comfort. I told him of my dread. 'God bless you, laddie,' he said with great heartiness, 'you've no call to worry like that. You'll think no more of putting your bayonet through a man than of putting your finger in a pot of jam. Fighting comes as natural as eating.' It was comforting to know that. I half believed it…

It is a sober fact that almost all of us were longing fiercely to get to the Front. Even what we had heard of the hardships for the Retreat from Mons, sometimes from the lips of wounded men, did not chasten our spirits. We envied those indomitable fighters their place in history.

There is a school of war-writing that derides those simple and honest emotions of ours, makes a mock of our eagerness to serve and our readiness to do our duty, and sees us only as poor, wretched animals, caught and tormented in a gigantic cage of steel and flame. It was not so…

Private William Andrews, The Black Watch, 2/4th The Black Watch (Royal Highlanders)

Last bivouac before embarking for France at the end of November 1915: men of the 20th Royal Fusiliers prepare to leave after more than a year's training.

Overleaf: *An unknown battalion of the Royal Warwickshire Regiment heads off to continental Europe and an uncertain future.*

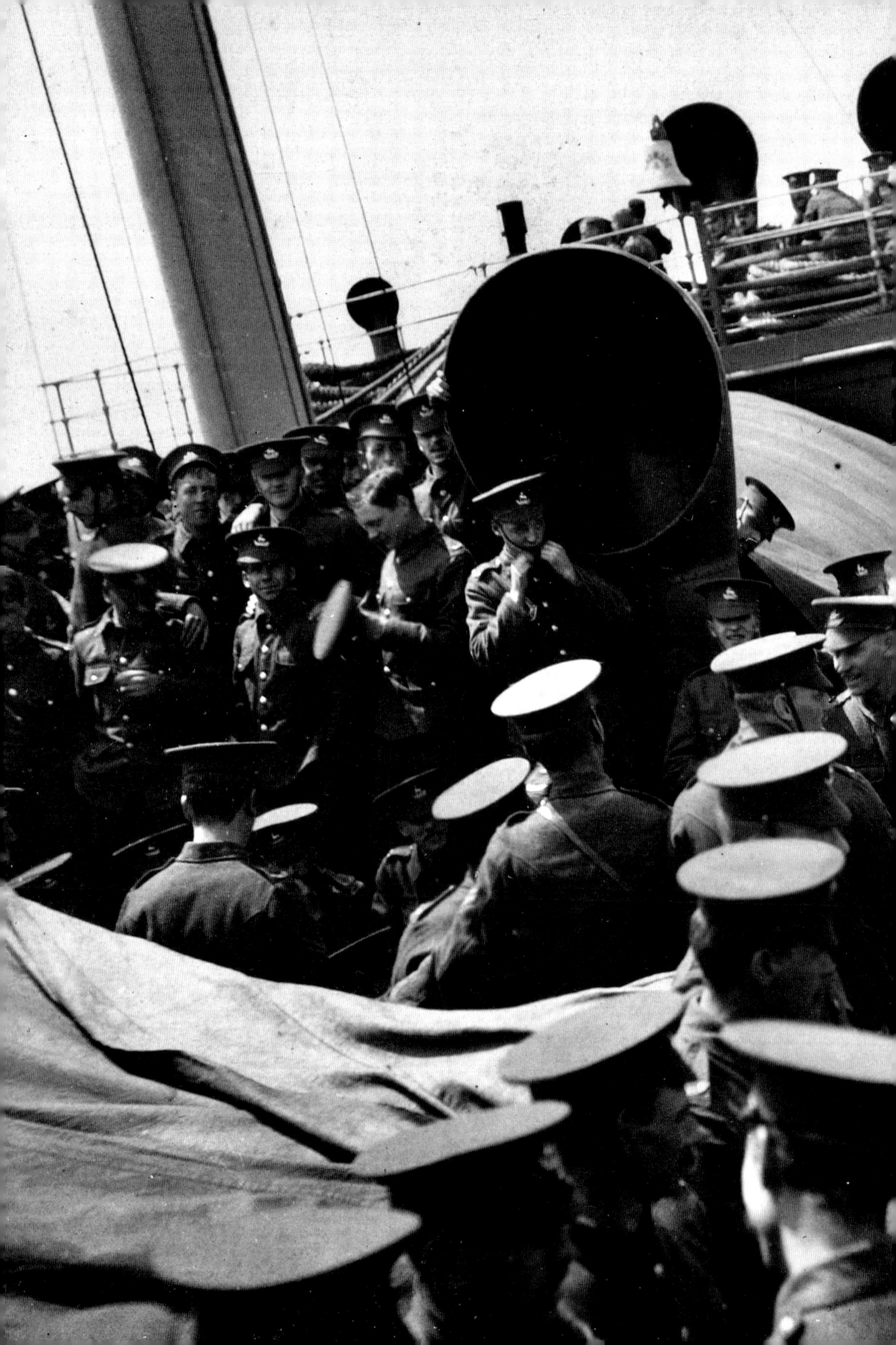

11 Grey Waters

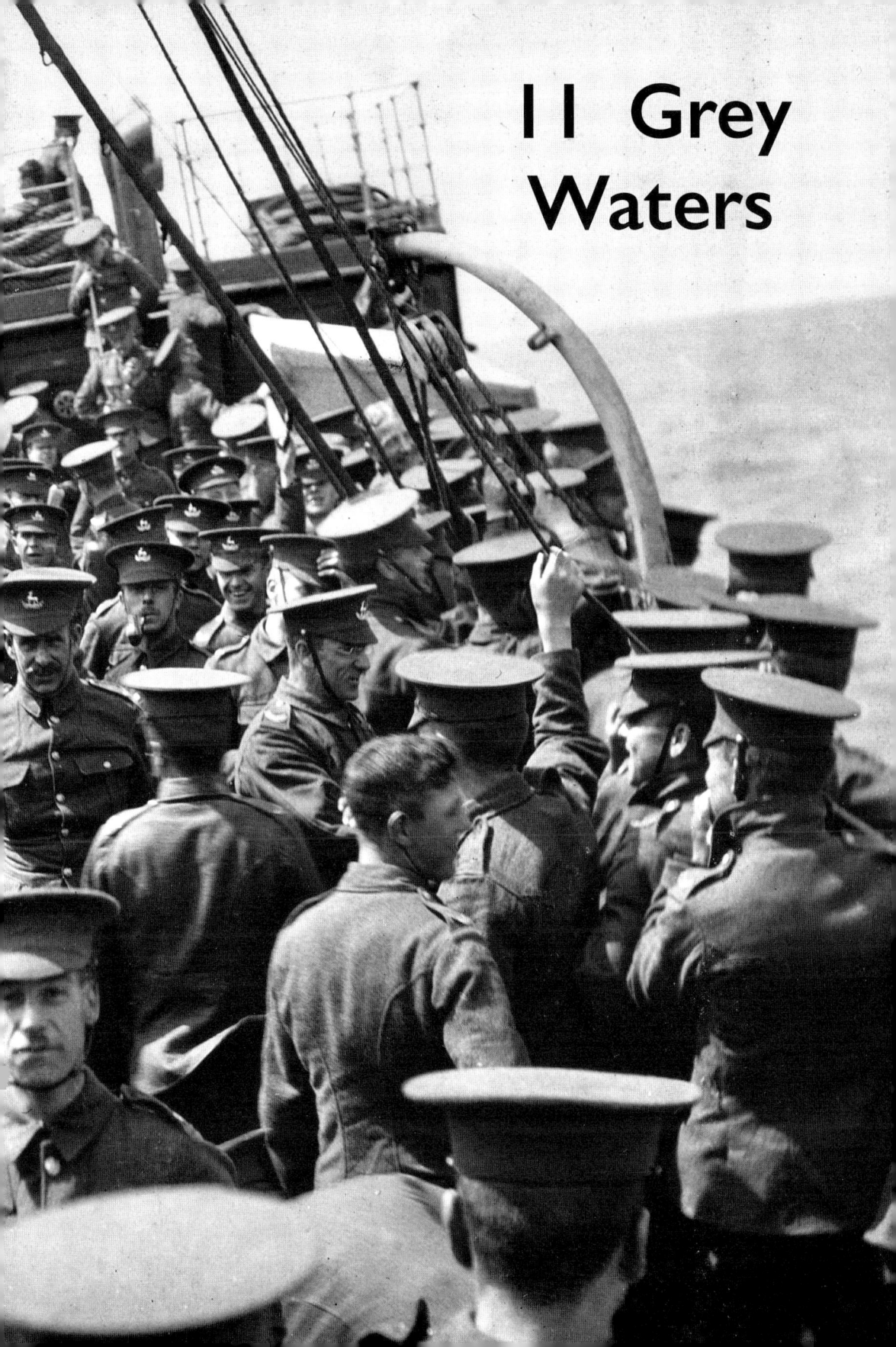

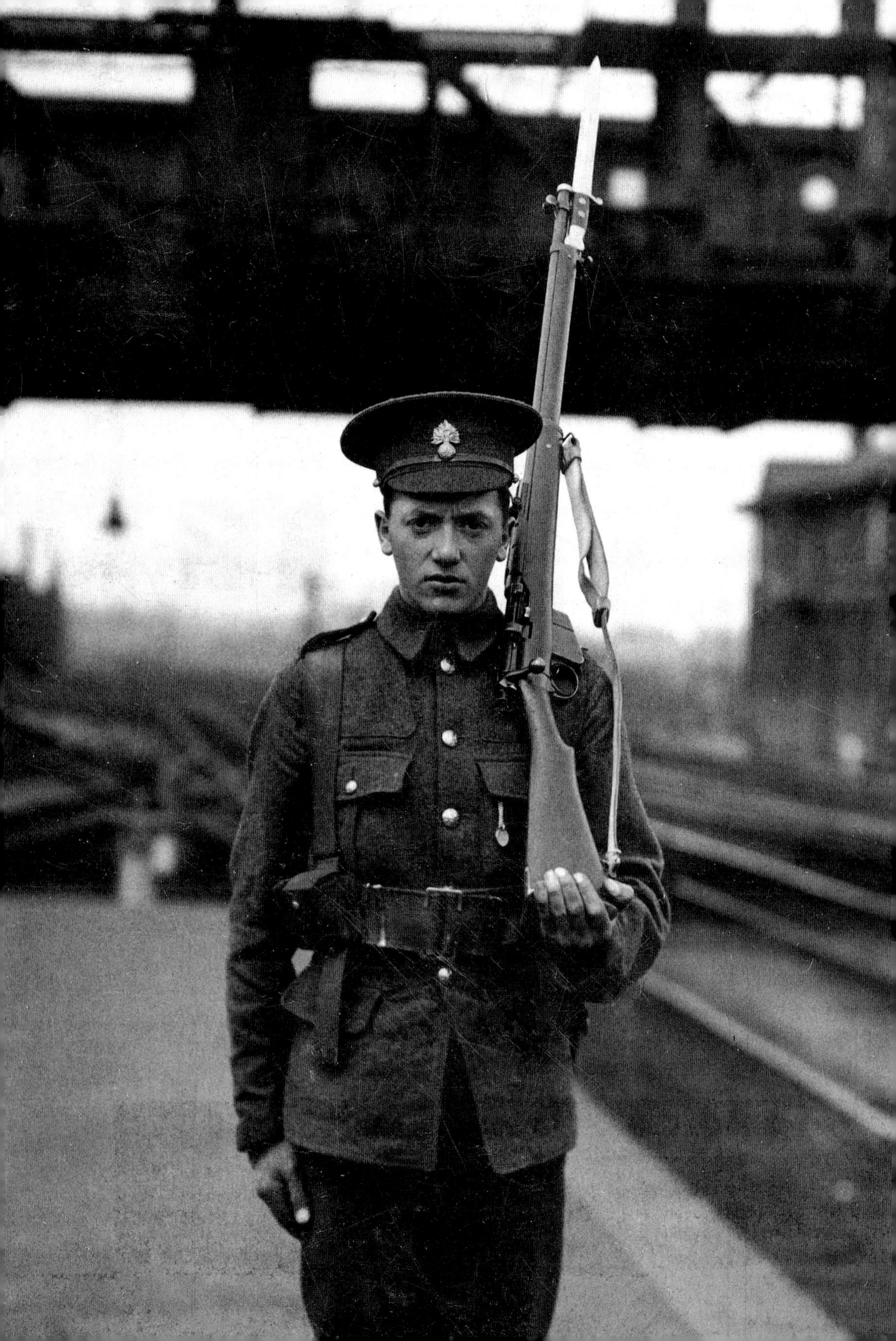

'I have an almost overwhelming terror of a violent death or of a wound, and it will be very difficult for me to do my bit in face of it, but somehow I think I'll do it – I think I'll find the strength to go through the great ordeal that is coming.'

Anonymous

[An] incident concerned a draft for France which was paraded for inspection by the GOC [General Officer Commanding] London Command (General Lloyd). It was supposed to be *en état de partir*, that is, with everything complete right down to the last pair of spare bootlaces, ready, if need be, to march straight off parade into battle.

After the formal inspection, a considerable number of men picked out at random were ordered to take their equipment and spread it all out for kit inspection. The result was embarrassing. Many of the beautifully squared packs had been made trim with pieces of wood down the sides and were filled with hay as being less burdensome than greatcoat and complete kit. The General went purple in the face and cursed us as the most unmitigated set of sweeps he had ever had under his command and the CO looked as though he wanted to crawl under the nearest stone. I expect he got into a good deal of trouble over the incident, but to us it was merely amusing. If one's platoon sergeant had cause to be dissatisfied with one's conduct, he could make life unpleasant, but generals were so far above us that their ravings were no more important to us than the growl of distant thunder.

Embarkation leave, permitting men to go home and say their farewells, was normally taken a matter of days before the order to entrain for the coastal ports. Leave could last forty-eight hours, it might be a few days, or conversely nothing at all: it was not an inalienable right.

Private John Nettleton, 2/28th (County of London) Battalion (Artists Rifles)

Opposite: Guarding a train station shortly before going abroad: a lovely portrait of an unknown soldier.

Private George Coppard, 6th The Queen's Own (Royal West Surrey Regiment)

Overseas leave started, and I went with the first batch. Some barrack-room lawyer told me that all entries on a soldier's crime sheet were expunged when he went overseas. On hearing this I was tempted to overstay my leave and, reckoning that there was some doubt about my eventual survival, I took three extra days. It was a stupid thing to do, but somehow I owed it to myself to do something in defiance of authority. I avoided the Red Caps, but on my return I was clapped in the guardroom forthwith… My punishment from the CO was seven days' Jankers, plus a nasty dressing-down. Overstaying leave was worked by a lot of the lads calculating that three extra days were well worth seven days' CB. The police sergeant had his work cut out, for there were more defaulters than work to keep them busy.

Men of the Birmingham Pals waiting for the leave train to pull in.

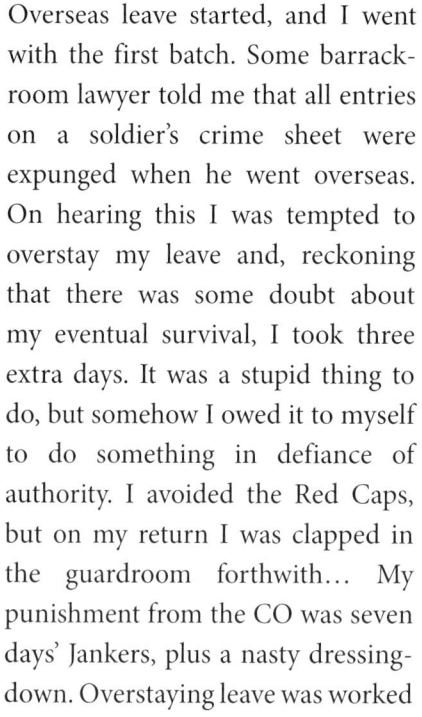

There was always a risk-reward calculation to be made in such circumstances, for the authorities' options for retribution varied significantly. Guardsman Jack Close, a former policeman in civilian life, approached Norman Cliff. He appeared to be in significant distress.

Guardsman Norman Cliff, 1st Grenadier Guards

Punishment had prevented him from going on leave. 'I'll be glad to go to France to get away from the life they lead me here,' he said, 'but I can't with a good heart if they don't let me see my little missus and kids first. I'd stand to be shot (with sudden passion) if only to have a look at them first.'

I advised him to apply for leave and if it was not granted to take it and put up with the consequences.

'But I haven't got the money to go without a free pass,' he replied hopelessly, 'and it's no good sending home for it 'cos the missus has all she can do to feed the kids.' I lent him enough and he disappeared.

Jack Close went home. On his return, Close was awarded fourteen days' detention.

I saw him on the small enclosed detention square. With full pack on a broiling day he and two others were being quick-marched around and around in a circle whilst a sour-tempered Sergeant badgered them to step faster and faster still. Close, a broken man before, staggered along looking a helpless wreck with not a spark of hope left. Indignation, almost to the point of nausea struck me.

Guardsman Norman Cliff, 1st Grenadier Guards

Shortly afterwards, Cliff's draft leave was granted and he made his way to his parents' home in Devon.

Precious days at Torquay seemed to flee almost before they began. I sat for whole afternoons at Mother's bedside, my heart heavy with the thought of the anxieties she endured and of how poorly I had repaid her sacrifices and love. Longing to speak the innermost confidences, yet sitting silent or talking only of trivialities, all the time trying to imprint on my mind her gentle features, whose lines of trouble could not mar her beautiful calm. I knew her heart ached, but her eyes were brave and her lips smiled. She must have longed for me to open my heart to her before I went, perhaps forever, and to pour out her love and prayers for me. But both of us, trying not to be overcome with emotion, silently exchanged thoughts we could not put into words. Of course, no sooner was I seated in the train for London than I became angry with myself for being tongue-tied and failing to express my love and gratitude to all at home for all I owed to them.

Guardsman Norman Cliff, 1st Grenadier Guards

Such an awkward farewell, such stoicism in the face of imminent danger was perhaps the sole option open to Cliff in such circumstances: weeping and wailing helped nobody. As one officer remembered, 'The time [had] arrived for dismal calls on friends and relatives, dismal on account of their unnatural hilarity and cordiality.' These leaving rites 'we generally term "horrors of war"', he wrote.

Rifleman Aubrey Smith, 2/5th (City of London) Battalion (London Rifle Brigade)

That last evening at home, the lump in the throat, my mother's brave attempt to appear as usual, the impulse I felt to throw my arms round her which must be checked lest her assumed cheerfulness break down in that moment, the emotion of my father's voice: all these excruciating feelings seemed to overwhelm me and make me dread the final parting. They were bad enough in later days, even when we were more accustomed to grief and our finer feelings were rendered more callous by the tragic events around us, it told upon one's parents and almost made one question whether one had done the right thing in being so anxious to leave home training for service in France. My own people came down to Haywards Heath for the weekend after the final leave. They talked about cheerful things, but the hours were tinged with sadness.

Embarkation leave: it was extraordinarily hard to see family members for the last time. Many men could not help but be subdued, appearing distant in the days before returning to the regimental depot.

My dear Mother

    I'm sorry you could not see me off quite at ease on Sunday. But I did so much enjoy the visit. You will not take it as any reflection on home when I say that I don't think I've ever enjoyed short visits to it so much before… I arrived back into a sea of rumours. Things started with the ugly reality of breakfast at six and a long morning in the rain on the Ash Ranges, firing machine-guns. No one really knows what is going to happen, and though the prophets fix on Monday, that seems to me an unlikely day to shift troops about. All we have been told definitely is to take plenty of food with us when we do go, since our transport is not going the same route. By all appearances next Sunday seems very likely, and perhaps Thursday evening might be the best time to go up to Waterloo [to say goodbye].

    Love from Arthur

Second Lieutenant Arthur Heath, 6th The Queen's Own (Royal West Kent Regiment)

I had to leave Manchester at 10.30 am on the Sunday to get back to Larkhill for seven that evening and my father came to the station to see me off. I remember him asking if there was anything I wanted and saying as we shook hands, 'Do your duty. Do it well. Run no unnecessary risks.'

Private Albert Andrews, 19th The Manchester Regiment (4th City)

We had a sort of farewell service at Broomfield yesterday morning, 9.30 am, the first church parade for about two and a half months. I was on guard, but being off at 6 pm was able to go to Chelmsford Cathedral, which is always full of off-duty men every Sunday night. The cleric didn't break in to his course of sermons on the Prodigal Son, which he has been giving, to say a word of advice or encouragement to the men, and not a word was said of their going, or any special hymn or prayer, although it is public news… Many of the men were frightfully disgusted at what may be their last service, possibly forever.

Gunner Cecil Longley, 1st South Midland Brigade, Royal Field Artillery

Of course everyone was very excited; one felt that a little of the real thing, after months and months of sham and boredom, must be a change for the good. The camp was in uproar most of the night.

    The actual process of mobilising, apart from the uncertainty of our movements and destination, was not very exciting. As far as I was

Second Lieutenant George Butterworth, 13th The Durham Light Infantry

An unknown infantry battalion at an open-air church service before overseas embarkation.

concerned, it consisted chiefly in making out lists of kit deficiencies and 'pinching' as much as possible from the quartermaster.

After April 1915, and in response to intense fighting around the town of Ypres and the Germans' first use of poison gas, an additional piece of kit was hurriedly produced and distributed to those about to embark overseas.

Private Sydney Fuller, 8th The Suffolk Regiment

Church parade at 9.30 am. Handed in one 'suit' of khaki, slippers, hairbrush, one towel, and one shirt, per man. Issued with gas respirators, which consisted of a pad of cotton waste wrapped in a length of black gauze or net. The cotton waste was saturated in solution, which, from the feel of it, was mainly 'hypo'. The whole respirator was carried in a small rubber-lined fabric pouch, tied with two strings. We were also each issued with a small can of non-freezing rifle oil.

Every man was in full marching order. His rifle was the 'Short Lee Enfield, Mark IV', his bayonet the long single-edged blade in general use throughout the British Army. In addition to his arms he carried 120 rounds of .303 calibre ammunition, an entrenching-tool, water-bottle, haversack, containing both emergency and the day's rations, and his pack, strapped to shoulders and waist in such a way that the weight of it was equally distributed. His pack contained the following articles: a greatcoat, a woollen shirt, two or three pairs of socks, a change of underclothing, a 'housewife' – the soldiers' sewing-kit – a towel, a cake of soap, and a 'hold-all', in which were a knife, fork, spoon, razor, shaving-brush, toothbrush, and comb. All of these were useful and sometimes essential articles, particularly the toothbrush, which Tommy regarded as the best little instrument for cleaning the mechanism of a rifle ever invented. Strapped on top of the pack was the blanket roll wrapped in a waterproof ground sheet; and hanging beneath it, the canteen in its khaki-cloth cover. Each man wore an identification disk on a cord about his neck. It was stamped with his name, regimental number, regiment, and religion. A first-aid field dressing, consisting of an antiseptic gauze pad and bandage and a small vial of iodine, sewn in the lining of his tunic, completed the equipment.

Private James Hall, 9th The Royal Fusiliers (City of London Regiment)

'General Edwards inspecting draft, 1.5.15' is the contemporary caption. The photographer, Second Lieutenant Reginald Elcock, serving with the King's Liverpool Regiment, would be in France before the end of the year, taking his camera with him. He survived the war.

Private Robert Sturges, 19th The Royal Fusiliers (City of London Regiment)

It is difficult to give any idea of the hundreds of things which have to be done at the last moment before a battalion leaves for the front. Clothing has to be given in, other clothing served out; identity discs, field dressings, service caps, iron rations, ammunition, clasp knives, etc. distributed; palliasses and pillows must be emptied of their straw, bed boards stacked, blankets rolled, and other things too numerous to mention.

I haven't the vaguest idea how I'm going to take everything. I have spent hours sewing field dressings, gas helmets, etc. inside my tunic, and I'm now engaged on an impromptu pocket. Some of us have bought extra haversacks, and we have also been served out with white bags for the iron ration. We have in addition to carry 120 rounds of ball ammunition on us (an incredible weight), a big army blanket and waterproof sheet, as well as full equipment and rifle; and then there is our wardrobe! I shudder to think how many things I have bought lately which 'exactly fit the breast pocket'. There is a large tin cigarette case (I thought it might protect my heart or something), a looking-glass, a writing case, a collapsible knife, fork, and spoon, a pocket medicine chest, a tobacco pouch, and a tinder lighter. All these things, as well as a bulky pocket-book, a soldier's Pay Book, pipe and matches, have to fit into the very small pockets provided in the tunic. I shall hardly be able to stand up…

That was written before the actual struggle began – the struggle of packing, I mean. Men were to be seen with perspiration pouring down their faces, vainly trying to cram into their packs and haversacks twice as much as they would hold. Desperate decisions had to be made as to whether this or that quite indispensable article should be left behind. Finally it was done somehow. When I tried on my various accoutrements, the weight, which hung upon my shoulders, pressed against my hips and glued my feet to the ground, was tremendous. A friend of mine weighed himself in full kit before starting and turned the scale at nineteen stone! One's appearance was rather comic; the pack was bulged out by the blanket and waterproof sheet, which it contained in addition to socks and shirts, etc.; the two haversacks, filled to over-flowing, stuck out like saddle bags on either side; the overcoat was rolled and looked like a horse-collar worn bandolier fashion, and finally the iron ration bag, suspended from any odd buckle, banged against one's legs at every step. The iron ration consists, by the way, of a tin of bully, a tin containing soups in solid form, I believe (I never opened one), and several large biscuits; it is only to be resorted to in case of emergency.

My chief concern at the moment is, however, the individual soldier and his personal belongings, and, if I relate my own experiences in this respect, I suppose I shall be relating the experiences of almost every soldier who has been through all the hurry and excitement of preparations for moving overseas.

The '<u>great day</u>'. Burnt the straw from our beds during the morning and handed in our blankets etc. 120 rounds of ammunition were issued to each man – the real article this time. Hitherto only blank had been issued, except when firing on the butts.

Private Sydney Fuller, 8th The Suffolk Regiment

After the first two Kitchener divisions (the 9th and 14th divisions) departed on 9 May and 19 May, Arthur Heath's 12th Division followed on 29 May. Most men assumed they were bound for the Western Front, unless there was evidence to the contrary.

On the eve of embarkation the atmosphere in camp was febrile. Behaviour was frequently raucous, with officers and NCOs overlooking all but the most exuberant activities so long as the men were ready to leave in the morning.

The men for draft were all smiles and excitement. Those other than Close who had not been able to bid farewell to their families drowned their distress in noise. Choruses rang through the barracks, hilarity and horseplay made pandemonium in the rooms. At night men streamed out of barracks to have a final spree, knowing that on the last night no one would be allowed out in case some might not return.

Thus on the eve of departure the canteen was the only resort left and it was packed with men singing and standing last drinks over and over again to their pals. Things became more and more uproarious

Guardsman Norman Cliff, 1st Grenadier Guards

until beer mugs began to fly about and bottles were smashed. All knew that whatever they did that night would not be marked against them unless it was sufficiently serious to bar them from the draft.

The fracas did not end with the closing of the canteen.

Guardsman Norman Cliff, 1st Grenadier Guards

A rush was made for the barrack rooms. One man fixed his bayonet and charged madly up and down, narrowly missing comrades who leapt nimbly left and right. Another loaded his rifle and shot off the gas shades one by one and then swung from the central gas pendulum. It was well into morning before comparative calm prevailed.

Private Sydney Fuller, 8th The Suffolk Regiment

Nine of the Battalion Signallers were warned to parade at midnight, when they were to leave the camp with the advance party. Towards evening, two of these nine were in very good spirits (canteen beer), and they gave us quite a good performance. One, under the combined influence of beer and Horatio Bottomley (his favourite author), gave us a stirring (?) speech, while the other man persisted in singing a song at the same time. As they stood on a form, clinging to one another to keep their balance, one singing, the other impressing on us the fact that we were going to France to 'C-r-rush German Milit'rism'. 'Comrades, we are going to fight for King and Country,' etc., the effect was very moving…

Unfortunately, they did not fall off the form, but it was funny enough as it was. While this was going on, we were having our hair cropped very short, as we had been told that short hair was healthiest when on active service. By the time we were finished, we were a most villainous-looking crew, enough to frighten anything. The advance party left the camp at midnight, as ordered, and as our high-spirited friends left with them, we got some sleep.

Alas, my poor hair! I had every blade ruthlessly clipped off a quarter of an hour ago. One tuft I managed to secrete in the palm of my hand as it rolled down my shoulders, and I enclose it herewith in memory of the glory that once was. I'm glad you can't see me now, or you would hope for my departure as soon as possible.

Private Robert Sturges, 19th The Royal Fusiliers (City of London Regiment)

Physically, the men were 'in the pink', as Tommy says. They were clear-eyed, vigorous, alert, and as hard as nails. With their caps on they looked the well-trained soldiers which they were; but with caps removed, they resembled so many uniformed convicts less the prison pallor. 'Overseas haircuts' were the last tonsorial cry, and for several days previous to our departure, the army hairdressers had been busily wielding the close-cutting clippers.

Private James Hall, 9th The Royal Fusiliers (City of London Regiment)

The Battalion will parade at 2 am tomorrow… Such were the words which, after a month of conflicting rumours, finally convinced us that this was the real thing at last. The long year of training was a thing of the past, and we were now standing on the brink of an entirely new phase of our lives. The future, though long and eagerly expected, was still almost completely unknown. After so long a period of regular and monotonous routine, the sensation of uncertainty, of not knowing where we should be in a week's time, was novel and exciting to say the least of it.

I suppose every one knows the feeling which he has before starting on a journey, especially when the place which he is leaving is well known to him, while his destination is vague and uncertain. All the old familiar things appear to take on a new aspect. The fact of leaving them seems to change their nature.

Private Robert Sturges, 19th The Royal Fusiliers (City of London Regiment)

Where possible, men sent final letters or notes to their families, usually to reassure them of their return.

Opposite: *Just prior to embarkation, and for reasons of hygiene, men had their hair clipped back to the scalp. These lads, serving with the 1/4th Royal Scots, would be on the Gallipoli peninsula within the month.*

Second Lieutenant Arthur Heath, 6th The Queen's Own (Royal West Kent Regiment)

My dear Mother,

In an hour or so we shall move. So my last thoughts in England are to you. I had myself photographed this morning. Enclosed is the receipt for a dozen, and the proofs will be sent to you in due course. One is just to amuse you by showing what my hair looks like now. The rest I hope are more flattering. If I never see you again, this will show you what I was like at the end of my time in England, and if I come back and settle down to civilian life again, it will be a memento of my curious past. I wish I could tell you how much I love you. But you know already. As I told you, don't bother if letters get through irregularly. We shall have a busy time till we get up into the trenches, and it won't be all leisure even then. So always take no news to be good news.

My love to you all,
Arthur.

In June 1915, Private Thomas Lyon was sent out with a draft of 300 men to replace casualties in the regiment's 1/9th Battalion. Leaving Dundee, the atmosphere was like a 'holiday excursion', wrote Lyon, the men hiding their true emotions from friends and relatives who joined throngs of people wishing them farewell and 'good luck'.

Private Thomas Lyon, 2/9th The Highland Light Infantry (Glasgow Highlanders)

It was dark when we assembled for the last time on the familiar parade ground, and rain was falling heavily. 'A regular wash-out for the last,' said Jimmy M__, who was my left-hand neighbour. We heard no word of command being given – only a dense roar from the crowd that lined the streets, then an answering cheer from our fellows further along the ranks. With the cheers there mingle the sounds of soldiers' voices 'O, Mary, bonnie Mary, will ye mairry me!' We knew that the ranks had begun to move off and as we joined in the cheering and singing we too formed fours and fell into step.

Progress was difficult, for the narrow streets were crowded with civilians and soldiers come to give us a send-off. These surged in upon us to shake us by the hand and bestow cigarettes and sweets on us. It was no easy thing to force one's way through the crowd, fully accoutred as we were. As we drew near to the station the crowds became denser and pressed in more closely on us, so that it became quite impossible to retain our formation of fours. Each man had perforce to fight his own way through the handshaking mob bestowing hurried goodbyes *en passant* to the pals he was leaving behind.

Some of the fellows around me tried to keep up their singing, but their voices became wavering and tremulous, and there were suspicious lapses in the notes from which one might deduce their true feelings. Latterly all attempt at singing was given up, and it was simply a case of shouting goodbyes on either side.

When as last we were all lined up on the station platform I found little Jimmy M__ beside me again, and his face was very white. 'It's too damn bad,' he was saying. 'The boys shouldn't have come tonight. It's rotten – leaving them behind after all those months together. Gad! I'd rather face the whole German army single-handed than go through that again. Thank heaven there'll be no more goodbyes.'

An unknown battalion on the march. In full kit, including the clothes he wore, an infantryman marched with an additional 59 pounds and 6¾ ounces.

Guardsman Norman Cliff, 1st Grenadier Guards

In the morning we paraded in full battle kit and, headed by the regimental band playing *The British Grenadiers*, marched over Waterloo Bridge with a few tearful relatives trotting alongside and occasionally a baby held out for a father to kiss. Rows of onlookers shouted 'Good luck!' and we wondered who amongst us might have return tickets…

Before departure we were given a farewell message from the King saying 'You are leaving home to fight for the safety and honour of my Empire.' Were we?

Second Lieutenant Geoffrey Fildes, 2nd Coldstream Guards

Outside, across the large expanse of grass that spread in front of the Officers' Block, groups of men were beginning to appear from the neighbouring barrack rooms. Somehow, the excitement of our departure drove away our usual appetites. Disquieting thoughts kept recurring; perhaps, even now, your servant might be late with your equipment? Hastily finishing our last meal, some of us repaired outside to make a final inspection of our belongings. Behind me I heard the familiar movement of the guardsman's salute. 'Your kit, sir! All correct.'

Indeed it was, like everything else the excellent fellow had done for me that day.

A movement toward 'the square' by the bunches of men around the side blocks now began. Among the khaki throng, the scarlet tunics of the Bandsmen from London showed up conspicuously; it was time to be getting on our equipment. Already my man was impassively waiting.

Webbing equipment, complete with full pack, constitutes another necessary evil of war. However, after a few moments to adjust a buckle or two, we were ready to move on to parade, feeling for all the world like an out-of-season group of Father Christmases.

Lieutenant & Quartermaster Joseph Goss, 8th The King's Own Scottish Borderers

[There] followed the task of loading wagons, preparatory to the transport moving off. S.A.A. [Small Arms Ammunition], tools and signalling equipment, all had to be packed according to mobilisation instructions. Stores and Officers' valises were packed on two baggage wagons which always accompanied the battalion when on the march. Great care was taken that officers' kits should not exceed the official weight, viz. 35 lbs. A meagre allowance, surely! But what could one

An atmospheric image of a battalion passing through a town's streets on the way to the docks and the Western Front.

do? Officers couldn't get their kits down to the prescribed weight without leaving some necessary article of clothing behind. In these circumstances, a good servant was a boon. He would pack his officer's valise so compactly that even the Quartermaster would be deceived. Each kit was scrutinised critically, but none was sent back.

As there was a surplus of subalterns, some had to be left behind. The selection rested with the Commanding Officer. He issued his orders. There were no cases of suicide among the band of outcasts; but in their minds lingered a feeling that the C.O.'s power of discrimination was a minus quantity, and that he had not selected the best men.

Teenager Basil Peacock was held back from a draft of men being sent to one of the Public Schools Battalions in France. Disappointed at being removed at the last minute for being under age, he became excited when the company sergeant major told him that should any man drop out Basil would take his place.

Private Basil Peacock, 27th (Reserve) Battalion, The Royal Fusiliers

There was one man missing from parade – our university lecturer – and this caused some commotion, as it was thought he had jumped the draft and deserted. A search party was sent through the building and in a few minutes the missing man appeared, his full marching order hanging about him like parcels on a Christmas tree. He held a small book in one hand and his rifle in the other, and trotted up to the draft conducting officer, gave a slight bow and said, 'I much regret to have kept you all waiting. Thinking I had half an hour to spare, I thought it advisable to visit the toilets and became so interested in this book of verse that time passed without my knowledge. My apologies to you, sir.'

Everyone, including the officer, roared with laughter; the CSM was so relieved that he had a full muster he simply called him a bloody fool and told him to fall in the ranks. The incident relieved the strain.

At the barracks of the Coldstream Guards and behind the windows of the officers' mess, faces appeared, then onto the mess steps those not on the draft assembled to wish comrades farewell. At the barrack gates, throngs of NCOs and men waited to shout their encouragement and support as the regimental colonel gave permission for the draft to go.

Second Lieutenant Geoffrey Fildes, 2nd Coldstream Guards

'Parade - 'Shun! Slope hah!'

The serried ranks sprang to life, giving forth the three movements of 'the slope'. The order to march was barely out before its echoes were drowned in a crash from the Band stationed on our flank. Short men though some of them were, their bearskins rose above the wall of khaki that lined the road. Now, I reflected, one was really off to the war.

'Good luck t'yer, Ted. Love t'Fritz.'

'Not 'arf! Same ter you,' would come the somewhat inconsequent reply. On every side arose a babble of greetings, some in what one felt to be real earnest, others jocularly ribald.

'Goodbye, sargint-major! Sorry I can't stop.' The note of chaff drew forth instant applause from those who were able to appreciate its full significance. A twinkle came to the eye of the sergeant-major.

'Take care of your mascot, lads,' came the reply, aimed not so much at the individual as at those in his vicinity.

And now, wheeling to the right, we passed the barrack guard, salute answering salute. A moment later, wheeling once more, we had left them behind us. Ahead of me, the long column, moving rhythmically in step and displaying a vista of caps and beautifully arranged packs, spread forward down the road. From my position in rear, I could note with appreciation the magnificent body of men. Five feet eleven inches was our actual height in those days, and they looked every inch of it. Powerfully built miners from Tyneside, strapping fellows from Birmingham and Devon, they were indeed good to look upon…

Presently we were descending the steep slope of the Castle Hill, and from the houses on one hand and the walls of the Castle opposite resounded the notes of 'The girl I left behind me'. Never until that moment had I understood the full beauty of that old English tune. Cheer answered cheer and hand replied to waving handkerchief, as we glanced up to window and balcony. There, you could not help noting every variety of human emotion. Assuredly, it was to no ordinary war we were bound.

Often I had read of such scenes as this, but it was hard to realise that the present moment was actual fact. It all seemed so unreal. My world had not acquainted me with such things beyond the artificial thrills of a patriotic drama. Behind the footlights one had heard the roll of drums and even the music now ringing in one's ears, but it had all been unreal; moreover, the knowledge that presently one would be motoring homeward to supper had not enhanced its appeal. But this was real: it was fact. Tears and smiles and sparks from the cobbled streets –yes, this was different.

The men were mostly old soldiers who had brought their wives and families to the town, and the farewells were heartrending. How many had made the last sacred parting at home that morning, yet how many

Captain Cecil Street, Royal Garrison Artillery

Right: *The 10th Battalion, The Lincolnshire Regiment, better known to posterity as the Grimsby Chums, takes part in a farewell march in their home town, although it was some time before the men embarked for overseas service.*

a loving heart had been unable to resist the temptation to come and take one last look at all it possessed in the world as it went away upon the unknown trail! Yet they were brave to the last, one hurried handgrip, the quick thrusting into a pocket of one final gift of love, wrapped up so carefully; one last whispered word, wherein the sob was choked back so that he might not hear, was all they allowed themselves, the last dear token. And then the great procession swept by, magnified through the mist of their tears till it seemed a dreadful convoy of huge black wagons of the dead, parting their beloved ones from them for ever, cutting their hearts in twain to the sound of the awful roaring of grim necessity. War has its sorrows, its pathos, but surely none so poignant as this, the tragedy of countless hearts upon a background of impressive pomp and display.

Opposite: An unknown battalion of the Gloucestershire Regiment leaving a town, surrounded by appreciative crowds wishing the men good luck.

The women were kissing their men. Factory girls in their shawls broke in among us. A red-headed girl flung her arms about me. 'Glory be to Jesus,' she cried again and again. Everyone pressed gifts upon us. But a few of the women from mean streets were sobbing. Useless for us to tell them that we were only to guard lines of communication. The women in the mean streets know by tradition what war is. And perhaps their own men were dead already.

Private William Andrews, 2/4th The Black Watch (Royal Highlanders)

Regimental or civic bands played tunes of farewell as men, many with sore heads from the previous night's ribaldry, jostled and shoved their way to find seats on trains. Private Robert Sturges heard the band, but the songs 'failed to rouse an atom of sentiment in us'. Weary, most of the men in his carriage slept their way to the coast.

In Cecil Street's motorised convoy, there had been seventy lorries, with additional cars and motorbikes. The convoy had been an impressive sight, kicking up great volumes of dust as it passed through village after village to the curiosity of inhabitants. There was some doubt in their minds, believed Street, 'whether the gigantic procession was really composed of soldiers, or was a mammoth travelling circus'.

Captain Cecil Street, Royal Garrison Artillery

We took six hours to cover thirty miles, including halts, not a bad performance for our first expedition, and arrived at the 'Rest Camp' at which we were to pass the night about dusk. Now Rest Camps are so called because under no possible combination of circumstances is there any possibility of any one obtaining any rest in them. One's stay there is fortunately very short, and the few hours of one's sojourn are amply filled by the many details that have to be attended to during a pause in movement. Nor is this all; the authorities in charge of the camp do their best to harass one, presumably because they have nothing better to do. They demand nominal rolls, require all manner of forms to be filled up, and generally behave with the greatest possible measure of obstruction. But in this particular case, the advance party that we had sent on ahead to make arrangements had found nobody in authority, and had commandeered huts for the men and found billets for the officers as best they could. It worked out all right, we left a couple of officers in what purported to be the Mess, there was no room for more, and the rest of us wandered off to a private hotel that we had been directed to. Here we spent a very comfortable few hours, and here I had the last real bath that was to be mine for many a long day.

From a station platform, Gunner Cecil Longley hurriedly scrawled a note to his family. The battery had had a 'weird night', he wrote. Their departure had been undertaken in near total secrecy, the battery leaving at midnight.

> Not a word was spoken from harnessing in to the time we got into the train on pain of arrest. I had to ride 200 yards in front of the battery as outpost guard, a man with a red lamp riding just behind, to warn any motorists that troops were coming.

Gunner Cecil Longley, 1st South Midland Brigade, Royal Field Artillery

Well, we had a magnificent and inspiring send-off. One belated man and his wife waved at us as we passed through Chelmsford and one policeman bid us good luck, otherwise we have sneaked out of England stealthily and one can hardly believe the finality of the business. Passing through the London stations was a bit more exciting, and our blobbed

The 20th Royal Fusiliers boarding a train at Worksop. These men were not yet destined for France, but it would not be long.

and variegatedly painted guns caused much comment… The veterinary officer is running though our horses finally and casting any unfits (only three) out of our battery, and remounts are here already to take their place.

We didn't know where we were going or how long we would be on the train, and as most of the lads had been drinking before they got into the carriages, they soon needed the toilet. Anyway, those who were further up the train, where I was, just opened the window and urinated. When we eventually stopped, some of the lads further down the train who had stuck their heads out of the window were saying, 'Oh, you could feel the steam from the engine,' but it wasn't that at all.

Private Jack Davis, 6th The Duke of Cornwall's Light Infantry

The men hung their newly shaved heads out of windows, waved, roared, shrieked, yelled, sang, and defeated official precaution. In the corner of my compartment, an elderly major slept. He knew all about departures, and was thankful for the opportunity of a few hours' peace. The rest of us chatted away about our anticipations. We were all very young and girded impatiently at the slowness of the train. At one point I saw the guise of an elderly friend and hoped I might survive to drink his port again.

Second Lieutenant Guy Chapman, 13th The Royal Fusiliers

In the train Martin Hay leant over to me and said: 'You know, I've never been out of England before. Have you?' I replied that I had, several times. 'I haven't,' repeated Hay, with a shake of his head. 'And I never thought that when I did, it'd be to go and fight. Why,' he added, in a burst of resentment, 'I may never see the place again!' He looked at me, demanding reassurance. But before I could answer, he went on: 'But *you* don't mind, do you? You don't mind leaving England.'

Second Lieutenant Alan Thomas, 6th The Queen's Own (Royal West Kent Regiment)

'I don't want to get killed, if that's what you mean,' I said feebly. 'I want to come back.'

Hay sighed and, shifting his gaze out of the window, relapsed into silence.

The embarkation that summer of Kitchener's New Army divisions became a flood. K1 was followed in July by K2, the 15th Division embarking for France followed shortly afterwards by the 17th Division. Within days, the 19th and 20th divisions had gone too. Last to go that month was the 18th Division with Vic Cole.

Lance Corporal Vic Cole and his friends embarked from Southampton, the 7th Royal West Kent Regiment, part of the 55th Brigade, being 'packed like sardines below the decks' of the iron-built paddle steamer the SS *Mona's Queen*. Private Sydney Fuller of the 8th Suffolk Regiment, part of the division's 53rd Brigade, detrained in Folkestone and marched straight onto the boats, leaving at 10 pm on the SS *Victoria*. Both ships belonged to the Isle of Man Steam Packet Company, who had some of their ships requisitioned by the Admiralty on the outbreak of war.

Private James Hall, 9th The Royal Fusiliers (City of London Regiment)

The men, transport, horses, commissariat, medical stores, and supplies of a battalion are entrained in less than half an hour. Everything is timed to the minute. Battalion after battalion and train after train, we moved out of Aldershot at half-hour intervals. Each train arrived at the port of embarkation on scheduled time and pulled up on the docks by the side of a troop transport, great slate-coloured liners taken out of the merchant service. Not a moment was lost. The last man was aboard and the last wagon on the crane swinging up over the ship's side as the next train came in.

Private I.L. (Dick) Read, 8th The Leicestershire Regiment

Our train came to a standstill at a dockside in the deep shadow of huge sheds and here we detrained and piled arms, divesting ourselves also of our equipment and jackets preparatory to a spell of real hard work, in the course of which we manhandled limber after limber within reach of the cranes on the quayside, which slung them into the holds of a

Craning ammunition, guns, and stores onto a ship hours before embarkation.

largish steamer which lay alongside. In addition to our own Brigade Transport, horses, mules, guns, limbers and supplies were being loaded simultaneously by other cranes and fatigue parties. It was not until we had paraded and filed up the ship's gangway in the late afternoon that we had time to ascertain her name and take a breather. She was the Ellerman boat *City of Dunkirk*.

Our kit being stowed in the after-holds, we made ourselves comfortable aft in the lee of a deck house, and took the advice of a friendly old sailor who stood close by, in readiness for recovering the stern wires about to be cast off by the shore gang.

Horses being stowed on board ship. These animals were being prepared for a much longer journey eastwards and the recently opened campaign on Gallipoli.

Once inside the dock gates everything worked with the precision of a machine. Three ships were loading that day, and were embarking our two batteries and a certain number of men and stores besides ourselves.

Captain Cecil Street, Royal Garrison Artillery

We were told off [directed], so many to each vessel, the stores to one, the guns and lorries to another. One big Blue Funnel cargo boat swallowed up the latter almost at a gulp, and found room for one Battery complete as well. The remainder were packed on to another big vessel and a smaller one, and by early afternoon we were all aboard. It was a wonderful sight to see the heavy lorries and their contents, weighing perhaps seven or eight tons in all, picked up by the silent hydraulic cranes and lowered into the holds as if they had been so many toys. There was no bustle and confusion, we were not even called upon to help in any way. The stevedores took charge of us, and carried out their duties with a speed that was astonishing.

Lieutenant Eliot Crawshay-Williams, 110th Battery, Royal Field Artillery

All day long solitary officers have been arriving at the great gates leading to the docks. There they have been questioned, and, on demonstrating their business, have been directed to the Embarkation Officer. No woman, except on special duty, is allowed inside the dock gates. Farewells must be said outside. Later in the day, say about 4 pm, trains full of jubilant soldiers have run right into the quays themselves. There they have disgorged their occupants, who have piled their arms and kit in the huge sheds once devoted to more peaceful purposes, and

The last few minutes before boarding the ship and leaving for the Western Front.

made themselves as comfortable as circumstances permit. Some have a talk, some lie and smoke, some just lie.

The detached officers who keep arriving first interview the Embarkation Officer. He gives them a green chit to enable them to draw two days' rations, and a note to another Embarkation Officer nearer the boat. After exchanging the green chit for a cardboard box containing about a dozen apparent dog-biscuits, a tin of milk, two small tins of pressed beef, a tin of 'Plum and Apple' jam, two little oval tobacco-like tins labelled 'Grocery Rations', and sundry mysterious paper packets, these officers proceed to the second Embarkation Officer. He is a genial old Colonel with a fire-and-brimstone manner, but a good heart.

'My senior officer', he bellows, 'says no one must take his baggage on board yet. But,' he goes on more confidentially, but still as if condemning a criminal, 'if I were you, I should run it as near the boat as I could in a cab, and then drop it on board at my own risk, of course. Anyone taking the best cabins', he finishes, 'is liable to be turned out if senior officers afterwards arrive.'

Then all go on board. After taking cabins (with due regard to the kind advice of our fire-eating friend), there is an hour to spend before we need finally 'join our ship'. Some spend it in driving round Southampton; some are once more 'seen off'. At last all assemble on board.

Then the men march on. First the RE in single file marshalled by a subaltern, and directed to their places by a capable ship's under-officer. Next the RHA and RFA. The leading draft are a somewhat weedy lot. 'Wouldn't change 'em with my chaps,' whispers a Territorial RHA Major to his neighbour. But the next lot are stronger and more disciplined-looking. I suppose it depends on the locality whence they are drawn. Then comes a third draft of artillery, and all are aboard.

We are only taking about 700 men over, and our boat is small and fast. The men themselves are quiet and well-behaved; an occasional 'Tipperary' or more recent ditty is the limit of their noise-making. And none are drunk. The only man who has evinced any signs of super-cheeriness is one of the boat's officers, who asks me who the

Commanding Officer is, and, when I say, 'Colonel Bowling', replies, 'Not my ole frien' Tom Bowling? I shall have to make the acquaintance of Colonel Bowling…' Then he goes off walking just a little too straight to be convincing.

Private James Hall, 9th The Royal Fusiliers (City of London Regiment)

Ship by ship we moved down the harbour in the twilight, the boys crowding the rail on both sides, taking their farewell look at England – home. It was the last farewell for many of them, but there was no martial music, no waving of flags, no tearful good-byes. Our farewell was as prosaic as our long period of training had been. We were each one a very small part of a tremendous business organisation which works without any of the display considered so essential in the old days.

We left England without a cheer. There was not so much as a wave of the hand from the wharf for there was no one on the wharf to wave with the exception of a few dock labourers and they had seen too many soldiers off to the front to be sentimental about it. It was a tense moment for the men, but trust Tommy to relieve a tense situation. As we steamed away from the landing slip, we passed a barge, loaded to the water's edge with coal. Tommy has a song pat to every occasion. He enjoys, above all things, giving a ludicrous twist to a 'weepy' ballad. When we were within hailing distance of the coal barge, he began singing one of this variety, 'Keep the Home Fires Burning', to those smutty-faced barge hands. Every one joined in heartily, forgetting all about the solemnity of the leave-taking.

The big steamer swung leisurely down towards the open sea, and I, who knew every inch of the waters she was travelling, every house and field on shore, felt a curious wonder as to when I should ever see them again. War as yet seemed so far off, it was quite impossible to realise that there was a very excellent chance of my never seeing them again, that men who had passed out of harbour with perhaps the same thoughts that mine then were, lay buried in the land to which we were journeying. Gradually the panorama slipped by, lit by the rays of the setting sun, until it became too dark for me to recognise its details any longer. Then I turned away to the duties that awaited me, which were many in number.

As we started our cruise down Southampton Water about four o'clock, we were all standing on deck waving our hands to well-wishers on shore and in neighbouring boats. We passed down that Water as in a dream. How would it be possible that here everything was going on as usual – the repairing of ships, the cranes working the South Western trains probably carrying passengers back to beloved Waterloo – when just over on the other side there was fighting, shelling, killing, mutilation and all the horrors of war? A ferry passed us conveying workmen to their homes; intent on their own cares, they gave but a fleeting glance at the cargo of home-sick ones just departing. The last glance we got of

Opposite: 'We are taking about 700 men over, and our boat is small and fast. The men themselves are quiet…' The moment of embarkation, and many men were wrapped up in their own private thoughts. How many would see England again?

Captain Cecil Street, Royal Garrison Artillery

Rifleman Aubrey Smith, 2/5th (City of London) Battalion (London Rifle Brigade)

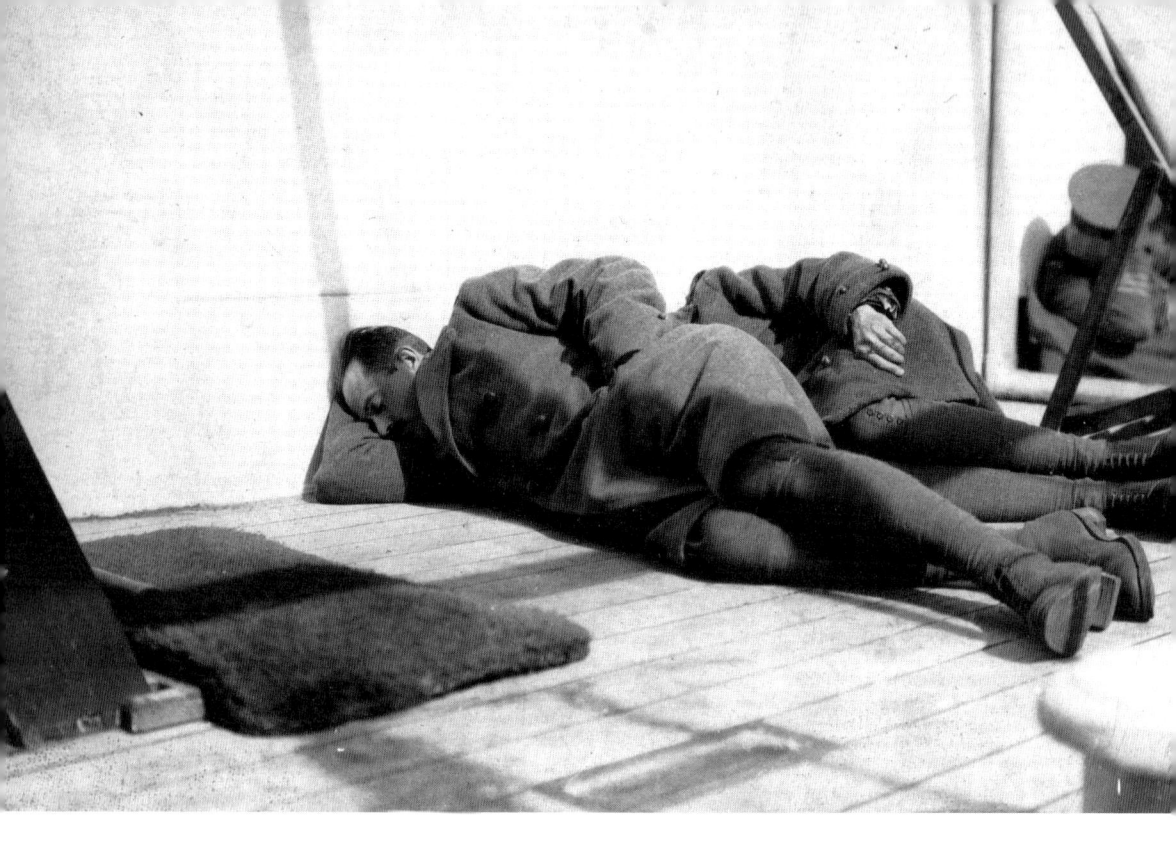

Halfway across and up on deck, officers and men take the chance to catch up on sleep.

England's shore was after dusk and we were approaching Portsmouth. A thousand pairs of eyes gazed upon it until twilight fell and scarcely a word was spoken.

Now there were only searchlights and signals to be seen. The former played upon us and our engines slowed down and finally stopped. The flashing lamps from the ships around us gave the impression that a myriad of vessels and forts were concerned with our arrival. For hours we lay there with the water lapping against our side, reflecting on the extraordinary might of our Navy.

Private I.L. (Dick) Read, 8th The Leicestershire Regiment

In the gathering twilight of the summer evening the engines stopped; the pilot went down the ladder and jumped into the dinghy which came alongside from his waiting launch. As he jumped, he waved and shouted 'Good luck, boys!' The engines restarted, and as bells tinkled on the bridge and below we all sang 'The Anchor's Weighed'. To the sustained farewells of this old song his little boat and the English coast were lost to view.

Lights drew near to us and we could make out the form of our escort on either side: then our engines moved again and our two destroyers dashed about on each flank, sometimes plunging forward and crossing our path, at others nestling close to our stern, the very embodiment of activity and the guarantee of our safe passage.

Rifleman Aubrey Smith, 2/5th (City of London) Battalion (London Rifle Brigade)

The wind had risen and already there was trouble with the horses below as the steamer pitched in the choppy sea. On either side of us raced a destroyer, ploughing through the white horses and throwing up great sheets of spray at the bows. At times we could see the length of their decks and the insides of belching funnels as they rose to the waves, by the light of occasional showers of sparks… Not feeling tired, we took a walk along the slippery decks, but the stink from the horse' quarters coming up from below drove us back again, and we thanked our lucky stars that they were not our responsibility.

Private I.L. (Dick) Read, 8th The Leicestershire Regiment

In spite of protests, the junior subaltern – myself – was detailed for duty somewhere in the bottom of the ship. I seated myself on a flight of steps and trusted that I should not be sick. The men lay tightly pressed together, rows of green cigars, and a great odour of sweaty,

Second Lieutenant Guy Chapman, 13th The Royal Fusiliers

Men of the 1/4th Royal Scots enjoying a bath on RMS Empress of Britain during a three-week-long journey to Egypt, before the battalion landed on Gallipoli. Their divisional commander would write, 'At least 50% of these men never returned.'

dusty humanity clotted between the decks. A jerky movement was imposed upon our smooth passage. I began to feel qualms. There was a bar in this part of the ship, much frequented by a party of Highlanders returning from leave. As they came down the stairs, each man jolted against me, and at each jolt, my nausea increased. At last, I rose and climbed wretchedly into the bows.

Second Lieutenant Alan Thomas, 6th The Queen's Own (Royal West Kent Regiment)

The sight of the destroyers which conveyed us across the Channel was exhilarating. They made us feel we were people who mattered. They also reminded us of Britain's command of the seas: and that pleased us, giving us a sense of our superiority. 'Fancy anyone imagining', somebody said, 'that the Germans stand an earthly!' Though I met people who felt they would never come back, I never met anyone who doubted that the Allies would win.

Second Lieutenant Victor Eberle, 475th Field Company (South Midland) Royal Engineers

For a long time I stood alone by the [SS] *Matheran*'s rail, watching the receding English coastline. Inevitably perhaps, in common with those of my fellow voyagers, and countless numbers who preceded and followed us, I had conflicting thoughts of the future and the past racing through my mind. Should I see England again? How would I react to active-service conditions?

I was setting forth on the biggest and perhaps the last venture of my life. Unexpectedly, I had been taken from a happy, but relatively humdrum life in my family's oil manufacturing and merchanting business, and exchanged it for that of a combatant on active war service.

I recall clearly now, as I watched the waves sweeping past the side of the ship. My thoughts traced out the changed course which my life had taken over the last eight months… In my thoughts of what the future might hold for us, as the English coast faded from sight, there was one which certainly did not occur to me. It was that out of the twelve officers who went overseas with the two original Field Companies in the South Midland Royal Engineers I should prove to be the only one left of them at the conclusion of hostilities, nearly four years later.

I awoke to the cries of gulls circling overhead. The ship was stationary and the sun shone strongly upon a sparkling sea as we stretched the stiffness from our limbs and sat up to take stock of our surroundings. We lay about a mile off shore from a considerable city, and around us lay shipping of many kinds. Just where we were I hadn't the faintest idea, but our [old seaman] friend told us that we were off Le Havre and that we were going in shortly.

Private I.L. (Dick) Read, 8th The Leicestershire Regiment

* * *

France lies before me as I write – a long, dark, narrow outline seen across a mile or two of grey waters. England lies somewhere beyond that grey haze that links together grey sea and greyer sky. For us England – home – lies somewhere in the past – and somewhere in the future.

The Great Adventure has begun.

Private Thomas Lyon, 2/9th The Highland Light Infantry (Glasgow Highlanders)

* * *

George Butterworth 1885–1916
Andrew Buxton 1879–1917
Donald Hankey 1884–1916
Arthur Heath 1887–1915
Frederick Keeling 1886–1916

Acknowledgements

I would like to say a big thank all to at Pen & Sword Books, in particular Jonathan Wright who has always been a great source of support and encouragement over many years: thank you, Jonathan. I would also like to thank Charles Hewitt for supporting this book and I remain ever grateful for the help of a highly professional team at Pen and Sword, including Heather Williams in production and Liv Camozzi in marketing, who have been so kind and helpful as we collectively worked to bring *Volunteers* to print. Once again, I would also like to thank Jon Wilkinson for the excellent cover. A thank you too to Tara Moran.

I would like to express my huge admiration and gratitude to Linne Matthews who is just a wonderful editor and always willing to go the extra mile to make sure that my books will always be the very best that they can be. And thank you too to Mat Blurton for this book's superb layout. It is never easy integrating images into a book and getting the look and the flow just right takes time and expertise, for which I am most grateful.

I am indebted to my agent, Jane Turnbull. Her kindness and support over the last two decades have been greatly valued and appreciated.

In preparing this book, I would like to mention my appreciation for the help given to me by Professor Karen Pratt. Karen has been a great family friend for many years and a very close friend of my late parents. I am so very grateful to Karen for reading the book and making many sensible observations and suggestions. Thank you, Karen. You have been so kind and generous with your time.

As always, I would like to pay tribute to my family, to my wife Anna and son Ben. They may be somewhat removed from the subject matter and the stresses and strains of writing, but they are always supportive and, more to the point, endlessly tolerant! I would also like to pay tribute to my late mother, Joan, who for so long encouraged me to write, helping in my development as an author in so many ways. Mum even had a very small part to play in this book too, so a final thank you.

I am grateful to Kevin Varty for the (extended) loan of Richard Hawkins' photograph album. I am also grateful to Michael Stedman for searching his old databases to find an image that I have been able to reproduce on page 122.

My gratitude for help and advice also goes to Taff Gillingham, whose knowledge of the Great War is legendary amongst those of us who adore the subject. He will always help me with advice and observations, particularly when it comes to uniforms and kit, subjects of which I know precious little! Thank you again, Taff.

And lastly, I would like to say thank you to the late Major Peter Field, a former officer in the Royal Corps of Transport. Many years ago, he spoke to me about his army career and gave me the opening story for this book.

Sources and Permissions

Published Books

Alexander, Jack, *McCrae's Battalion: The Story of the 16th Royal Scots*, Mainstream Publishing, Edinburgh, 2003

Bardgett, Colin, *The "Lonsdale Battalion" 1914–1918*, The Cromwell Press, Melksham, 1993

Carter, David, *The Stockbrokers' Battalion in the Great War*, Pen & Sword Military, Barnsley, 2014

Carter, Terry, *Birmingham Pals*, Pen & Sword Military, Barnsley, 1997

Churchill, Winston S., *The World in Crisis 1911–1918*, Odhams Press, London, 1923

Cooksey, Jon, *Barnsley Pals, the 13th and 14th Battalions York & Lancaster Regiment*, Pen & Sword Military, Barnsley, 1986

DeGroot, Gerard J., *Blighty: British Society in the Era of the Great War*, Longman, London, 1996

Hart, Peter, *Voices from the Front*, Profile Books, London, 2015

Hart, Peter & Bain, Gary, *Laugh or Cry: The British Soldier on the Western Front 1914–1918*, Pen & Sword Military, Barnsley, 2022

Hurst, Steve, *The Public Schools Battalion in the Great War*, Pen & Sword Military, Barnsley, 2007

Macdonald, Lyn, *1914–1918 Voices and Images of the Great War*, Michael Joseph, London, 1988

Marks, Dean, *Bristol's Own*, Dolman Scott, Gloucestershire, 2011

Messenger, Charles, *Call To Arms: The British Army 1914–18*, Weidenfeld & Nicolson, London, 2005

Milner, Laurie, *Leeds Pals*, Pen & Sword Military, Barnsley, 1998

Peel, Mrs C.S., *How We Lived Then*, The Bodley Head, London, 1929

Scott, William Herbert, *Leeds in the Great War, 1914–1918*, Libraries and Arts Committee, Leeds, 1923

Sherriff, Robert, quoted from *Promise of Greatness*, Panichas, George A. (ed.), Cassell, London, 1968

Simkins, Peter, *Kitchener's Army: The Raising of the New Armies 1914–1916*, Pen & Sword Military, Barnsley, 2007

Stedman, Michael, *Manchester Pals*, Pen & Sword Military, Barnsley, 1994

Turner, William, *Accrington Pals, the 11th (Service) Battalion, East Lancashire Battalion (Accrington)*, Pen & Sword Military, Barnsley, 1998

van Emden, Richard, *Britain's Last Tommies*, Pen & Sword Military, Barnsley, 2005

Wilson, Keith, *The Rasp of War: The Letters of H.A. Gwynne to the Countess Bathurst 1914–1918*, Sidgwick Jackson, London, 1988

Published Memoirs

Andrews, William Linton, *Haunting Years*, Hutchinson & Co, London, 1930

Burder, Rev. C.V., *Hell On Earth*, Big Ben Books, London, 2010

Butler, Douglas, H., *Where they Kill Captains*, Vanguard Press, Cambridge, 2018

Buxton, Andrew, *The Rifle Brigade, A Memoir*, Robert Scott, London, 1918

Carrington, Charles, *Soldier from the Wars Returning*, Hutchinson, London, 1965

Chapman, Guy, *A Passionate Prodigality*, Ivor Nicholson & Watson, London, 1933

Cliff, Norman D., *To Hell and Back with the Guards*, Merlin Books, London, 1988

Coppard, George, *With a Machine Gun to Cambrai*, Papermac, Basingstoke, 1986

Craig, Colonel J., *Home Service*, Alexander Gardner, Paisley, 1920

Crawshay-Williams, Eliot, *Leaves from an Officer's Notebook*, Edward Arnold, London, 1918

Cuddeford, Douglas, *And all for What?*, Heath Cranton, 1933

Dolden, A. Stuart, *Cannon Fodder*, Blandford Press, Pool, 1980

Douie, Charles, *The Weary Road: Recollections of a Subaltern of Infantry*, The Strong Oak Press, 1988

Eberle, Victor F., *My Sapper Venture*, Pitman Publishing, 1973

Ellison, Norman, *Remembrances of Hell*, Airlife Publishing, Shrewsbury, 1997

Fielding, Rowland, *War Letters to a Wife*, Spellmount Classics, 2001

Fildes, Geoffrey, *Iron Times with the Guards*, John Murray, London, 1918

Fuller, Sydney, *War Diary*, privately published, undated

Gibson, Ashley, *Postscript to Adventure*, J.M. Dent, London, 1930

Greenwell, Graham, *An Infant in Arms: War Letters of a Company Officer 1914–1918*, Lovat Dickson & Thompson, 1935

Hall, James Norman, *Kitchener's Mob: The Adventures of an American in the British Army*, The Riverside Press, 1916

Hankey, Donald, *The Beloved Captain*, Geoffrey Bless, London, 1956

Hanson, Ivor J., *Plough & Scatter*, Haynes Publishing, Yeovil, 2009

Heath, Arthur George, *Letters of Arthur George Heath*, B.H. Blackwell, Oxford, 1917

Jackson, John, *Private 12768*, Tempus, 2004

Jacomb, Charles, *Torment (A Study in Patriotism)*, A. Melrose Ltd, London, 1920

Keeling, Frederick, *Keeling: Letters & Recollections*, Macmillan Company, London, 1916

Lauder, Harry, *A Minstrel in France*, Hearst's International Library, New York, 1918

Longley, Cecil, *Battery Flashes*, John Murray, London, 1916

Lyon, Thomas M., *In Kilt & Khaki*, The Standard Press, Kilmarnock, 1916

Martin, Arthur Anderson, *A Surgeon in Khaki*, Longmans, Green & Co, London, 1915

Mellersh, H.E.L., *Schoolboy into War*, William Kimber, London, 1978

Nash, T.A.M., *The Diary of an Unprofessional Soldier*, Picton Publishing, 1991

Nettleton, John, *The Anger of the Guns*, William Kimber, London, 1979

Parker, Ernest, *Into Battle*, Leo Cooper, Barnsley, 1994

Peacock, Basil, *Tinker's Mufti*, Seeley Service & Co., London, 1974
Read, I.L. (Dick), *Of Those We Loved*, The Pentland Press, Edinburgh, 1994
Roe, F.P. *Accidental Soldiers*, privately published, London, 1981
Smith, Aubrey, *Four Years on the Western Front*, Odhams Press, London, 1922
Spicer, Lancelot Dykes, *Letters from France 1915–1918*, Robert York, London, 1979
Street, Cecil John Charles, *The Making of a Gunner*, Eveleigh Nash, London, 1916
Sturges, Robert, *On the Remainder of our Front*, by Private No. 904, Harrison & Sons, London, 1917
Thomas, Alan, *A Life Apart*, Victor Gollancz, London, 1968
Tucker, John, *Johnny Get Your Gun*, William Kimber, London, 1978
Tyndale-Biscoe, Julian, *Gunner Subaltern*, Leo Cooper, London, 1971

Unpublished Memoirs
Andrews, Albert William, *Orders Are Orders*, privately printed, 1987
Butterworth, George, 1885–1916, privately printed, 1918
Dillon, Norman, unpublished memoirs
Easton, Tom, *The 2nd Batt. Tyneside Scottish*, unpublished memoirs
Goss, Joseph, *A Border Battalion*, privately printed, Edinburgh, 1920
Harbottle, George, *Civilian Soldiers 1914–1919*, privately printed, 1982
McCauley, John, unpublished memoirs

Unpublished Memoirs – author's collection
Cole, Vic, *An Englishman's Life*, 1973

Unpublished Letters – author's collection
Lieutenant Thomas Butler-Stoney

Interviews conducted by the author with the following Great War veterans and civilians:
Private Robert Burns, 7th The Queen's Own Cameron Highlanders
Private Horace Calvert, 2/6th The West Yorkshire Regiment
Private Jack Davis, 6th The Duke of Cornwall's Light Infantry
Second Lieutenant Norman Dillon, 14th The Northumberland Fusiliers
Emily Galbraith, civilian (London)
Second Lieutenant Richard Hawkins, 11th The Royal Fusiliers
Percy Johnson, civilian (London)
Private John Rea Laister, 2nd The King's Royal Rifle Corps
Private Frank Lindley, 14th The York and Lancaster Regiment (2nd Barnsley Pals)
Private Reginald Spraggins, 1/4th The Suffolk Regiment

Photographs
All pictures are taken from the author's private collection unless otherwise stated.

Photographs of Lieutenant Richard Hawkins
By kind permission of Kevin Varty. Pages: 133, 141, 151, 320

Index

Aldershot, 117, 134, 177, 211, 236, 260, 354
   camp, 107, 150
Andrews, Albert, 301, 337
Andrews, William, 64–5, 115–19, 187–90, 206, 267, 279, 329, 351
Archduke (Franz Ferdinand), 39
Arisaka *see* rifle
Armstrong, Brig Gen, 178
Artillery Company camp, 96
Ashmole, Richard, 133
Asquith, Prime Minister Herbert, 2, 56–7

Banks, Rowland, 223
Barnet, Maj, 124, 149–50
barracks, 54, 65, 95, 98, 99, 100–103, 110, 115, 117, 130–1, 153, 159, 166, 167, 189, 204, 217, 220, 251, 326, 341–2, 348–9
   Bedford, 131
   Bodmin, 100–101
   Bramshott, 283
   Bristol, 103
   Caterham, 111–12
   Deepcut, 176
   Ely, 83
   Fenham, 137
   Hertford, 131
   Hounslow, 77, 110, 132
   Maidstone, 97, 101
   Malplaquet, 260
   Stoughton, 102, 121
bayonet, 339
   supply of, 227, 229, 230
   training/practice, 242–5, 258, 292, 300, 302, 329, 342
Bedford, 130, 131, 146, 224, 272

Beith, John Hay, 166–7, 218–20, 235, 238, 240, 241–2, 263–4, 266, 270, 272, 275, 279, 290, 296–7, 299, 302–305, 309, 318, 323–4, 326, 327
Belgium, 28–9, 35, 45, 53, 56, 79, 129, 227, 323
bell tents, 40, 104, 121, 199–200, 257–8
   provision of, 95, 104, 121–2, 203, 263, 266, 326
   living in, 101, 199, 201, 209, 257–8, 260–1
Bellerby, John, 250, 314
billeting (on civilians), 265–75
Bing, Harold, 44
Blaikie, Capt, 302–305
blue serge uniform ('Kitchener Blue'), 227–9, 254, 318
Boase, Capt, 206–207
Bodmin, 98, 99, 101, 104, 107, 117
bomb throwing, 244, 258, 281, 297, 311–12
Booth, Cpl, 189
Bowling, Col, 358
Boy Scouts/scouting, 22, 24, 27, 28, 155, 181
Boys' Brigade, 24, 79, 155, 172
Bramshott camp, Hants, 283
Bristol, 44, 103, 137, 138, 180, 199, 216
British Army, 1, 6, 8, 12, 34–5, 58–9, 111, 137, 183, 193, 194, 222–3, 229–30, 339

British Army formations:
Divisions:
   2/1st Highland Division, 284

Brigades:
  123rd (Tyneside Scottish) Brigade, 133–4
Regiments:
  Argyll & Sutherland Highlanders, 35, 265
    1/6th Argyll & Sutherland Highlanders 40–1, 66, 146
    2/6th Argyll & Sutherland Highlanders, 146, 223–4, 230, 284
    1/10th Argyll & Sutherland Highlanders, 166–7, 218–20, 235, 238, 240, 241, 263–4, 266, 272, 275, 279, 290, 296–7, 299, 302–305, 309–10, 318, 323–4, 326, 327
  Black Watch (Royal Highlanders), 115
    2/4th Black Watch, 115–16, 118, 187, 188–9, 190, 206–207, 267, 279, 329, 351
  2nd Border Regiment, 224
  11th Border Regiment (Lonsdale Battalion), 143
  The Buffs (East Kent Regiment), 246, 247
  6th Queen's Own Cameron Highlanders, 283, 316–17
  7th Queen's Own Cameron Highlanders, 239
  Coldstream Guards, 152, 348
    2nd Coldstream Guards, 346, 348–9
  Devonshire Regiment, viii, 154, 237, 328
    8th Devonshire Regiment, 235, 322
  16th Duke of Cambridge's Own (Middlesex Regiment), 147
    Public Schools Battalions/Brigades, 86, 129, 146–8, 151–2, 153, 302–303, 347–8
  Duke of Cornwall's Light Infantry (DCLI), 98
    6th Duke of Cornwall's Light Infantry, 13, 72–3, 98–101, 104–105, 107, 122–3, 124–5, 149–53, 168–9, 187, 189, 190, 194, 208–209, 211–12, 214, 215–17, 249, 252, 253, 255, 319, 320, 321, 323, 325–6, 327, 353
    7th Duke of Cornwall's Light Infantry, 72, 122, 218
  2/6th Duke of Wellington's Regiment (West Riding Regiment), 230
  13th Durham Light Infantry, 260–1, 337–8
  10th East Yorkshire Regiment, 244, 298
  Essex Regiment, 146, 155
    1/4th Essex Regiment, 273
    10th Essex Regiment, 156, 213
  Gloucestershire Regiment, 138, 179, 298, 350
    1/4th Gloucestershire Regiment, 212
    1/6th Gloucestershire Regiment, 138, 180, 194, 195, 201–202, 204, 207, 216
    2/6th Gloucestershire Regiment, 160, 191, 231, 251, 257, 278
    12th Gloucestershire Regiment, 198–9, 237, 312
  1/6th Gordon Highlanders, 272–3
  Grenadier Guards, 192
    1st Grenadier Guards, 111–12, 237, 244, 334–5, 341–2, 346
  2/9th Highland Light Infantry (Glasgow Highlanders), 87, 157, 158, 170–1, 173, 174, 184–5, 190, 191, 199, 200–201, 202, 203–205, 207–208, 243,

247–8, 251–2, 259–60, 284–6, 287–8, 292, 293–6, 319–20, 344–5, 363
Irish Guards, 258
King's (Liverpool Regiment), 129, 268, 339
   1/6th King's (Liverpool Regiment), 268–9, 270, 275
   11th King's (Liverpool Regiment), 312
8th King's Own Scottish Borderers, 139, 177, 230, 245, 269, 311, 317, 346–7
1st King's Own (Yorkshire Light Infantry), 130
9th King's Own (Yorkshire Light Infantry), 132
8th Leicestershire Regiment, 354–5, 360–1, 363
London Regiment, 70–1
   1/5th (City of London) Battalion, London Rifle Brigade (LRB), 70–1, 86, 172
   2/5th (City of London) Battalion (LRB), 173, 297, 318–19, 336, 359–60, 361
   1/14th (County of London) Battalion (London Scottish), 69–70, 71
   1/28th (County of London) Battalion (Artists Rifles), 70–1, 72, 81–3, 84–6, 110, 112, 119–20, 145–6, 148, 168, 185, 224, 235, 333
   2/28th (County of London) Battalion (Artists Rifles), 119–20, 146, 185, 224, 235, 333
Northumberland Fusiliers, 133, 177
   1/6th Northumberland Fusiliers, 229
   9th Northumberland Fusiliers, 305–307
   14th Northumberland Fusiliers, 174–6, 178–9, 182, 205
   21st Northumberland Fusiliers (2nd Tyneside Scottish), 188, 213–14, 215, 217
1/4th Oxford and Buckinghamshire Light Infantry, 289
7th Prince of Wales's Leinster Regiment, 256
Rifle Brigade, 134, 148
   6th Rifle Brigade, 288
   7th Rifle Brigade (The Prince Consort's Own), 158, 165, 167, 177–8
   12th Rifle Brigade, 228
Royal Army Medical Corps, 74–6, 80, 210, 217, 274, 315, 321
Royal Engineers, 321, 362
   475th Field Company (South Midland) Royal Engineers, 362
Royal Field Artillery, 83–4, 98, 131, 192, 199
   1st South Midland Brigade, Royal Field Artillery, 199, 226, 263, 280–1, 285, 286–7, 309, 337, 352–3
   87 Brigade, Royal Field Artillery, 273–4
   110th Battery, Royal Field Artillery, 324, 327–8, 356
Royal Garrison Artillery, 83
   23rd Siege Battery, Royal Garrison Artillery, 238–9
Royal Horse Artillery, 176, 182, 283
10th Royal Dublin Fusiliers, 125
Royal Fusiliers, 120, 132–3, 148, 153, 213, 223, 225–6, 236,

INDEX

249–50, 253–4, 265, 309–11, 319–20, 339–40, 343, 353–4
9th Royal Fusiliers, 110, 112–13, 120–1, 136–7, 153, 173, 186, 221–2, 223, 225–7, 236, 246, 249–51, 253, 262, 265, 300, 310, 311–12, 314, 319, 339, 343, 354, 358
10th Royal Fusiliers (Stockbrokers' Battalion), 146
11th Royal Fusiliers, 133, 151, 320
18th Royal Fusiliers (1st Public Schools), 125–6
19th Royal Fusiliers (2nd Public Schools), 340, 343
20th Royal Fusiliers (3rd Public Schools), 148, 223
21st Royal Fusiliers (4th Public Schools), 153
1/4th Royal Scots (Lothian Regiment), 343
16th Royal Scots (Lothian Regiment), 244, 245
Royal Warwickshire Regiment, 32–3, 137, 158, 221, 329–30
  14th Royal Warwickshire Regiment, 1st Birmingham Pals, 243
  15th Royal Warwickshire Regiment, 2nd Birmingham Pals, 10, 161
6th Royal West Kent Regiment, 8, 9, 52, 81, 90, 97, 125, 165–6, 168, 184, 194, 262, 299–300, 310, 313, 328, 337, 344, 353–4, 362
7th Royal West Kent Regiment, 97–8, 101–102, 105–106, 121, 122, 123, 180–2, 228, 246–7, 321–2, 354
Royal West Surrey Regiment, 102, 246

6th Royal West Surrey Regiment, 102, 121–2, 202, 211, 240, 265, 334
Scots Guards, 112, 186, 189, 289
3rd Sherwood Foresters (Nottinghamshire and Derbyshire Regiment), 110
16th Sherwood Foresters (Nottinghamshire and Derbyshire Regiment, 231
7th Somerset Light Infantry, 282
Suffolk Regiment, 83–4, 98, 209
  8th Suffolk Regiment, 98, 103–104, 124, 155, 172, 193, 201, 202, 205–206, 209–10, 218, 220, 227, 229, 302, 318, 338–9, 341, 342, 354
2/6th West Yorkshire Regiment, 191–2
1/8th West Yorkshire Regiment, 250, 314
12th West Yorkshire Regiment, 156–7
15th West Yorkshire Regiment, 156–7, 225, 248–9

British Expeditionary Force (BEF), 1–2, 58, 79, 112, 130, 229, 231, 319
British Empire, 21, 22, 50, 52, 58, 130, 346
British Government, 2, 4, 44, 56–9, 104, 130, 222, 226, 250
Buckingham Palace, 45–6, 146
Bullock, Sgt, 192
Bullswater camp, Surrey, 149, 260
Burns, Robert, 239
Bury St Edmunds depot, 83–4, 98, 155
Butler, Lt, 130
Butler, Douglas, 212
Butler-Stoney, Thomas, 256, 258

Butterworth, George, 99–100, 101, 104–105, 124–5, 149, 150–2, 211–12, 214, 260, 261, 337–8, 363
Buxton, Andrew, 55, 84–6, 153, 224, 288, 363

Calvert, Horace, 191–2
Cambridge, 119, 129
Campbeltown, 40
Canada, 21, 37, 231
Carlisle camp, Cumbria, 143
Carr, Lt Col, 132–3
Carrington, Charles, 3, 55, 134–5, 144
Chapman, Guy, 254, 256, 258, 353, 361–2
Churchill, Winston, 3, 45, 56
Cliff, Norman, 111–12, 237, 244, 334–6, 341–2, 346
Clipstone camp, Notts, 236
Close, Jack, 334, 335
Codford camp, Wilts, 186
Colchester camp, 97, 120–1, 132, 229
Cole, Vic, 8–9, 13–28, 46, 80, 86, 90, 97, 101, 105, 121–3, 180–1, 199, 228, 246, 321, 354
Coppard, George, 102, 121, 122, 202, 211, 240, 265, 270, 334
Craig, Col J., 40–1, 66, 146, 223–4, 230–1, 284
Crawshay-Williams, Eliot, 53, 324–5, 327, 356
Crystal Palace, 15, 18, 19–22, 23, 24, 27, 80
Cuddeford, Douglas, 33–5, 38, 112, 186, 189, 289

Davies, Jim, 46–7
Davis, Jack, 79, 353
Deepcut *see* barracks

Dick, Col Douglas, 284
Diggle, Philip, 143
Dillon, Norman, 137, 174–5, 178–9, 182, 205, 208
Dolden, Stuart, 69–70, 71, 73
Douie, Charles, 37
drill hall, 65, 115, 138, 230
    Bromley, 81, 86, 90
    Glasgow, 87
Drinkwater, Harold, 158, 161

Easton, Tom, 188, 213–15, 217
Edward VII, King, 24
Egypt, 56, 57, 77, 89, 140, 268, 361
Elcock, Reginald, 339
Ellis, Francis, 107, 150, 152, 158
Ellis, Roland, 107, 149, 150, 152
Ellison, Norman, 268–70, 274–5
Empire Day, 15, 17, 317
Erbele, Victor, 362
Essex, 120, 132, 133, 216, 279, 298
Europe, 2, 33, 37–8, 39, 47, 50, 53, 130, 313

Feilding, Rowland, 95
Fildes, Geoffrey, 56, 81–3, 119–20, 146, 224, 235, 346, 348–9
First Lord of the Admiralty *see* Churchill, Winston
food:
    canteens, 100, 189, 214–15, 264, 341–2
    complaints about, 55, 209–13
    cooking, 95, 208
    food parcels, 214
    hunger, 65, 100, 246
    quality and preparation of, 203, 206–13, 215, 266, 289, 291
    queuing for, 103, 204–205
France, 39, 43, 45, 53, 58, 74, 77, 79, 80, 112–13, 129, 130, 140, 141,

143–44, 146, 161, 199, 227, 229, 328–9, 333–4, 347, 353–4, 363
Freeman, 'General', 302–304,
Freeman, Hardy and Willis, 303–305
Fuller, Sydney, 83, 98, 103–104, 124, 155, 172, 193, 201–202, 205–206, 209–10, 217–18, 220, 227, 229, 302, 318, 338–9, 341–2, 354

Galbraith, Emily, 48–9
George V, King, 38, 47, 48, 49, 81, 322, 346
German Army, 8, 45, 56, 79, 299, 338, 345,
    106th (Saxon) Infantry Regiment, 28
German Empire, 324
German High Seas Fleet, 35
Germans, 4, 27–8, 38, 46, 63, 89, 109, 285, 314, 362
Germany, 5, 33, 34–5, 39, 43, 45–50, 52–3, 57–8, 78, 231, 244
Gibson, Ashley, 148, 223
Glasgow, 38, 66, 87–8, 121, 170, 279
Goss, Joseph, 230, 311, 317, 346–7
Great Britain, 1–2, 35, 183–4, 222
Greenwell, Graham, 289

Hale, Ewart, 237
Hall, Col, 147
Hall, James, 66, 68, 77–8, 110, 112, 120–1, 136–7, 186, 221–2, 225–7, 236–7, 246, 249–53, 262, 265, 300, 311–12, 314, 319, 339, 343, 354, 358–9
Hankey, Donald, 158–60, 165, 167–8, 177–8, 363
Hanson, Ivor, 44
Harbottle, George, 229, 298
Hardie, Kier, 44

Hardy, 'General', 303–304
Hardy, Ronald, 177, 303
Hardy, Thomas, 153
Hawkins, Richard, 132–3, 140, 141, 151
Hay, Martin, 328, 353
Heath, Arthur, 129, 138, 140, 165–6, 168, 184, 194, 262, 299–300, 310, 313–14, 337, 341, 344, 363
Heaton Park camp, Manchester, 122, 195
Hemming, Harold, 157
Hollingworth, Clifford, 248
Horse Guards, 323
Horse Guards Parade, 45, 78
Hounslow depot, 78, 112, 123, 133
    see also barracks, Hounslow
Hughes-Games, Claude, 138

illness:
    enteric fever (typhoid), 216, 217, 218, 220
    influenza, 150
    smallpox, 217
    spotted fever, 148
    see also vaccination/inoculation
India, 21, 77, 89, 130, 132, 140, 154, 231, 310
Indian Army, 254
Isle of Man Steam Packet Company, 354

Jackson, John, 283, 316–17
Jacomb, Charles, 34
Japan, 58, 231
Johnson, Percy, 248

Kaiser Wilhelm, 8, 45, 48–50, 80, 324
Keeling, Frederick, 13, 42–3, 47, 52–3, 63, 71–3, 98–9, 107, 117, 119, 152, 168–9, 187, 189–90, 194,

208–10, 215–17, 249, 252–5, 258, 319–21, 323, 325–7, 363
King's shilling, 68, 79, 98, 102, 132
Kitchener, Lord, 2–6, 8, 56–9, 66, 71, 85, 88, 112, 129, 130, 140, 142, 144, 228, 281, 282, 283, 321
'Kitchener Blue' *see* blue serge uniform
Kitchener's New Army, 3, 5, 6, 8, 12, 58–9, 71, 72, 78, 80, 86, 89, 120, 129, 130, 132, 140, 154, 157, 177, 189, 208, 221, 223, 230, 231, 237, 254, 255, 256, 265, 283, 319, 354
Knight, Albert, 273–4

Laister, John, 63–4, 76–7
Lauder, Harry, 34, 37, 39
Lauder, John, 34, 37, 38
Lawson, Charles, 146–7
Lee, Georgina, 50
Lee, Joe, 190
Lee-Enfield *see* rifle
Lindley, Frank, 192
London, 5, 13, 15, 18–24, 26–8, 33, 35, 45–9, 55, 57, 58, 66, 68, 69–70, 72, 77, 96, 98, 119–20, 133–4, 142, 213, 280, 333, 335, 346, 352
Longley, Cecil, 11, 199, 214, 226, 263, 280–1, 285–7, 309, 337, 352–3
Lonsdale, Lord, 143
Lyon, Thomas, 87–9, 157–8, 170–1, 173–4, 183–5, 190, 191, 199–204, 207–208, 243, 247–8, 251–2, 259–60, 284–8, 292–6, 319–20, 344–5, 363

Machell, Percy, 143
Mafeking Day, 15
Maidstone depot, 90, 97–8, 101–102, 121
 see also barracks

Malplaquet *see* barracks
Manchester Pals, 122
Martin, Arthur, 74–6
Mary, Queen, 38
McAllister, Sgt, 316
McCauley, John, 224–5
Melbourne, Australia, 34, 37
Melhuish, Ian, 282
Millerand, Alexandre, 281
Mona's Queen, SS, 354
Mons, 79, 140, 302, 309, 319, 329
Morris, 107, 150, 152
musketry, 235–9, 253, 292, 298, 310–11, 318, 320–1

Nash, Thomas, 201–202, 204, 208, 212, 216
Naval Reservists, 43
Nettleton, John, 185, 333
Newcastle upon Tyne, 116, 137, 213, 229
Nisbet, Hugh, 50, 52
Northumberland, 121, 175, 178, 182, 188, 205, 213, 217
Northumberland Fusiliers' depot, 133, 137

OTC, 133–4, 144–6, 147, 148, 176, 180
 camp, 130, 137
Ovens, Brig Gen, 149, 151–2

Paris, 33, 45, 68, 79
Parker, Ernest, 103, 211, 216
Parker, George, 110–11
Parkhouse camp, 317
Pattern Infantry Equipment, 222
Peacock, Basil, 54, 116–17, 347–8
Pearson, Arthur, 225
Philip, David, 244, 245
Pirbright, 260
 camp, 152

Pollard, George, 267
Post Office, 142, 144, 228, 272, 287–88
Prior, Lt Col Arthur, 181
Pulley, George, 80, 86, 90, 97
Purfleet, 121, 246–7
   camp, 121, 165, 180, 246

Read, Dick, 355–6, 360–1, 363
Rest Camps, 352
rifle:
   Arisaka, 231
   Long Lee-Enfield, 227
   Long Lee-Metford, 223, 229
   Short Lee-Enfield Mark III, 229
   Short Lee-Enfield Mark IV, 339
   antiquated/old, 298–9
   cleaning/maintenance, 190, 267, 291, 310, 338, 339
   inspection, 166, 180, 190,
   Royal Ordnance Factories, 229
   supply of, 143, 180–1, 227, 229–31, 324, 340
   training, 112, 169, 235–44, 297, 298–9, 310, 311, 320–1
   see also musketry
Roe, Frederick, 137–8, 153, 179–80, 194–5
Rubery, Lt, 161
Runcie, Alex, 272–3
Russia, 34, 35, 39, 43, 45, 227
Russians, 35, 53

Salisbury Plain, 137, 161–2, 186, 262–3, 280–1, 308–309, 316, 325
Schlieffen Plan, 45
Scotland, 34, 40, 66, 72, 115, 121, 129–30, 181, 284
Scots festival, 279
Sea Scouts, 24
Sherriff, Robert, 135–6
signallers, 11, 181, 247, 320, 322, 342

Simpson, Albert, 230
Smith, Aubrey, 70, 172–3, 297–8, 318–19, 336, 359, 361
Smith, John, 272
Smith, Ralph, 312
Snailham, James, 321
South Africa, 15, 33, 37, 77, 120–1, 140, 154, 175, 226, 268, 310
Spicer, Lancelot, 129–30, 132
Spraggins, Reginald, 83–4
Stoughton *see* barracks
Street, Cecil, 1, 6, 89–90, 95–7, 106–107, 113–15, 171–2, 193, 238–9, 271–2, 349–52, 355–6, 359
Studholme, Lancelot, 256, 258
Sturges, Robert, 340–1, 343, 351
Sweden, 183, 84
Swedish Drill, 184

Ternan, Trevor, 133–4
Territorial battalions, 89, 153, 191, 224, 268
Territorial Force, 6, 8, 34, 39–40, 59, 85, 89, 129, 138, 146, 177, 180, 265, 267
Thomas, Alan, 52, 328, 353–4, 362
Town Clerks' Army, 59
Toye, Pte, 107, 124–5
Tucker, John, 141–2
'Twig', 116–17
Tyndale-Biscoe, Julian, 130–2, 176–7, 182, 239, 283

University Training Corps, 129, 130
USA, 58

vaccination/inoculation, 217–18, 220, 256, 325
Victoria, SS, 354
Voigt, Frederick, 206

Wagstaffe, Capt, 290, 304, 324
War Office, 1, 4, 7, 55, 58, 95, 125, 131, 132, 134, 137–8, 142–3, 144, 147, 148, 175, 213, 221–2, 262–3, 265, 266, 299, 310, 314
War Office manual, 176
West Kent depot, 90
Western Front, 3, 4, 9, 38, 89, 144, 231, 292, 341, 347, 356
Whittaker, Maj, 180
Willis, 'General', 303, 305
Winchester depot, 134
Windmill Hill camp, Wilts, 137
Woodcock, Dr Herbert de Carle, 73, 76–7
Worrell, Bill, 228